Volume 1

Parent/Teacher Handbook

Teaching Younger Children Everything They Need to Know About

The Bible

Dr. Edward A. Buchanan

0-8054-2711-2

Published by Broadman & Holman Publishers
Nashville, Tennessee

Dewey Decimal Classification: 649
Subject Heading: CHILD REARING \ BIBLE \ CHRISTIAN
EDUCATION OF CHILDREN

Scripture quotations are taken from the following versions: Holman Christian
Standard Bible® Copyright © 1999, 2000, 2001, 2002, 2003 by Holman Bible
Publishers. Used by permission. The New American Standard, © Lockman
Foundation, 1960, 1962, 1963, 1968, 1971, 1972, 1973, 1975, 1977; used
by permisison. New International Version, copyright © 1973, 1978,
1984 by International Bible Society.

1 2 3 4 5 6 7 8 9 10 09 08 07 06 05 04

DEDICATION

To my wife and best friend, Gladys

ACKNOWLEDGMENTS

In preparing this handbook, I have deeply appreciated the help of my student assistants and my secretary. I would like to express special thanks to Broadman & Holman Publishers for their help in turning this project into a reality.

Edward A. Buchanan
May 2003

Table of Contents

General Introduction for Parents and Teachers

The content for this book grows out of a conviction that we need to provide our children with a greater understanding of the Christian faith. The world is growing increasingly hostile to Christianity and to those who practice their Christian faith. If the next generation of believers will possess faith and be able to articulate that faith, they will need to have a solid foundation of background knowledge about their faith. We must become more intentional about helping our children know what it means to be a Christian and teach them how to tell others about the strength they receive from their faith in Jesus Christ.

Our Culture

We live in a culture where tolerance is accorded to many outlandish and bizarre groups but not to Christians. The exclusivism of the gospel of Jesus Christ is offensive to many in our world. Other religious groups, who are very evangelistic and militant to bring Christian believers into their folds, are bombarding us with their false doctrines. If we care about our children, it is essential that we help them gain an adequate knowledge to combat these influences and ideologies.

As parents, we are often too busy with our own concerns to spend adequate time with our children and oversee their growth and development. We come home frazzled from the hectic pace of work and even from our leisure activities. We fail to nurture our children to hold the values and beliefs that we have found essential to the well-being of our lives. We assume that there will be time, and someday we will help them. Or we believe that the church will be able to teach them all they need to know to become Christians and to grow in their faith.

Our culture works in opposition to many of the things that we believe. It has been estimated that by the time a child graduates from high school, he or she will have watched twice as many hours of television as was spent in the classroom. Television homogenizes its viewers. It does not matter whether a child of five or an adult of twenty-five is watching the television screen. Both persons see the same things. For the adult, the prominent themes of violence and sex may not be too significant. But to the child of five, these themes can be very harmful. The child may not understand all of the innuendos, the meaning of the language, or the visual scenes, but the impact upon the child is significant. Even children's cartoons are filled with images of violence. Movies provide another source for visual images that may not enhance, but cause difficulty for the child to pattern behavior in healthy ways.

Overt sexual themes are also prominent in our television shows and movies. They pose another hazard for our children, who are not equipped to deal with adult scenes, language, and situations. The philosophy of "Just do it!" pervades our culture. The problems reach a zenith in the teenage years with promiscuity, pregnancy, and abortion. Negative role models who support such a philosophy only make these problems more prevalent. Many of the role models come from the professional sports and rock music worlds. Often the morals of these persons do not provide healthy lifestyle models for our children and youth.

Our schools are plagued with violence. Frustration and dissatisfaction result in shootings. Schools have become a haven for illegal drugs and alcohol. Suicides have also become a significant problem in many schools. All of these situations are compounded by the fact that the level of learning in schools has continued to drop over the past two decades.

Psychologist David Elkind has observed that while many of these problems may manifest themselves in the adolescent years, the roots for these behaviors stem from childhood. Inappropriate behaviors may be ignored in childhood, but they cannot be ignored during the adolescent years, when drugs, drinking, and promiscuity take a painful and distorted toll on the lives of our youth.

While we might continue to analyze endlessly the negative aspects of our society and its effects on our children, the question of what a parent can do to counteract these evil forces requires our urgent attention. The first essential is for parents to spend time with their children. At the first and second grade levels, select wholesome materials, like the stories in this and other books, then read aloud. At bedtime, establish a pattern of having your child sit in your lap and read aloud for ten to fifteen minutes. Then discuss what you both have heard. In doing so, you will develop a deeper and more intimate relationship with your child and at the same time provide a healthy basis for your child to withstand the evils of our society.

Helping Your Child Learn

Current research on learning clearly indicates that there are things that can be done to help children develop healthy attitudes, espouse Christian values, and live out these values in appropriate Christian behavior. Perhaps the foremost principle of learning is that a person needs a solid knowledge base of prior learning. For someone to become a Christian and live in accordance with Christian principles, it is imperative to develop a full understanding of the Christian faith. It has been estimated that about half of the young people from one of our major denominations lose their faith when they go off to college. Perhaps one of the reasons is that they never had a solid foundation in the first place. They are often ill-equipped to face the temptations of college life and the onslaught of a college culture that ridicules their faith and beliefs.

A second principle for effective learning is learning that is presented in a meaningful and structured format. Our learning needs to be organized. For example, if you were studying the Gospel of Mark, it would be helpful to have a chart of the way in which the Gospel is structured. Such a chart would provide some pegs on which to hang the individual parts of the text. For the Bible, a time line can help us better retain and recall the information that was gained from the study. Such devices will be included in this study to assist your child to better learn the material.

A third principle of learning that is critical is modeling. This means that we learn by observation. Parents provide children with their most important role models. As a result of the amount of time spent with parents, the child will pick up attitudes, values, beliefs, and behaviors from the parent.

Long before these became principles of learning in today's educational context, the Bible described parents teaching children in Deuteronomy 6:7: *"Repeat them [commandments] to your children. Talk about them when you sit in your house and when you walk along the road, when you lie down and when you get up."* Note that parents are expected to provide instruction in the precepts of God that lead to godly behavior. That has not changed. God is love, but He has set the moral requirements for us to follow, and He expects obedience. Unless we know what God expects in His moral precepts, we cannot live our lives in accordance with them. Children need to learn God's expectations and follow them. These expectations are not given to limit our behavior unnecessarily. On the contrary, they are provided to help us live lives that are free from guilt and anxiety.

Basic Christian Learning

To help with the process of understanding Christian faith, each person needs some basic knowledge of the Bible, persons, events, terms, symbols, and phrases that are included under the term *Christian*. This is called Basic Christian

Learning. Basic Christian Learning begins with study of the Scripture. Scripture is foundational to everything that we believe. Since the Bible is God's message to us, every Christian needs to be thoroughly grounded in the Bible. This study will begin by providing a solid foundation in Scripture. But Basic Christian Learning includes more than Bible study. Here are some examples of the kinds of items that are included under the heading of Basic Christian Learning. What does a Christian believe? If you are Presbyterian, how did Presbyterianism develop? If you are Baptist, how did you become Baptist? As much as we might wish that each of our denominations came from the New Testament church, there was a historical process that brought about the development of each of the denominations. Some of the cultures of the past have been much more Christian than our present culture. Children, youth, and adults need to understand past Christian cultures. Christianity has not always been ridiculed as it often is today. Some of the greatest work in art, music, and literature has been inspired by the Christian faith. Consider Michelangelo's magnificent ceiling in the Sistine Chapel in Rome. Or consider the inspiration that led to George Handel's great masterpiece, the *Messiah*. Isaac Watts was a hardened and profane slave trader, but his conversion to Christ led to reformation in his life and inspired him to write the great hymn "Amazing Grace." John Bunyan was not educated but was inspired by his faith in Christ to write one of the masterpieces of English literature *Pilgrim's Progress*.

Basic Christian Learning includes all of the above and many other related topics. It is intended to provide a fundamental understanding of our Christian faith and to stir the imagination of our children to live their Christian faith in the midst of a world that needs the good news of the gospel.

With a background in Basic Christian Learning, a child and young person is prepared to face some of the issues of defining, defending, and living the Christian faith inside and outside the church. Teaching in Sunday school and preaching in the church become more meaningful when set against a background of an understanding that Basic Christian Learning can provide. Common understanding can foster deeper relationships between parents and their children, as they share a common bond of understanding of their Christian faith. Witnessing to Christian belief is no longer an onerous task but a joyous privilege. Christian faith is not only to be believed; it is to be practiced. With basic knowledge of Christian behavior, a Christian can respond to the moral and ethical issues of a non-Christian world that one confronts each day. As the missionary William Carey once observed, "Expect great things of God; attempt great things for God!"

About This Book

Every effort has been made to prepare these materials with a vocabulary and style that are age appropriate. The book begins with the foundation of Christian faith—the Bible. We have purposely provided stories from the Bible that follow the historical biblical sequence of material. This will help your child develop an appreciation of how God has dealt with persons down through history. It culminates in the supreme expression of God's love for humanity by sending His own Son, Jesus Christ, to live and die in order that we might have life eternally with God. Other sections include geography of the Bible and customs of Bible times. Since the Bible is not a product of our culture, it is important to understand geography and customs to rightly interpret the Scripture.

The Old Testament is imbued with God's dealing with His people Israel. To understand the Old Testament, some knowledge of Jewish customs and worship is necessary. A section on this material is provided.

It is not necessary to read the book through from cover to cover. You will probably want to present some portion of the Bible section each day. This is a good time to help your child develop the habit of studying the Bible. Follow the reading of the Bible with a short time of prayer. Develop a close and intimate relationship with your child so that he or she will enjoy this time that you share together. Read aloud the Bible stories and follow that with a story from another part of the book. With first and second graders, it is not necessary to focus upon the time sequence. By third grade you will want to frequently refer to the time line and provide a foundation for understanding the time sequence. Refer to the time line in the learning activity.

Enlarge upon the learning presented in this volume. Talk with your child about what he or she is learning in school. Try to relate principles from this book to subjects that the child is learning in school and church. Visit museums, attend plays and concerts, and though you may find it difficult to visit the Holy Land, you can do that through videotapes. There are many available that explore Palestine and Europe and other civilizations that are discussed in this volume. Explore your church library, school library, and the public library. Each will have materials that will relate to your child's experience.

Above all else, make these learning experiences fun for your child! These can be some of the richest and most rewarding times that you will spend with your child. Enjoy them. You will never pass this way again!

Introduction to the Children's Bible

Through the centuries the stories of the Bible have been told and retold from generation to generation. Its precepts lie at the very heart of our culture. The Bible is a very special book and continues to be the world's best-selling book. It has affected the history of Western civilization and has been part of the structure of our society. For children it is able to fire their imagination and inspire the ideals of a godly heritage.

But the Bible is more than a collection of stories. The Bible is special because God Himself guided its writing. The Bible had thirty-five different authors and was written over many centuries; nevertheless, there is a unity to the Book. This unity comes from the power of the Holy Spirit, who superintended its writing and guides those who read it today to understand and come to know God.

It is exciting to read the Bible. In the past, people read the Bible in their search for God. Many people still read the Bible today for the same reason. But as they read, they discover that God is reaching out to them. God wants people to know Him and know that He loves them; God wants people to enjoy a relationship with Him.

The stories of the Bible are about real people, whose lives have been changed by their relationship with God. The Bible tells the stories of persons who have been good and bad, who have experienced successes and failures, who have felt love and anger. The Bible can stir our feelings as well. But most importantly, the Bible demonstrates the love God has had for people down through thousands of years of human history.

People have difficult questions about life that cannot easily be answered. What is the meaning of life? Does God exist? Does the great God, who created the universe, care about us? Why do people suffer? How can a person find happiness? How should we live our lives? What is right and wrong? How can a person come to know God? The Bible addresses these and many other questions that people ask.

The truths of the Bible do not change. But over the millennia, civilizations change. The world in which the Bible was written is very different from the world of the twenty-first century. We watch television, use computers, listen to music CDs, and drive cars. Life in the ancient world had none of those things. Even though the material world of things change, the inner hopes, dreams, longings, and desires of people are not all that different from one civilization to the next. The Bible speaks to these dreams and hopes today, as it has spoken to longings and desires of persons for centuries past. For example, the problems of sin and guilt are just as real today as they were when David reigned as king over the people of Israel several thousand years ago. So, to understand the Bible today, we learn about the folkways and customs of the ancient world and allow the Bible to speak to us and to our deepest longings in today's world.

The term *Bible* originally meant a scroll or book, which was written on papyrus. Papyrus was an aquatic plant that grew in Egypt. It was dried and used as paper. In order for the written material to be used, it was rolled into a scroll.

Today the Bible carries the meaning of two great collections of holy books. They are known as the Old Testament and the New Testament. A *testament* is a covenant, an agreement between two parties. In this case the covenant is between God and man.

The Old Testament is composed of thirty-nine books of law, poetry, history, and prophecy. The Old Testament was written across a period of fifteen hundred years. It tells about the beginning of time and focuses upon God's chosen people, the Israelites, later known as Jews. The Old Testament tells the history of the Jewish people.

The New Testament is made up of twenty-seven books. They were written during a period, beginning about ten years after Jesus' resurrection and ending about AD 100. The Gospels tell about the good news that God came in Jesus to bring us back into a relationship with Himself. Jesus' life, ministry, and teachings are described. The history of the early church, the letters of Paul, and other writings tell us how we should live as followers of Jesus. Some of the writings tell about the future and the end of time.

In the section of this book called "Children's Bible" not all of the sixty-six books will be recounted. This is intentional. The stories are presented in chronological sequence. Great effort has been expended to include only those stories that carry the history of the drama of redemption from the time of Adam and Eve in the Garden of Eden to the advent of God's Son, Jesus Christ, and His death on the cross and resurrection to bring salvation to all who will believe. The unfolding drama of chronological Bible storying has been used in many cultures throughout the world to show how God dealt with sinful humanity to bring them into a personal relationship with Himself.

You will want your children who are in first and second grade to become thoroughly familiar with the Bible stories. They need to come to a deep appreciation for the depth and richness of the Bible. By third grade they should be able to discover the sequence of the historical framework in which God has worked throughout history. As you read the stories, you will want to refer back to the time line that comes after this introduction. As children study contemporary events in history with the events of Bible history, they will be able to make connections between the events of general history and the unique events of Bible history.

The stories of the Bible have been written in language that a child can understand and to which he can relate. Difficult words are only used when they are important to understanding the text of the Bible.

You will want to follow up the stories with questions about what your child understood about the story. At the beginning and throughout each section, the biblical reference has been provided. This will allow you, if you desire, to examine the context for yourself and supplement the reading from this text with your own additional material from the Bible itself.

More important than all of these instructions is the fact that the Bible has inspired men and women and boys and girls for millennia. The Bible is the most important book from our religious heritage. It is essential that you inspire your child to a love and appreciation for this Book that has changed lives throughout history and is still changing lives today.

Children's Bible

Discovering God

Who is God? The Bible tells us that no person has ever seen Him. God is spirit. He exists in three persons: Father, Son, and Holy Spirit. God is sovereign and all-powerful. God is the Creator of everything that exists. God is present at all times and in every place. God knows everything.

There are some qualities of God that we should examine more closely. God is holy. The term *holiness* means that God is separate from anything that is sinful, not pure, or wrong. God is absolute perfection. God created the standard of perfection. God hates sin and will not allow it to come into His presence.

> ### LOVE
> *God is love. God loves the angelic beings that He created. God loves all men and women and boys and girls. It is in God's nature to love.*

The Bible tells us that God is love. This is much more than just a warm feeling. God created us to enjoy His love. He reaches out to sinful humans and seeks them. He wants them to turn from sin and become part of His family. Love is God's highest perfection. His love shows itself in His promises. We may fail to keep our promises, but God never fails to keep His promises.

God created angels, or spirit beings. The Bible does not tell us a great deal about these beings. What the Bible does share helps us better understand God and His creation. These beings are identified as spirits, angels, cherubim, and seraphim. They were created sinless and given superior intelligence and strength.

The term *angel* carries the idea of a messenger. Angels were created to serve God. Their existence gives us a better understanding of God's vast creation. Jesus is higher than the angels and the object of their worship. They take joy in doing God's will. They obey God and do all that He wants them to do. They provide for us a good example. They are aware of what happens here on earth. They rejoice when even one person comes into the family of God. The Bible tells us that human beings were created a little lower than the angels.

The Bible tells us that God created Lucifer as the head of the angels. His name means the "morning star." He was created with great power and intelligence. But Lucifer decided that he wanted to be as powerful as God Himself. He rebelled against God. The prophet Isaiah (Isaiah 14:13–14) describes that rebellion against God. The Bible does not give great detail about the rebellion of Lucifer. He became known as Satan. The name *Satan* means "enemy." He became the enemy of God.

Satan brought with him other angels, who also rebelled against God. These demons help Satan. They do his bidding and they defy God.

Satan also became the enemy of mankind. Satan is still the enemy of mankind. He opposes God and tries to hurt Christian believers in any way that he can. Our task is to stay close to God. He will protect us from the power of Satan and his evil forces.

If this were the end of the story, it might not have a happy ending. But the Book of Revelation tells that one day God will make it all right. God will one day punish Satan and his demons forever. Their sin, rebellion, and wickedness will receive its reward. In the meantime they do everything that they can to disrupt and defeat the purposes of God.

The Old Testament

GOD CREATES
GENESIS 1–2

Our world is very old. But God was living long before He created the earth, sun, moon, and stars. With the word of His mouth, God called the world into being. During that time the earth did not have trees, animals, or people. It was dark, and there was nothing. But God's Spirit moved on the surface of the waters. The presence of God's Spirit can be seen even in the act of creation.

God said, "Let there be light" (Genesis 1:2). Light came upon the world. God separated light from the darkness. The light He called day and the darkness, night.

God then divided the sky from the water on the earth. God completed the second day of creation.

On the third day of creation God called the land out of the sea. He brought forth plants, flowers, and trees on the land. Plants flowered, bloomed, and bore fruit. God completed the third day of creation. God was pleased with His creation that He had brought into being.

Next, God divided day from night. He created seasons, days, and years. He created the sun to provide the light by day. He made the moon to serve as light for the night. God put the stars in the heavens. At the close of the fourth day, God saw that His creative acts were very good.

On the fifth day God created the fish of the sea. He also brought the birds of the air into being. God told the birds and fishes to multiply. God was satisfied with His creation.

On the sixth day God created the animals that live on the earth. God made domestic animals—like cows, sheep, and horses—that graze. He also made wild animals, such as bears, lions, and snakes. God saw that all His creation was good.

But God was not finished. He said, "Let us make man in our image, in our likeness" (1:26). (God is three Persons in one.) He created Adam from the dust of the earth and breathed into man the breath of life. Adam was given responsibility to care for all of God's creation. God placed Adam in a wonderful paradise, the Garden of Eden.

God searched through all of His creation. He could not find a partner for Adam. So God put Adam to sleep. He took a rib and formed Adam's wife, Eve. Both Adam and Eve were very happy in the Garden of Eden.

Finally, God ended His creation and rested on the seventh day. He was very pleased with all that He had created. So God set the seventh day apart from the rest of the week. It became a special day for rest and worship.

SIN ENTERS THE WORLD
GENESIS 3–4

Adam and Eve were very happy in the Garden of Eden. It was a magnificent and beautiful Paradise. In the evening of each day, they would walk with God. God provided everything for their enjoyment. They did not know evil or sin.

Among the animals of the Garden was the snake (serpent). One day Eve was walking in the Garden. A serpent came and asked her if God had said, "You must not eat from any tree in the garden" (Genesis 3:1). Eve answered that they could eat of any fruit except the tree in the center of the Garden. She told the serpent that God had said that if she and Adam ate or even touched the tree, they would die.

The serpent told her that they would not die, but would become like God by knowing good from evil. The serpent placed doubt in Eve's mind about God's love for them. The serpent lied.

Eve was misled by Satan who was disguised as a serpent. She looked at the fruit, and it was appealing. She took and ate of it. Then she gave some to Adam, and he also ate of the fruit. Immediately, they were aware they had disobeyed God. They were embarrassed that they did not have clothes to cover themselves. They sewed fig leaves together and covered themselves with the leaves.

When God came to meet with Adam and Eve, they hid from Him. God knew that they had disobeyed. Adam blamed Eve, and Eve blamed the serpent.

God condemned the serpent to crawl forever in the dust. God told Eve that she would have pain and sorrow at childbirth and that her husband would rule over her. To Adam, God said that all his life he must work hard to provide for his family. But God promised that one day a Redeemer would come. The Redeemer would one day make peace between God and man. God made garments of skin for Adam and Eve. To prevent them from living forever by eating of the fruit of the Tree of Life, God drove them from the Garden and placed cherubim to guard its entrance.

Adam and Eve had two sons. Cain was the elder, and he was a farmer. Abel was the younger, who raised sheep. Each brought a sacrifice to worship God.

God was pleased with Abel's sacrifice but not with Cain's. Cain took Abel to the field and murdered him.

God was displeased with Cain and condemned him to wander across the earth. God still loved Cain and placed a mark on him so no one would hurt him. Adam and Eve's sin now grew into murder at the hand of their own son.

NOAH AND THE FLOOD
GENESIS 6–9

Generations passed and the population grew. The world became more evil. God was sorry that He had created man. He decided to destroy all the people from the earth with a great flood.

Only Noah, his wife, three sons, and their wives found favor with God. They had not acted wickedly before God.

> **SIN**
>
> *Sin means to disobey God. God hates sin. We cannot please God when we sin. The Bible provides many examples of sin. Look at the examples of Adam and Eve and Cain. As you read the Bible stories, look for examples of sin and what happens when a person sins.*

So God told Noah what He planned to do. He told Noah to build an ark for his family and the animals. The ark was to be built of cypress wood and covered with tar. It was 450 feet long, 75 feet wide and 45 feet high (6:15). The people laughed at Noah for building a boat.

After it was built, God told Noah to bring into the ark a male and female of each animal. Noah brought food for his family and the animals for a year. Then Noah and his family and the animals entered the ark. God shut the door and sealed it. Noah obeyed God and did all that God told him to do.

When all were safely in the ark, the rains came. The peoples of the earth tried to scramble to safety. The waters rose until everything was covered and all life was destroyed, except those in the ark. It rained forty days and forty nights.

Months passed before the ark began to settle on land, finally coming to rest on Mount Ararat. Noah sent a raven out of the ark. It returned because the waters still covered the earth. Next Noah sent a dove out of the ark. It returned with a leaf. After another

God sends a rainbow as a promise.

week he sent the dove again, and this time it did not return. Now Noah knew that the waters had gone down. He opened the window and saw dry land.

God called Noah to leave the ark and release the animals. Noah and his family made a sacrifice to thank God for preserving them.

God promised never to destroy the earth with a flood again. To seal His promise, He placed the rainbow in the sky that followed a shower in which the sun continued to shine. At such times it is still visible today and continues to show God's promise.

THE TOWER OF BABEL
GENESIS 11

Hundreds of years passed after the Great Flood. As the generations went by, the population grew much larger again. People moved to cities for protection and to live with one another. They learned to make bricks and to use tar as mortar to hold the bricks together. All of the people spoke the same language. This allowed them to communicate and carry out their plan to build both a city and a tower.

One particular group settled on the plains of Shinar. This was located between the two great rivers, the Tigris and the Euphrates. These people built their great city on the flat land of the plain. Then they began to build a tower that would reach to the heavens. They were arrogant toward God.

God came down to watch what they were doing. He knew that their attitudes and actions would cause trouble. God did not want them to commit the same evil that the people had done before them, during the time of Noah. By staying together in the same place, they would only increase their wickedness.

Before they could complete their tower, God acted. He confused their speech, creating a "babel" of different sounds. The peoples could not understand each other. Tribes now spoke different languages and were forced to migrate to other parts of the world. The unfinished tower remained. It was called the Tower of Babel, since God confused their speech. The city on the plains of Shinar became known as Babylon.

ABRAHAM, THE MAN OF FAITH
GENESIS 11:27–23

Abram's Call and the Promise
(Genesis 12)

This story from the Bible changes focus from God's relation to all people. The story narrows to one family, the family of Terah. Terah took his family from the city of Ur, located near the Persian Gulf, to Haran, a city between the Tigris and Euphrates Rivers. Abram, as the oldest son, led the family when Terah died in Haran.

God said to Abram, "Leave this country. Go to another country that I will show you. I will make of you a great nation. I will bless you." God also told Abram that, "I will bless all the peoples of the earth through you."

Abram and Sarai, his wife, and all of their family left for the land of the Canaanites. Abram's nephew, Lot, and his family also journeyed to the land. Even though the Canaanites were in the land, God promised Abram that He would give the land to Abram and his descendants. Abram built an altar to worship God.

The land had a famine at the time Abram settled there. Abram took his family to Egypt. He told Sarai to tell Pharaoh that she was his sister. Sarai was very beautiful. Abram feared that Pharaoh might kill him if he knew that Abram was her husband. Instead God brought a plague on Pharaoh's household. Pharaoh gave gifts to Abram and sent him away. Abram went back to the place where he had built an altar, near Bethel. Abram settled there and became very rich.

Abram and Lot Separate (Genesis 13)

The flocks and herds of Abram and Lot grew.

The herdsmen began to fight one another. Abram wanted to keep peace with his nephew.

Abram told Lot to choose the place where he wanted to live. He said, "If you choose the land on the right, I will choose the land on the left. If you choose the land on the left, I will choose the land on the right."

Lot chose the best land along the plain of the Jordan. Lot pitched his tents near Sodom and Gomorrah. The men of Sodom were wicked and displeased God.

After Lot left, God spoke again to Abram. God told Abram to look to the east and west, north and south. As far as Abram could see, God gave the land to Abram.

God Renews His Promise (Genesis 15)

Time passed. How would God make His promise come true? Abram and Sarai were getting older. God told Abram to bring a cow, a goat, and a ram. Each was cut in half, and the halves were separated. Along with these Abram brought a dove and a pigeon. The birds were not cut.

After dark, God renewed His promise to Abram. He promised that Abram's descendants would increase. He told Abram that his descendants would spend four hundred years in another country before God would bring them back to this land of promise.

Then God sealed His promise. A burning torch passed between the halves of the animals. God committed Himself to Abram. This is similar to our signing a contract today.

Hagar Has a Son (Genesis 16)

Sarai was growing old. She still did not have a child. Sarai told Abram to start a family with her servant, Hagar. After Hagar was going to have a baby, she was mean to Sarai.

Sarai complained to Abram. Abram told his wife to decide what she wanted to do with Hagar. Sarai mistreated Hagar, and Hagar fled.

In the wilderness Hagar began to cry. God sent an angel to her.

He asked, "What are you doing here?"

"I'm running away from my mistress," said Hagar.

The angel told her to return to Sarai, and God would bless her. God would make her descendants numerous. The angel told Hagar that she should name the boy Ishmael, which means, "God hears."

FAITH

Faith means to trust God completetly. God is always working in our best interest. He wants us to trust Him. Abraham exercised faith. He believed God. He did what God told him to do. Because he acted in faith, God made a promise to Abraham. What was the promise?

God Appears to Abraham Again (Genesis 17–18)

God appeared to Abram again. God renewed His promise to make a great nation from Abram. He told Abram, "No longer will you be called Abram,

---

COMPARISON OF ADAM AND ABRAHAM

Recall that Eve was tempted to doubt God. Satan told her that God was trying to keep the knowledge of good and evil from her. He prevented her from eating of the tree. She disobeyed God and ate. She gave to Adam, and he disobeyed God.

Their disobedience led to sin and death. Abraham believed God and obeyed God. Abraham went from Haran to the Promised Land. Even when Abraham and Sarah were beyond the child-bearing years, God gave them a son. Abraham obeyed God in his willingness to sacrifice his son. Abraham became the father of the Hebrew nation. God was pleased with Abraham. What differences do you see between Adam and Eve and Abraham and Sarah?

but your name will be Abraham. He also said, "Your wife's name will no longer be Sarai. Her name will be Sarah."

Sodom and Gomorrah Destroyed (Genesis 19)

The Lord sent two angels to the wicked city of Sodom. Lot was sitting in the gate. Lot asked the strangers to come to his home.

At night a crowd gathered. They wanted Lot to hand the strangers over to them. Lot refused. The angels struck the crowd with blindness so they would not find Lot's door.

The next morning the angels insisted that Lot, his wife, and two daughters leave the city and not look back. They fled to the city of Zoar. Lot's wife lagged behind. God rained burning sulphur on the cities. Lot's wife disobeyed God's angels and looked back. She was turned to a pillar of salt. But Lot and his daughters were saved.

When Abraham awoke that morning, he could see the smoke rising from the cities. The sin of Sodom and Gomorrah brought God's punishment, but Lot was saved because God remembered Abraham.

Isaac Is Born (Genesis 21)

God promised He would give Sarah a son in her old age. Abraham was one hundred years old when Sarah bore him a son. It was the very time that God had promised. They named their son Isaac.

Abraham loved both his and Hagar's son Ishmael and his son Isaac. Trouble between Ishmael and Isaac arose. Sarah was very upset. Sarah wanted Hagar and Ishmael sent away. God told Abraham to do as Sarah wanted.

Hagar and Ishmael were sent away and went to the desert in Beer-shedba. After their food and water were gone, Hagar put the boy in the shade. Hagar walked away. She began to cry.

God's angel came. He said, "Do not be afraid. God will not allow Ishmael to die. Go to him."

Hagar went to Ishmael. God showed her that a well of water was close. She filled her water skin and gave Ishmael water.

Ishmael grew up in the wilderness. He became skilled with a bow. As an adult he married an Egyptian woman.

God Tested Abraham (Genesis 22)

Meanwhile Isaac grew to manhood. God tested Abraham's faith. He told Abraham to take his son Isaac to Mount Moriah. There God told Abraham to sacrifice his son on an altar to God. With a sad heart, Abraham obeyed. As they climbed the mountain, Abraham told the servants to stay behind.

When they drew close, Isaac said to his father, "We have fire and wood. Where is the lamb?"

Abraham answered, "God Himself will provide the lamb."

When they arrived, they built the altar. They laid the wood on the altar. Abraham placed his son on the altar and raised the knife. At that moment Abraham heard the voice of God's angel.

"Abraham! Abraham!"

Abraham replied, "Here I am."

"Do not harm your son. I know that you fear the Lord, because you have not kept your son from me."

Abraham looked around and found a ram caught in the bushes. Abraham called the place, The Lord Will Provide. Again, God promised to bless Abraham's family. From them would come descendants. They would be as many as the stars in the sky or the sand on the seashore.

ISAAC MARRIES REBEKAH
GENESIS 24

Sarah died. Abraham was aging. Abraham was very concerned that Isaac find a godly wife to carry on the family line, but he did not want her to come from among the Canaanite women. These women did not worship or fear the God of Abraham.

Abraham asked his trusted servant to go back to Abraham's homeland. His family had lived in the area between the Tigris and Euphrates Rivers. From Sarah's family, the servant would find a wife for Isaac.

Laden with many camels and gifts, the servant came to the city of Nahor. He came in the evening at a time when the women came to draw water from the well. There he prayed to God. The servant had learned well from his master, Abraham. He asked God to give him success. "May the woman that I ask to give me a drink from her water jug respond by saying, 'Let me also give water to your camels,' and so be the one for Isaac."

Before the servant finished praying, Rebekah came to the well. The servant went to her and asked if he might have a drink.

Rebekah answered, "Drink and I will draw water for your camels also." The servant was pleased and excited. He gave Rebekah a gold nose ring and two gold bracelets. The servant discovered that she was the daughter of Bethuel. Bethuel was the son of Abraham's brother, Nahor. The servant then asked if he and his party might stay at the home of her father. She invited them to come.

The servant knelt and worshiped God. God had led the servant to the relatives of Abraham. Rebekah ran home to tell her family all that had happened.

That evening the servant and his companions were cared for well. Before the servant would dine with Rebekah's family, he insisted on telling the reason for his visit. Both her father, Bethuel, and her brother, Laban, saw the hand of the Lord. They agreed that Rebekah should return to Abraham's home and become the wife of Isaac. They called Rebekah and asked if she were willing to go. She agreed to go.

On the next day the servant, his companions, Rebekah, and her maid left for her new home.

The servant took Rebekah to Isaac. Isaac saw the camel train and came to meet it. Rebekah saw Isaac and asked the servant who he was. When she learned that he was Isaac, she veiled herself, as was the custom, and dismounted from the camel.

The servant told Isaac about all that had happened. Isaac led Rebekah to his mother's tent where Isaac and Rebekah were married. Isaac loved Rebekah and was comforted at the loss of his mother, Sarah.

God wants to be involved in the major decisions of our lives, just as He was in Isaac's choice of a lifelong companion.

JACOB LEARNS TO TRUST GOD
GENESIS 25–33

Jacob Takes Rights from Esau
(Genesis 25, 27)

After many years without any children, Isaac prayed for his wife. God answered, and she had twin boys. Even before birth they struggled. Finally, at birth Jacob, the younger boy, held to the foot of his older brother, Esau. This was a sign suggesting that he would get the blessings of his older brother.

Esau was rugged and covered with hair. He became a hunter and the favorite of his father. Jacob stayed at home and so was the favorite of his mother.

One day Jacob was at home cooking lentil stew. Esau hunted all day and came home very hungry. He asked Jacob for some of his red stew. Jacob agreed, if Esau would sell him his birthright, or inheritance. Esau ate the stew and bread, and, in exchange, Jacob got the inheritance of his older brother.

Years passed. Isaac was old and could not see. Isaac called to Esau, "Go and hunt for some game. Then come and prepare my favorite meat dish. After I have eaten, I will bless you, my son."

Rebekah listened to the instructions of Isaac. She called to Jacob, "Go find two goats from the flock. I will cook them and prepare your father's favorite dish." She cooked the meal and covered the smooth skin of Jacob's arms and neck with goatskins so that Isaac would believe he was the rough-skinned Esau.

Jacob went to his father, who felt his arms. Jacob said, "I have prepared the meal." Isaac said that even though the voice sounded like Jacob's, he believed that his son, Esau, had come.

After Isaac had eaten, he blessed Jacob and Jacob left. Then Esau arrived. He brought Isaac's favorite dish. Isaac realized that he had been deceived. But Isaac had already given his blessing to Jacob. Esau wept. The best that Isaac could do was promise that one day Esau would lose the burden of his brother's control.

Esau was angry with his brother. He said that after Isaac's death, he would kill Jacob.

Jacob Meets God (Genesis 27–28)

Rebekah overheard Esau's plot to kill his brother. She called Jacob and told him, "Go and stay with my brother Laban. Your brother wants to kill you. You will be safe in Haran." She told Isaac that she did not want Jacob to marry any of the godless local women. So Jacob left his home and went to Haran.

Jacob set out for Haran. When he reached a certain place, he decided to stop for the night. He placed his head on a stone and slept. While he was asleep, he had a dream. He saw a staircase leading to heaven. God's angels were ascending and descending the staircase. God spoke to him, "I am the God of Abraham and your father Isaac. I will bless you. I will make your family great. Through your family all of the peoples of the world will be blessed."

The next morning Jacob renamed the place Bethel, or the House of God. He set the stone on which he had slept as a memorial to the place where he met God.

He promised the Lord that if God would care for him and protect him, he would serve God. He also promised to give God a tenth of all that he had.

Jacob Finds a Wife (Genesis 29–30)

Jacob arrived in Haran. He met some shepherds and asked, "Where are you from?"

They replied that they were from Haran. Jacob asked if they knew Laban. They answered that they did. At that moment the shepherdess, Rachel, came with her sheep. Jacob removed the large stone from the well. He watered Rachel's sheep. Then he kissed Rachel and told her that she was his cousin, the son of her aunt, Rebekah. Rachel ran home and told her father, Laban.

As soon as Laban heard the news, he ran to meet Jacob and invited him to come home and stay with their family. Rachel was so beautiful to Jacob that he fell in love with her. Rachel's older sister, Leah, had poor eyesight and was not as pretty. Jacob contracted to work for seven years if Laban would let him marry Rachel. Laban agreed.

After seven years Laban held a wedding feast. Since the bride was veiled, Jacob did not know that Laban had tricked him and given him Leah as his bride. According to the custom of the land, Laban insisted that the older daughter had to marry first. In exchange for another seven years, he could also marry Rachel. Jacob agreed because of his love for Rachel. At the end of the next seven years, he finally married Rachel.

Leah bore many sons for Jacob. Rachel was jealous of her sister. Finally, God heard Rachel's cry, and she had a son, Joseph. Jacob's sons were Reuben, Simeon, Levi, Judah, Issachar, Zebulun, Joseph, Benjamin, Gad, Asher, Dan, and Naphtali. Each son became the father of a tribe. Jacob had one daughter, Dinah.

Jacob wanted to return to his homeland, but Laban encouraged him to stay a while longer. God blessed Jacob, and his flocks increased, while Laban's were not growing as quickly. Laban's sons became jealous.

Jacob gathered his family and his flocks, and they prepared to leave quickly. Laban pursued but made peace with Jacob. He sent him on his way.

Jacob Meets Esau (Genesis 32–33)

Jacob knew that he still had to face his brother. He did not know whether Esau was still angry with him. Jacob sent word to Esau that he was returning home. The messengers told Jacob that Esau set out to meet him with four hundred men.

Jacob feared Esau. He divided his family, goods, and cattle. He thought that if Esau killed one group, the other would be able to escape. He sent them across the river Jabbok. He was alone until a stranger came and wrestled with him. They wrestled all night. By morning the stranger touched Jacob's hip and twisted it. The stranger wanted to leave. But Jacob would not let go until the stranger blessed him.

The man asked, "What is your name?"

"My name is Jacob," he said.

"Your name shall no longer be Jacob, but Israel. You have wrestled with God and with men and succeeded." The stranger blessed Israel. Israel called the place Peniel, because he met God there and did not die.

Soon a cloud of dust appeared on the horizon. Esau was coming with his four hundred men. Israel bowed to his brother. Instead of fighting, Esau and Jacob embraced and were reunited. Esau welcomed his brother home.

GOD CARES FOR JOSEPH
GENESIS 37–50

Joseph Has a Dream (Genesis 37:1–11)
Jacob (also called Israel) and his family lived in the land of Canaan, where both Abraham and Isaac had lived before him. Of all his sons, Jacob loved Joseph the best. He was the son of his most beloved wife, Rachel. Joseph was born to Jacob in his old age. Jacob was especially fond of Joseph, so he had a coat of many colors woven for Joseph. At age seventeen, along with his brothers, Joseph tended his father's flocks. Upon his return home, Joseph brought Jacob a bad report about his brothers. That's when his brothers became very jealous.

To add to their anger, Joseph had a dream. He dreamed that they were binding sheaves of grain. All at once Joseph's sheaf rose above the others. All of the others bowed down to Joseph's sheaf. The brothers hated him more.

Joseph had a second dream. In this dream the sun and moon and eleven stars bowed down to him. Even his father rebuked Joseph for this dream. He said, "Will your mother and I and your brothers all bow down to you?" But Jacob remembered the dream.

Joseph Sold to Slavery (Genesis 37)
One day, Jacob's sons were grazing their herds. Jacob sent Joseph to see how the brothers were caring for the herds. When they saw him coming, they plotted to kill Joseph. Only Reuben wanted to save him, and he suggested they throw him into an empty well. Reuben thought that later he could rescue Joseph. The brothers agreed, so when Joseph arrived, they took his coat of many colors and threw him into a deep well.

A caravan of Midianite traders came that way. Judah told his brothers, "We can't make any money killing Joseph. Let us sell him as a slave." The brothers liked the plan. They dipped his coat in blood and decided to tell their father that a wild animal killed him.

When Jacob saw the coat, he wept bitterly. "It is my son's coat. He has been killed by a wild animal." Jacob mourned for his son and would not be comforted.

Joseph Thrown into Prison (Genesis 39–40)
The traders sold Joseph to one of Pharaoh's officers, Potiphar. God blessed Joseph. Soon Potiphar made Joseph head over his household.

Joseph was good-looking. Potiphar's wife found herself desiring him. She told him of her desire. He replied, "My master has trusted me with everything. I cannot deceive him by taking his wife. God would not be pleased with that!"

The woman became very angry. One day when Joseph had work to do inside the house, she saw that they were alone. There were no other persons in the house. When Potiphar returned home, his wife accused Joseph of being alone with her. Potiphar had Joseph put in prison.

God did not forget Joseph. After some time in prison, Pharaoh was angry with his cupbearer and baker. They were also put in prison.

One night each had a dream. Neither knew the meaning of the dreams. When Joseph heard that they were saddened, he said he would ask God the meaning. For the cupbearer the dream meant that he would be freed and go back to work for Pharaoh. Joseph asked him to remember him and help him to get out of prison.

For the baker the dream was not good. In three days the baker would be hanged. Joseph's interpretation turned out as he said. But the cupbearer forgot about Joseph.

Pharaoh Had Dreams (Genesis 41)

Two years went by, and Joseph was still in prison. Pharaoh had two dreams. None of the magicians of Egypt could tell Pharaoh the meaning of the dreams. The chief cupbearer then remembered Joseph. He told Pharaoh what happened to him and that Joseph had interpreted his dream.

Pharaoh sent for Joseph and told him the two dreams. As Pharaoh stood on the bank of the Nile River, he saw seven healthy cows come out of the water. Seven unhealthy cows ate the healthy cows.

Then in the second dream, there were seven healthy ears of grain. Seven unhealthy ears followed these. The unhealthy ears ate the healthy ones.

Joseph said that God was telling Pharoah what He was going to do. There will be seven years of plenty in Egypt. These will be followed by seven years of famine. Joseph told Pharaoh to choose a wise man to store grain during the years of plenty for the years of famine. Pharaoh wisely chose Joseph and made Joseph second in command. He gave Joseph a wife, Asenath. They had two sons, Manasseh and Ephraim. God blessed Joseph though all these years.

The plentiful harvest and famine happened just as Joseph had said. During the first seven years Joseph stored one-fifth of the harvest for the years of famine. Once the famine began, the people cried to Pharaoh. Pharaoh sent them to Joseph. Joseph opened the supply of corn, and the people were fed.

Jacob's Sons Go to Egypt (Genesis 42)

The famine spread throughout Palestine. Jacob and his family were not spared. Joseph's brothers traveled to Egypt to get food. Joseph was governor and was in charge of selling grain to the people. Since he was dressed as an Egyptian, his brothers approached him, bowed down, but did not recognize him.

Joseph knew these were his brothers, but he accused them of coming to Egypt as spies. They tried to assure Joseph that they were not spies. He asked about their family. The brothers told Joseph that there were twelve brothers. One had died, and the youngest, Benjamin, was with their father.

Joseph told them that they must send one brother to their father and bring Benjamin back to Egypt. Then Joseph had the brothers put in jail for three days. At the end of that time, he said that they could go home, but one would have to remain in jail until they returned.

Since they believed Joseph to be an Egyptian, Reuben spoke in Hebrew to his brothers. Reuben told them that their sin against Joseph was the cause of their present situation. Remember that Reuben wanted to save Joseph. Joseph turned away from them and cried.

Then he had Simeon bound and placed in prison until the brothers returned. The brothers went home and told their father what had happened. Imagine their surprise to find that the money they paid for the grain had been returned, along with the grain.

Jacob said to Reuben, "You have taken away my sons. Joseph is gone. Simeon is gone. And now you want to take Benjamin."

Joseph Makes Himself Known (Genesis 43–47)

Time passed. Jacob's family suffered in the famine. The brothers wanted to make a second trip to Egypt. They reminded their father that they could not go without Benjamin. Judah promised to protect Benjamin. Sadly, Jacob agreed. He told them that they must take extra money and provisions to the ruler in Egypt.

They arrived in Egypt and went to Joseph. He had them come to his home. The brothers were frightened, but the dinner went well. When the time came for the brothers to leave Egypt, Joseph had the steward secretly place his own cup in Benjamin's sack. The brothers received their grain, and Joseph had the money restored to them also. Then they began their trip home.

Joseph's steward followed them, caught up with them, and accused them of stealing Joseph's cup. They assured him they did not have it. The brother's said that if any one of them had the cup, he should be killed. When it was found in Benjamin's sack, they all were very upset.

When Joseph's brothers returned to Egypt, Judah begged for Benjamin's life. Joseph could not restrain himself any longer. He made himself known to his brothers and told them that he was not angry with them. "You sold me into slavery. But God meant it for good and He brought me here." Joseph forgave his brothers of the wrong they had done to him by selling him into slavery in Egypt. Joseph asked them to bring their father and return to Egypt.

Jacob's sons returned to their father. They told him all that had happened. Jacob was excited to know that his son, Joseph, whom he loved, was alive and in Egypt. They told Jacob that Joseph wanted him to leave Palestine and move to Egypt.

So Jacob gathered his family, and they moved to Egypt. Pharaoh welcomed Jacob's family. Jacob blessed Pharaoh. Jacob's family settled in the land of Goshen.

The Famine and the Death of Jacob and Joseph (Genesis 47–50)

Famine throughout the region grew more severe. The people begged for food. They paid for their grain until their money ran out.

After the money was gone, the people came to Joseph and asked to buy food with their cattle, horses, and other animals. Another year passed, and the people had given their money and their animals to Pharaoh. The people told Joseph that they had no money and no cattle. All they had left was their land and their bodies. The people became slaves to Pharaoh. One-fifth of their harvest went to Pharaoh. Joseph greatly increased the wealth of Pharaoh.

For seventeen years Jacob lived in Egypt. Before he died, Jacob brought all of his sons before him and blessed them. He told his sons, "Bury me in with my fathers in the cave which Abraham had bought." When all was complete, Jacob died and was taken to the land of his family.

Joseph's brothers feared that after Jacob died he would hurt them. But Joseph reassured them that God had brought him to Egypt. Joseph freely forgave his brothers.

After many years, Joseph himself was about to die. He told his brothers, "God will visit you and bring you to the Land of Promise. Take my bones and bury them in the land of our fathers." With the passing of Joseph, the era of the Patriarchs came to an end.

MOSES' BIRTH AND CALL
EXODUS 1–5

The Israelites in Egypt (Exodus 1)

Several hundred years passed after the death of Joseph. The Israelites grew and became a very large group of people in Egypt. The new Pharaoh did not know Joseph and did not feel any responsibility to him. He became anxious about the size of the population of these foreign people. He feared that in the event of a war, the Israelites might help the enemy.

Pharaoh enslaved the people and made them serve him. The Egyptians made the Israelites work very hard. They worked in work gangs under cruel taskmasters. The people of Israel worked in the fields to produce food. They also worked in Pharaoh's building programs by making bricks and mortar. Even though the work was hard, the people of Israel continued to grow.

When Pharaoh was not successful in limiting them by making them work hard, he called the midwives. These are the women that help mothers in childbirth. He told them to kill all of the boy babies and to allow the girl babies to live. The midwives were loyal to God and did not carry out Pharaoh's order. When Pharaoh failed to limit the number of births, he commanded his people to throw boys into the Nile River and allow only the girls to live.

The Birth of Moses (Exodus 2:1–10)

A man from the tribe of Levi and his wife had a son. The boy was healthy. She kept him hidden at home as long as she could. Then she wove together a basket of bulrushes from the riverbank. She lined the basket with pitch so it would float in the water.

She placed the baby in the basket and set it afloat in the river. Every day the baby's sister watched from a safe distance. When Pharaoh's daughter came to the river to bathe one day, she saw the basket among the reeds. She had one of her servants pull the basket from the water. When she opened the basket, she found the baby crying. She said, "This must be one of the Hebrew children." She felt sorry for the baby.

Miriam came to Pharaoh's daughter and asked, "Shall I go find a nurse from among the Hebrew women?" Pharaoh's daughter sent her to find a nurse.

She brought the baby's mother. Pharaoh's daughter sent her to nurse the baby and bring him back when he had grown into a healthy child.

When they returned, Pharaoh's daughter made him her son. She needed to find a name for the child. She called him Moses, because he had been taken out of the water. He grew up and was educated in the household of Pharaoh.

Moses Runs Away to Midian (Exodus 2:11–25)

Even though Moses was raised in the household of Pharaoh, he never forgot that his family was Hebrew. Moses saw that the people of Israel were treated badly by the Egyptians. One day he saw an Egyptian mistreating one of the Hebrews. To protect the Hebrew, he killed the Egyptian.

The next day he saw two Hebrews quarreling with each other. The Hebrews were annoyed that Moses interfered. They asked if he intended to kill them as he had killed the Egyptian the day before. Moses became frightened that his deed was known. He knew that if Pharaoh heard about the incident, his life was in danger.

He fled from Egypt and traveled to the land of Midian. Moses was resting at a well. The seven daughters of Jethro, a priest in Midian, came to draw water for their sheep. A group of shepherds tried to chase the young women away. Moses protected the young women. Moses helped them fill their jars with water.

When his daughters came home early, Jethro wanted to know how they got done so quickly. They told him about the young Egyptian who had helped them at the well. He told them to go quickly. "Invite the young man for dinner."

Moses came to dinner. Later he married Zipporah. Moses named their son Gershom, which means "stranger here." Moses realized that he was a stranger in Midian.

God Calls Moses (Exodus 3–4)

Years passed and Moses lived in the home of Jethro with his wife and son. He tended the flocks of his father-in-law.

One day as he was tending his flock near the mountain of God, he saw a strange sight. There was a bush that was burning, but it was not burned completely. Moses turned aside to look at the strange sight.

As he approached the bush, a voice called to him, "Moses, Moses!" Moses answered, "Here I am." The Lord said to Moses, "Do not come any further. The ground on which you are standing is holy. Take off your shoes."

God told Moses, "I have seen the suffering of my people in Egypt. I have come to take them out of Egypt and to bring them into the land that I promised to their fathers. I am going to send you to Pharaoh to bring my people out of Egypt."

Moses objected, "Who am I that I should go to Pharaoh?"

God answered, "I will be with you. When you have come to this mountain, you will serve me."

Moses said, "Perhaps the people will ask, 'What is the name of God who has sent you?'"

God said, "I AM WHO I AM has sent you. I am the God of your fathers, Abraham, Isaac, and Jacob."

God promised to give Moses signs to convince Pharaoh that he should let the people go. God showed His power to comfort Moses. He told Moses to throw his staff on the ground. The staff became a serpent. When Moses picked it up again, it was a staff.

Then God told Moses to put his hand inside his robe. When he brought it back out, it was diseased. When he put it back in again, he was healed.

God also promised Moses that Aaron would speak for him.

When God finished speaking to Moses, Moses went into the wilderness and found Aaron as God had said. Together they went to the people, and the people believed.

MOSES DELIVERS ISRAEL FROM EGYPT
EXODUS 5–13

Moses Appears to Pharaoh (Exodus 5–6)

Moses and Aaron went to Pharaoh. They told Pharaoh, "The God of Israel says, 'Let my people go into the wilderness to worship me.'"

Pharaoh answered, "Why do you take the people from their work?"

Pharaoh commanded, "Make the people work harder. Do not give the Hebrews straw to make bricks. Do not reduce the number of bricks that they will produce. They are lazy and want to worship their God, when they should be working." The taskmasters drove the people harder. They did not give them straw any longer. They beat the people and demanded that they produce the same number of bricks.

The people went to Pharaoh and complained. He said they were idle because they wanted to worship their God. When Pharaoh refused to listen, the people went to Moses. They told Moses it was his fault they had to work harder without straw.

Moses went to God. He asked God why the people were suffering. He asked God why God did not deliver the people.

God said to Moses, "Now you will see My power. Pharaoh will send the people out of Egypt. Before that happens, Pharaoh's heart will be hardened. I will show mighty signs, and then he will let my people go."

Moses went back to Pharaoh. Moses and Aaron did as God told them. Pharaoh said to Moses, "Work a miracle."

Aaron threw down his rod before Pharaoh. It became a serpent. Pharaoh called his magicians. They threw the rods on the ground. The rods became snakes. But Aaron's snake ate the snakes of Pharoah's men.

God Sends the Plagues (Exodus 7–10)

God sent Moses and Aaron to the Nile River. He told Moses to strike the river Nile with his staff. The river turned to blood. The fish died. The river smelled bad. There was no drinking water from the Nile for seven days. Still Pharaoh would not let the people go because his magicians were able to turn the river to blood also.

Again Moses went to Pharaoh and told him that God said, "Let my people go." Pharaoh refused.

Aaron struck the land with his rod. The rivers and streams filled with frogs. Pharaoh asked Moses to remove the frogs, and he would let the people go. On the next day the frogs died. They were piled in heaps. The land smelled bad. But as soon as the frogs were killed, Pharaoh would not let the people go. The magicians copied what Moses and Aaron had done.

God told Moses and Aaron to strike the dust. The grains of dust became gnats. The whole land was filled with gnats. This time the magicians could do nothing. They admitted that God was punishing Egypt. Pharaoh would not listen.

A plague of flies swarmed across the land. The flies entered into the homes of all the Egyptians, but not into the homes of the Hebrews. Pharaoh asked Moses to plead his case before God. Pharaoh promised to let the Israelites go. As soon as the flies were removed, Pharaoh would not let the people go.

God told Moses to speak to Pharaoh again. If Pharaoh refused to let the people go, then God would bring disease upon the animals of Egypt. The plague affected only the Egyptians. God protected the Hebrews. But Pharaoh refused to let the people go.

God told Moses and Aaron to take ashes to Pharaoh. They threw the ashes into the air and boils and sores plagued all the Egyptians. The magicians were also plagued. Pharaoh would still not let the people go.

Because Pharaoh refused to let the people go, God sent a hailstorm on the people of Egypt. Thunder crashed and lightening flashed and accompanied the hail. The crops of flax and barley that were growing now lay flat. Cattle and people died. Pharaoh again asked Moses to plead with God to stop the plague. Even Pharaoh's servants asked him to change his mind. Pharaoh called Moses and told him to take the people and go worship God. When Moses said that the people and their herds must leave Egypt, Pharaoh did not keep his word.

God said that He would make Pharaoh know that God was Lord. God told Moses that the children of Israel would one day look back and see the delivering hand of God. They would see how God dealt with the

Locusts came in swarms.

Egyptians, who did not worship Him. God told Moses to ask Pharaoh, "How long will you refuse to humble yourself and not let my people go? Because you will not listen, I will send a plague of locusts." The locusts came in swarms. There were so many that the sky was darkened. The trees that escaped the other plagues were now eaten by the locusts. Pharoah once again promised to let the people go. God sent a strong wind, which pushed the locusts into the Red Sea. As soon as the plague was stopped, Pharaoh did not do as he had promised.

Because Pharaoh refused to let the people go, God covered the land with darkness. The people of Israel had light in their homes, but the people of Egypt did not. Pharaoh called Moses and said, "You may take your families, but your flocks must stay." Then Pharaoh changed his mind again and would not let the people go. Pharaoh told Moses that if he ever came into his presence again, Pharaoh would kill him. Moses answered, "It is true, you will never see my face again."

The Last Plague (Exodus 11–12)

The Lord said to Moses, "I will send one last plague upon Egypt. Pharaoh will let you go." God said, "The people will find favor in the sight of the Egyptians. The Egyptians will give them gold, silver, and other treasures." God also instructed Moses and the people that they should prepare for the Passover. God would pass over the people of Egypt. The firstborn child of every family in Egypt would die. The firstborn animals in each home would also die. But nothing would happen to the Israelites.

That night was painful to the Egyptians. Every household suffered from the death of the firstborn. But no one among the Israelites was hurt.

The people of Israel ate their dinner and prepared to leave Egypt. Pharaoh called for Moses and Aaron. Pharaoh was experiencing grief at the loss of his own son. Pharaoh told them to take their families and leave Egypt. He said that they should take all of their herds and cattle. The Egyptian people gave the Hebrews gold, silver, and precious jewels to take on their journey.

The people of Israel had been in Egypt for 430 years. That night God sent His people from Egypt toward the Promised Land in Palestine.

God wanted the Egyptians to know that He was Lord. The gods of Egypt included the Nile River god, the sun god, and nature gods. The plagues were sent to show those were false gods. God demonstrated His power. God showed the Egyptians that He was more powerful than any of their gods. Finally, in the last plague God demonstrated that He had power over life and death. Pharaoh's pride had kept the people of Israel from leaving Egypt to worship God. He caused the Egyptians much suffering.

MOSES AND THE TEN COMMANDMENTS
EXODUS 14–17, 19–20, 32

Crossing the Red Sea (Exodus 13:17–15:27)
The people were camped beside the Red Sea. In the distance they could see the Egyptians coming. Pharaoh had not learned his lesson. He was angry because he lost his slaves. The Egyptians pursued the Hebrews.

The people of Israel were afraid. They complained to Moses. Moses said, "Do not be afraid. Look for the salvation of God. The Lord will fight for you."

God told Moses to lift up his staff and stretched his hand over the sea. The waters parted. The angel of God guided the people of Israel across the sea. The people walked on dry land and were shielded from the Egyptians by a cloud.

The Egyptians began to follow. Their chariots bogged down in the mud. Some of the Egyptians wanted to turn back. They saw that God was on the side of the Israelites. But Pharaoh pressed forward.

When the Israelites were safely across the sea, Moses stretched out his rod. The wind stopped, and the waters returned to the riverbed. The Egyptians were drowned. None of the Egyptians escaped. On that day God demonstrated His power and protected the Israelites. The Israelites sang to God and praised Him for His deliverance.

Provision of Food in the Wilderness (Exodus 15–16)
The people entered the desert. They did not find food or water in the desert. They complained to Moses about their situation. Moses went to God. God provided for their needs.

The waters of Marah were bitter. The people complained. God told Moses to throw a piece of wood into the waters. The bitter waters now became sweet and pleasant to drink.

The people of Israel were camped between Elim and Mount Sinai. They began to complain to Moses and Aaron. "You have brought us out here to die. We have no food. We could have been in Egypt and enjoyed the good food there. Instead you brought us out here to kill us with hunger."

The Lord told Moses, "I will rain bread from heaven. Each person should gather only enough for that day. On the sixth day each person should gather a double portion. On the Sabbath day there will be no bread from heaven. But the bread gathered before the Sabbath will not go bad. I will also provide quail in the evening."

Moses told the people all that God had said. The people did not know what to call the bread. They called it manna. It was white and tasted like wafers with honey. For the next forty years, as the people wandered in the wilderness, God provided manna and quail for them to eat.

In spite of the plagues and the destruction of the Egyptians, the people still complained and did not trust God. God expects His people to trust Him.

Everything He does is in their best interest. What was true then is still true today.

The Ten Commandments (Exodus 19–20)

The people of Israel had been wondering in the wilderness for three months. They came to Mount Sinai. They encamped at the foot of the mount. Moses went up into the mountain. He prayed to God. God told them that in three days He would speak to the people.

> #### ATONE
> Atone means to bring together. The sin offering was made in order for humans to find fellowship with God. God is very sad when we sin. The sacrifice makes it possible for us to again relate to God.

In the meantime the people needed to make themselves holy.

God made His presence felt by the people. Fire, smoke, and quaking in the mountain made the people aware of God's presence. The sound of a trumpet was heard. The people were told not to approach the mountain as Moses appeared before God to receive the Ten Commandments.

God said to Moses, "I am the LORD your God, who brought you out of Egypt, where you were slaves."

"You shall not have any other gods before me."

"You shall not make any statue to serve or worship. If you serve false gods, you and your children will suffer. But if you keep my commandments, you will experience my love."

"You shall not take the name of the Lord carelessly, but with reverence."

"You shall keep the Sabbath day holy. You may work during six days, but the seventh day is holy to the Lord. The Sabbath day is a holy day."

"Show respect for your mother and father, that you may live long on the earth."

"You shall not kill."

"You shall not be unfaithful to your husband or wife."

"You shall not steal."

"You shall not speak falsely against your neighbor."

"You must not envy another person's possessions."

At the end of God's commandments, the mountain shook. The sounds of thunder, lightning, and trumpet came forth. Smoke came from the mountain. The people were afraid. Moses said to the people, "Do not be afraid! God wants to test you. He shows His power, so that you will not commit sin."

The Ark of the Covenant (Exodus 25)

God spoke again to Moses from the mountaintop. He said, "Tell the children of Israel to make an offering to Me. Ask only of the people that are willing to give Me an offering of gold, silver, bronze, blue, purple, and scarlet thread, linen, animal skins, acacia wood, spices, incense, and precious stones. From these things I will make a sanctuary to live among the people."

The sanctuary was the Tabernacle. It would be taken down and moved when the people moved from place to place. The Tabernacle would be the place where the people would come to worship God. The Tabernacle was the responsibility of the

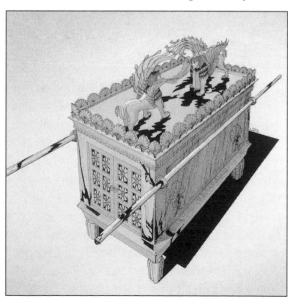

Artist rendering of the Ark of the Covenant.

27

priests, who would conduct the offerings to God and attend to the holy places inside the Tabernacle.

God also told Moses to prepare the Ark of the Covenant. This would be made of acacia wood and covered inside and outside with gold. On the top of the Ark would be placed two cherubim facing each other and between them would be the Mercy Seat. This would be the Holy of Holies. As the people moved, they would take the Ark of the Covenant with them and set up the Tabernacle in the new location.

The Golden Calf (Exodus 32)

Moses talked to God for many days. The people thought he was not coming back. They told Aaron, "We do not know about this man Moses. He is not returning. Let us make a god, whom we may serve."

Aaron told the people, "Bring your gold from your sons and daughters and your wives. We will fashion a golden calf to worship."

The people said, "These are the gods who brought us out of Egypt." The people built an altar. The next day they had a feast to the Lord. They ate and drank and danced.

God knew what the people had done, and He was very angry. He told Moses that He would destroy the people of Israel. He promised to make a great nation out of Moses' family.

But Moses begged for the people. He told God that the people of Israel would be laughed at by the people around them. He pleaded that God would spare them. Because Moses prayed, God relented.

Then Moses had to face the people. He was very angry. In his hand he carried the two tablets of stone with the Ten Commandments. In his anger, Moses broke the Ten Commandments over the golden calf. God brought a plague of disease upon the people for their disobedience and sin. But He spared the people from death. Sin and disobedience always bring punishment when we disobey God. The people became obedient and followed what Moses told them.

WORSHIP AND THE TABERNACLE
EXODUS 26–27, 30, 35–38

Worship for the Hebrews took place in the Tabernacle. The Tabernacle, or Tent of Meeting, was the place that God designed for worship among His people. God gave Moses directions for building the Tabernacle. The people donated an offering to God the materials for construction of the Tabernacle. The Tabernacle could be taken down and moved, when necessary.

Walls made from finely woven linen enclosed the courtyard. There were sixty supporting pillars of bronze. The length was about 150 feet, while the width was 75 feet. Inside the courtyard behind the entrance was the altar for burnt offering. On the altar, animals were sacrificed while prayers were made to God. Next behind the altar was the laver. The laver was used by the priests to wash their hands.

Behind the laver was the Tabernacle. It was divided into two rooms. The first room was larger and contained several items. The first was the bronze altar of incense. This was lighted every morning. To the left of the altar was the gold menorah or seven-branched candlesticks. To the right of the altar was the table of twelve loaves of bread. These were changed once each week and stood for the twelve tribes of Israel.

Toward the back of the Tabernacle was a smaller room. It was called the "most holy place." It was also called the "Holy of Holies." It contained the Ark of the Covenant. The Ark of the Covenant was a wooden box. The wood was overlaid with gold. On top of the Ark were the seraphim, or angels. Inside the Ark were the tables of stone on which were etched the Ten Commandments. It also had a pot of manna from the food that the people ate in the wilderness. Later, when the leadership of the priesthood was questioned, God selected Aaron. The rod of Aaron bore almonds (see Numbers 17).

Sin is very important to God. Only God can forgive sin. The worship of the ancient Hebrews required sacrifice for sin. When we understand the worship of Israel, we can better understand why Jesus had to come. Unlike the sacrifices on the altar of burnt offerings, Jesus' death on the cross was a sacrifice once for all. His death and resurrection provide salvation for us. Many of the contents of the Tabernacle tell us about Jesus' sacrifice for us.

JOSHUA LEADS THE PEOPLE TO THE PROMISED LAND
JOSHUA 1–6

Joshua Becomes Leader (Joshua 1)

Moses was not permitted to go into the Promised Land. God allowed Moses to climb Mount Nebo, which overlooked the Promised Land. From there Moses could see the land of Canaan. Then Moses died. The people wept for Moses for thirty days. Moses had already chosen his successor to be Joshua.

The people now had a new leader. God spoke to Joshua: "Moses, my servan,t is dead. You will take my people into the Promised Land. As I was with Moses, so I will be with you. I will not fail or forsake you. Be strong and of good courage. Do not forsake the law that I gave to Moses. Meditate upon my Word. Be careful to do everything written in my Word. Then you'll make your way prosperous and have good success." God promised to go with Joshua wherever he went.

Joshua told the people about his instructions from God. He told the people, "We will arrive in three days when we cross the Jordan River. We will take the land that God promised to our forefathers."

The people responded, "All that you have commanded we will do. Just as we obeyed Moses, we will obey you. If anyone refuses to obey you, that person will be punished. Be strong and of good courage."

Joshua Sends Spies to Jericho (Joshua 2)

Jericho was an important city that lay just beyond the Jordan River. It had to be captured before Joshua and his army could conquer the rest of Palestine. Joshua sent two spies to Jericho.

Rahab's home was in the wall of Jericho. It was an ideal place for the spies to look at the city. Rahab said she knew that God had protected the Israelites on their flight from Egypt. All of the people of Jericho realized that God was fighting for the Israelites. They were afraid. She made the spies promise that if she protected them, they would save her and her family after the Israelites came to the city.

Rahab hid the spies under stalks of flax. When the king of Jericho sent men to find the spies, Rahab protected them. She sent the men into the mountains to find them. Meanwhile, Rahab let the spies down by rope during the night. She told them to wait three days in the hills and then return to their camp. By that time the king would have given up the search.

The sign by which the Israelites would know to protect Rahab would be the scarlet cord hanging from her window. This was the same cord by which the spies escaped from the wall of Jericho.

Crossing the Jordan River (Joshua 3–5)

God gave Joshua clear instructions about crossing the river Jordan. The Lord intended to do a miracle. The people would cross the river on dry land. God would guide them in a special manner. God's guidance would indicate to the neighboring peoples that God was protecting His people.

The Israelites left their encampment and followed the Ark of the Covenant. The priests carried the Ark. Since it was harvest time, the water of the river was very high. As soon as the priests set foot in the water, the water parted. All of the people of Israel crossed the river on dry land. This was the second time God had parted the waters for the Israelites.

God instructed the people to select stones from the places where the Ark had stood. The stones were to be carried to the homes of the people. They would serve as a reminder of the

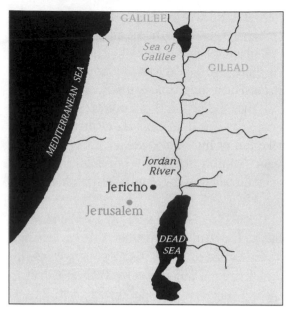

miracle that God performed on that day. God said, "Whenever a child asks, 'What is the meaning of the stones?' The family member should reply, 'The stones make us remember how God guided us across the River Jordan.'" It was a day in which He allowed Israel to experience God's power. All of the neighboring peoples could see that God was protecting and guiding His people.

Jericho Is Defeated (Joshua 6)

The wall surrounding Jericho protected it. No one was allowed to enter or leave the city. The people of Jericho were afraid. God said, "I have given you Jericho this day. Your soldiers will march around the city once each day. You'll repeat this for six days. On the seventh day your soldiers will march around the city seven times. Then the priests will blow the ram's horn seven times. All of the people will shout. The wall will go flat. Until the seventh day you should not make a sound." Each day the priests carried the Ark. Other priests blew the trumpets. The people did not say anything. After they marched around the city one time, they went back to camp. They repeated this for six days.

On the seventh day they marched around the city seven times. The priests blew the trumpets for the seventh time. Joshua said to the people, "Shout, for God has given you the city. It is yours. Do not take anything from the city."

On that day the people of Israel were victorious over the city of Jericho. God fought for the people of Israel. Only Rahab and her family were saved. Joshua remembered the promise that the spies had given to her.

To conquer Canaan, Joshua and his army continued to fight for control of all Palestine. The miraculous victory at Jericho provides understanding of the work that Joshua did because he listened to and obeyed God. God was with him and the Israelites as they carried out the task. The Book of Joshua does not give a complete account of all that happened. By the time Joshua finished, most of the land belonged to the Israelites.

As the land was conquered, Joshua divided the land among the twelve tribes of Israel. Each of the tribes had its own symbol that it had carried during the exodus. Three of the tribes stayed on the east of the Jordan River. Moab and Edom were two countries that were south of the Dead Sea. Moab and Edom remained enemies of the people of Israel for years to come.

SAMSON AND THE JUDGES
JUDGES 13–16

After the Israelites had settled in Palestine, there was a period of time in which they were ruled by judges. They had no king. The people did not always live up to the commandments of God. When they sinned against God, they were punished. Many times the punishment came from neighbors, who would steal or fight against the Hebrew people. Then the people would pray to God. God would hear their prayer. He would send a judge to settle the problem.

Manoah and his wife were from the tribe of Dan. They did not have any children, so God promised to give them a son. They were told that they must not give the child wine or shave his head.

When the boy was born, his parents named him Samson. Years later Samson fell in love with a Philistine woman. The Philistines were a group of people who did not believe in God. They lived by the Mediterranean Sea. For forty years the Philistines caused problems for the people of Israel. God saw the difficulty this caused His people.

Even though his parents did not approve of a marriage with a Philistine, they went with Samson to the woman's home and asked her to marry him. On the way to Philistia, a lion confronted them. Samson tore the lion apart with his bare hands. Several weeks later bees had made a nest in the lion. Samson simply reached in and took the honey.

On his wedding day Samson posed a riddle to his guests. He said, *"Out of the eater came something to eat, out of the strong came something sweet."* He asked his guests, "What does this mean? If you can tell me what it means, I will give you thirty linen garments and thirty sets of garments. If you cannot tell me, then you will give me the sets of garments." They agreed.

Samson's wife begged him to tell her the answer to the riddle, but he refused. Finally, after seven days, his wife went to him crying. "If you loved me, you would tell me," she said. Samson could not take it any longer and told her. She told the guests and Samson lost. In his anger he killed thirty Philistines and brought the garments to the ones who solved the riddle. Samson never saw his wife again.

Sometime later Samson fell in love with another Philistine woman named Delilah. The Philistines promised to pay Delilah if she would find out the secret of his strength. Delilah begged Samson to tell her the secret. He told her, "If you bind me with seven new cords, I will lose my strength." When Samson fell asleep, Delilah bound him with seven new cords. She cried, "The Philistines are upon you!" Sampson woke up and burst the cords.

After several more tries, Sampson did not tell Delilah the secret of his strength. She grew very angry and complained that he did not love her.

Finally, he told her that if his hair was cut, he would lose his strength. When he fell asleep, the Philistines cut his hair. When he awoke, his strength was gone. The Philistines blinded him and took him to their prison. For a long time Samson suffered for his foolishness. The Philistines put him to hard labor.

One day they brought him to their temple to make fun of him. They gave credit to their god, Dagon. Samson asked a little boy to take him to the two main pillars of the temple. His hair had grown long. He prayed to God, "Give me strength again this once." With all his might he pushed on the two pillars. The temple collapsed. Many men and women and all the leaders of the Philistines were killed. Israel was avenged of the Philistines.

SAMUEL, THE LAST OF THE PROPHETS
1 SAMUEL 1–15

The Philistines were a seafaring people. It is believed that they came from an area around the Aegean Sea. This is near Greece. They arrived in Palestine during the period of the Patriarchs. There are Egyptian records that show these peoples fighting with the Egyptians. They were well organized and were a serious threat to the children of Israel during the time of the judges and the beginning of the reigns of the kings.

The Birth of Samuel (1 Samuel 1)
A man by the name of Elkanah had two wives. His wife, Peninnah, had children, but his other wife, Hannah, did not have any children. Although Hannah's husband loved her, Peninnah made fun of Hannah.

Hannah was deeply hurt. She went to the temple where Eli was the High Priest. There she wept before God. She asked God to give her a son. She promised that he would serve God all of his life. Eli felt sorry for her and asked God to hear her prayer. Eli blessed her as she left.

God heard her prayer. The next year she had a son. When he was a little older, she took him to Eli.

She said to Eli, "I am the woman who prayed for a son. God heard my prayer and sent me Samuel. My son will enter the service of God." Eli cared for the boy and taught him the ways of God.

God Calls Samuel (1 Samuel 3)

One night as Samuel was sleeping, he heard a voice calling, "Samuel, Samuel." He got up and ran to Eli and said, "I am here. You called me." But Eli answered, "I did not call you. Go back to sleep."

God called Samuel a second time. Again Samuel ran to Eli. Eli told the boy to go back to sleep. When it happened the third time, Eli realized that God was calling to Samuel. He told Samuel that if God called, he should say, "Speak Lord, for your servant is listening."

God called the fourth time. This time Samuel answered as Eli had told him. God told Samuel that he would take Eli's place. Eli's sons did what was the evil in God's sight. They would never fulfill the role of their father as priests in the temple.

The next morning Eli asked Samuel to tell him all that God said. As difficult as it was, Eli accepted God's will. God blessed Samuel and guided him through the years that he judged Israel. Unlike Samson, Samuel was a very godly judge and did what was right in the eyes of God.

Israel Asks for a King (1 Samuel 8–15)

Years passed and Samuel grew old. Samuel lived in Ramah and judged Israel from there. He also had two sons who became judges. They did not follow in the footsteps of their father. They took bribes and were dishonest in other ways.

A group of elders came to Samuel. They told Samuel that the people wanted a king. Samuel was not happy with their request. He prayed to God. God assured Samuel that it was God, not Samuel, that the people rejected.

Samuel told the people that a king was not best for them. He warned them a king would take their sons and daughters. Their sons would serve a king in the army. Their daughters would serve the king as cooks and bakers. Their crops and herds would be taxed. When the day came that they were sorry for choosing a king, God would not hear.

God selected Saul to be the first king. At first Saul was very humble. He led the people to war against the Philistines. But then he disobeyed God. Though God rejected Saul, he remained on the throne for some years after his disobedience. He lost the blessing of God. Disobeying God always leads to disaster.

God Chooses David (1 Samuel 16)

Samuel was saddened by the failure of Saul. God told Samuel to stop being sad. He told Samuel to take a horn of oil and anoint a new king. God told Samuel to go to the house of Jesse in Bethlehem.

Samuel told the people of Bethlehem that he was there to worship God. They did not need to be afraid. When he came to the home of Jesse, he asked Jesse to bring his sons. All of Jesse's seven sons came before Samuel. God told Samuel that none of these sons should be anointed. Samuel asked, "Do you have another son?"

Jessie said that his youngest son was still in the field. He was tending the sheep. Samuel would not eat with the family until David was brought home.

When he arrived, God told Samuel, "This is the one." Samuel anointed David with the oil in front of his family. Then Samuel returned home to Ramah. Some time later Samuel died.

DAVID BECOMES KING
1 SAMUEL 16–2 SAMUEL 24; 1 KINGS 1–2

Because God left Saul, Saul was suffering from serious problems. Saul asked his advisers to provide someone who could play the harp to soothe him. Thy young boy David was chosen. David went back and forth between caring for his sheep and playing the harp for Saul.

David and Goliath (1 Samuel 17)

David's father called him home from tending the sheep to carry food to his three older brothers. They were serving in the army of King Saul. Saul's army was fighting the Philistines.

The Philistines had a champion in Goliath from Gath. Goliath was a giant. He stood over nine feet tall. He had been a warrior from his youth. The Philistines stood on a mountain. On the mountain across the valley stood the army of Israel. Each day Goliath made fun of the armies of Israel.

When David arrived and saw what Goliath was doing to the Israelite army, he began to ask among the soldiers what was happening. Saul's army was afraid. David was shocked that the Israelites would allow Goliath to make fun of God's army. His brothers expressed their anger at David. But when Saul heard that David was asking about the giant, he sent for him.

David said he would fight the giant, but Saul was not sure that he wanted to send David against the giant. But David reminded him that he had killed a lion and a bear that threatened his father's sheep. David did not believe that the Philistine was any more difficult than a lion. Then the king offered David the king's armor to wear. When David put on the armor, it was too heavy. He decided to face Goliath without any kind of armor. David chose five smooth pebbles from the brook. He placed them in his pouch and went to meet Goliath.

Goliath saw David coming toward him. He cursed David and said, "Am I a dog that you come after me with sticks? Come to me and I will feed your body to the birds."

David answered, "You come to me with your armor and sword. But I come to you in the name of the Lord of Hosts. You have made fun of God to the armies of Israel. Today He will deliver you to me. The battle is God's. He will be victorious."

Goliath came toward David. David put his hand in the pouch and withdrew a pebble. He placed it in his sling, swung with all his might, and let the stone go. The pebble struck the giant in the forehead. Goliath fell dead and David cut off his head.

Then the army of the Philistines fled. The army of Israel chased the Philistines. The Israelites took as their own all the goods that were left in the camp of the Philistines. David brought a great victory to the armies of Israel.

King of Judah and Israel (2 Samuel 5–7)

David's success caused Saul to be angry and jealous of David. Saul's son Jonathan became a friend of David's. Jonathan indicated to David that he must flee for his life or Saul would kill him. Finally, Saul and his son died in another battle with the Philistines.

Later, the men of Israel met at Hebron. They asked David to become their king. David became king when he was thirty years of age. He reigned in Hebron for seven and a half years.

David intended to rule Israel from the city of Jerusalem. Jerusalem was under the control of the Jebusites. From the time of Joshua, the people of Israel were not able to control the city of Jerusalem. It stood high on a hill and was well protected. David's men were able to get into the city through the water tunnel. Once inside they were able to defeat the Jebusites.

David asked the Lord if he should fight the Philistines. God told him to go against them. With the Lord's blessing, David and his men won.

A second time the Philistines came out to fight against David and his army. Again David called upon God to give him wisdom and a course of action. This time God told him to circle behind the Philistines. David achieved a great victory against the Philistines by obeying God. During his reign, David was able to defeat the threat of the Philistines. David rejoiced before the Ark of the Lord and offered sacrifices to God.

To honor God, David wanted to build a temple to the Lord. He wanted to remove the Ark of the Covenant from the Tabernacle and place it in a permanent Temple. He brought his desire to God.

God spoke to the prophet Nathan. "Tell David my servant that I will make a great name of him and his family. I will not remove my blessing from his household. His kingdom shall last forever. But I want his son to build the Temple."

David was satisfied. He answered God in prayer and worshiped God.

David and Bathsheba (2 Samuel 11–12)

In the springtime David usually went to war with his men. One year he sent his men out to fight the Ammonites and he stayed home. David grew restless. As the king was walking on the roof of his house one day, he saw a beautiful woman bathing on a nearby roof.

David asked who the woman was. He was told that she was Bathsheba. She was a wife of Uriah, the Hittite. David courted Bathsheba and fell in love with her. Some time passed, and Bathsheba sent word that she was carrying his child.

David thought he could cover up his sin and he called her husband home from the battlefront. But Uriah felt guilty about leaving his troops, so he would not spend time with his wife. Instead, he slept at the door of the palace.

David asked, "Why did you not go home to your wife?"

Uriah answered, "It would be wrong for me to eat and drink and spend time with my wife while my men are in the field."

David then sent a letter with Uriah telling the general to placed Uriah in the front line. In time, word came from the field that the battle was going badly for the Israelites. The messenger also told David that Uriah had been killed.

After Bathsheba mourned her husband's death, she married David. Their son was born soon after. David thought that he had covered up his sin.

But God was very displeased with David. God sent Nathan to tell David a story. Nathan said, "There was a rich man who had large herds. There was a poor man who had only one lamb. One day a traveler came to the home of the rich man. The rich man was not willing to use an animal from his flock to feed the traveler. Instead, he took the lamb from the poor man and had it cooked for their feast."

David became very angry. He told Nathan, "The rich man should give four times to the poor man. The rich man deserves to die!"

Nathan said to David, "You are that man! Because you have sinned, God will not allow your son to live. There will be trouble in your own home. But if you put away your sin, your life will be spared."

> ### REPENT
> Repent means to tell God you are sorry for sin and to turn away from that sin. When the prophet Nathan told David that God was angry with his sin, David asked God's forgiveness. That is why his life was spared. God desires repentance for sin. He is willing to forgive, if we repent.

Absalom's Revolt (2 Samuel 14–18)

As the years passed, David's family had many problems. It happened just as God had promised. Sin always brings punishment. A family feud followed between the family of Tamar and the family of Jonadab. They were both David's children by different marriages. Tamar's brother was David's favorite son, Absalom. David intended that Absalom should succeed him as king of Israel.

Absalom protected his sister. He killed his half brother, Jonadab. For that David sent him away. Absalom went to Hebron. While he was there, he tried to take the kingdom away from David. He went to the city gate. At the city gate he would settle problems that were brought for David. Slowly he began to win the people away from his father David.

Absalom raised a large army. When he believed that his army was strong enough, they fought with David's men. Even though David's army was able to defeat the rebels, many men lost their lives. Absalom was trying to escape as he rode through the forest. His long hair became caught in a tree. As he hung there, Joab, David's general, ran a spear through Absalom. The revolt was ended.

David was happy that his throne had been saved. But he grieved over the loss of his son, Absalom.

David's Death (1 Kings 1–2)

David was getting old. His servants covered him with blankets in order to keep him warm. After Bathsheba became David's wife, she had another son, Solomon. Bathsheba worked very hard to have David name Solomon as the new king, and David agreed.

As the time of David's death drew near, he called his son Solomon. "I am going to die," David said. "You must be strong and follow God. Walk in His ways and keep His commandments, as are written in the Law of Moses. If you do, you will succeed." The king continued to give Solomon advice.

David had been king for forty years when he died. He was buried in Jeresalem. Solomon was crowned the new king.

SOLOMON BUILDS THE TEMPLE
1 KINGS 2–11

The Wisdom of Solomon (1 Kings 2–3)

After David's death, Solomon became king of Israel. Solomon strengthened his ties with Egypt. He married the daughter of Pharaoh.

When Solomon began to reign in Israel, he walked in God's way. God appeared to Solomon in a dream. God said to Solomon, "Ask what you want, and I will give it to you."

Solomon said to God, "You have made me king over this great people. I am only a young man and lack wisdom to reign. Give me wisdom that I may rule as You want me to rule."

God was pleased with Solomon's request. God told Solomon, "You have asked for wisdom. You have not asked for long life, riches, or the lives of your enemies. Because you have asked wisely, I will give you riches and honor. If you walk as your father David walked, I will also give you long life."

Soon after the dream, two women appeared before Solomon. They lived in the same house. Each woman had a baby. But one woman's baby died. The woman whose baby had died switched the babies during the night. They came to Solomon to settle the dispute of who was the baby's mother.

Solomon said, "Bring my sword. Let me cut the baby in half and give each of you half."

The mother of the living child said, "Do not kill the child! Give the child to the other woman."

The other woman said, "Divide the child. He shall belong to neither of us."

Solomon said, "The woman who said, 'Do not kill the child!' is the real mother. Give the baby to her."

The people of Israel saw the wisdom of Solomon. They respected the king. They believed that such wisdom could only come from God.

Solomon Builds the Temple (1 Kings 6–8)

Solomon reigned four years before he started to build the Temple to the Lord. It had been 480 years since the people of Israel left Egypt.

The Temple of the Lord was about 98 feet long. It measured 33 feet wide. Its height was about 49 feet tall. The foundation and outer walls were built of stone. Cedar beams were floated down from Lebanon. These were used to finish the Temple in the ceiling. The inside walls were also made of cedar.

The outside and inside were both decorated with gold. The altar was made of cedar and decorated

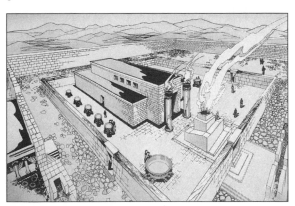

Solomon's Temple.

with gold. The whole inside of the Temple was covered with gold. Some of the decoration included cherubim that were carved from olive wood and covered with gold.

After seven year the Temple was finished. The priests and the leaders of the nation joined King Solomon to bring the Ark of the Covenant into the Temple. It was placed in the inner sanctuary. On top of the Ark there were two cherubim, and the mercy seat was between them. This is the place where God met His people. The Ark of the Covenant now contained only the two tablets of stone with the Ten Commandments.

The Queen of Sheba (1 Kings 10)

The Queen of Sheba heard about the fame and fortune of King Solomon. She decided to look for herself. She came with many servants and many camels. She asked the king many difficult questions. Solomon was able to answer them all. The Queen was amazed by his wisdom. She said, "Everything I have heard about you is true. I had to come and see for myself. Your wisdom and wealth go beyond all that I have heard. I bless the Lord your God, who has given you such success."

The Queen of Sheba gave Solomon many presents. She gave him spices, precious stones, and a large quantity of gold. In addition to her gifts, Hiram gave Solomon wood and precious stones. From the trees, Solomon made the pillars in the Temple.

Solomon gave the Queen of Sheba many gifts also. Everything she desired, he gave her. Then she left Solomon and returned to her own country.

Solomon's Death and the Division of the Kingdom (1 Kings 10–12)

God blessed Solomon with wealth, a large army, and many servants. He lived in luxury. He even expanded his kingdom.

Solomon made a serious mistake. He married many foreign wives. They came from countries that worshiped idols. Solomon soon turned toward sacrificing to the idols of his wives. This displeased the Lord. He spoke to Solomon, but Solomon did not listen.

Then God came to Solomon and told him, "Because you have gone after other gods, I will take the kingdom from you. For the sake of your father, David, I will not remove you from the throne. I will allow your son to rule over one tribe. Your servant will become king in your place. He will rule over the rest of the country."

Jeroboam was a son of one of the king's servants. One day the prophet Ahijah met Jeroboam along the road. The prophet was wearing a new robe. He took the robe and tore it into twelve pieces. He gave ten of those pieces to Jeroboam. He told Jeroboam, "God has promised to give you ten tribes of Israel. You will become their king. But for David's sake God has promised not to give all of the kingdom to you. God has promised to give Jerusalem to Solomon's son. God says, 'I have chosen to put my name in that city.' If you will follow God and keep His commandments, God will bless you and your descendants."

Solomon heard about the meeting of Jeroboam with Ahijah the prophet. He was very angry. He tried to kill Jeroboam. Jeroboam escaped and stayed in Egypt until Solomon died.

Solomon reigned over Israel for forty years. He was buried in Jerusalem. His son Rehoboam reigned in his place. Rehoboam was not wise in ruling Israel. He placed heavy tax burdens upon the people. As the prophet had promised, the northern ten tribes withdrew. They wanted their own king. The kingdom was now divided—Israel in the North and Judah in the South.

Jeroboam returned from Egypt to Israel and ruled as king. Jeroboam was afraid that the people would return to Jerusalem to worship. He thought that the people would turn to Rehoboam. He feared that they would kill him. He had two golden calves made for the people to worship. He placed one in the city of Bethel and the other in the city of Dan. He appointed priests to serve in these places of worship. God was very displeased.

ELIJAH, THE PROPHET TO ISRAEL
1 KINGS 17–2 KINGS 2

Elijah, Prophet in the Wilderness (1 Kings 17)

Years passed and the people of Israel continued to turn away from God. What started with Jeroboam continued to grow worse.

Finally, King Ahab came to the throne of Israel. Israel included the northern ten tribes. His wife Jezebel was the daughter of the king of Sidon. They made idols and caused the people to worship them. They worked hard to oppose the prophets of God.

God afflicted the land of Israel with a drought. He called Elijah to be His prophet to the northern ten tribes of Israel. God told Elijah, "Go to the brook Kerith. You will find water. I will send a raven to bring food." Elijah obeyed God and was fed just as God said. After some time passed, the brook became dry.

God said to Elijah, "Go to a city of Sidon and live there. I have commanded a widow to provide you with food."

Elijah obeyed. He met a woman outside the city who was gathering sticks. He called to her and asked for some food.

The woman answered, "I have nothing but a jar of flour and a little oil. I need this for my son or we will starve."

Elijah answered, "Do not be afraid. Go and make a cake for me. Then make a cake for you and your son. The Lord God of Israel has promised that the flour and oil will not run out until it rains again." When the woman went to her home, she found that it happened just as Elijah had promised.

After some time the woman's son became ill. At last he died. The woman was heartbroken. She asked Elijah, "Why have you brought this tragedy upon me?"

Elijah said, "Bring the boy to me." Elijah took the boy to his chamber. He put the boy on his bed. Three times he stretched out across him. As he did, he prayed, "O Lord, please let this child's life return." God answered his prayer. The boy revived.

Elijah took the boy into his mother. His mother said, "Now I know that you are a man of God."

Elijah and the Prophets of Baal (1 Kings 18)

Elijah met King Ahab. Ahab said to Elijah, "So you are the one who is causing trouble for Israel."

"I have not made any trouble for Israel. You and your family have caused this trouble for Israel," said Elijah. "You have stopped following the Lord's commands. Why don't you bring people from all over Israel to Mount Carmel? Bring fifty of the prophets of Baal. Bring 450 of the prophets of the Asherah. Have them meet me at Mount Carmel."

On that day they all met at Mount Carmel. Elijah asked the people, "How long will you continue to disobey God? If God is Lord, then follow Him. If Baal is God, then follow him."

The people said nothing.

Elijah said, "I am the only one of God's prophets left. Baal has 450 prophets. Get two bulls. Let the prophets of Baal choose one. Let them cut the bull and place it on the wood. Set no fire. Let them call upon their god to send fire. I will do the same. The one who answers with fire is the one we will serve."

The people said, "We will do it."

The prophets of Baal prepared their sacrifice. From morning until noon they cried, "O Baal, answer us." No one answered. They danced around the altar. They even cut themselves with knives. They continued until evening, but nothing happened.

Elijah said to the people, "Come here to me." Elijah took twelve stones for each of the tribes of Israel. He cut the bull and placed it on the wood on the altar. He dug a trench around the altar and called to the people to bring jugs of water and pour the water on the altar. He did this three times.

Then Elijah called upon God. "Lord God of Israel, show the people this day that you are Lord."

The fire fell from heaven. It burned up the sacrifice, the wood, the stones, and the water in the trenches. On that day, God showed the people that He alone was God. The prophets of Baal were false prophets indeed.

Elijah told the men to gather the prophets of Baal. For their sin they were put to death.

Elijah told Ahab that the drought was over. "Look toward the sea. The clouds are forming." Then a mighty wind rose and the rain fell.

Elijah at Mount Horeb (1 Kings 19)

Queen Jezebel asked Ahab what had happened to her prophets. She was very angry and promised to take Elijah's life. Elijah heard about her threats, and he fled to the mountain of God for safety. Mount Horeb was the same mountain on which Moses met God.

God came and spoke to Elijah. He said to Elijah, "What are you doing here?"

Elijah told God, "The people of Israel have rejected You. They have broken down Your altars and put your prophets to death. I alone am left."

God said to Elijah, "Go stand on the mountain, for I am about to pass by."

Elijah was in a cave when a mighty wind tore the mountain. It shattered the rocks. Elijah hid. But God was not in the wind.

Next came an earthquake. But God was not in the earthquake. This was followed by fire. But God was not in the fire. Next came a gentle whisper. Elijah hid his face and went to the mouth of a cave. There, God spoke to Elijah, "Go to the desert of Damascus, where I have many tasks for you. You will find Elisha there. He also will be my prophet."

Elijah did as he was told. Elisha followed God's call and became the attendant for Elijah.

Naboth's Vineyard (1 Kings 21)

Naboth owned a vineyard that was next to the palace. King Ahab offered to buy the vineyard to expand his property. Even though he offered a good price, Naboth refused to sell. Naboth said that God had given him this inheritance.

This made the king very angry. His wife, Jezebel, told the king that she would get the property for him. She held a feast in honor of Naboth. Two men were sent to accuse Naboth of saying things against God and the king. This crime was punishable by death.

It all happened just as Jezebel had said. Naboth was stoned to death.

Ahab was very excited. He went to explore the new vineyard. But he soon saw that he was not alone. Elijah was there. Elijah told him, "You have gotten this vineyard by shedding the blood of an innocent man. Just as you have killed Naboth, both you and Jezebel will die a violent death."

Ahab was ashamed of what he had done. He would not eat or sleep. He dressed in sackcloth. He was very depressed.

God said to Elijah, "Have you seen how Ahab has repented? I have decided to show mercy to him. Judgment will not fall on him during his life, to bring him to a violent death. It will happen to those who come after him."

Elijah Is Taken to Heaven (2 Kings 2)

Elijah was getting old. He knew that the time had come for him to leave. He went on a journey with Elisha. When they were leaving Gilgal, Elijah said, "You remain here, while I go on further." But Elisha loved the prophet and insisted on following.

They went on further and came to Bethel. The prophets in Bethel said, "Do you know that God will take Elijah today?"

"Yes, I do! Let us not talk of it any further," answered Elisha.

"Stay here and I will go on further," said Elijah.

Elisha said, "As God lives, I will not leave you."

They came to the river Jordan. Elijah took his cloak and struck the water. The water parted, and the two men passed over on dry ground.

Elijah said, "Tell me what I can do for you before I leave."

"Let me have a double portion of your spirit," said Elisha.

"Your request is difficult," said Elijah. "If you see me taken up, God has granted your request."

They continued on their way, walking and talking together. Suddenly, a chariot of fire appeared and took Elijah away. Elisha saw this awesome event. He cried out, "My father! My father!" Elisha did not see Elijah anymore.

In sadness he tore his clothes. He picked up Elijah's cloak that had fallen. He began the sorrowful walk back the way he had come. When he reached the river Jordan, he cried, "Where is the God of Elijah?" He struck the water as Elijah had done. It parted for him and he walked across dry land. God showed him that day that He would be with Elisha just as He had been with Elijah.

JONAH'S STORY
JONAH 1–4

Jonah, the prophet, lived around the time of Elisha. God told him to go to the city of Nineveh located in the country of Assyria. The people there were warlike and cruel. In God's eyes they were sinful.

The people of Israel were afraid of the Assyrians, so Jonah feared to go to Nineveh. He wanted God's judgment to fall upon the people of Assyria. Jonah thought that if he could run away from God, he wouldn't have to go. He ran away to the seacoast city of Joppa. There he took a ship that was headed for Tarshish (probably southern Spain).

Jonah did not realize that no one can run away from God. As soon as the ship had set sail and was out in the deep water, a storm came up. The wind howled. The waves grew higher. All who were on the ship feared for their lives.

Jonah was sleeping. The captain came to Jonah and woke him up. He said, "Wake up! Perhaps if you pray to your God, He will save us from drowning."

Meanwhile, the sailors were casting lots. They were trying to discover who was responsible for the storm. The lots fell upon Jonah.

When Jonah came on deck, the sailors asked, "Who are you? From what country have you come?"

Jonah answered, "I am from Israel. I worship the God of heaven, who created all things."

Since he had already told them that he was running away from the Lord, they were very afraid. They asked him, "What have you done? What shall we do with you?"

"I am the cause for your trouble. Throw me overboard. The sea will become calm, and your lives will be saved," said Jonah.

Instead, the men rowed harder and tried to save Jonah from being thrown into the water. But the sea and the storm grew more violent. They cried out to God. Finally they threw Jonah into the water.

God had prepared a great fish. The fish swallowed Jonah. He did not die. He spent three days and three nights inside the fish. Jonah was very miserable. He cried to God when he thought his life was about to end. God heard his prayer and caused the fish to vomit Jonah on the land.

God told Jonah a second time to go and preach in Nineveh. This time Jonah obeyed.

When he got to Nineveh, Jonah cried, "Forty more days and God will destroy the city of Ninevah!"

The people of Nineveh believed that God would carry out their destruction. They put on sackcloth in sorrow for their sin. When news reached the king, he took off his royal robes. He wore sackcloth and sat in the dust as a sign of repentance. He issued a law that all people in his country should repent of their violence and their sins.

God saw that the people repented and were sorry for the evil they had done. God decided not to bring the destruction upon the people of Nineveh.

This really made Jonah angry. He sat on a hill overlooking the city, awaiting its destruction. During the heat of the day, a vine grew and protected him from the sun. The next day a worm entered the vine and it withered. Jonah stayed unhappy. He wanted to die.

God saw Jonah's unhappiness. He said to Jonah, "You are unhappy because the vine withered. You did not create the vine. I have thousands of people in the city of Nineveh who do not know what is right. I love these people. They have repented and turned away from their wickedness. I do not want to destroy them."

During the years that followed, the people of Israel grew more and more wicked. From the time of Jereboam, there had been no good kings on the throne in Israel. None of the kings had obeyed the Lord or followed in His ways. God used the country of Assyria to bring judgment upon the people of Israel. In 722 BC, the Assyrians took the Israelites into captivity. They were taken from the homeland to Assyria. Life was difficult in captivity. As a family of peoples, the ten tribes disappeared.

MERCY
Mercy means that God does not give us what we deserve. God planned to destroy Nineveh because of their sin. He showed mercy to them. He did not destroy the people of Nineveh, because they repented.

YOUNG JOSIAH BECOMES KING
2 KINGS 22–23

Israel had gone into captivity because they did what was evil in God's sight. While all of the kings of Israel had been evil, there were a few good kings in Judah. One of those good kings was Josiah.

Josiah came to the throne when he was only eight years of age. He did not follow the evil of his fathers. He tried to do what was right in the sight of the Lord. He followed in the way of his ancestor David.

In the eighteenth year of his reign, Josiah had workmen repairing the Temple. Hilkiah, the high priest, found the Book of the Law in the cornerstone of the Temple. When Shaphan, the king's messenger, brought money to the Temple to assist in its repairs, Hilkiah gave Shaphan the Book of the Law. Shaphan read the Book of the Law. He took it to King Josiah, who listened to the commandments of God.

Josiah became upset. He knew that he and the people had not followed the laws of God. They had worshiped idols. They had disgraced the Temple of the Lord. He tore his royal robes. He cried out to God for forgiveness. Then he sent Hilkiah to Huldah, the prophetess, to ask the Lord about the future.

Huldah sent a message to the king. "God says, 'Because you have repented I will not bring destruction upon your house. The sin of the people is too great. I will punish them, but not during your lifetime. You will have peace while you are on the throne.'"

King Josiah called all the people together. In their hearing he read the Book of the Law. The king renewed the covenant with the Lord in the presence of all the people. The people also promised to keep the covenant.

King Josiah ordered that Hilkiah, the high priest, and the other priests who served the Lord take all of the things dedicated to the worship of Baal and burn them. He also ordered that the priests of Baal be put to death.

The priests of the Lord were instructed to go throughout the land and tear down the altars to idols. They were to destroy the altars and get rid of the priests. Many of the kings who had come before Josiah had set up altars to gods of the surrounding nations. These had to be destroyed. The worship of the pagan gods in Judah was forbidden. There had not been a king like Josiah. He followed the way of the Lord.

When Passover came, the people celebrated as it was written in the Law of Moses. It was celebrated in Jerusalem.

The pharaoh of Egypt went to help the king of Assyria in battle. King Josiah and his army went out to face the pharaoh. King Josiah was killed in battle on the plains of Megiddo. Josiah's servants brought his body back to Jerusalem, and he was buried there in his own tomb.

Four more kings served on the throne of Judah. All four of these kings did what was evil in the sight of God. Zedekiah was the last of these kings. He and the people of Judah were taken into captivity in Babylon.

JEREMIAH AND THE FALL OF JERUSALEM
JEREMIAH; 2 KINGS 23–25; LAMENTATIONS

The priests of the Temple continued to perform sacrifices, but they did not lead the people closer to God. God sent a long line of prophets, beginning with Elijah and continuing through the end of the Old Testament. Through the prophets, God told the people of Israel and Judah that they needed to repent and change their way of life. The people of Israel and Judah needed to follow God's Law, which was given to Moses. In addition, the prophets foretold the coming of the Messiah.

Jeremiah began his prophecy around the middle of Josiah's reign. God told Jeremiah that He had set him apart before birth to be His prophet.

Jeremiah protested, "O, Lord, I am just a child. I cannot speak."

God answered, "Do not say you're just a child. Go everywhere that I send you. I have put my words in your mouth. Do not be afraid, for I will protect you."

He told Jeremiah to tell the people of Judah, "If you will put away your idols and turn to Me, I will forgive you and bless you. If you continue to forsake Me, you will be destroyed. I will bring a distant nation against you. They will take your homeland and your sons and daughters. With their swords they will destroy your cities.

"Yet I will not destroy you completely. I will take you to a foreign land. But today a disaster is coming!"

Jeremiah at the Potter's house
(Jeremiah 18–19)
God told Jeremiah to go down to the potter's house. Jeremiah saw the potter working at his wheel. He

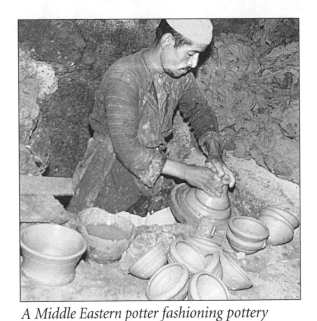

A Middle Eastern potter fashioning pottery in the same manner used in biblical times.

took a lump of clay and shaped it into a pot. It did not form as the potter desired. It was not perfect. The potter took the clay and made another pot.

God said to Jeremiah, "Can I not do as the potter does? The house of Israel is clay in My hands. I will do with it as I please. If a nation repents to Me, I will not bring disaster as I planned. If a nation does what is evil in My sight, then I will destroy them.

"Say to the people of Judah, 'This is what the Lord says. I am preparing a disaster for you. But if you turn from your evil ways, I will forgive.' But they will reply to you, Jeremiah, 'It is useless. We will follow our own way.'"

God continued, "Go and buy a jar from the potter. They have run after the gods of other peoples. I will bring their plans to ruin, and they will be taken into captivity.

"Break the jar in front of them. This is what God says, 'I will smash this nation so they cannot be repaired. I will bring disaster upon you.'"

PUNISHMENT
Punishment means to receive the penalty for sin. God's people sinned. The punishment was captivity in Babylon. Why did God send His people away from the Promised Land to Babylon?

Disaster Falls upon Judah
(Jeremiah 23–24, 38–39; 2 Kings 25)

The people did not listen. They continued to burn incense to the idols. They continued to worship the idols. They continued to be dishonest and to commit wickedness. There were false prophets who said that Jeremiah's prophecy was not right.

Jehoiachin was on the throne in Judah when God taught Jeremiah through another object lesson. There were two baskets of figs. One basket of figs held good fruit. The other basket was rotten. No one would want to eat from the second basket.

God told Jeremiah that the good fruit was like the good people in captivity in Babylon. They would repent of their sins, and God would forgive them. The other basket contained the evil Judeans and King Zedekiah. They would not survive.

The last king of Judah was Zedekiah. He was an evil king. Some of the king's men had Jeremiah thrown into a well. Zedekiah told the soldiers to do what they pleased with Jeremiah. Jeremiah would have died there if one from the king's household had not rescued him.

The warnings of Jeremiah fell on deaf ears. The people would not listen. They continued in their evil ways. Almost two hundred years had passed since Israel had been taken into captivity by Assyria. During that time the Assyrian power declined. A new power dominated the world. It was Babylonia. Their king was Nebuchadnezzar.

Nebuchadnezzar marched on the city of Jerusalem with his army. The army held the city captive. No one could enter or leave Jerusalem. The people were starving and dying. King Zedekiah escaped with a small band of men. He was captured by the army of Nebuchadnezzar and blinded. Zedekiah and the people who remained in Jerusalem were taken to Babylon in captivity.

Lamentations for the Loss of Jerusalem and Judea (Lamentations)

The fall of Jerusalem and the prisoners taken into captivity from Judea caused great sadness to Jeremiah. He wrote the bulk of Lamentations, which is a series of five poems.

Once Jerusalem was a great city among the nations. Now it had gone into ruin. There was no one to comfort her. Those who once opposed her had now become her master. The anger of the Lord destroyed the great nation of Israel. The enemies of the Lord scoffed at the destruction of Israel.

But there was a message of hope. One day God's anger would end. The punishment and exile would end. The sin would be forgiven. Jeremiah prayed to God that Israel might one day return to the land of Zion and that all would be restored.

DANIEL AND THE PRINCES OF ISRAEL
DANIEL 1–12

Daniel Is Taken Prisoner in Babylon
(Daniel 1)

Before the fall of Jerusalem in 586 BC, King Nebuchadnezzar had marched on Palestine and taken many of the people prisoners. Along with many treasures that he stole from the Temple, he took the prisoners back to Babylon. Babylon became a world power and overtook Assyria. It was located in present-day Iraq, near Baghdad.

Nebuchadnezzar was very interested in some of the royal children. They were invited to live in the king's palace, to eat of the king's food, and to be educated in science, language, and the arts of Babylon.

Among the princes who were brought from Judah were Daniel, Hananiah, Mishael, and Azariah. Daniel had decided not to eat from the king's table. It contained food that was against the laws of Israel. The head of the household liked Daniel. He was afraid that he might lose his life if he didn't obey the king's orders. Daniel suggested that he and his three friends be allowed to eat the kind of food that they desired for ten days. If, at the end of that time, they did not appear to be healthy, then they would eat the king's food. The steward agreed.

At the end of ten days, the steward examined the boys. They all appeared to be healthy. They looked better than the young men who had eaten at the king's table. There was no longer any question that Daniel and his friends could eat their own food.

For three years the boys were instructed in Babylonian learning. At the end of that period, the steward brought them before Nebuchadnezzar.

The king asked them many questions. He found that they had grown in knowledge and wisdom. They were better equipped than many of the magicians and astrologers of Babylon. By following God's way, Daniel and his friends were blessed, even in a foreign land.

Nebuchadnezzar's Dream (Daniel 2–3)

King Nebuchadnezzar had a dream. He did not remember what happened in the dream. He called all of his wise men and astrologers to tell him the dream and its meaning. They could not tell him, so he decided to kill all of his advisers.

Daniel heard about the threat of the king. The threat included Daniel and his friends. Daniel asked the commander of the king's guard to take him to Nebuchadnezzar. He told the king that he needed some time to discover the dream and its meaning. The king granted his request.

Daniel returned home and asked his friends Hananiah, Mishael, and Azariah to pray for him. During the night God revealed the dream and its meaning. The next day Daniel went to the king. He told the king what he had dreamed.

Nebuchadnezzar saw a very large statue. Its head was gold. Its chest and arms were silver. The stomach and thighs were bronze. The legs and feet were iron and clay. As he watched, a large rock hit the statue, and it was broken into pieces. The rock then became a mountain and covered the whole earth. That was the dream.

Then Daniel interpreted the dream. The gold was the Babylonian Empire. One day another empire, represented by the silver, would replace it. Later a third kingdom would arise. It was the bronze part of the statue. Eventually, the third empire would be overthrown and replaced by a fourth. The mixture of iron and clay meant that this empire would not remain united.

The rock represented the kingdom God would set up. That kingdom will last forever. Human hands will not set up this kingdom. Daniel ended by saying, "That is the dream and its meaning. It is true. It will come to pass."

Nebuchadnezzar was so excited that he bowed down before Daniel. He honored him by placing him in a position of power in the kingdom. He also honored Daniel's friends and made them rulers of provinces.

Daniel's Friends in the Fiery Furnace (Daniel 3)

Nebuchadnezzar had a huge statue constructed on the plains of Dura. He sent out a decree that ordered everyone to bow down before the statue.

Daniel's friends refused, and Nebuchadnezzar became furious. He said that he would throw them into a fiery furnace. He instructed the guard to heat the furnace seven times hotter than normal.

Shadrach, Meshach, and Abednego (their Babylonia names) told the king, "God may protect us. But even if he does not, we will not bow down to an image. It will dishonor our God."

They were bound and thrown into the fiery furnace. The king looked into the fire. Instead of three men walking around in the fire, Nebuchadnezzar saw four men. They were not bound. The king was amazed!

The king shouted, "Shadrach, Meshach, and Abednego, come out of the fire. Your God has protected you."

All the men of the royal house gathered around Shadrach, Meshach, and Abednego. They saw that their clothes were not burned, and their hair was not singed.

The king ordered that no one should say anything against the God of Shadrach, Meshach, and Abednego. He then promoted the young men to high positions in the kingdom of Babylon.

The Writing on the Wall (Daniel 5)

King Nebuchadnezzar died. His son, Belshazzar, came to the throne. Belshazzar hosted a great feast for a thousand of the lords in his kingdom. As they were drinking, Belshazzar had an idea.

He called his servants to bring the gold and silver vessels that his father had captured from the Temple in Jerusalem. The goblets were filled with wine. The lords of the kingdom and the women at the feast drank to the idol gods of gold, silver, brass, iron, wood, and stone.

Suddenly, a hand appeared on the wall. It inscribed the following words: MENE, MENE, TEKEL, PARSIN. The king was frightened. His knees began to shake. The color of his cheeks changed.

Belshazzar called all of the astrologers and the wise men of the kingdom. He called them to interpret the meaning of the writing on the wall. He promised to clothe the one who could interpret the meaning in purple and to give him a gold chain to wear around his neck. But no one could tell the meaning of the words.

The queen entered the banquet hall. She said, "Oh King, live forever! Do not be afraid. There is a man in your kingdom who has understanding and wisdom. He served your father. His name is Daniel."

Belshazzar brought Daniel to the banquet hall. By this time Daniel was much older. The king said to Daniel, "You were one of the exiles from Judah. My father brought you to Babylon. I have heard about you and your wisdom given by the gods. Can you give the interpretation of the writing on the wall? If you can, I will give you a gold chain, clothe you in purple, and make you the third highest ruler in the kingdom."

Daniel answered, "You may keep the gifts and give the reward to another. Nevertheless, I will interpret the writing on the wall. The God of heaven gave your father, Nebuchadnezzar, power over many nations. When he became boastful, he was reduced to eating like cattle. But you, his son, have not humbled yourself before the Lord of heaven. You have taken the goblets from the Temple and not honored them.

"This is the meaning of the writing on the wall:

"MENE means that God has judged your reign, and it is over.

"TEKEL means that God has weighed your life in the balance, and He is not pleased with you.

"PARSIN means that your kingdom will be given to the Medes and Persians."

Belshazzar commanded that Daniel receive the golden chain and be clothed in purple. The king made him third ruler in the kingdom.

That night Belshazzar was killed. Darius the Mede took the kingdom.

Daniel in the Lion's Den (Daniel 6)

The new king, Darius, placed one hundred twenty princes over his kingdom. Over the princes he placed three presidents. Daniel was one of the presidents. Among the three, Daniel was the leader.

The other presidents and princes became very jealous of Daniel. They began to watch his life in order to find something that they could criticize. But they could find no fault in Daniel.

They decided to find another way to overthrow Daniel. They went to King Darius and said, "Oh King, live forever! All of the rulers of your kingdom want you to enforce an edict. No one may pray to any god or man except you, oh King. This will be enforced for thirty days. No one can change this law of the Medes and Persians."

Daniel knew about the law. But he went to his chamber and opened the window toward Jerusalem and prayed to God. This was no different from his normal prayer.

The evil men were watching. As soon as Daniel prayed, they went to the king. They said, "Oh King! You made an edict. No one may pray to a god or man, except you, oh King. If he does, he will be thrown into the den of lions."

The king agreed. Then they charged Daniel with disobeying the king's decree. They said he makes petition to his God three times a day.

King Darius was upset when he realized what had happened. He tried all day to find a way to save Daniel from the lions. But he could not.

At last he commanded that Daniel be thrown to the lions. He said, "May your God save you from the lions." The king placed his seal across the stone. That night the king did not sleep. He would not eat. He would not watch any entertainment.

He came near to the den. In distress the king cried out, "Daniel, servant of God. Has your God been able to deliver you from the lions?"

Daniel answered, "Oh King, live forever! God sent His angels to shut the lion's mouths. I did nothing wrong before God. I did nothing wrong to you, oh King."

The king was overjoyed. He called to have Daniel taken up out of the den. Daniel was not hurt. He had trusted in God, and God had heard his prayers. The king commanded that the evil men who tried to kill Daniel be thrown to the lions. The lions ate the evil men.

King Darius wrote a decree (or law) to peoples of all nations. He sent a message of peace. He told them they must fear the God of Daniel. He told how God rescued Daniel from the lions. During the reign of Darius, Daniel did well. He also prospered during the reign of Cyrus.

OBEDIENCE
Obedience means to obey. Daniel and his friends obeyed God by only praying to Him.

ESTHER SAVES THE JEWISH PEOPLE
ESTHER 1–9

The King's Banquet (Esther 1–2)
The Persian king, Ahasuerus, reigned in Susa. His Greek name was Xerxes. His kingdom extended through 127 provinces, from India to Ethiopia. The people of Judah were still in captivity in Persia.

In his third year as king, Xerxes held a banquet to celebrate his royal glory. He invited the princes, officers of the army, and other nobles. The furnishings were beautiful. The banquet lasted for seven days. It was held in the garden of the king's palace.

Queen Vashti held a banquet of her own for the women of the palace. Queen Vashti was very beautiful. On the seventh day of the feast, King Xerxes, summoned his wife. He wanted to show her off at his banquet.

Queen Vashti refused to come. The king became very angry. He summoned his wise men. He asked what should be done with Queen Vashti. The wise men told the king that if her behavior were allowed, all women would disobey their husbands. They advised the king to remove her from her throne. King Xerxes followed their advice.

A successor to the queen was to be sought throughout the land. All of the beautiful women of the provinces were brought to the palace. For twelve months they were provided with cosmetics. They were bathed in oils. They were made beautiful. At last they were brought before the king.

Among the young women was Esther. As a child, her parents had died. Her uncle, Mordecai, brought her up and was concerned for her. Esther was very beautiful. The king fell in love with Esther. King Ahasuerus married Esther and made her his queen.

Mordecai uncovered a plot to kill the king and told Esther about it. He named the two who wanted to kill King Ahasuerus. Esther went to the king. She told him about the plot. The king discovered that what Mordecai had said was true. The evil men were hanged.

Haman Plans to Destroy the Jews (Esther 3–4)
The king promoted Haman over the other princes. He was second in command only to the king. Xerxes commanded that all the princes bow down to Haman. Mordecai refused and that made Haman very angry.

Haman decided to get rid of Mordecai, and with him all of the Jews. The king gave him permission to do what he wanted. He also gave Haman a sign of power, the king's signet ring. Whatever Haman decided to do would carry the king's authority.

Mordecai learned about the plot to kill all Jews. He put on sackcloth and encouraged Jews throughout the city to do the same. They fasted and prayed. Then Mordecai sent an urgent message to Esther asking her to go to the king to save her people.

Esther replied, "The king has not summoned me for thirty days. If I go to the king and he does not extend his golden scepter, I will be put to death."

Mordecai sent word to Esther, "Do not imagine that you will be spared. If Jews are killed, you will be killed also. For such a time as this you have become queen."

Esther said, "Bring all the Jews together. Have them fast for three days. I will go to the king. If I die, I will die."

Esther Holds a Banquet (Esther 5–6)

Esther put on her royal robes. She went to the king. King Xerxes extended his golden scepter. He asked her, "What is troubling you my queen? What is your request? I will give you up to half my kingdom."

Esther said, "I want to invite you and Haman to a feast."

The king was very pleased. He commanded Haman to come with him to the feast that Esther had prepared. Again the king asked Esther what was her request. She asked that they come again to a banquet on the next day. Once again he agreed.

Haman was very pleased. He believed that the queen was honoring him. As he left the palace, he passed Mordecai. Mordecai refused to bow before him. Haman again became very angry.

That night King Xerxes could not sleep. He ordered his servants to bring him the book of records. In the book he found that Mordecai had saved his life. He asked if Mordecai had been rewarded. The king's servants told him that nothing had been done.

Haman had commanded that a gallows be constructed because he planned to hang Mordecai that day from the gallows.

In the morning the king asked Haman what should be done to honor a man whom the king wanted to honor. Haman immediately thought that the king wanted to honor him. He suggested that the king put the royal robes on the person he wanted to honor and take them to the city square on horseback. All should know that the king was honoring this person. Haman did not know that Mordecai was the man whom the king wanted to honor.

Instead of hanging Mordecai from the gallows, Haman was required to take him through the city square to honor him as the king had commanded.

When they returned from honoring Mordecai, the king's men brought Haman to drink with the king and Queen Esther. Again the king was pleased with Esther. He asked her what she wanted him to do. She told of the plot to kill her people.

The king was furious. He asked, "Who is this wicked person?"

Esther answered, "It is the wicked Haman!"

The king became so angry that he left the banquet. He went to the garden to walk. Haman realized that he was in trouble. He went to the queen to beg her mercy.

Just then the king returned and thought that Haman was trying to harm his queen. He became more enraged. He had his servants take Haman to the gallows that had been prepared for Mordecai. Haman was hanged.

The king could not reverse the decree against the Jews. It had been signed with his signet ring. In place of that, he sent letters throughout the one hundred twenty-seven provinces that the Jews were to defend themselves against all of those who wanted to harm them.

Mordecai was elevated to second in command. He served King Xerxes for the rest of his life. Mordecai established the Feast of Purim in honor of Queen Esther. She was the brave young woman who had saved God's people from the wicked plot of Haman.

THE RETURN TO JERUSALEM
EZRA 1–10; NEHEMIAH 1–13

The End of the Captivity (Ezra 1–6)

In the first year of his reign, King Cyrus of Persia encouraged many of the Jews to return to Jerusalem. Zerubbabel, grandson of the last Jewish king, and Jeshua, high priest, led the people back to Jerusalem to rebuild the Temple. Many of the Jews chose to stay in the land where they had been resettled. These people gave money, food, and other gifts of gold and silver to those who returned to Jerusalem.

Cyrus wanted the people to rebuild the Temple. Many of the heads of households from the tribes of Benjamin and Judah agreed to go. The Levites' also went. Many of the treasures that Nebuchadnezzar had taken from the Temple were given to those who returned. They were to be placed in the new Temple. Altogether there were more than fifty-four hundred articles taken back from Babylon to the Temple. More than forty-two thousand people returned.

Soon after they arrived, they set up the altar. They began to sacrifice to God throughout the day. They also began to restore the Temple. This was a major undertaking. For some of the people this was a joyful experience. They had not seen the Temple. They had only heard about it from their parents. To them the new Temple was an answer to prayer.

For others this was a very sad occasion. They could recall the beauty of the original Temple. The new Temple did not measure up. It was smaller and not as beautiful.

The enemies of Judah tried to keep the Temple from being rebuilt. They made life difficult for the workers. Whenever they could slow down the work, they did so. This continued through the reign of Cyrus.

When the new king, Darius, came to the throne, he allowed the people to continue their work. The people who opposed the work on the Temple wrote a letter to Darius. They told him that the Temple should not be rebuilt because there was no proof it had been ordered by the king. Darius searched the archives for a decree from Cyrus, who had been king before him. When he found the edict, he gave orders that the people around should not hinder the building. In the sixth year of king Darius, the Temple was finished.

Ezra Leads a Second Group Back to Jerusalem (Ezra 7–8)

More than fifty years passed after the Temple was completed. Ezra was a scribe who carefully studied the Law of God and pleased God by teaching God's Law. He determined to return to Jerusalem and bring more Jewish people back to their homeland. He went to the king and asked for his help. Artaxerxes, the new Persian king, gladly sent Ezra to lead many Jewish people to Jerusalem. There they could serve God and worship in the Temple.

In his letter the king commanded that Ezra go to Jerusalem to see that God's Law was being carried out. The king also gave money for sacrifices in the Temple. The treasurers from the provinces were to provide supplies. Officials in the Temple were not to be taxed. Ezra was to set up a system that would judge persons who did not obey God's Law.

The people had been resettled in Babylon and Persia. It was not an easy task to ask them to take all that they had and move to Jerusalem. The journey took four months and was very dangerous. Without Ezra's trust in God, it would have been impossible. He asked the king for a military escort.

All of the articles from the Temple that had been taken by Nebuchadnezzar to Babylon were returned. Ezra was careful to certify all the articles that had been taken from the Temple.

The people who returned offered sacrifices to God. They delivered the king's orders to the princes. Then they helped the people who lived in Jerusalem. They also helped people who served in the Temple. They asked for God's forgiveness for the sin that had become part of the community while they were in captivity.

Nehemiah Rebuilds the Wall
(Nehemiah 1–7)

Nehemiah was the cupbearer for the king. The cupbearer was important because he tasted any food that came to the king. If it were poison, the cupbearer would suffer, but it would protect the king. He became a trusted friend of the king. The king was in his winter palace at Susa, the same palace where Esther had served as queen.

About ten years had passed since Ezra led the people back to Jerusalem. One day in the palace a group of Jewish men returned from Jerusalem. Nehemiah and others asked about the situation in Jerusalem. They discovered that there was trouble. The walls had broken down, and the gates of the city were burned.

For many days Nehemiah was sorrowful, did not eat, and prayed to God. The holy city of Jerusalem was a disgrace. The people of God had not carried out the Law that had been given by Moses. Nehemiah recognized that God had scattered the Jewish people among the nations because they failed to carry out His Law. But when they obeyed God, God promised to bring them back to the land of promise. Nehemiah asked God to give him success with the king to return and rebuild the walls.

When Nehemiah came into the presence of the king, he was very sad. The king was very concerned. Nehemiah told King Artaxerxes what had happened in his homeland. The king asked Nehemiah, "What is it you want?"

Nehemiah told the king he would like to return to Jerusalem and rebuild the walls. The king asked how long he would be gone. Nehemiah gave him a certain time. The king granted his wish and sent him back to Jerusalem. He also gave him permission to obtain the needed supplies to rebuild the walls.

Nehemiah looked over the situation in Jerusalem. He gathered the men and the materials needed. There were other evil men who did not want the walls to be rebuilt and opposed the work of Nehemiah. The workers had to carry their swords at their sides as they continued to build. Some of the workers guarded the walls around the clock. A trumpet was used to call the people to defend the walls if the enemy appeared.

Because Nehemiah had to return to the king, the work had to be done quickly. At the end of fifty-two days the walls and the gates were rebuilt. God gave Nehemiah and the workers success at their task, and the people worshiped God. The walls were dedicated. The Sabbath and the feasts were restored.

Worship was restored in Jerusalem. His people again honored God's name. Even though there were several prophets who ministered to the people, the sacred Scriptures of the Old Testament ended with Malachi. There were prophecies about the coming of a Messiah. The people of Judah lived in hope that soon these prophecies would be fulfilled. But four hundred years passed before the Messiah did come. The events surrounding the Messiah, Jesus, are described in the New Testament.

Construction of the Temple.

The New Testament

JEWISH LIFE AT THE BEGINNING OF THE NEW TESTAMENT

Since God last spoke through one of His prophets at the end of the Old Testament, many things had happened in the world. Alexander the Great had defeated Persia. Alexander came from Macedonia. This was north of Greece. The philosopher Aristotle had educated Alexander. Alexander's contribution was to leave the world with a common language, Greek. The New Testament was written in Greek. Since Alexander left no heirs, his empire was divided. After Alexander, Rome rose to world power. The Romans were skillful with their military forces on land and sea. They were more effective than some of those who had ruled in the past. Greek was kept as the common language. The Romans controlled the people they conquered. Many of these people were brought back to Rome as slaves. Rome brought peace in the world. Among their conquered peoples were the people from Judea. The people of Judah were suffering under the strong arm of Roman rule.

A Jewish group known as the Zealots used every opportunity to fight against the Romans. They would ambush the Roman soldiers. When they were caught, the Romans would crucify them. This made an example for all to see.

Herod the Great became king of Judea. Herod came from Idumea, a country south of Judea. Herod built his palace in Jericho. Herod was not Jewish. He established a relationship with Caesar. Caesar allowed Herod to rule in Palestine. The Roman army supported him.

The Romans had allowed the Jews to continue their worship. Remember that the Temple had been rebuilt more than four hundred years earlier. Cyrus, king of Persia, had sent a group of Jews back to Palestine. Zerubbabel led them. Now the Temple was badly in need of repair. To gain favor with the Jews, Herod rebuilt a very large Temple.

There were other Jewish religious groups, such as the Pharisees. The Pharisees wanted to keep Judaism pure. They would have nothing to do with non-Jews, known as Gentiles. The common people believed that the Pharisees were very religious, and they respected them highly.

The high priest and members of the Sanhedrin were usually from a group known as the Sadducees. The Sadducees were less religious and more interested in political power. The Sanhedrin was like a Jewish court. They protected the Jewish laws. The Sanhedrin could punish Jews who failed to live by Jewish law.

In addition to the Zealots, Pharisees, and Sadducees, there were the Essenes. The Essenes worshiped God and looked for the coming of the Messiah. They were very godly. They lived a very simple life in a community along the Dead Sea.

Many people in Judah were looking for the coming of the Messiah. They were very poor. Herod and the Romans taxed them heavily. They looked for God to deliver them. They remembered how He helped them in Egypt, Babylon, and Persia. All the people expected that God would help them now.

Zachariah in the Temple (Luke 1)
Zachariah was a priest in the Temple. His wife was Elizabeth. They were a husband and wife who pleased God because they followed God's Law. Both of them were getting older in age, and they had no children.

One day Zachariah was performing his service as a priest. When the priests gathered together, they chose one of their number to burn incense on the altar in the Temple. Many of the people were outside praying.

Zachariah did his work at the altar. Suddenly, an angel of the Lord appeared to Zachariah. Zachariah became very afraid.

The angel said to Zachariah, "Do not be afraid. God has answered your prayer. You will have a son. His name shall be John. You will have great joy and delight. Your son will not drink any alcoholic drink. He will be filled with the Holy Spirit. He will call the people back to repentance. He will come with the spirit and power of Elijah to prepare the people for the Lord."

Zachariah asked the angel, "How is this possible? My wife and I are too old to have children."

The angel answered, "I am the angel, Gabriel. I stand before God. I have been sent to bring you the good news. You will not be able to speak until the day that this is accomplished."

The people became anxious because Zachariah stayed so long in the Temple. Finally, when Zachariah came out, he made signs to the people since he could not speak. The people realized that he had seen a vision.

After he had carried out his responsibilities, Zachariah went home. His wife, Elizabeth, conceived a child. She was very happy. She knew that God had heard her prayer and was allowing her to have a child.

The Annunciation (Luke 1)

God sent His angel Gabriel to visit a virgin named Mary. She was engaged to a man named Joseph, a carpenter. Both Mary and Joseph lived in the town of Nazareth. They could trace their ancestors to King David.

The angel said to Mary, "Greetings! God is with you. You are blessed among women."

Mary was anxious about the greeting. She did not know what it meant. But the angel continued, "Do not be afraid; you will be the mother of a son. You will call Him Jesus. He will be great and be called the Son of the Most High. His reign will last forever."

"How can this happen to me?" asked Mary. "I am not yet married."

"The Holy Spirit will come upon you, and the Most High will overshadow you. Your Son will be the Son of God. Even now your relative Elizabeth is having a child in her old age. Behold, with God nothing is impossible."

Mary answered, "I am the handmaiden of the Lord. Let it happen as you said." The angel left Mary.

Mary went quickly to visit her cousin Elizabeth. When Elizabeth heard the greeting of Mary, Elizabeth's baby moved inside her.

Elizabeth said, "You are blessed among women. Blessed is the Son that you will have. How is it that you have come to me?"

Mary answered:
"My soul glorifies the LORD!
My spirit rejoices in GOD *my Savior,*
GOD *has looked with favor on His humble servant.*
From this time on all generations will call me
  blessed,
The Mighty One has done great things to me—
Holy is His name.
His mercy extends from one generation to the next.
He has performed mighty deeds,
He has put down the proud,
He has exalted the humble.
He fills the hungry, but sends the rich away.
He has helped His servant Israel.
He remembers His mercy
to Abraham and His descendants forever."

Mary stayed with her cousin Elizabeth for the next three months. Then she returned to her own home in Nazareth.

The Birth of John the Baptist (Luke 1)

After Mary left, Elizabeth gave birth to a son. The neighbors were happy with her. Elizabeth was no longer childless.

Eight days after the child was born, he was circumcised. From the time of Abraham this practice identified him as a member of God's people, the Jews. At that time the child was also named. They wanted to name him Zachariah after his father. But Elizabeth said, "No, he shall be called John."

They said, "How can you name him John? None of his relatives are named John." They made a sign to his father that he should tell them by what name the baby would be called.

Zachariah asked for tablet. On it he wrote, "John." They were all surprised that the baby should be called John.

At that moment Zachariah was able to speak again. He praised God.

All the people that heard it were astonished. They were filled with awe toward God.

THE BIRTH/EARLY LIFE OF JESUS
MATTHEW 1–2; LUKE 2

Jesus Birth in Bethlehem (Luke 2)

Augustus Caesar issued a decree. All the nations ruled by Rome would be counted and taxed. Each person had to return to the home of his family. Joseph and Mary had to go to Bethlehem, the home of David. Mary was close to giving birth to her son, Jesus.

Mary and Joseph traveled from Nazareth to Bethlehem. It was a long trip. Mary was very tired and uncomfortable. She rode on the back of a donkey.

When they arrived in Bethlehem, they looked for a place to stay. There were many other travelers returning to the home of their ancestors. There was no room for them in the inn.

They found a cattle stall. There Mary gave birth to Jesus. Mary wrapped Jesus in linen cloths. She laid Him in a manger. A manger was used to feed the animals. Mary, Joseph, and the baby were sheltered from the outside and kept warm with fresh hay among the animals in the cattle stall.

At the same time there were shepherds in the fields watching their flocks. In the sky an angel suddenly appeared, glorifying God. The shepherds trembled. They were very afraid.

But the angel said to them, "Do not be afraid! I bring you good news! Today in David's city a Savior is born. He is Christ the Lord. This will be a sign for you. You will find the baby wrapped in cloths and lying in a manger."

Suddenly the sky was filled with heavenly beings. They were praising God. They were saying:

"Glory to GOD in the highest! And on earth, peace to men upon whom his favor rests".

When the heavenly beings had left, the shepherds said among themselves, "We must go to Bethlehem to see this thing that has happened. The Lord has made it known to us."

They came quickly. They found Mary and Joseph. They found the baby lying in a manger, wrapped in cloths. It was just as the angel had told them.

They went out and spread the news. They told others just as the angel had told them. They told what they saw when they came to Bethlehem. All those who heard were filled with wonder.

Mary kept all of these things in her heart. The shepherds went back to tending their sheep. They rejoiced in what God had told them and in what they saw with their own eyes.

Jesus Presented in the Temple (Luke 2)

After eight days Jesus was presented in the Temple in Jerusalem. This was according to custom, similar to John. He was given the name Jesus, as the angel had told Mary before Jesus was born. Mary and Joseph followed the instructions that had been given by Moses.

The firstborn son was always dedicated to the Lord. The sacrifice consisted of offering a pair of turtledoves or two young pigeons.

In the Temple was an elderly man named Simeon. Simeon was a godly man who was looking for the salvation of Israel. Through the Holy Spirit, God had promised that Simeon would not see death until he saw the Lord's Christ. God's Spirit guided him to know that this baby was the one.

He took the child in his arms and prayed, "Now Lord, let your servant die in peace. My eyes have seen your salvation. He will be a light to the Gentiles. He will be glory to Israel."

Jesus' parents were surprised at the things that were said about Him.

Simeon spoke again, blessing Mary and Joseph. Then he turned to Mary and said, "This child is destined to cause the falling and rising of many in

Israel. A sword will pierce your own heart. The thoughts of many hearts will show forth."

As Simeon was speaking, a prophetess, Anna, came up to the family. She was eighty-four years of age. She had been a widow for many years. She spent her time in the Temple, night and day, fasting and praying.

She gave thanks to God for the promised Savior. She spoke of Jesus to all who were looking for the Savior to come.

Everything was done according to the Law. Then Mary and Joseph took the baby and returned home.

The Wise Men Travel from the East (Matthew 2)

Three wise men came from the East. These wise men were astrologers and astronomers. They studied the stars. When they saw the star, they knew that the King of the Jews had been born. They traveled far to find the King.

They came to Jerusalem and asked, "Where is He who is born King of the Jews? We have seen His star in the East. We have come to worship Him."

Herod was very troubled. He was afraid that a new king would take his throne.

He called the priests and the scribes together. He asked them where the Messiah would be born.

They told him that the prophet Micah wrote:
But you, Bethlehem, are not the least,
though you are small among the clans of Judah,
out of you will come one who will rule Israel,
who will be the shepherd of my people.

Hearing this, Herod asked the wise men when the star had appeared. He sent them to Bethlehem. He said, "When you have found Him, return and tell me so I may worship him also."

When they left Herod, the wise men journeyed to Bethlehem. The star guided them to the house where they found Mary and her son Jesus. They bowed down and worshiped Him. They opened their treasures and presented Him gifts of gold, frankincense, and myrrh.

God warned them in a dream not to return to Herod, so they left Bethlehem and went home by another way.

The Flight to Egypt (Matthew 2)

After the wise men left, the Lord's angel appeared to Joseph. He told Joseph that Herod wanted to harm the child and destroy Him. He told Joseph to leave immediately, taking Mary and the child to Egypt. He promised to bring word when it would be safe to return.

That night Mary and Joseph and the Baby fled to Egypt. Hosea the prophet had said, "Out of Egypt I have called my Son." This was a fulfillment of that prophecy.

Herod soon realized that the wise men had returned another way. Herod was a cruel and angry man. He sent the soldiers to Bethlehem to kill every boy child under the age of two. He did this because of what the wise men had told him.

As soon as Herod died, an angel of the Lord came to Joseph in a dream. He told Joseph, "Those who have tried to kill the Child are dead. Take the Child and his mother and return to Israel."

At first they planned to go to Judea, but Joseph learned that Archelaus reigned in Judea. He was the son of Herod. Joseph was afraid to go there. He took Mary and Jesus to the town of Nazareth in Galilee.

Another prophecy from the Old Testament was fulfilled. It said that the Messiah would be called a Nazarene.

The miracle of Jesus' birth is that Jesus, who is God's Son, came to mankind. God Himself could not get tired or hungry. God never felt lonely. But God loves us so much that He wanted to understand what we think and feel in life, so He sent His Son Jesus. That means Jesus was able to experience and feel just as we do.

> ### LOVE
> *Love comes from God. God's love is shown to us by sending His own Son to earth as a gift to bring us to Himself. Jesus lived among us and died on the cross to show His love to us.*

Jesus in Jerusalem (Luke 2)

When Jesus was twelve years of age, His parents came to Jerusalem. This was in keeping with the Law of Moses. There they celebrated the Feast of the Passover. Jesus was preparing to become an adult in Jewish society.

After the celebration of Passover, Mary and Joseph traveled back toward Nazareth. They were in the company of others from Nazareth. Probably there were family members among this group. They most likely thought that Jesus was in the company of others from their group. Later they discovered that He was not among them.

At Passover there were large crowds in Jerusalem. There were dangers that His parents must have feared. Filled with anxiety, they returned to the Holy City in search of Jesus. As any parents, then or now, they loved their Son and did not want anything to happen to Him. When they got back to Jerusalem, they began to hunt frantically for Him. They must have been very upset.

After three days, they found Him in the Temple sitting among the older men of learning. He was asking questions and answering their questions. They were amazed at His wisdom. For a lad of twelve, He had understanding of persons much older.

His mother asked Him, "Why have You done this to us? Your father and I have searched all over for You."

Jesus answered, "Why were you looking for me? Did you not know that I must be about my Father's work?" His parents did not understand the meaning of what He said.

Jesus returned to Nazareth with His parents. He was obedient to His parents, and God was pleased. God blessed Him.

JOHN THE BAPTIST
MATTHEW 3–4; MARK 1; LUKE 3

The years passed. Both John and Jesus grew to manhood. Luke tells us that it was during the fifteenth year of Tiberius Caesar that John came preaching. Pontius Pilate was the governor in Judea. The area that Herod the Great had ruled was now divided among his sons. Annas and Caiaphas were the high priests at the Temple in Jerusalem.

John lived in the wilderness. He chose to live a life of simplicity. Matthew says that John dressed in very rough clothes. He ate very simple food. His diet included locusts and honey.

God called John to preach repentance to the people. The prophet Isaiah had said:

"A voice of one calling in the desert,
Prepare the way for the Lord,
Make his paths straight for him.
Every valley shall be filled,
Every mountain and hill made low,
The crooked roads shall become straight,
the rough ways smooth.
All mankind will see God's salvation"

Crowds of people came out to listen to John. His message was stern. "You must produce fruits that are righteous. You must repent! If the fruit of the tree does not produce, it will be cut down."

The people asked, "What shall we do?"

John answered, "If you have two coats, share one. Tax collector's should collect no more than required. Soldiers should not take money unfairly or accuse people falsely. Be content with your pay."

Many people wondered if John was the Christ. But John assured them, "I baptize only with water. But the One who comes after me will baptize with the Holy Spirit and with fire." John prepared the way for Jesus.

Jesus' Baptism and Temptation
(Matthew 3–4)

While John was preaching in the wilderness, Jesus came to John and asked to be baptized. John did not want to baptize Jesus. He told Jesus, "I should rather be baptized by You."

Jesus insisted that it was right for John to do the baptism. John finally agreed. When Jesus came up out of the water, the heavens opened. The Spirit of God descended upon Him as a dove. A voice from heaven said, "This is My Son, hear Him."

Following His baptism, the Holy Spirit led Jesus into the wilderness to be tempted by the devil. Jesus fasted and prayed for forty days and nights.

Satan came to Jesus and said, "If you are the Son of God, take these rocks and turn them into bread."

Jesus was hungry, but He would not give in to Satan, so He answered, "Man does not live by bread alone. He must live by every word that comes from the mouth of God."

The devil took Him to Jerusalem. He brought Jesus to the top of the Temple and said to Him, "If You are the Son of God, throw Yourself off the Temple. God has promised to give His angels charge over You."

Jesus said, "Do not put the Lord God to the test."

This time the devil took Him to a very high mountain. He showed Jesus all the kingdoms of the earth. Satan said, "I will give all of this to You, if You worship me."

Jesus said to Satan, "Get away from Me, Satan. It is written in the Word, 'Worship the Lord God. Serve Him only.'"

At this point, Satan left Jesus. The angels came to minister to Him.

God cannot be tempted. But when God became Jesus in human flesh, He could understand the temptations that we experience. God loves us so much that He was even willing to experience temptation. But unlike us, Jesus did not sin.

JESUS CALLS THE DISCIPLES
MATTHEW 4, 10;
MARK 1–3; LUKE 5–6

Jesus called His disciples and trained them for the time when they would carry on His work. He chose them after He had spent time in prayer. Jesus prepared them for all they would face when He was gone.

Jesus was standing by the Sea of Galilee when a large crowd of people gather around Him. He asked if He could use Simon's boat. The boat was pushed away from the shore so Jesus could teach all the people from the boat.

When Jesus finished teaching, He told Simon, "Push out into the deep water. Let your nets down."

Simon said, "We have fished all night and caught nothing, but I will do as You say."

They caught such a large number of fish that the nets began to break. Simon called his partners to

Fishermen leave their nets to follow Jesus.

help bring in all the fish. Simon turned to Jesus and said, "You should go away from me, for I am a sinful man."

Jesus answered, "Do not be afraid. Come follow Me. You will not need to go to sea for fish. Instead, I will lead you to bring men to follow Me." Simon came and followed Jesus.

James and John, sons of Zebedee, were also fishermen. They too left their nets to follow Jesus.

Jesus called a tax collector named Levi and said, "Follow Me." Levi, who was called Matthew, immediately left his work as a tax collector and followed Jesus.

Tax collectors and others came to dinner with Jesus. When the Pharisees saw that He had dinner with sinners, they criticized Him. They asked His disciples why He sat with sinners. Jesus heard their complaints. He answered them by saying, "If the people are well, they do not need a doctor. It is only those who are sick who need a doctor. I came to heal the sick."

One night Jesus went off to pray. He spent the entire night in prayer to God. The next day He called all of His disciples. He chose twelve and called them apostles.

The twelve apostles included Simon (called Peter); the brother of Peter, Andrew; James and John; Philip and Bartholomew; Matthew and Thomas; James, the son of Alphaeus; Simon the Zealot; and Judas, the son of James. Judas Iscariot was also among them.

Jesus came and stood on a level plain. A large crowd of His disciples and many other people came to listen to Jesus and to be healed. Some had evil spirits. Jesus healed them also. Many tried to touch Him. They felt His power.

Jesus healed them all.

THE WEDDING AT CANA
JOHN 2

There was a wedding in Cana in Galilee. Jesus' mother, Mary, was invited. Jesus and His disciples were also attending the wedding. The wine at the wedding had run out early. Mary said to her Son, "They do not have any wine."

Jesus answered, "Why are you involving Me?" Jesus was not yet ready to tell the world who He was.

Mary said to the servants, "Do whatever He tells you to do."

There were six large water pots set outside. They were used to wash the people as they entered the house. This was Jewish custom. Each pot held about thirty gallons of water.

Jesus told the servants to fill each of the water pots. They filled them to the top. Then Jesus told the servants to draw some and give it to the master of the banquet. The master, who did not know what Jesus had done, was astonished. But the servants knew what Jesus did.

The master of the banquet called the groom. He said to the groom, "Most people use the best wine first. They bring the cheaper wine when people have been drinking and do not notice. You have saved the best wine until last." This was the first miracle that Jesus performed.

At the wedding at Cana, Jesus showed His love for His mother. He cared for the groom, who would have been embarrassed if the wedding party ran out of wine. He cares even in the small things of life.

JESUS TEACHES AND HEALS
IN CAPERNAUM
MARK 1–2

Jesus' Popularity Grows (Mark 1)
After Jesus called the disciples, they went to Capernaum in Galilee. Jesus taught in the synagogue. His teaching surprised the people. He talked with authority. His teaching was more powerful than that of the scribes.

While He was teaching, a man with a demon said, "What do we have to do with You, Jesus? I know You, Jesus of Nazareth. You are the Holy One of God!"

Jesus told him, "Be quiet! Come out of the man!"

The demon threw the man on the ground. With a loud voice he came out of the man.

The people were amazed! They asked each other, "What kind of new teaching is this? Even the evil spirits obey Him."

The news about Jesus spread quickly throughout Galilee.

After Jesus left the synagogue, He went to the home of Simon and Andrew. He took James and John. Simon's mother-in-law was in bed with a fever. Jesus came, raised her up, and the fever left her.

That evening it seemed as if the entire city was at the door. People came from all around Galilee to be healed of sickness and disease. Some came to have demons cast out of them. Jesus would not allow the demons to speak.

Early the next morning Jesus left the house, went to a quiet place, and prayed. Simon and the others came looking for Him. When they found Him, they said, "Everybody is looking for You."

He left and went to the synagogues in Galilee and preached. He healed and cast out demons.

A man came who had the disease of leprosy. The man fell on his knees and said to Jesus, "If You want to, You can make me clean."

Jesus had compassion on the man. He said, "I will. Be clean!"

That moment the leprosy left him, but Jesus told him not to tell anyone.

However, the man left and began to tell people everywhere that Jesus had healed him. Jesus could no longer openly go to the cities because there were too many people. He stayed in areas that did not have many people, but the people still came to find Him.

Jesus Heals the Man with Paralysis (Mark 2)

Several days later Jesus returned to Capernaum. He was in a house. Many people came to hear Him teach. Four men brought a friend with paralysis to Jesus to be healed. But the house was so crowded there was no way they could get through the door to Jesus.

They went to the roof and removed the tiles to carefully lower the man on the pallet in front of Jesus.

Jesus saw their faith. He said to the man with the paralysis, "Your sin is forgiven."

Some of the scribes began to criticize Jesus. They said, "Only God can forgive sin."

Jesus was aware of what they were thinking and saying. He said to the scribes, "Why are you thinking so? Is it easier to say, 'Your sin is forgiven, or take up your bed and walk?' So that you may know that the Son of Man has power to forgive sin"—He turned and said to the man with paralysis—"Take up your bed and walk."

The man picked up his pallet and went home. The people were amazed. They glorified God.

Jesus went to the seashore and continued to teach.

When Jesus saw a human need, He met that need. When people were sick, He had compassion on them and made them better. He showed us that God is love. He taught us that we must love as God loves.

THE SERMON ON THE MOUNT
MATTHEW 5–7

Jesus saw the crowds of people. He went up on the mountain to teach them. He sat down on the grass. His disciples came and joined Him.

He said, "Happy is he who is humble. Happy is he who repents and is sad. Happy is he who is gentle. Happy is he who loves to do what is right. Happy is he who gives mercy. Happy is the person who is pure. Happy is the person who tries to make peace. Happy is the person who suffers for doing right. Happy are you when you are insulted because of Me. In each case, be happy, for your reward is in Heaven.

"You are like salt to those around you. You give seasoning to life. But if the salt loses its taste, it is good for nothing.

"You are light in a dark world. Your light must not be hidden. Your light must shine forth and lead people to God."

Jesus said, "I did not come to get rid of the Law or the prophets. The Law and prophets must be followed and obeyed.

"The Ten Commandments said that you must not murder. But I say to you, anyone who is very angry with another person may also be guilty.

"You cannot worship God and be angry with another person. Go first to the other person and make peace. When you have gotten rid of your anger and make peace with the other person, then come and worship God.

"A saying of old was 'An eye for an eye, and a tooth for a tooth.' But I say to you, if someone slaps you on the right cheek, let him slap the left also. If someone wants you to go one mile, go two.

"You've heard it said, 'Love your neighbor and hate your enemy.' But I say to you, love your enemy and do good to those who treat you badly.

"Do not pray out loud in public so others can see how religious you are. Go to your closet and pray to God in private. God, who hears your prayer in private, will reward you openly.

"Therefore, you should pray like this:
Our Father in heaven,
Your name be honored as holy.
Your kingdom come.
Your will be done on earth as it is in heaven.
Give us today our daily bread.
And forgive us our debts, as we also have forgiven
our debtors.
And do not lead us into temptation, but deliver
us from the evil one.
For Yours is the kingdom and the power and
the glory forever.
Amen.

"Do not be afraid, God knows your needs. Look at the birds. Your heavenly Father feeds them. Are you not of more value than they? He will feed you also.

"Do worry about what you wear. Even Solomon was not clothed better than the lilies of the field. Do not worry about tomorrow. Have faith in God.

"Ask and you will receive. Seek and you will find. Knock and it will be open to you. God answers prayer."

At the close of His sermon, Jesus told about the two foundations. He said, "To those who hear and act, they are like the wise man who built his house on the rock. The rain fell and the flood rose. The house stood firm on the rock.

"To those persons who do not act on what they hear, they are like the foolish man who built his house on the sand. When the rain fell and the flood rose, the house shifted and collapsed."

Jesus taught many other things to His listeners. The crowds continued to gather and listened intently to His teaching.

Jesus taught that God hates sin. He taught us how to please God. In this sermon He taught about the kind of life that God wants us to live.

JESUS CALMS THE STORM
MATTHEW 8; MARK 4; LUKE 8

Jesus had been teaching all day. He was very tired. He said to the disciples, "Let us go to the other side of the lake."

They climbed into one of the fishing boats and began to sail across the lake. Since Jesus was so tired, He went to the back of the boat. He fell asleep on a cushion.

Soon a storm arose on the lake. The wind howled. The waves overwhelmed the boat. The water came into the boat, and it began to sink.

The disciples went to the back of the boat. They awakened Jesus. They said, "Master, do You not care that we perish?"

Jesus arose. He told the wind to stop. He said to the sea, "Be still!" Immediately, the wind stopped, and a great calm came over the sea.

Jesus turned to the disciples. He said, "Why were you afraid? Where is your faith?"

The disciples were in awe. They said to each other, "Who is this man? Even the wind and the waves obey Him."

Jesus showed the disciples that He had power even over the forces of nature.

THE FEEDING OF THE FIVE THOUSAND
MATTHEW 14; MARK 6; JOHN 6

Jesus took the disciples away from the crowd to a place where they could rest. They got into a boat and crossed to the other side of the Sea of Galilee. The people saw them going, so they began to walk along the shore to the other side.

When Jesus and His disciples arrived and saw all the people who had followed, Jesus felt compassion for them. It appeared to Him that they were sheep without a shepherd. He began to teach them many things. He healed their sickness and disease.

The day was slowly coming to an end. The disciples said to Jesus, "The hour is late. Send the people away. We do not have any food."

Jesus said to Philip, "Where can we buy bread to feed the people?" Jesus already knew what He was going to do, but He wanted to test the disciples.

Philip answered, "A large quantity of bread would not be enough to feed this group, even for each person to have a little."

Andrew said to Jesus, "There is a boy in the crowd who has five barley loaves and two fish. But what good is that among so many?"

Jesus said, "Ask the people to sit down on the grass." He took the loaves and fish and blessed them. Then He distributed the loaves and fish to the disciples. They took the food to the people. He kept giving them loaves and fish until all were satisfied.

After they were finished eating, the disciples went around to pick up the leftovers. They picked up twelve baskets of leftovers. Altogether, they had fed five thousand men, women, and children.

This miracle led many of the people to understand that Jesus was not an ordinary man. He was sent from God.

JESUS TELLS THE STORY OF THE GOOD SAMARITAN
LUKE 10

One of the lawyers tried to cause Jesus to make a mistake. He said to Jesus, "Master, what do I need to do to gain eternal life?"

Jesus answered, "What does the Law say? Have you read the Law?"

The lawyer said, "You shall love the Lord your God with all your heart, strength, and mind. You shall love your neighbor as you love yourself."

Jesus responded, "You have answered well. If you do this, you will live."

But the lawyer was not satisfied. He then asked Jesus, "Who is my neighbor?"

Jesus told this story:

There was a man traveling from Jerusalem to Jericho. The road was very rocky. Robbers hid among the rocks. When this man passed by, they attacked him. He was very badly beaten. They left him, thinking he was dead.

The man heard some footsteps. He pulled his head up to see the robes of the priest. He must have thought, *Surely the priest will help me.* The Law prescribes help for someone in need. When the priest saw the man, he moved to the other side of the road and went on his way.

Soon, the man heard more footsteps. Again he pulled his head up enough to see the robes of the Levite. Levites assist the priests in the Temple. It seemed just as important for the Levite to help. Like the priest, he studied the Law also. But he too was just too busy. He also passed by on the other side.

Yet again the injured man heard footsteps on the road. This time he could tell that the man was a Samaritan. The Jews and Samaritans did not get along very well. He would not get much help from a Samaritan, he must have thought.

But the next thing he knew, the Samaritan was bandaging his wounds and pouring oil on them. The Samaritan gently placed the wounded man on his own donkey. They went to an inn. He gave the innkeeper money to pay for helping the wounded man. If more money was needed, he promised to pay the innkeeper on his next trip.

Jesus asked, "Which of these was the neighbor?"

The lawyer answered, "The one who showed mercy."

Jesus answered, "Go and do the same."

THE PARABLE OF THE LOST SON
LUKE 15

There was a man who had two sons. The younger son said to his father, "Father, I would like to have my inheritance." So his father gathered his two sons and gave them much of his wealth.

Not many days later, the younger son gathered all that he had. He started on a journey to a country far away.

With the money that his father had given him, the young man lived a wild life. It was not long before his money ran out. To make matters worse, there was also a famine in the land where he was living.

The young man tried to find work. He finally got a job feeding pigs in the field. He was so hungry that he ate the same food that he fed to the pigs.

Soon he thought about his situation. He remembered that his father had more than enough food. It would be much better for him to be at home. He thought to himself, *I will say to my father, "I have sinned against you. I am no longer worthy to be your son. Make me one of your hired hands."*

With a plan made, he traveled back toward his home. While he was yet a long way off, his father saw him. He ran to his son and embraced him. The young man told his father that he had sinned against him and was not worthy to be his son. But his father would not hear of it.

His father had a servant bring the best robe. He held a feast in honor of the son who had returned. "My son who was dead is now alive." There was music and dancing.

The older son came home from working in the field. He heard the music and saw the celebration and asked one of the servants what was going on. When he was told that his brother had returned, he became very angry.

His father begged him to come and join the party, but the older son refused.

He said to his father, "I have served you all these years. You never held a dinner in my honor. We never had music or dancing to celebrate. When this son of yours returns from spending your money foolishly, you celebrate with his friends."

His father said, "I always have you with me. All I have his yours. We need to celebrate because your brother, who was lost, is now found. Your brother, who was dead, is now alive."

God loves people like that. He is merciful and loving. He rejoices when sinners repent.

JESUS WITH THE CHILDREN
MATTHEW 19; MARK 10

One day the disciples had gathered around Jesus. They asked Him, "Who will be the greatest in the kingdom of heaven?"

Jesus brought a child in front of them. He told the disciples, "Unless you become as a little child, you cannot enter the kingdom of heaven. Whoever takes on the humility of a child will be the greatest in heaven. Woe to the person who causes one of these little children to fall or sin. He will be severely punished."

On another occasion there were parents who brought their children to Jesus. They wanted Him to bless them. They wanted Him to put His hands on them and pray for them. But the disciples became very irritated.

Jesus said, "Allow the little children to come to Me. Do not hold them back. The kingdom of heaven belongs to persons like them."

Jesus loves all children.

Jesus laid His hands on them and blessed them.

Jesus was concerned for children. He did not ignore them. He loved them and nurtured them. He is still concerned for children today.

JESUS RAISES LAZARUS FROM THE DEAD
JOHN 11

Mary and Martha were sisters. They had a brother named Lazarus. Jesus was a close friend with all three. One day as Jesus was passing through the village of Bethany, He stopped at their home.

They welcomed Him. Both Mary and Martha sat at the feet of Jesus. They listened to Him teach them. Mary continued to listen. Martha went to make preparation for their meal.

Martha wanted to do her best for Jesus. She was cooking and baking. She worked very hard to make Jesus' visit special.

There was so much to do. Martha became upset when Mary did not come and help her. She went to Jesus and said, "Lord, I have so much to do. My sister Mary sits and listens to You while I have to make the preparations myself. Please tell her to come help me."

Jesus had compassion on Martha. He said to her, "Martha, Martha. You are concerned about so many things. Mary has chosen the better part. All these things do not distract her. Rather, she has chosen to listen."

Time passed. Mary, Martha, and Lazarus were with Jesus on other occasions. Mary performed a beautiful act for Jesus. It was the custom in a hot and dusty land to wash the feet of your guests with water. But Mary loved Jesus so much that she poured perfume on Jesus' feet and dried them with her hair.

Jesus loved Mary, Martha, and Lazarus. Word was sent to Jesus that Lazarus was very ill. They said, "Lord, Lazarus, the one you love, is very ill."

Jesus did not leave immediately. He said, "His illness will not end in death. God's glory will be seen. His Son will be glorified."

Then Jesus said to His disciples, "We need to go back to Judea." The disciples were afraid that His enemies would stone Him there. They did not want to go, nor did they want Jesus to go.

At first Jesus said to the disciples, "Lazarus sleeps." The disciples' first response was, "Let him wake up." But then Jesus told them Lazarus was dead. He said God allowed it so that they might believe. Thomas said to the other disciples, "Let us go and die with him in Judea."

When they arrived in Bethany, word came that Lazarus had been in the grave for four days. Martha came out to meet Jesus. She said, "Lord, if You had been here, Lazarus would not have died. But I know that whatever You ask, God will grant it.

Jesus said, "Martha, your brother will live again."

Martha answered, "I know he will rise in the resurrection. I believe that you are the Christ, the Son of God." After saying that, Martha returned home. She whispered to Mary, "Jesus is here. He wants to see you."

There were many people in their house. They were trying to comfort Mary. They saw her leave quickly and followed her. They saw that she was going to the tomb to mourn Lazarus's death.

When Mary arrived, she said, "Lord, if only You had been here, Lazarus would not have died."

Jesus was moved when he saw Mary crying. He also saw all those who had come to comfort her. He said, "Where have you taken him?" They answered, "Come and see."

When Jesus arrived at the tomb, He was again deeply moved. He asked them to remove the stone. They did so. Jesus prayed, "Father, I thank You for hearing Me. Let the people here know that You sent Me." Then Jesus called to Lazarus, "Come out!"

Lazarus was still wrapped in the grave clothes. He had a cloth over his face. Jesus told them to free him and remove the clothes.

On that day Jesus demonstrated that He had power over life and death. Many of the Jews believed in Him.

Other people ran to tell the Pharisees what Jesus had done. The chief priests and the Pharisees became very angry. They called for a meeting of the Sanhedrin. The Sanhedrin, the Jewish court that protected the Jewish laws, were very jealous of Jesus. They saw that the people followed Him. They began looking for a way to get rid of Jesus.

JESUS ENTERS JERUSALEM
MATTHEW 21; MARK 11; LUKE 19

The Passover was coming soon. Jesus came to Bethphage. That was a town near Bethany and the Mount of Olives. Bethany was the town where Jesus stayed the night before. From the Mount of Olives one could see the holy city of Jerusalem.

Jesus sent two disciples to a village to find a colt. He told them that they should untie the colt. "Someone will certainly ask why you are untying the colt," said Jesus. "You will answer, 'The Master needs him.' Then bring the colt to Me." Zechariah, the prophet, had said in the Old Testament writings that the king would come, riding on a colt.

The disciples went to the village. They found the colt, untied it, and spoke to the owners as Jesus said. They put their garments on the colt for Jesus to ride.

Jesus came riding to Jerusalem. The crowds who had gathered for the Passover placed their garments in the road. Others cut branches of palms and placed them in His path. The crowds shouted, "Hosanna," "Hosanna!" Hosanna meant, "Save now."

But some of the Pharisees were annoyed. They said to Jesus, "Tell your disciples to be quiet."

Jesus said, "If they did not shout, the stones would cry out!"

As Jesus came close to the city, He cried. He said, "I wish that today you would know what would bring you peace."

After He entered Jerusalem, He went to the Temple. He found out that the people were not allowed to bring their sacrifices to the Temple. They had to purchase the lambs and other animals that were sacrificed. In the Temple there were traders who sold animals for sacrifice. This was very wrong.

Jesus became angry with them. He drove them out of the Temple. He said, "My house is a house of prayer. You have made My house a den of thieves."

Jesus continued to teach each day in the Temple. The chief priests and scribes became more angry. They were jealous of the crowds that followed Jesus. They wanted to stop Him from teaching, so they gathered together to find a way to get rid of Jesus.

THE LAST SUPPER
MATTHEW 26; MARK 14;
LUKE 22; JOHN 13

Judas Plans to Betray Jesus
(Matthew 26)
Judas Iscariot heard about the plans of the chief priests to get rid of Jesus, and he went to the chief priests. He asked them, "What will I get if I give Jesus to you?"

They answered, "We will give you thirty pieces of silver."

They made the agreement. Then Judas looked for a chance to betray Jesus to the chief priests.

Meanwhile, Jesus' disciples asked Him, "Where would You like us to eat the Passover?"

Jesus said, "Go to the city. You will find a man there.

"Tell him, 'The Master says, my time has come. With My disciples, I will keep the Passover at your house.'"

The disciples did as Jesus bid them.

The Last Passover
(Luke 22; John 13)

Jesus ate the Passover meal with His disciples in the upper room. Jesus arose from supper. He tied a towel around Himself. He poured water in a basin. Then He began to wash the disciples' feet. He dried them with the towel.

When Jesus came to Peter, Peter protested. He did not want Jesus to wash his feet. Jesus said, "What I am doing, you may not understand now. You will understand later."

Peter answered, "You will never wash my feet."

Jesus said, "If I do not wash your feet, you will not be with Me."

Then Peter said, "Lord, do not watch my feet only, but my hands and head."

The Jesus said, "I only need to wash your feet."

After washing the disciples' feet, Jesus asked, "Do you understand what I have done? As your Master, I have washed your feet. You need to wash each other's feet. I have shown you an example. The servant is not greater than his Master. Since you know what to do, you will be happy if you follow My example."

Jesus grew very sad. He said, "One of you will betray me."

The disciples turned to each other. They were upset and asked each other, "Am I the one?"

Peter motioned to John to ask Jesus. Jesus told him, "It is the one who dips bread with me." Then

Jesus dipped His piece of bread and handed it to Judas.

Satan entered Judas at that moment. Jesus said to him, "What you are going to do, do it quickly."

The disciples did not understand what He was saying. Judas left immediately and went into the darkness of the night. The disciples thought Judas was going to use money for the poor or to buy food.

Jesus told them, "I am giving you a new commandment. Love each other. I have loved you. You should also love each other. In this way, all will know that you are My followers."

Jesus told Peter, "You will not be able to follow Me."

Peter asked, "Why?"

Jesus said, "Will you die for Me? The rooster will not crow until you have denied Me three times."

The Lord's Supper
(Matthew 26; Mark 14; Luke 22)

Jesus knew that the time had come that He would soon die. He told the disciples He wanted to eat His last Passover with them. When the meal ended, Jesus took the bread. He gave thanks to God. He broke it and gave it to the disciples. He said, "This is My body which is broken for you. Do this to remember Me."

Jesus took the cup. He gave thanks to God. Then He said, "Drink this. This is the cup of the New Testament. My blood is shed for you. I will not drink again of the fruit of the vine until the kingdom of God comes."

The disciples still did not understand what Jesus was telling them, that He would die soon and then rise from the grave.

The Garden of Gethsemane
(Matthew 26; Mark 14; Luke 22; John 18)

Jesus and His disciples left the upper room and made their way to the Garden of Gethsemane. As they walked, Jesus began to comfort His disciples. He promised them that He would prepare a place for them. One day they would come to live with Him forever. Jesus told them the way to the Father was through the Son. He promised to send the Holy Spirit. He told them of His love for them. He warned them that many would suffer because they belonged to Him. Finally, He prayed for them, asking God to protect and care for them.

Jesus and the disciples had been to the garden before. This was a quiet place away from the noise of the city. He told the disciples, "Stay here for a little while. I will go a little further and pray."

He took Peter, James, and John a little farther into the garden with Him. He told them to stay and pray while He went on alone a little further.

Jesus was in great sorrow. He knelt down and prayed, "Father, if it is possible, take this cup from Me. Nevertheless, not My will, but Yours."

He returned to the three disciples, Peter, James, and John. The events of this day and the fear that they had for Jesus caused the disciples to be very tired. Jesus found them asleep. He asked them, "Could you not stay awake a little longer? Watch, that you do not enter into temptation."

He went away a second time and prayed. He returned to Peter, James, and John. Again, He found them asleep and spoke to them as He had before.

He went away a third time. He prayed the same prayer. Again, He found them asleep. This time He said, "The time has come. The one who will betray Me is close at hand."

Just then Judas Iscariot came with a large crowd of people. Judas said, "Hello, Master." Then Judas kissed Jesus.

Jesus answered, "Friend, why have you come?"

Just then, Peter took out his sword and struck the ear of the servant of the high priest. Jesus told Peter to put his sword away. He said, "I must carry out the will of my Father." Out of fear, all the disciples left Him.

The men who had come with Judas took Him. They bound Him and led Him away.

THE TRIALS AND CRUCIFIXION OF JESUS
MATTHEW 26–27; MARK 14–15; LUKE 22–23; JOHN 18–19

The Trial before the Sanhedrin
(Matthew 26; Mark 14; Luke 22; John 18)

Jesus was bound and brought to the Sanhedrin. Caiaphas, the high priest, asked Jesus about what He believed. Jesus answered, "I was in the Temple and taught there. I did nothing in secret. Why do you ask Me what I taught?" The officer slapped Jesus for answering the high priest in such a manner.

Jesus said, "I only told the truth. Why did you slap Me?"

These men hated Jesus so much that they hired men to lie about Him. But even these false witnesses could not bring a charge against Jesus. The witnesses did not even agree among themselves. Jesus answered nothing to their false charges.

Finally, the high priest asked Him, "Are you the Christ? Are you the Son of God?

Jesus answered, "I am. You will see Me come in power and great glory."

The high priest tore His clothes while others spit on Jesus. Caiaphas said, "Do we need any more testimony? He has spoken blasphemy. Do we need any more witnesses?"

The members of the Sanhedrin agreed. They said He was worthy of death. Some of them began to spit at Him, to beat Him, and to mock Him.

Peter Denies Jesus (Mark 14)

All of Jesus' disciples had left Him. Peter, however, followed as close as he dared. He was standing by the fire, warming himself. One of the servant girls to the high priest said, "You also were with Jesus of Nazareth!"

Peter denied it. He said, "I do not know what you are saying." Peter went out to the porch. At that moment the rooster crowed.

Another maid saw Jesus. She said to the group, "This man is one of them."

Peter again denied any relationship with Jesus.

A little later some who stood there said, "This man talks like a Galilean. You must be one of them."

Again, Peter cursed and said, "I do not know the Man."

Again the rooster crowed. Peter remembered the words that Jesus had said to him. "Before the rooster crows twice, you will deny Me three times." He thought about it and went out and cried bitterly.

Judas Regrets Betraying Jesus (Matthew 27)

When Judas saw that Jesus was condemned to death, he was sorry for what he had done. He went back to the chief priests with the thirty pieces of silver and said, "I have sinned. I have betrayed an innocent man." The priests answered, "That is your problem." Judas threw the silver coins on the floor of the Temple. He went out and hanged himself.

The priests said, "We cannot put this money back in the treasury. It is a price of blood." They decided the best way to use the money was to buy the potter's field. This would be a burial place for strangers who died in Jerusalem.

Jeremiah, the prophet, had proclaimed long ago that thirty pieces of silver would buy the potter's field.

Jesus Before Pilate (Matthew 27; Mark 15; Luke 23; John 18)

Jesus stood before the Roman governor, Pilate. He asked Jesus, "Are You the king of the Jews?"

Jesus said, "You have said so."

The priests accused Jesus of many things, yet Jesus said nothing in His defense. Pilate was amazed.

At the feast of Passover, it was custom for the governor to release one prisoner. Barabbas was a notorious prisoner. He had killed many.

Pilate told the people that he could release Jesus of Nazareth or Barabbas.

Pilate sat in the judgment chair. His wife sent word to her husband, "I had a dream about this man Jesus. Do not have anything to do with Him."

The chief priests had stirred the people. They cried out to release Barabbas because they wanted to get rid of Jesus.

Pilate asked them, "What shall I do with Jesus?"

They cried, "Crucify Him! Crucify Him!"

Pilate saw that he could do nothing to change their minds. He had a bowl of water brought. In front of the people, he washed his hands. He said, "I am innocent of this Man's blood."

The people shouted, "Let His blood be on our hands and those of our children."

Pilate released Barabbas. He had Jesus beaten. He prepared Jesus to be crucified.

The Roman soldiers made sport of Jesus. They took off His robe and placed a scarlet robe on Him. They took a crown of thorns and placed it on His head. They put a reed in His right hand. They began to strike Him. They spit upon Him. When they got tired of that, they put His clothes back on Him. They led Him away to be crucified.

The Crucifixion of Jesus (Matthew 27; Mark 15; Luke 23; John 19)

They came to a place called Golgotha. It was known as the place of the skull. They offerred Jesus vinegar mixed with gall. The purpose was to deaden the pain. When Jesus tasted it, He would not drink it.

They nailed Him to the cross and mocked Him. They said, "He saved others, but Himself He cannot save."

The soldiers took His clothes. They cast lots to see who would get them.

Pilate had an inscription written at the top of the cross. It was in letters of Greek, Latin, and Hebrew. It said, "THIS IS THE KING OF THE JEWS."

Two thieves were also crucified with Him. There was one on His left and another on His right. The one made fun of Jesus. He said, "If you are the Christ, save yourself and us."

Jesus died on the cross.

The other thief did not mock Jesus but said to the first thief, "Do you not fear God? We suffer because we did wrong. But this man has done nothing wrong." Then he turned to Jesus and said, "When You come into Your kingdom, Lord, remember me."

Jesus answered, "Today you will be with Me in Paradise."

Standing by the cross were John, the apostle; Mary; Mary Magdalene; and Salome. They all loved Jesus and refused to leave.

For three hours darkness covered the land.

Finally, Jesus cried with a loud voice and gave up His life. At that moment the veil in the Temple was torn from top to bottom. The death of Jesus made it possible for those who believe in Him to go directly to God. No longer was it necessary to go through the priests to come close to God. No longer was it necessary to have to sacrifice animals to atone for sin. By dying on the cross, Jesus shed His blood and paid the price for everyone's sin. He opened the door for those who believe in Him to become part of God's family.

SALVATION

Salvation means to be delivered. God provided salvation from sin for all who put their trust in Jesus. Jesus died on the cross to bring salvation to all who will believe.

The Burial of Jesus (Matthew 27; Mark 15; Luke 23; John 19)

Joseph of Arimathea had arranged with Pilate that he might take the body of Jesus and bury Jesus in his own tomb. With the help of Nicodemus, they wrapped the body in linen and anointed it with spices. Both Joseph and Nicodemus were secret followers of Jesus.

The tomb was new. No one had ever been buried there before. It was carved out of the rock. A large stone was rolled in front of the door. When they had completed their preparations, Joseph and Nicodemus departed.

Many of the women who had stood by Jesus at the cross also came to the tomb. They wanted to see where it was located. The Sabbath was coming. But they would return on the first day of the week.

The chief priests and the Pharisees went to Pilate. They said, "This deceiver said that He would rise from the dead on the third day. Let us make sure that His disciples do not steal His body. They will tell the people that He has risen from the dead. This would be a worse error."

Pilate told them that they could seal the stone and place soldiers to watch in front of the tomb.

THE RESURRECTION AND APPEARANCES OF JESUS
MATTHEW 28; MARK 16; LUKE 24; JOHN 20–21; ACTS 1

The Resurrection of Jesus
(Matthew 28; Mark 16; Luke 24; John 20)

The Sabbath Day came to an end. It was the first day of the week. Mary and Mary Magdalene came to the tomb. As they came close, they felt the shock waves of an earthquake. The angel of the Lord descended from heaven. The face of the angel was like lightning, and his clothing was pure white.

The soldiers who were assigned to guard the tomb were frightened. They seemed like dead men.

The angel spoke kindly to the women. He told them not to be afraid, that Jesus had risen just as He said. He invited them to see the place where Jesus was buried. He encouraged them to go quickly and find the disciples. He said Jesus would be found in Galilee.

The women left with great joy. They ran to tell the disciples. As they were running, they met Jesus. They fell at His feet and worshiped Him. He told them, "Do not be afraid! Go to the disciples and tell them that I have risen. I will go to Galilee."

The soldiers who were assigned to guard the tomb went to the chief priests. They told all that had happened. The chief priests met together. They paid the soldiers a large sum of money to tell the story that His disciples had taken Him away during the night. They promised to protect the soldiers if the governor found out. The soldiers did as they were told and convinced some that the disciples had taken Jesus body.

The Disciples on the Road to Emmaus (Luke 24)

There were two disciples who were walking together toward their home in Emmaus. They talked about all that had happened in Jerusalem to Jesus.

Jesus came along the road and met the disciples. They did not know it was Jesus. Jesus asked them, "Why are you so sad? What are you talking about?"

One of the disciples, Cleopas, asked Jesus, "Are you new to the city of Jerusalem? Do you not know what has happened during these days?"

Jesus answered, "What things?"

They said, "Those things about Jesus of Nazareth. He was a Prophet and taught the Word of the Lord. The chief priests and rulers had Him crucified. We had hoped that He would redeem Israel. Some of our women went to the tomb this morning. They did not find His body. They saw a vision of an angel, who said that He was alive. Others also went to the tomb and did not find Him."

Jesus then began to teach them. They still did not know that it was Jesus. He started with Moses and all the prophets, then taught them all about the Scriptures. He taught them about himself.

When they came to the village, it appeared to the disciples that their guest was going to go further. They persuaded Him to stay with them.

Jesus sat at dinner with these disciples. When He broke bread and gave it to them, they recognized Him, and immediately He disappeared from their sight.

They were so excited that they ran back to Jerusalem. There they found the eleven apostles gathered together. They told them that the Lord had risen. The disciples already knew that the Lord had risen. Peter had actually seen Him and talked with Him.

Jesus appeared to them. Thomas was not with the disciples at this time. He said that unless he could touch the nail prints in Jesus' hands and put his hand into Jesus' side, he would not believe. Later when the disciples were gathered again, Jesus came into their midst. He called Thomas to come and put his hand on the nail prints and in His side. Thomas cried, "My Lord and my God!"

Jesus in Galilee (Matthew 28; Acts 1)

Finally, the eleven disciples went to Galilee. This was a place Jesus had promised to meet them. They stood upon a mountain. Many believed, but a few doubted.

Jesus said, "All power is given to Me. Go to all the world and teach the gospel. Baptize them in the name of the Father, Son, and Holy Spirit. Teach them to follow all that I've commanded you. I am with you always."

After Jesus had instructed His disciples, He was taken out of their sight. He disappeared into a cloud.

They were gazing into heaven. Two men came and stood by them. They were wearing white garments. They asked the disciples why they were gazing into heaven. They said the same Jesus will come again one day. He will do it in the same way that they saw Him go away.

THE DAY OF PENTECOST
ACTS 1:12–26

After the ascension of Jesus, the eleven disciples continued to meet regularly for prayer in an upper room. Mary and some of the women joined in prayer as well. Judas, who had betrayed Jesus, was no longer with the disciples.

Since there were only eleven of the twelve, whom Jesus had chosen, the apostles decided that it was time to replace Judas. They prayed and asked God to guide their choice of a successor to Judas. Matthias was chosen to serve with the eleven.

Pentecost was an ancient feast day, that was commanded back in Exodus 19. Pentecost came fifty days after the Feast of Passover. In Leviticus 23 it was called the "First Fruits" harvest. In the Jewish synagogue, the Book of Ruth is read to the congregation. Every feast day in Jerusalem brought crowds of Jews from all across the ancient world to worship in the Holy City. Pentecost was no different.

THE BIRTH OF THE CHURCH
ACTS 2

This Pentecost was very different from the ones in the past. As the followers of Jesus were gathered together, there suddenly came a sound from heaven. It must have been very loud because many people came rushing to the scene. A violent wind came from heaven. Over the top of the apostles came small flames of fire that flickered over their heads. Just as Jesus had promised, the Holy Spirit of God came to the followers of Jesus.

Each of the apostles began to talk in a tongue that was not his own language. The people stood and watched in amazement. Many persons, from different parts of the world, heard the apostles talk in their language. There were people from Phrygia, Pamphilia, Crete, Libya, Rome, and other parts of the world that were present in the crowd.

The people were amazed! They wanted the apostles to explain what had happened. Why had these men from Galilee started to talk in a language that was not their own? Some of the bystanders began to laugh and make fun of the disciples. These people said that the disciples had drunk too much wine.

The apostle Peter stood up in the middle of the crowd and began to preach. He told the crowd that these men were not drinking. They had received the Holy Spirit of God. Then Peter started back in Jewish history with the prophet Joel. Joel had prophesied that God's Spirit would one day be poured out. In that day, said Peter, God will do wonders. He told the crowd that Joel's prophecy was fulfilled this day.

Peter continued to tell the crowd that God was doing this because Jesus had come in their midst and fulfilled the prophecies. The people knew about the crucifixion of Jesus on the previous feast day of Passover. Then God raised Jesus from the dead. Jesus was made Lord and Christ by God.

The people felt very guilty about what had been done to Jesus. Many asked Peter and the other apostles, "What shall we do?"

Peter answered, "Repent, turn away from your sin. Be baptized in the name of Jesus Christ. You will receive the Holy Spirit of God. God's promise is for you and your children and to all whom the Lord will call."

On that day many persons followed God. They turned to Christ and received Jesus as Savior and Lord.

About 3,000 persons became followers of Jesus. After they were baptized, they were added to the church. On that day the church was born. God's Spirit had come to those who became followers of Jesus.

The church, made up of the followers of Jesus, grew. The believers grew in their understanding of the teaching of the apostles. They continued to observe the Lord's Supper, as they had been taught by Jesus Himself. The apostles did many signs and wonders for the new church. There was a close fellowship among the believers. God continued to add many persons to the church in those days.

PETER AND JOHN AT THE TEMPLE
ACTS 3–4

Peter and John went to the Temple to pray. There was a crippled man at the gate called Beautiful. When the crippled man saw Peter and John, he begged for money.

Peter said, "Look at us!" The man thought that he would receive some money. So he looked. Peter then said, "We have no money to give to you. But what we do have, we will give to you. In the name of Jesus of Nazareth, get up and walk."

Then Peter helped the man to his feet. The man rose to his feet. He began jumping and walking. He praised God for the miracle of his healing. The people who were watching recognized the beggar. They knew he was the one who sat at the gate called Beautiful. The people were amazed and did not know what to think about this miracle.

Peter used the opportunity to preach to the crowd. He told them that it was not surprising. God had promised this in His Word. The prophets from Samuel forward had told that the day would come when God would cause such miracles to happen. He told them about Jesus. Faith in the name of Jesus by this crippled beggar had caused his healing. They were witnesses.

Peter was still speaking. The priests, Sadducees, and the Temple guard came and arrested Peter and John. They were very disturbed because Peter and John preached about the resurrection of Jesus. It was late in the afternoon. They could not do anything that day, so they threw Peter and John into prison.

Meanwhile, many of the people who heard Peter believed. There were many who became followers of Jesus that day. The church continued to grow.

On the next day the Sadducees, priests, and elders asked how they had the power to heal. Peter and John boldly answered in the power of the Holy Spirit. They did the miracle of healing the beggar, who could not walk, in the name of Jesus. The members of the Sanhedrin were surprised by the answers of Peter and John. They could not deny that the man had been healed.

They were not sure what to do with these men who spoke so boldly about Jesus. Finally, they let Peter and John go. But they warned them to stop speaking about Jesus. Peter and John would make no such promise. They told the Sanhedrin that they had to obey God and not man.

Peter and John went back and told the church all that had happened to them. The disciples continued to preach about Christ. The church continued to grow.

THE STONING OF STEPHEN
ACTS 6–8:1

Many of the widows in the church were not given enough care. The apostles became concerned. They spoke to the members of the church. They told them that the church should choose seven men to minister to the widows and others. They were to be men who were godly and filled with the Holy Spirit. The apostles would continue in prayer, preaching, and teaching the Word of God.

The church liked the idea. They chose seven deacons. The apostles laid hands on them and prayed for them.

Among the deacons was Stephen. Stephen was a man of faith and filled with the Holy Spirit. He ministered in the church. God did miracles through him. God was with Stephen. Stephen preached about Jesus.

There were Jewish men from other parts of the world among his hearers. They began to argue with Stephen. But they were no match for Stephen, who was led by the Holy Spirit. They could not deny his wisdom. The men became angry and convinced other men to lie about Stephen. These men said that Stephen had said evil things about God and Moses.

Soon the Jewish people and the leaders were very angry. They brought Stephen before the Jewish court of the Sanhedrin. The accusers told the court that Stephen had spoken evil of the Temple. They also accused Stephen of telling people that Jesus of Nazareth would destroy the Jewish customs.

The members of the Sanhedrin looked at Stephen. His face shone like the face of an angel. The high priest then asked Stephen if what the men said was true.

To answer, Stephen began to tell the history of Israel from Abraham and his family. Then he told them about Moses and others. Finally, Stephen ended his answer by telling the Sanhedrin that they had resisted the Holy Spirit. They were resisting the Holy Spirit now. He said that they were blind and missed the work of God in Jesus. They had killed Jesus!

At that moment, Stephen looked up and saw Jesus sitting at the right hand of God. The Sanhedrin would listen no more. They were furious! They dragged Stephen outside and threw stones at him. He looked to heaven and prayed that God would take his spirit. He prayed that God would not judge them for killing him.

Stephen died. Saul, the Pharisee from Tarsus, agreed with what they did. He was a young man at the time. Saul stood by and held the clothes of those who stoned Stephen.

GROWTH OF THE CHURCH
ACTS 8–11

The disciples were traveling around preaching and teaching about Christ. Philip was led by the Spirit of God to an Ethiopian. The man was reading from Isaiah the prophet. He did not understand what he was reading. Philip showed him that Jesus was the One who was described in Isaiah. The man came to Christ and was baptized.

CONVERSION OF SAUL
ACTS 9:1–31

Saul was a young Jewish man. He was a Pharisee, a member of the strictest group of Jews. He came from the city of Tarsus in Asia Minor. His father was a Roman citizen. That gave Saul the right of citizenship from Rome as well. Recall that Saul approved of the stoning of Stephen.

It should be no surprise that he was now on his way to Damascus to capture Jews who had become Christians. With permission of the high priest, Saul was going to bring these people back to Jerusalem to stand trial. He brought with him persons who would take these Christians back to Jerusalem.

Because Saul was a Pharisee, he probably did not travel close to the other men. Rather, he would travel behind them. In that way he would not associate with people who were not as pure as he was.

His whole group was traveling along the road to Damascus. Suddenly, as they drew near to Damascus, a bright light shone around Saul. He fell to the ground. A voice came from heaven, "Saul, Saul, why are you persecuting Me?" Jesus called to Saul. Saul answered, "Who are You, Lord?"

Jesus told Saul, "I am Jesus. Get up off the ground. Go to Damascus and find Ananias. He will tell you what you are to do."

The people who traveled with Saul were amazed! They heard a voice, but they could not see anyone. Then they found that Saul was blind. They had to lead him to the city of Damascus. He was in the city for three days. He could not see. He did not eat anything.

Meanwhile, the Lord appeared to Ananias in a vision. Jesus told Ananias to go to the street named Straight. There in the home of Judas he would find

Saul praying. He told Ananias to lay hands on Saul so he might receive his sight.

Ananias told the Lord that Saul had done evil to Christians. But Jesus told Ananias that Saul was chosen to preach the gospel to the Gentiles. Saul would indeed suffer for his faith in Jesus.

Ananias did as he was told. He restored Saul's sight. He baptized Saul. Saul ate and was strengthened. Saul immediately began to preach the gospel.

Very quickly the Jews wanted to kill Saul. But the disciples let Saul out of the city. They helped him down to the road by lowering him in a basket. He was then able to get to Caesarea. From there he returned to his home in Tarsus.

After that God protected the church. For a period of time the church had peace and continued to grow.

PETER AND CORNELIUS
ACTS 9:32–10:33

The apostle Peter was in Joppa, a city along the seacoast. He was staying with a tanner, who made leather. Peter had ministered there in Joppa. Dorcas was a godly woman. She served the people. But she became ill and died. Peter was called, and through his prayer, God raised Dorcas from death back to life.

Cornelius was a centurion in the Roman army. Cornelius was the leader of an Italian group of soldiers. Although, he was a Gentile, he was a God-fearer. In other words, Cornelius was becoming a Jew. He had not yet completed all of the steps. (A Gentile is a person who is not a Jew. Jews stayed away from Gentiles).

One day Cornelius was in prayer. It was late in the day. An angel of the Lord appeared to Cornelius and told him that God had heard his prayers. God was pleased with Cornelius. The angel told Cornelius to send two of his men to Joppa to find Peter. They were to ask Peter to come to Caesarea.

Cornelius did as he was told. He asked two of his servants, to be accompanied by a trusted and believing soldier, to go to Joppa. Cornelius related what the angel told him.

On the next day the men left to find Peter.

While the men were on the road, Peter was on the roof. He was hungry. He saw a vision of a sheet coming down in front of him. On the sheet were animals that Jewish law called "Unclean!" Peter watched, and then a voice told him to kill the animals and eat.

But Peter said, "No, Lord. I have never eaten any animals that were unclean."

God told Peter, "What I have called holy, you should not call unholy."

This happened three times. Peter was puzzled! He was thinking about what he had seen. Then the Spirit came to Peter and told him to go to the street. There he would find three men. The Spirit told Peter to go with the men.

Peter went as he was told. He found the three men at the gate. Peter asked them why they had come. The men answered that Cornelius had been praying and saw a vision. He was directed to find Peter. Peter was to go with the men to Caesarea. It was late in the day, so the men came and stayed at Simon the tanner's home that night.

On the next day they went to Caesarea. Cornelius explained the vision God had given him. Peter then preached about what had happened to Jesus. The forgiveness of their sins would come through the death of Jesus Christ. This was the very same thing that happened to the Jewish believers.

Peter was still speaking, when the Holy Spirit came upon these Gentile believers. It happened in the same way that it happened to the Jewish believers in Jesus Christ. All of the Jewish believers were amazed! They did not expect that the Holy Spirit would come to the Gentiles as He had come to the Jewish believers.

Seeing this happen, Peter said, "Can we refuse these believers to be baptized?" Cornelius and the others were taken to the water and baptized. Peter continued there for several days, ministering to the new believers.

Many of the members of the church in Judea heard about Peter bringing the Word of God to the Gentiles. They were very upset. Peter went to the church in Jerusalem and explained all that had happened. He told them about the vision he had of the sheet coming down with the unclean animals. Then he reminded them of Jesus' words: "John baptized with water, but you will be baptized with the Holy Spirit." Therefore, if the Holy Spirit came to them, in the same way He came to us, then God is bringing Gentiles into His church also. This satisfied the church.

PETER TAKEN TO JAIL
AND RELEASED
ACTS 12

Herod Agrippa was the son of Herod the Great. He ruled part of Palestine. He wanted to please the Jews. Herod found that when he arrested followers of Jesus and put them in prison, he pleased the Jews. Some, like James the brother of John, he put to death.

The time of year was Passover. Herod had his soldiers arrest Peter. Four squads of soldiers were given charge over Peter to make sure that he could not escape. On the night before Herod was going to bring Peter before the Jewish people, Peter was sleeping between two guards. Peter was chained to the two guards. There were guards in front of the door, watching the prison also. During the time Peter was in prison, the followers of Jesus were praying for his safe return.

Suddenly, in the middle of the night, a light shone in Peter's cell. An angel of the Lord appeared to Peter. The angel said, "Get up quickly." The angel led Peter past the guards and out of the prison. Peter thought he was having a dream. But when they were out of the prison, the angel left him. Peter now knew that God had rescued him from Herod and from the Jewish people.

Peter went to the home of Mary, mother of John Mark. He knocked on the door. When Rhoda, the servant girl, heard his voice, she was very excited. She did not open the door but went back to tell the disciples, who were still in prayer. They did not believe her.

Peter kept knocking until someone finally came and opened the gate. They were all amazed. Then Peter told them what God had done to protect him. Peter left the area.

On the next day, the soldiers were very upset. They did not know what happened to Peter. Herod was cruel. He had the soldiers killed for letting the prisoner get away. Herod tried to pass himself off as a god. Instead, the true God struck him down and he died.

Many of the believers who had been scattered at the death of Stephen left Jerusalem for Phoenicia, Cyprus, and Antioch. It was in Antioch that the followers of Jesus were first called Christians. Many of the followers of Jesus in Judea were suffering from the famine that arose at that time.

Barnabas and Saul were sent by the church at Antioch to Jerusalem to relieve the suffering there. They returned from Jerusalem to Antioch with John Mark. They determined to go on their first missionary journey. From this point on, Saul was now known as Paul.

THE TRAVELS OF PAUL
ACTS 13–28

Even though the Romans were cruel, there were many benefits that they provided. The gospel would not have been spread as easily during another period of time. Three things were important to the spread of the gospel.

First, all roads led to Rome. Before the Romans, transportation was very difficult. They created a network of roads. Paul often traveled along these roads. When he came to the sea, there were ships on which he could sail.

Second, the Peace of Rome, or Pax Romana, meant that there was no war. If war had been part of the Empire, it would have been hard to preach the gospel.

Third, the common language spoken throughout the Roman Empire was Greek. To communicate among people of different races and different countries Greek was used. The New Testament was written in Greek so all could understand.

After Paul became a Christian, he began to preach and teach about the gospel of Jesus Christ. Wherever he went he witnessed to the saving power of Jesus. He started churches in the cities where he visited. When he received reports of difficulties from the churches that he started, he would write them a letter. These letters are an important part of the New Testament.

The gospel was preached, and the church was growing. Paul came to the church at Antioch. There were prophets and teachers there. They fasted and prayed. The Holy Spirit told them, "Set apart Barnabas and Paul. I have work for them to do." Paul and Barnabas were sent by the church at Antioch to preach the gospel in parts of the world where it had never been heard.

Paul's First Missionary Journey (Acts 13–15)

They went to the seacoast and set sail for Cyprus. In Salamis, they went to the synagogue and preached about Jesus, the Christ. They went across the island to Paphos. They continued to preach about Jesus. In Paphos, there was a false prophet who was a sorcerer. He tried to stop their preaching, but the Holy Spirit prevented him.

Paul and Barnabas sailed from Cyprus to Attalia. This was on the coast of what is today Asia Minor. They went to the synagogue of Antioch in Pisidia. They preached about Jesus and His resurrection on the Sabbath. The next week they preached again, and the whole town came to hear them. They said, "The Lord has told us that we must carry this message throughout the world."

Then they traveled to the synagogue in Iconium. The Jews stirred up the Gentiles, and both groups wanted to kill Paul and Barnabas. They fled to Lystra, but the Jews stirred up the people there as well. They had to flee for their lives again. This time they went to Derbe where they were received warmly.

After this welcome visit, they turned around and retraced their steps through Lystra, Iconium, and Antioch of Pisidia. They strengthened the churches that they had established in each of the cities.

Before they went on another missionary journey, they went to Jerusalem for a conference with the elders in the church there. Because of their reports of success among the Gentiles, the Jews in Jerusalem had become very concerned. At the conference, the Jewish Christians decided to support their Gentile brothers in Antioch. Paul and Barnabas came from the church at Antioch. Peter supported the work of Paul and Barnabas. James, a member of Jesus' family, did not believe at first. But after Jesus' resurrection, James became a follower and a leader in the church in Jerusalem. He led the group in support of Gentiles becoming part of the church. The church only asked that the Gentiles live godly lives and avoid certain practices that were sensitive to Jews. This was an important event for the growth of the church.

Paul's Second Missionary Journey (Acts 15:36–18:22)

Paul and Barnabas had a disagreement over taking John Mark on their next missionary journey. Barnabas took John Mark with him to Cyprus to continue to preach there. Paul took Silas as his new companion. They traveled overland to Tarsus. Then they went by way of Derbe, Lystra, Iconium, and Antioch in Pisidia. They strengthened the Christians in the churches in those cities. Continuing across Asia Minor, they came to the seaport city of Troas. Paul intended to stay in Asia Minor, but during the night he had a vision of a Macedonian saying, "Come over and help us!"

The next day they boarded a ship and sailed to the island of Samothrace. Then they sailed across the Aegean Sea to Neapolis. Here they followed the Roman road called Via Egnatia. It led them to Philippi where they established new churches. They went on to also start churches in Thessalonica and Berea. Their first European convert was Lydia. She was a businesswoman who sold purple dye. This was used for robes of royalty. She entertained Paul and Silas and established a church in her home.

While they were in Philippi, they met a young slave girl. An evil spirit possessed her. Day after day, she kept shouting, "These are servants of the Most High God." Finally, Paul commanded this spirit to come out of the young girl.

The owners of the slave became irritated. Their source of income had stopped. They brought Paul and Silas before the rulers of the town, who had Paul and Silas beaten. Then, they had Paul and Silas thrown into prison. Their feet were placed in irons. About midnight, Paul and Silas were singing hymns. A violent earthquake broke the irons.

The jailer was frightened, and he assumed that the prisoners had escaped. He was about to take his life. Paul called him and said, "Do not harm yourself! We are all here!" When the jailer discovered that Paul and Silas and the other prisoners had not escaped, he asked them, "Sirs, what must I do to be saved?"

They answered, "Believe on the Lord Jesus Christ. You will be saved and your household." The jailer brought them into his house. He washed their wounds. He gave them food. The jailer and all his family became Christians that day.

The next day the rulers of the town ordered the prisoners to be released. But Paul said, "We are Roman citizens. Let the rulers of the town come themselves and escort us out of the city." The rulers came and apologized and let them go. Paul and Silas went to the home of Lydia and encouraged the believers before they left.

Paul and Silas went on to Athens and Corinth. Their experiences there were no less memorable.

Athens was the ancient classical city in Greece. It was the home of the philosophers. Paul preached the resurrection of Christ in that city. Many laughed, but some believed.

The city of Corinth was a seaport city. All the evil vices of a seaport could be found there. Paul stayed in the city and established a church there. Many came to Christ and were baptized, but there was also much opposition to his message in the local synagogue. The Jews brought charges against Paul, but Gallio, the Roman proconsul, dismissed the charges.

Paul and two friends, Priscilla and Aquila, left Corinth and set sail from the city of Cenchrea. They stopped briefly in Ephesus, then returned to Jerusalem. From Jerusalem they traveled by land back to Antioch.

> *GRACE*
> *Grace means bringing joy because of God's love. Paul wrote about grace in many of his letters. God gives us grace, which is abundant love. We do not deserve His grace, but He delights to give it to us because of His love.*

The Third Missionary Journey
(Acts 18:23–21:14)

On Paul's third missionary journey, he and Silas traveled again through Asia Minor to Ephesus. Paul spent his longest time in Ephesus. God gave Paul special power to cure the sick. Even some who practiced magic became Christians and burned many of their books.

One of the events in Ephesus created a great stir. Ephesus was the city of the great temple to Diana. She was a pagan goddess. The silversmiths made images of Diana and of the temple.

Paul's preaching caused many people to stop buying the images. This loss of income angered the silversmiths. Demetrius called a meeting of his fellow workers. They stirred up the towns-folk. All of the people rushed into the arena and shouted, "Long live Diana of the Ephesians!" For two hours they shouted. Paul tried to go to the arena. His friends insisted that for his safety he stay away.

The town clerk came to address the assembly. He said, "Men of Ephesus, the whole world knows about Diana of the Ephesians. We are unlawfully assembled today. These men have not taken anything. They have not destroyed our property. We have courts in which the cases may be decided. We will have to give account for this assembly. There is no reason for it." Then he dismissed the group.

Paul and his companions retraced their steps through Macedonia and down to Corinth. Then they circled back and went to Jerusalem.

Paul's Journey to Rome (Acts 27:1–28:16)

When Paul arrived in Jerusalem, it was the time of Pentecost. Paul was warned that he should not go to Jerusalem, but Paul wanted to keep a vow in the Temple.

He entered the Temple. Someone started an uproar. They claimed that Paul had brought Gentiles into the Temple. The mob became unruly. Roman soldiers came from the Tower of Antonia to escort Paul out of the Temple. Paul defended his actions before the Roman centurion. To protect him, he was placed in jail.

After months in jail, his case was heard before Felix, a governor. Two years passed and nothing happened. Festus became governor. He heard Paul's case but could find no fault for which Paul had been imprisoned. Then Paul appealed to Caesar. This was a right of every Roman citizen. Festus agreed to the appeal in Rome.

The trip to Rome by ship was dangerous. Paul and the other prisoners encountered a shipwreck on the rough seas. Finally they arrived in Rome where Paul remained under house arrest for a year. He preached Christ to all of the Roman soldiers who attended him. Many of the people in Caesar's household came to know Christ.

When no one came to accuse Paul, he was set free, but he remained in Rome for two years and continued to preach about God.

We do not have any other record of the other events in Paul's life. He expressed a desire to go to Spain. Many believe that he went on to Spain and preached the gospel there. Later he was brought back to Rome during the persecution and was killed for his faith in Christ.

THE BOOK OF THE REVELATION
REVELATION 1–4, 18–22

The Book of Revelation is different from the other books that we have read. It gives instruction to the seven churches in Asia Minor. The rest of the book tells about things that will happen in the future. This is a very different kind of writing from the stories that we have read in the Bible before.

The writer is the apostle John. The Emperor Domitian exiled John from the church he pastored in Ephesus. He was sent to the island of Patmos. This island in the Mediterranean Sea is very rocky. The Emperor intended that John should die there. Instead, Jesus showed him the future. While it seems at times that evil is winning, the message of the Revelation is that God is in control and will win the victory. In the meantime, it is important for Christians to hold on to the truth and live the truth. They are on the winning side.

The Seven Churches (Revelation 1–3)

John was told to write to the churches: Ephesus, Smyrna, Pergamum, Thyatira, Sardis, Philadelphia, and Laodicea. To the church at Ephesus, Jesus said, "I know your deeds. But you have left your first love. Repent!"

To the church it Smyrna, the Lord said, "Some of you will be put in prison for your faith. Some of you will suffer for your faith. But the one who endures will not suffer in the second death."

Jesus said to the church at Pergamum, "You remained true to My name. Yet some of you are doing sinful things. Repent! If you do not repent,

I will fight against you. Listen to what the Spirit tells you."

Jesus spoke to the church at Thyatira. He said, "I know you have remained true. You are doing more now than at the beginning. But you allow Jezebel to mislead my servants. She is not willing to repent. Hold on to what you have until I come. To the one who overcomes, I will give power over nations."

To the church at Sardis, Jesus said, "I know what you are doing. You are dead. Wake up and live. Yet there are some people in the church at Sardis who have not sinned. The one who overcomes will be dressed in white. His name will be written in the book of life."

Jesus spoke to the church at Philadelphia. He said, "You have been faithful. I will keep you from suffering. The time is coming when many will suffer. Hold on to what you have. The New Jerusalem will come. Your name will be there."

To the church at Laodicea, Jesus said, "You are neither cold nor hot. You are lukewarm. I will get rid of you. The ones I love, I discipline. Be faithful and true. Repent. If you overcome, you will sit with Me on My throne."

The Throne in Heaven (Revelation 4)
John was caught up in the Spirit. A voice called from heaven, "Come here. I will show you what will come next."

John was standing before the throne in heaven. It was very beautiful. Surrounding the throne were twenty-four elders. They were dressed in white and had crowns of gold. Before the throne was a sea of glass.

In the center of the throne were four living creatures. Day and night they would cry, "Holy, holy, holy is the Lord God Almighty, who was, who is, and is to come."

The twenty-four elders bow down before the throne and worship God. They put their crowns at His feet. They say, "You are worthy, our Lord and God, to receive glory and honor and power, for You created all things, and by Your will they were created and have their being."

Judgment (Revelation 20)
God's judgment will fall upon Satan. He will be doomed forever. All those who follow Satan will stand before the Great White Throne. God will judge them. The persons who died will be resurrected and judged. The persons who are alive will be judged. Anyone whose name was not written in the book of life will be judged and meet the second death.

The New Jerusalem and the River of Life (Revelation 21–22)
John then saw a new heaven and a new earth. The earth and heaven passed away. God will live with His people. They will no longer be separated. God will wipe away every tear from their eyes. There will be no more death. The new heaven and the new earth are very beautiful. There will be no more need of a Temple because God will live with His people. This is the future hope of all those who follow Jesus.

Jesus said, "Happy are all who keep the words of this book." An angel said, "Worship God!"

The Spirit said, "Come. Anyone who is thirsty, come and drink freely from the gift of water, which the Lord provides. I warn anyone who hears the prophecy of this book to follow and believe."

Religious Practices

INTRODUCTION TO PARENTS AND TEACHERS

While Christian worship originally grew out of Jewish worship, it soon changed to become more distinctly Christian. The Sabbath was no longer the primary day of worship. Even though many Christians kept the Sabbath along with their worship on Sunday, the Sabbath observance soon disappeared. Worship took place on the first day of the week, the Lord's Day. Some of the elements of Jewish worship remained in the Christian service, but soon these were changed or at least modified to become more Christian.

The festival days of the Jewish calendar were replaced by the veneration of saints in the Catholic churches. Later, Protestant churches and free churches no longer venerated saints and, as a result, cut those days from the annual calendar. Three holidays were retained—Easter, Pentecost, and Christmas. Some of the liturgical churches also retained other Christian holidays, such as Epiphany—the day on which Jesus was manifest to the world through the coming of the wise men and the day on which He was baptized and manifest made to the world as the Savior.

Before Easter, there was a period of preparation—Lent. The period of Lent allowed Christians to prepare for the holiest days of the Christian year, when we celebrate the death, burial, and resurrection of Jesus. Some denominations, such as Baptists, have avoided Lent. They believe that it has become an empty ritual and has done little to enhance the spiritual lives of those who practice it.

Consider, for example, Mardi Gras that preceeds Ash Wednesday at the beginning of Lent. Mardi Gras has become an excuse for carousing and reveling. It does little to enhance the spiritual lives of many who participate in it.

The period of Advent occurs before Christmas. The intent of Advent is to prepare for the celebration of Christmas. Many denominations, including

Christmas cards celebrate the season.

Southern Baptists, observe Advent. Activities such as lighting the Advent candles and preparing the Advent wreath are helpful for children to come to a better understanding of the spiritual significance of the Christmas season.

When our family was growing up, it had always been tradition in our homes to open gifts on Christmas morning. We continued that tradition with our children and used Christmas Eve as the time to teach our children about the true meaning of the Christmas celebration. We would read the Christmas story and use some other means to retell the story. Through the centuries, Christian art has focused strongly on the narrative of the birth of Jesus. There are many examples from the annunciation to Mary to the actual birth in a stable. These can be used, along with manger scenes, to retell the story. Also, attending a Christmas Eve service in church can enhance and reinforce the story.

For many Christians the idea of Santa Claus has become repugnant and controversial. Historically, however, Santa Claus was originally St. Nicholas. St. Nicholas of Myra in the fourth century was a Christian who went about giving gifts. The story is told that there were three noble women who had lost their inheritance. To avert selling their children into slavery, Nicholas anonymously threw three bags of gold into their home. Interestingly, the crest of the saint contained three balls, representing the three bags of gold that he delivered to the women. During the Middle Ages his crest was taken and misappropriated by the pawn dealers as a sign of their business. Over the years St. Nicholas' Christian magnanimity has been replaced with a secular Santa Claus. Italian sailors stole his remains in 1087 and took them to Bari, Italy. His final resting place can still be seen there today.

We need to reclaim our heritage. Our children have a right to know that the true Santa Claus originated as a Christian. The stories of St. Valentine and St. Patrick are no less interesting and are weighted with Christian meaning. We will discuss St. Patrick later. St. Valentine was a Christian who went to Christians who were imprisoned during the Roman persecutions. He would slip notes of encouragement to them through the bars. These became known as Valentines. We still follow the original custom today, but the Christian meaning of valentines has been lost. To our culture, these memories have lost their original Christian meaning and have been replaced by secular images.

As a parent or as a teacher, try to find ways to encourage and enhance the Christian aspects of our holiday celebrations and to return them to their original meaning. We are in danger of losing these special memories to a pagan society. Three examples will illustrate my point. 1) In Independence Hall in Philadelphia, the painting of the First Continental Congress praying was removed by the Department of Interior because it had Christian meaning. 2) Recently, a publisher instructed a chronicler of the life of C. S. Lewis to remove any Christian overtones to the Chronicles of Narnia. 3) Some of the textbook publishers have agreed to teach the history of the twentieth century and ignore the foundation of the Pilgrims and Puritans, who came to America to worship God. They did not come to found a nation that was godless and pagan. It may be difficult to counteract the secular culture, but at least we can inform our children about the truth of Christians having a significant impact upon our Western culture.

Just as the Jews have survived by passing on their traditions during these thousands of years, it is imperative that Christians pass on our heritage from one generation to the next. One of the purposes of this series of books is to help parents and teachers to learn and understand some of the stories of the Christians of the past so that we can pass them along to the next generation. If we fail at this, our children may have a totally fallacious understanding of how America began, or worse, they may find Christmas to be nothing more than the midwinter celebration that has been proposed by some school districts. This is far from the instruction that the psalmist gave to the people of Israel in Psalm 78. The psalmist indicated that the people of Israel should rehearse the history in order that the new generation might know how God led them in the past so they would not repeat the sins and mistakes that led the people into difficulty in the past.

While most of the Jewish practices had their origin in the Old Testament, that was not always true for the practices of the early church. Remember, the Old Testament was composed over several thousand years. Practices and worship experiences grew out of that long period of history. By contrast, the New Testament took place in a very short period, and the complete text was completed within the space of no more than two hundred years.

Church history plays a significant role in the development of some church practices. The emergence of denominations is an attempt to recover the New Testament church practice. You may want to explore with your pastor what your particular denomination believes about certain church practices. Teach your children what is included in this volume and then teach specifically any beliefs that are distinctive to your denomination.

THE LORD'S DAY

The first day of the week, Sunday, was designated as the "Lord's Day." That was instituted almost two thousand years ago. It was very different from the Jewish Sabbath. The Lord's Day did not represent the day on which God rested from creating the universe. The Lord's Day meant the day on which Jesus arose from the dead. Just as the Sabbath each week celebrates God's creation of the universe, the Lord's Day celebrates each week Easter and the resurrection of Jesus. This is the day on which our salvation was accomplished. As a result of Jesus' death on the cross and His resurrection, we can by faith become members of the family of God. God's amazing grace is given to us. We only have to accept Jesus into our hearts by faith and we become members of God's family.

How the Lord's Day Originated in the New Testament

The Lord's Day appears in the New Testament both in the ministry of Jesus and in the writings to the churches. The first suggestion that this would be a special day is found in each of the Gospels. All four Gospels tell about the women and the disciples who went to the tomb on the first day of the week to find Jesus. Several of the accounts tell us that Mary Magdalene and the other Mary went early to the tomb with spices. A great earthquake frightened the guards, and the stone was rolled away from the tomb. An angel appeared and he told them not to be afraid. Jesus had risen from the dead. This was a special day indeed!

To the early church there was a parallel here with creation. Recall that on the first day of the week God created light (see Genesis 1:3–5).On the first day of the week after the crucifixion, a new light appeared. It shown brightly and got rid of the darkness. The new light was the resurrection of Jesus. The Sabbath recalled God's creation of the world for the Jewish people. For Christians this has been replaced by the Lord's Day, which recalls the resurrection of Jesus.

Jesus continued to support the idea of the first day of the week by His appearances to the disciples. On the resurrection day, Jesus appeared to the two disciples on the road to Emmaus. Along the way Jesus explained all that must happen to the Savior. The two disciples did not understand until they sat down to eat together. Jesus broke bread and they recognized Him (see Luke 24:13–35).

This experience also carried another idea that would affect the future of the church. They broke bread together on the Lord's Day. Recall the Last Supper that Jesus had with His disciples. He said, "This is My body, which is given for you. Do this in remembrance of Me" (Luke 22:19b). Now it was the disciples turn to carry out Jesus' instructions. On the first day of the week, when they met together for worship, they would participate in the Lord's Supper together.

Jesus commissioned the disciples to tell the good news of the gospel. Jesus came and appeared to the disciples on the first day of the week following the resurrection (John 20:19–23). Thomas was not with the other disciples at that time. Remember, Thomas said he would not believe unless he could put his finger in the nail-pierced hands of Jesus and put his hand in Jesus' side. A week passed and on the first day of the next week, Jesus appeared again to the disciples. This time Thomas was present. He saw and he believed (see John 20:24–29).

All of these examples point to the fact that it was Jesus Himself who made the first day of the week an important day for worship. The disciples did follow Jesus' leading. We can see this in the records of the early church.

The disciples met on the first day of the week to break bread together. This happened some years later and is described in Acts 20:7. In 1 Corinthians 16:1–2 we read that Paul instructed the churches at Corinth and Galatia to take an offering at their worship service on the first day of the week to help the poor in Jerusalem. Further support for the first day of the week appears in

Revelation. John wrote that he was exiled by the Roman Emperor Domitian to the island of Patmos, because of his faith in Jesus Christ. It was during that experience when he was worshiping on the first day of the week that he received the Revelation (see Revelation 1:9–10).

By the end of the first century, Ignatius, an early Christian writer, said that the Christians stopped keeping the Sabbath and worshiped on the Lord's Day. One of the earliest Christian books that is not in the New Testament was the Didache. It describes the church meeting on the Lord's Day to hold the Lord's Supper together.

Justin Martyr, another early Christian writer, tells us that the Christians met on the first day of the week to worship. The writer tells us that one of the reasons was that God created light on that first day. God got rid of the darkness. Jesus' resurrection also got rid of darkness. Other references suggested that the Lord's Day was the eighth day of the week. They did not mean that the week had eight days. They meant that Jesus opened the door to a new creation of God.

The Roman Emperor Constantine became a Christian. In the fourth century he made a law for the empire. In honor of the death, burial, and resurrection of Jesus, all work should stop on the Lord's Day. As we shall see later, this law affected worship on Sunday generations later.

Bread and wine were used to celebrate the Lord's Supper.

How the Lord's Day Is Celebrated Today

Almost two thousand years later, the Lord's Day has gone through many changes. During the Middle Ages a person might be fined for not attending church. Following the Reformation, some churches not only required church attendance but also did not allow persons to do anything on Sunday. The Puritans kept Sunday holy to the Lord. They kept Sunday in a manner similar to the way the Jews kept the Sabbath.

In our world most people do not work on Sunday, but they do not keep Sunday separate for God either. Sports have become a major attraction for Sunday afternoons. The Lord's Day should be a joyous occasion to celebrate Easter anew each week. The Lord's Day is a time to worship. We will look next at the place we worship—the church.

CHRISTIAN CHURCH

The term *Christian church* is used in two ways. The first and most common way is to describe a building that is used for Christian worship. There are large church buildings, and there are small church buildings. Some church buildings are located in the city, while others may be found in the country. Some of the very large Christian church buildings are constructed in the shape of a cross. We will look at some of these buildings in the section on Christian art and architecture.

The other way that the term *Christian church* is used is more important. It comes from a Greek word that means the people are "called out." They are called out by Jesus Christ to be God's people in a sinful world. This means that members of the church must be holy and set apart to God.

There are two purposes that have generally become recognized as the reason why a church exists. The first purpose is for Christians to be obedient to the Great Commandment. It is found in Matthew 22:37–40. Jesus said, "You shall love the Lord your God with all your heart, with all your soul, and with all your mind. You shall love your neighbor as yourself." That means that I must love God with my whole being. It also means that I need to love others as I love myself.

The second purpose is to carry out the Great Commission. It is found in Matthew 28:18–20. Jesus said, "Go, therefore, and make disciples of all nations, baptizing them in the name of the Father and of the Son and of the Holy Spirit, teaching them to observe everything I have commanded you. And remember, I am with you always, to the end of the age." This is a task or job for Christians to do. We need to go and spread the good news that God sent Jesus. God wants all persons to love and follow Him. That is why He sent Jesus to die on the cross to save people from their sins. The people of the church spread the Good News in their places of work and in their schools. They witness to God's love among their neighbors and also send missionaries all over the world to spread the gospel.

The Christian church tries to obey the Lord Jesus Christ in five ways. First, the church worships God. Worship means to give honor and respect to God. It also means to obey God. In the Christian church service, worship is given to God through singing hymns to God. Our hymns adore and honor God. In the church we also honor God by reading and paying attention to His Word, the Bible. We also worship through listening to the preaching of God's Word. Finally, we obey God by doing what He teaches us through His Word. God also wants us to worship Him during the week in our family worship. Worship helps us obey the Great Commandment.

The second way the church obeys God is through teaching. The Great Commission commands us to make disciples. This requires teaching. We teach God's Word in Sunday school and church. We teach what it means to be a Christian.

We also teach how to live the Christian life in a world that is not Christian and does not love Jesus Christ. Without teaching, it would not be possible to do the other things for which the church is responsible.

The third way that the church obeys Christ is through its witness. We tell the good news that Jesus Christ came to save sinners. This is in obedience to the Great Commission. God calls us not only to be a people who worship and honor Him, but He also desires that we tell others about His saving love that sent Jesus to earth to make salvation possible. We do this by our own personal witness. We tell our friends about God and His love for them. The church also sends missionaries to other countries around the world to tell people about Jesus and His love for them.

The fourth way that the church obeys the Lord is through fellowship. This is part of the Great Commandment: "You shall love your neighbor." Jesus made this more clear, when He said, "By this shall all people will know that you are My disciples, if you have love for one another" (John 13:35). The church must be a place where followers of Jesus love and care for each other. It must not be like other places in the world, where there is jealousy, anger, and hatred. The church needs to be a place of caring and genuine love. In the church, people need to find a second family that cares for them. When one of our members hurts, we all hurt. When one of our members is happy, we rejoice with them.

The final way that the church obeys Christ is through its ministry in the world. When we minister to persons in our world, we express the love of Christ that was expressed in the Great Commandment. There are many ways by which the church can express the love of God to people in the world. We can comfort persons who have

> ## THE GREAT COMMISSION
> ### MATTHEW 28:19–20
>
> *"Go, therefore, and make disciples of all nations, baptizing them in the neame of the Father and of the Son and of the Holy Sprirlt, teaching them to observe everything I have commanded you. And remember, I am with you always, to the end of the age."*

lost family members. We can help persons who do not have enough to eat. We can reach out to persons who are suffering in a great tragedy, such as a hurricane or terrorist act. We do not expect anything in return. We minister on behalf of Jesus to persons who need to experience God's care and love.

In these ways the mission of the church is carried out in the world. The church is God's representative on earth. Jesus is no longer here in person. But the Spirit of Jesus can be present in the world through those who are believers in Christ. The church must worship, teach, witness, care for one another, and minister to carry out its mission in the church and in the world.

> THE CHURCH DOES THE FOLLOWING:
> • *Worship* • *Teach* • *Witness*
> • *Fellowship* • *Minister*

THE CHRISTIAN CHURCH YEAR

Recall the celebration of the Jewish year. It was built around the agricultural harvests. The New Year's, Day of Atonement, and Passover feasts were added. These holidays were related to God's redemptive acts in the life of the Jewish people. Redemption is very important to an understanding of what Jesus did for us. When we come to the Christian church, there are only three holidays upon which all Christian groups agree. They are Christmas, Easter, and Pentecost. In the Christian faith, all three of these holidays are related to our redemption in Christ.

> ### REDEMPTION
> *Redemption means "to buy back." From birth we are lost in sin, and the penalty for sin is death. God loves us. He sent Jesus to earth to die on the cross and to rise again. God accepted the death of Jesus in our place. When we believe in Him, He becomes our Redeemer.*

CHRISTMAS

Christmas is one of the most beautiful times of the year and is loved by almost everyone. There are shoppers looking for gifts to give to their loved ones. The sound of familiar Christmas carols is heard on the radio and even in the busy shopping malls. Through the mail we receive Christmas cards from friends and relatives. Santa Claus may be seen in the shopping centers. Christmas trees are decorated with colored balls and ornaments. Christmas is different from other holidays. Friends and family gather on Christmas and celebrate together. Candy and presents are under the Christmas tree. Shops, schools, and businesses are closed on Christmas Day. So how did Christmas become the important holiday that it is today?

To answer that question, we have to go back to the Gospels of Matthew and Luke to find the meaning of the Christmas story. The accounts of the Christmas story are different in Matthew and Luke. It seems that Matthew tells the story from the line of Joseph. Luke tells the story from the memories of Mary, the mother of Jesus.

THE CHRISTMAS STORY

The Genealogy or History of Jesus (Matthew 1:1–17)

Since the New Testament opens with this verse, let's begin with Matthew's account—a record of the genealogy of Jesus Christ, the Son of David, the Son of Abraham" (Matthew 1:1). Then Matthew goes on to tell us about Abraham, who was the father of Isaac. Matthew lists the fathers that came between Abraham and Jesus. The first seventeen verses of this genealogy contain the names of many different persons. We may be tempted to pass over this list and not read it. But wait; let's see if we can understand what Matthew is trying to tell us.

We need to go all the way back, even before Matthew's account, to the Garden of Eden. Remember when God discovered that Adam and Eve had eaten of the tree of the knowledge of good and evil? God told Eve that she would have difficulty and pain in childbirth. He also told her that the Redeemer would come through her line. Sin got worse during the next generations.

Matthew's account begins with Abraham. God called Abraham to go to the Promised Land of Palestine. Abraham wanted to follow and obey God. God was pleased with Abraham. God made a covenant, or promise, to Abraham. Abraham would be the father of many nations. Through Ishmael came the line of Arab tribes. Today many of these people believe the religion of Islam.

But in his old age, Abraham had a son, Isaac. Isaac was the father of the Hebrew peoples. It was through Isaac that the promised Messiah would come. In Genesis 18:18 God promised that a mighty nation would come through Abraham. But more than that, God promised that through Abraham all the nations of the earth would be blessed. The plan of God was becoming clearer. The promised Messiah would come through Abraham.

Many more generations passed. Then David became king over Israel. God made a promise to David (see 2 Samuel 7:12–16). God promised David that sometime after David died, a descendent would come from the line of David. He would establish David's kingdom forever. God promised that He would be a father to this One, who would be God's Son.

Psalm 2 was written by David. Psalm 2 applied to David after he conquered Jerusalem from the Jebusites. But David could not possibly be all that the psalm describes. The psalm more fully describes the One who was to come after David as God's promised Messiah.

Several hundred years passed. The people of Israel sinned against God. Things went from bad to worse. God punished the people of Israel and sent the northern ten tribes into captivity in Assyria. Then, in 586 BC the people of Judah were surrounded by the Babylonian army of Nebuchadnezzar. The Temple to the Lord was destroyed. The people of Judah were led away into captivity.

Jeremiah the prophet was not a happy man. He saw the things that would happen to the people of Judah. He was himself punished by the king of Judah because Jeremiah told the people and the king what was going to happen to them. It was not going to be happy. The people would suffer. But in the middle of that sad picture, God spoke kindly to Jeremiah. God told Jeremiah that a new day would come. God would restore the throne of David (see Jeremiah 33:14–18). And the One who will come will carry out righteousness. This one will be the Messiah. So in the midst of his sorrow and grief for the people, God gave Jeremiah a promise.

Remember that Cyrus, the king of Persia, let the Jewish people return to Palestine. Several hundred years passed again. During this time the Old Testament ended. Four hundred years went by. The people were looking for the promised Messiah. That is where the New Testament begins. God has kept His promise. Matthew tells us that the promised Messiah has come in the person of Jesus. The genealogy is important because Jesus is both the Son of Abraham and the Son of David. Jesus came to earth not just for God's chosen people, Israel. Jesus came as the Messiah for the entire human race. It no longer matters whether one is a Jew or Gentile; everyone can find a relationship with God through Jesus.

Why was the genealogy included? It would seem that there were two reasons. First, for the Jewish boy growing up in Jewish schools, memorizing was important. Matthew gives fourteen generations from Abraham to David. He adds fourteen generations from David to the captivity in Babylon. Another fourteen generations are given from the return to Palestine and the coming of Jesus. This would have been easier to memorize.

Secondly, remember that the Jewish calendar is based on the lunar, or moon, month. The lunar month lasts twenty-nine and a half days. The moon goes through fourteen days of passing from the new moon to the full moon. Then it goes through another fourteen days from full moon to new moon. Compare that with the fourteen generations from Abraham to the greatness of David (or full moon phase). Then the decline takes place in the next fourteen generations to the captivity. But the moon continues to grow until it reaches full moon phase again. This is represented in the next fourteen generations to the coming of Jesus Christ.

The fourteen generations are important to understanding how Jesus fulfills the promises of God. The promises first came to Abraham as the father of the Jewish people. They were renewed to David as God's servant king. It looked as if God's plan would not be reached when the Temple was destroyed and the people were taken into captivity. But a group returned to Israel, and God's plan was complete in the coming of Jesus Christ.

Mary and Joseph of Nazareth (Matthew 1:18)

Beyond some simple facts, we do not know a lot about Mary. Mary must have been a Jewish girl about twelve or thirteen years of age. Mary means "the Lord's beloved." Like Joseph, Mary was also from the line of King David. Mary was related to Elizabeth, the mother of John the Baptist and wife of Zechariah. Zechariah was a priest. Elizabeth was of a priestly family. Mary must also have been from a priestly family. But Mary's family must have been very poor.

Joseph was probably between twenty-five and thirty years of age. Men married at an older age than women in New Testament times. Joseph was a carpenter. Since sons followed their fathers in their occupation, Joseph's father must have been a carpenter also. Matthew tells us that Joseph's father was Jacob. We are not told why either family lived in the little city of Nazareth.

Nazareth is not mentioned elsewhere in the Old Testament or in the Jewish writings. Nazareth was located in the hill country between the Sea of Galilee and the Mediterranean Sea. It is 1,230 feet above sea level. There was only one well in the town of Nazareth. It is probably the well from which Mary would have drawn water as a girl. It is known today as Mary's Well. In New Testament times there was a Roman road from the town of Capernaum, along the Sea of Galilee, to the Mediterranean coast. Today it has the largest Arab population in Palestine.

Joseph probably talked with his parents about his interest in Mary, the peasant girl in town. He probably asked his parents if they would consider talking with Mary's parents about marriage with Mary. Joseph's parents would have talked about Mary and her family. When they agreed that Mary would be a good girl to have in their family, they would have prepared to go and talk with Mary's parents. Marriage was not built upon romance, as it is in our country today. Marriages were arranged by the parents of the groom and the bride.

Jacob then would have called on Mary's family. Mary's wishes would have been considered. If she did not like the man chosen by her parents, she would likely have made that known to them.

When Mary's parents were over their surprise about the visit of Jacob, they would have talked seriously about the possibility of marriage for their daughter. Most likely, they would have agreed on a bride price. Girls were valuable to their parents. It was customary for the husband's parents to pay for the loss of the daughter in the household. In turn, Mary's parents would have talked about the dowry that would come with their daughter. The dowry was given to the groom but was returned to the bride if her husband died. Both families were poor. But marriage was an agreement between the two families. They would have to come to an agreement.

With the agreement reached, Joseph would be brought to Mary's home. The parents would give their blessing to the couple. They would celebrate the engagement with a traditional glass of wine. Mary and Joseph would be formally engaged to be married. In Palestine, engagement was serious. It meant that they were married, even though the ceremony had not yet taken place. If Joseph died before the marriage took place, Mary would be considered a widow. During the time of their engagement, Mary would still have lived at home with her parents. She would go to Joseph's home and they would spend time together. They would plan their wedding together.

The Annunciation and the Wedding
(Luke 1:26–56; Matthew 1:18–25)

While they were engaged, one day the angel Gabriel came to Mary. In the Old Testament there were often appearances of angels. The people were looking for the coming of the Messiah. The angel said, "Rejoice, favored woman! The Lord is with you." Imagine how Mary must have felt. She was both surprised and a little scared. You and I would probably feel the same way.

Listen to what the angel told her:

Do not be afraid, Mary, for you have found favor with God.
Now listen: You will conceive and give birth to a son,

and you will call His name JESUS.
He will be great
and will be called the Son of the Most High,
and the Lord God will give Him the throne of His father David.
He will reign over the house of Jacob forever,
and His kingdom will have no end.

(Luke 1:30b–33)

Mary asked the angel how this was possible, since she was not intimate with a man. The angel answered:

The Holy Spirit will come upon you,
and the power of the Most High
will overshadow you.
Therefore the holy child to be born
will be called the Son of God. (Luke 1:35b)

Mary answered the angel Gabriel this way:

Consider me the Lord's slave. . . .
May it be done to me according to your word.

(Luke 1:38)

Mary never questioned the angel. She accepted the news that the angel Gabriel brought to her. She was willing to obey God. That must have been difficult, since she knew that she would have to tell Joseph about her situation. Would he believe her? Would he have her stoned? Would he divorce her? She would have to trust God, just as Queen Esther had trusted God to protect her several hundred years earlier.

For a few months Mary went into the hill country to meet her cousin Elizabeth. When she arrived, Elizabeth greeted her:

Blessed are you among women,
and blessed is your offspring! (Luke 1:42b)

Mary responded with some of the most beautiful words in Scripture:

My soul proclaims the greatness of the Lord,
and my spirit has rejoiced in God my Savior.

(Luke 1:46b–47)

Mary stayed with her cousin Elizabeth for three months. As she returned home, she still had to tell Joseph what had happened. She must have been frightened. But she could not avoid telling him now.

When Joseph got the news, he was terribly upset. He had come to love Mary and did not want any harm to come to her. But he could not marry her as she was already expecting a child. So Matthew tells us that he decided to divorce her quietly. He would draw up the papers and have two persons witness the divorce. Then Mary could go away and have the baby.

While Joseph was troubled about this, an angel of the Lord appeared to Joseph in a dream. The angel told him, "Don't be afraid to take Mary as your wife, because what has been conceived in her is by the Holy Spirit. She will give birth to a son, and you are to name Him Jesus, because He will save His people from their sins" (Matthew 1:20–21). Joseph awoke from his sleep and did what the angel told him to do.

Joseph and Mary were married. The wedding parties then were similar to weddings today. They marched to the place where the ceremony would take place. Then the couple would have a feast for all of the wedding guests. After the wedding, Mary came to live with Joseph for the next five months. They must have been happy months as they looked forward to the baby. But then they must have worried about what the townsfolk would say.

They did not have to worry long. Caesar Augustus sent out an order that all the people in the Roman Empire would have to be enrolled in the census. Each would have to go to the home of their ancestors. Since Joseph was from the line of David, it meant that he would have to go back to Bethlehem. He and Mary would go to Bethlehem, and the baby could be born there. This would prevent any gossip about the birth of Jesus in Nazareth.

The Birth of Jesus (Luke 2:1–7)

Mary and Joseph left Nazareth and traveled for four or five days. It must have been a difficult trip for Mary. She was very uncomfortable. But when they arrived in Bethlehem, there was no room in the inn.

Jesus was born in a manger similar to this.

They had to settle for a stable. It was probably a cave behind the hotel. The cattle lived in the stable. There was fresh hay to keep them warm. In the winter it gets cold in Bethlehem at night.

On that beautiful night Mary gave birth to her son Jesus. She wrapped Him up tightly with cloth. This would hold Him snug and warm. Then she laid Him in a manger, or food tray, for the animals. The Son of God was not born in a palace or even in an ordinary house. His birth took place in a common animal stable. Imagine what Mary and Joseph were thinking as they sat together in that stable holding the baby Jesus. The One they were holding was the One who would save His people from their sins.

Today the Bethlehem church is above the grotto, which is the place where Jesus was born. This is the oldest church in the world, and it is still in use. The inside of the church is dark. It is also cool and damp. Since it belongs to the Orthodox Church, it is lighted with many lamps and has the smell of incense. One has to pause and think about the birth that took place there so many years ago.

Bethlehem is a small town. It is located about five miles southwest of Jerusalem. Bethlehem means "house of bread." Bethlehem is mentioned several times in the Old Testament. Remember that Ruth met and married Boaz in Bethlehem. Boaz was a farmer of grain for bread. David was born in Bethlehem. Probably the most important claim to fame for Bethlehem was the birth of Jesus. Today Bethlehem is home to about thirty thousand people.

The Shepherds Come to the Manger
(Luke 2:8–20)

One of the chief occupations among the people of Palestine was shepherding. Caring for sheep was done by allowing them to graze on the grasses away from the cities. At night the sheep would be placed in a pen. It was usually made of stones that were piled on top of each other to make a low wall. The opening was closed by the shepherd sleeping with his body across the empty space in the wall. In this way the shepherd could prevent a wild animal from sneaking into the sheep pen and killing one of the sheep. It also prevented thieves from stealing the sheep.

Luke tells us that on this particular night the shepherds were caring for their sheep in the usual way. It was a quiet night until the sky was filled with light. The angel of the Lord came to the shepherds and told them the glorious news. In the city of David a Savior, Christ the Lord, was born that very night. The sign to the shepherds for finding the baby was that He was wrapped in swaddling clothes and lying in a manger.

Along with the angel came a heavenly host of angels praising God. They said, "Glory to God in the highest, and on earth peace, good will toward men." For a world that had been taken over by sin, this was good news indeed. Jesus came as the Prince of Peace. He is described as the One who will bring peace (see Isaiah 9:6–7).

Having received the announcement of Jesus' birth, the shepherds were ready to go to Bethlehem to see this wonderful event. They left the sheep on the hillsides and went immediately in search of the baby. In a small town like Bethlehem, the birth of a child under these strange circumstances was news. Probably there were those in Bethlehem who knew about the birth and directed the shepherds to the stable and to Mary, Joseph, and the baby Jesus.

When they had seen the baby, they went out and told all the people they met about the wonderful vision of the angels that they had seen. They told about seeing the baby and his parents in the stable. They probably did not sleep much that night. Rather, they glorified God for what He had done and what they had seen. The praise that they voiced was probably a song. It likely came from the Psalms. They returned to their flocks.

But these were probably not ordinary shepherds. From the ancient writings of the Jewish people, we learn that regular shepherds were not allowed within the confines of the settled areas. There is a field southwest of Bethlehem that has been identified as the place where the shepherds saw the heavenly vision of the angels. That would be within the settled areas and not permitted for the average shepherds.

It is likely that the shepherds that were caring for the sheep were Levites. They were not ordinary shepherds. Rather, they were raising the sheep for sacrifice in the Temple. Their sheep were without blemish or spot. They were perfect for sacrifice. The Levites would have known the Old Testament writings. They would have understood the coming of the Messiah. They would have appreciated what the angels of the Lord were telling them. Most of all, they would have worshiped the baby, Christ.

Presentation of Jesus in the Temple
(Luke 2:21–39)

After eight days, Jesus was circumcised. This was done according to the Law of Moses. Jesus was identified as a Jew. At the circumcision ceremony, they named their Son. Back when the angel announced to Mary that she would have a son, the angel said that His name would be Jesus. Jesus is the Greek name for the Hebrew name Joshua. Both mean "salvation is from God."

The Old Testament prescribed that after giving birth to a male child, a mother should go to the Temple for her ceremonial cleansing (see Leviticus 12:2, 4). She had to sacrifice a lamb. If she was too poor to afford a lamb, then two pigeons would do. Mary chose to sacrifice the two pigeons.

Parents were required to dedicate the firstborn son to the Lord (see Exodus 13:2). There was also a payment of money to redeem the firstborn son (see Numbers 18:16). These were the normal requirements under the Law. Then something wonderful happened.

An old man named Simeon came up to Mary, Joseph, and Jesus. The Holy Spirit was upon Simeon. He was a godly man. For years he had been in the Temple looking for the coming of the Messiah. The Spirit promised Simeon that he would not die before he saw the Messiah. Now the Spirit came upon Simeon. Simeon took the baby Jesus in his arms. He prayed to God that now that he had been permitted to see the Messiah, he could go to be with the Lord.

He prophesied that Jesus would be a light to the Gentiles and the glory of Israel. Both Joseph and Mary were amazed at what was said about their Son Jesus. Simeon blessed the family.

Then Simeon spoke of Jesus as the One who would affect the lives of many in Israel. Simeon was using the text from Isaiah 8:14–15 to show that Jesus would not be accepted by everyone. And then Simeon said to Mary that she would suffer when Jesus was rejected. Simeon understood what was happening. He stood between the Old Testament and the promises to Abraham, and the New Testament and the opening of salvation to the Gentiles.

As Mary and Joseph were trying to understand all that Simeon had said, they met Anna. Anna was a prophetess from the tribe of Aser. The tribe of Aser had not been taken into captivity with the other tribes and was reunited with Judah after the return from Babylon. Anna was eighty-four years of age and had been a widow for many years.

She had come to the Temple every day to worship and pray. Now she too had seen the promised Messiah. She thanked God and told everyone she met about the promised Messiah that had come.

The Magi Come to Bethlehem
(Matthew 2:1–12)

About the time that Jesus was born in Bethlehem, a star appeared in the sky. To most people it would not have meant much of anything. But to the Magi, or astrologers, in the East, it meant the birth of a king. Astrologers were among the most educated persons of Jesus' day. They were educated in mathematics, astronomy, science, and other things, such as magic. But when they saw the star, they recognized that the birth of a king had occurred in Palestine. They were very excited and gathered together their followers and began to make the long trip to Palestine.

Astronomers are still interested in discovering what star appeared in the East. It is possible that God placed a unique star in the sky to proclaim the

The Magi present Jesus with gifts.

birth of Jesus. But it is more likely that the star was a natural star that would have appeared in the heavens. Several possible stars might have appeared together. Every eight hundred and five years, the planets Jupiter and Saturn come near each other, and a year later they are joined by the planet Mars. We know that these planets were together near the time of Jesus' birth. The planet Jupiter was known to the ancient astrologers as "the king's planet." Although we cannot tell for sure, this is one possible sighting of the Magi that would have attracted their interest.

We cannot even be sure from what country these Magi, or wise men, came. Persia was the most likely place. Persia was known for their astrologers. The traditions of the early church, from the early art on the walls of the catacombs, believed that they were Persians. We also know that about six hundred years later, the Persians invaded Palestine. They did not destroy the Church of the Nativity because the headdresses of the Magi were Persian.

Whatever their origin, recall the prophecy of Simeon when Jesus was presented in the Temple— that Jesus would be a light to the Gentiles. These were the first Gentiles to recognize the light that Jesus would bring.

Think about the excitement that the Magi felt as they prepared for this long journey to Palestine to welcome the birth of a king. There would be months of travel. They needed camels that could endure the hot tropical sun and carry them safely to the new king. They needed food rations for the long journey. Probably they brought tents for sleeping. And of course, they must bring gifts to the new king. Probably they brought their servants to attend to them on the long journey and to help protect them from the dangers that such a trip might have. This king was special indeed. No one would make such a trip unless the king was very special. These men from the East did not know all of the Jewish prophesies about the Messiah. They only knew that they wanted to see the new king

and worship him. These men were Gentiles, but they knew about the meaning of the stars that they saw in the heavens.

When the Magi arrived in Palestine, they went straight to Jerusalem and to the palace of Herod. They expected that a major event of the birth of a new king would happen in the capital or at least the present king on the throne would know of the birth. Instead, Herod was very upset. Herod the Great was from the land of Idumea. He ruled because the foreign power of Rome gave him the power to rule. His wife, Mariamne, was Jewish, but Herod had her killed. He rebuilt the Temple. But Herod was hated by the Jews. He was a foreigner and not from the House of David. Therefore, the birth of a new Jewish king was a threat to Herod. He called the priests together to find out where the Messiah would be born. They went back to the Old Testament Scriptures in Micah 5:2 and told Herod that the Savior would be born in Bethlehem. Herod asked the wise men about what time the star had appeared. He wanted to know about how old Jesus was at that time. Herod sent the Magi to Bethlehem and told them to return again and tell him where the king might be found. Herod said that he wanted to worship the new king, but his real purpose was to get rid of this threat to his kingship.

Imagine what a stir these Magi would have caused in the little town of Bethlehem. They came with the camel caravan and their servants. They stopped at the home of Mary and Joseph. Jesus was no longer a baby. He had grown into boyhood. There they found Mary and Joseph and the young child. They were very happy. These wise men knelt before Jesus and worshiped him. They opened their treasures and presented Jesus with gifts of gold, frankincense, and myrrh. Gold represented Jesus as king. Gold was given to a king in tribute as a mark of respect. It was prophesied in Isaiah 60:6 and Psalm 72:10 that they would come from afar and bring gifts of gold and incense. Frankincense was a rare and expensive incense. Incense was used in the

Temple by the priests before God in worship. Frankincense reminds us that Jesus became our priest before God. Finally, there was myrrh. Myrrh was also rare and expensive. It was harvested from a plant and used in medicine, perfume, and embalming. Myrrh was a reminder of the death that Jesus would suffer. It was later used with Jesus in his burial (see John 19:39).

A strange thing happened to the wise men as they prepared for the long journey back to their home country. They were warned in a dream by God not to return to Herod. Herod had no intention of coming to worship the new king. Herod wanted to harm the new king. So the Magi left Bethlehem and returned to their homeland by another way.

The Flight to Egypt (Matthew 2:13–23)

That night, after the Magi had left to return home, Joseph also had a dream. It was a frightening dream. Herod was intent on killing the child Jesus. In the middle of the night, Joseph woke Mary and the boy Jesus. They went to the donkey stall and loaded all their earthly belongings and left before the dawn of a new day. It would have been a lonely trip to Egypt. The trip would have been at least twice as long as the trip that Mary and Joseph had made from Nazareth to Bethlehem. It probably would have taken them about a week and a half to travel the distance of about sixty miles. The Bible does not tell us where they went in Egypt, but there are many local traditions that are very old to suggest the trip and the destination.

The usual route for traders would have taken them south from Bethlehem to Hebron. There they would have turned west to the old Philistine city of Gaza on the coast of the Mediterranean Sea. From there they would have traveled along the coast to Egypt. The family would have been very welcome in Egypt. There was a very large Jewish population in Egypt at that time.

The Bible does not tell us where Mary, Joseph, and the boy Jesus stayed in Egypt. The Church of St. Sergius is located in old Cairo. The Egyptian Christians claim that the family stayed there for three months. There is even a niche in the wall where Jesus was supposed to have slept. Mary, Joseph, and the boy Jesus were safe there in Egypt. The trip to Egypt fulfilled an ancient prophecy: "Out of Egypt I called My son" (Hosea 11:1).

Meanwhile, back in Jerusalem, Herod anxiously awaited the return of the Magi. When they did not return, Herod became very angry. He called out the troops. He sent them to Bethlehem and had them kill all male children from two years and younger. Herod was so cruel! This event also fulfilled a prophecy from Jeremiah 31:15. There would be bitter crying over the loss of the children.

It was not long until Herod the Great died. An angel appeared to Joseph and told him that it was safe for their family to return to the land of Israel. After Herod's death, the land was divided among Herod's sons. Archelaus ruled in Judea. While the Bible does not talk about Archelaus, we know from history that he was at least as cruel as his father. Joseph decided not to return to Bethlehem. Instead, he took Mary and Jesus back to Nazareth. It was there in Nazareth that Jesus grew to manhood.

Early Church Practices

We have examined the details of the original Christmas at the birth of Jesus in the previous section. It may seem hard to believe, but in spite of all the special events surrounding Christmas, it was not very important to the early church. For the Christian believer, there is no more important holiday than Easter. Easter was the day on which Jesus rose from the dead and salvation came to us. Easter was related to the Old Testament Jewish holiday of Passover. Christmas was not related to a Jewish holiday. There is no record of Christmas before the third century.

Celebration of Epiphany

By the end of the second century, the church in Egypt began celebrating the holiday of Epiphany on January 6. Epiphany gained popularity in other churches. It represented God coming in the flesh to save persons who would believe from their sin. Epiphany represented Jesus' birth through the appearance of the shepherds and the journey of the Magi. Epiphany also was used to declare Jesus as the Messiah at His baptism. The dove alighted on Jesus and that was God's indication that Jesus was the Lord's Messiah. Jesus had come to save all who would put their trust in Him. Epiphany also represented the performing of Jesus' first miracle in turning the water to wine at the wedding at Cana.

EPIPHANY

Epiphany means the "manifestation" or showing forth of Jesus as the divine Son of God. It is still celebrated in many churches. The celebration of Christmas showed that Jesus was fully human in His birth. Epiphany came at the end of the twelve days of celebration of Christmas. Epiphany marked the appearance of Jesus' divine nature in the coming of the wise men, the descent of the dove at His baptism, and Jesus' first miracle at Cana.

Celebration of Christmas

Celebration of Christmas is known to have taken place in Rome by AD 336 on December 25. There is no reason to assume that Jesus was not born on December 25, but the Bible does not provide details on the time of year when Jesus was born. In the year AD 274, the Roman Emperor Aurelian wanted to unite the Roman Empire by adding a pagan feast day. He chose the "Unconquered sun god." It was to be celebrated on December 25. The Romans did not have an effective way to determine what day was the shortest day of the year, so they settled on December 25. The date suggested the change from increasing darkness to the expanding light of day in the calendar. Christians were able to offer their own alternative to this pagan holiday in the birth of Christ.

It was prophesied that the Messiah would be the "sun of Righteousness" (Malachi 4:2). The theme of light is also found in John's Gospel. John 1:9 indicates that Jesus was the true light that gives light to every man who enters the world. Jesus is the light of the world (see John 8:12 and 9:5).

Christmas became well established and replaced Epiphany as the most important event. It continues to be the most important holiday of the Christian year even today. In the early church, Lent was a forty-day period that served for Christians as a period of preparation before the holy days of Good Friday and Easter. It is not surprising that the early church decided that it would be good to have a period for preparation before Christmas and the celebration of the coming of Christ.

Since Christmas is celebrated on December 25 and Epiphany is celebrated on January 6, there are twelve days between the two holidays. Many churches in America do not celebrate Epiphany on January 6. Other churches in America and many in Europe celebrate both holidays. From the twelve days between the two holidays came the Christmas song "The Twelve Days of Christmas."

Advent

The four Sundays before Christmas and the days that led to Christmas Eve were designated as Advent. Advent is a time of preparation for the coming of Jesus. During the Middle Ages, Advent meant that the people had to restrict their diet. They were not allowed to eat as much. In those days it was a harsh period, similar to Lent. But today it is celebrated as a happy occasion to help families prepare for the coming of Christ. Advent is also used as a reminder that Jesus not only came the first time as a baby in Bethlehem, but Jesus will come again. It will be a time of joy for those who have become part of God's family by faith in Jesus as their Lord and Savior. It will be a time of judgment for those who do not know Jesus Christ as their Lord and Savior.

Many Christian groups celebrate Advent by lighting a new Advent candle on each of the four Sundays and the fifth candle on Christmas Eve. Along with lighting the candles, appropriate Scriptures are read.

Some denominations also use the Jesse Tree to help celebrate the significance of the Advent season. Jesse was the father of King David. Jesse began the royal line that led to the coming of Jesus. The prophecy in Isaiah 11:1–5 tells that from the stem of Jesse shall come the Anointed One. This Anointed One is Jesus. There are twenty-nine symbols of the stories that surround the Christmas story. One of the symbols is placed on the tree each day until Christmas. This is a family experience that helps family members to appreciate the true meaning of Christmas.

Another practice associated with Advent is to display an Advent calendar. The Advent calendar is used through the month of December and has little openings that lead from the first day of December to Christmas day on the 25th of December.

New Year's Day

A week after Christmas we celebrate New Year's Day. In 46 BC Julius Caesar changed the calendar. Before that time March 1 was the beginning of the New Year. The Romans made New Year's Day as a celebration to the pagan god Janus. They would have their feasts and become drunk. Sometime after the celebration of Christmas came into the church calendar, Christians used the celebration of the New Year to establish a Watch Night service. On New Year's Eve, Christians would gather at church and make this a time of reflection about the goodness of God during the past year. They would also make this a time of prayer for the coming year. In this way they were closer to the ancient Jewish practice of celebrating the New Year as a time of reflection, confession of sin, and looking to the salvation of God.

CHRISTMAS TRADITIONS

The Bible events are most important for our understanding of Christmas. There would be no Christmas without the birth of Jesus. There are many traditions that have grown up during the celebrations of Christmases past. These customs did not come from a world that does not honor Jesus. Yet the world would like to take these customs away from us and make us think that they had nothing to do with the birth of the Christ child. These customs had their beginnings in Christian celebrations of Jesus' birth. As Christians, we need to use these customs and celebrate them for their Christian roots.

Christmas Greens

The use of greens to decorate a home or church comes from pre-Christian times. The ancient Romans used green boughs and flowers to decorate their homes and pagan Temples. Many European countries used this kind of decoration. European people used this decoration to bring a touch of green during times when the days were short and the winters were long.

It is not surprising that when Europe became Christian there was opposition by some of the church leaders toward using greens in Christian homes and churches. But support for the continuation of the custom came from Pope Gregory the Great and others. They reinterpreted the greens in the light of the birth of Jesus. This was particularly true in countries in northern Europe, such as England. The Scandinavian countries such as Norway, Sweden, Finland, and Denmark used greens to decorate also.

After the Reformation, Protestant churches began to use green to decorate their places of worship. Since many plants did not grow in the cold, the choices were limited. Ivy and holly were used for decoration. Holly was considered to be a very good choice. The old English Christmas hymn "The Holly and the Ivy" is a good example.

Not only did holly have green leaves, but it had red berries as well, which added color. Holly also had thorns and bitter bark. All of these characteristics were used to symbolize the birth of Jesus, as the red berries were borne by the holly. The red berries also symbolized the blood that Jesus shed on the cross. The thorns and bitter bark symbolized His death.

St. Nicholas (later Santa Claus) (c. AD 271–342)

In our day, there is probably no one who is more a symbol of the commercialism of Christmas in America than Santa Claus. But that was not always the case. Let's think first about St. Nicholas. Then we will try to understand how he became known as Santa Claus in a red suit.

Nicholas was born in Patara and became bishop of Myra. Both Patara and Myra are located along the seacoast in the southern part of Asia Minor or present-day Turkey. (See the map below.) The church in Myra was probably started by one of the missionary churches from the area that the apostle Paul had visited.

During his boyhood years, Nicholas's parents died of a plague that spread through the area. His

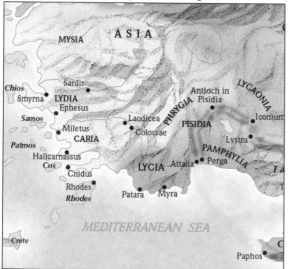

Map showing the cities of Myra and Patara (where St. Nicholas was born).

parents left him with a good inheritance. Nicholas turned to a life of helping people and of prayer. When the bishop of Myra died, Nicholas was invited to become the bishop there. He was especially kind to children, and they loved him.

One of the stories for which he is most remembered describes a father of three daughters. The father was very poor. He could not afford to help his daughters as they grew older. He did not have the money to provide each of them with a dowry. A dowry was a sum of money or very expensive gifts that a girl had to bring to the marriage. In the event that something happened to her husband, the dowry would help to take care of her. In those days, a dowry was required before a girl could marry. The girls were desperate and would have been sold into slavery.

Nicholas came to their rescue. Each night he threw a bag of gold through the window of their home. On the third night their father hid in the shadows outside their home to discover who had done this kind deed. The bag of gold fell into a stocking beside the fireplace. When Nicholas was discovered, he asked the father not to tell about his help. But the father broadcast the deed and told about the stocking. This made Nicholas famous, and the stocking by the fireplace became his mark, even today.

On another occasion Nicholas was traveling from his home to Jerusalem. A violent storm on the Mediterranean Sea threatened to cause the ship to wreck. Nicholas prayed to God for the safety of the passengers and crew. God answered and the sea became calm. After that, sailors would ask Nicholas to pray for them as they set sail.

Nicholas lived in a time when the Romans persecuted Christians. Nicholas was put in prison for his faith. But he stood firm for his Christian beliefs.

Deeds of Christian charity like these caused Nicholas to be called St. Nicholas. He is pictured as a bishop. In his later years, he had a long white beard. He was dressed in a white robe with a dark red cloak. On his cloak, or mantle, are three gold balls, symbolizing the gift to the poor man's three daughters. As a bishop, on his head he wore a dark red miter. In his hand he carried a staff shaped like a shepherd's staff. This symbolized his care for the Christian flock of people that God had entrusted to him.

Asia Minor was later conquered by the Moslems. A group of sailors from Bari, Italy went to Myra. They went to the church where St. Nicholas was buried and opened the crypt. They took the remains of St. Nicholas and returned to their ship. The town soon discovered what had happened and was in an uproar. But the sailors took his remains back to Bari. Today they are still in the church that was built in his honor in Bari.

In many parts of Europe, where St. Nicholas is still honored, he is still dressed in the same way. He is greatly beloved in Belgium, Holland, Germany, and Russia. He still brings gifts to children. In Amsterdam, Holland, he arrives, not on Christmas, but on December 6. In Holland alone there are 23 churches named for St. Nicholas.

His Dutch name is Sinterklaas. That is important because when the Dutch settled in New Amsterdam (present-day New York City) they brought Sinterklaas with them. The English took over New York City, and his name became Santa Claus.

In 1823 the Troy *Sentinel*, newspaper for the city of Troy, New York, published the poem "'Twas the Night before Christmas." Santa Claus became an instant success. Instead of the bishop of Myra, he became a chubby man with a white beard. He wore buckles on his boots and belt. This is the way Santa Claus is pictured today.

Christmas Tree

Evergreen trees were popular in Europe in pre-Christian times. Unlike other trees, the fir tree would stay green and even grow in cloudy, cold weather. It did not need the warmth of the summer sun to flourish.

One story comes from the life of St. Boniface. He became a martyr for his faith in God in the year 755. Boniface lived in England. He loved God dearly. At age thirteen, against his father's wishes, Boniface began to study in the monastery for a life of service to God. He became a missionary to Germany. The people there were pagans and worshiped the god Thor.

One day as he was walking through the forest, Boniface happened upon a pagan sacrifice. The pagan Druid priests had taken a prince and were about to sacrifice him to Thor. The sacrifice was to take place under a large oak tree. Boniface tore down the altar and freed the young prince. He cut down the oak tree, and in its place grew an evergreen tree. He told the Druid priests that the fir tree was special. It was a tree of Christ. He proceeded to tell them the story of the gospel.

Several hundred years later, the leader of the Protestant Reformation, Martin Luther, was walking home on a cold, wintry night. It was during the Christmas season. The snow was shimmering in the moonlight. The stars were beautiful in the winter sky. Luther thought about God and the beauty of nature that God had provided. He thought that he would like to take this scene home to his family and share the joy that Christmas brings.

Luther went home and got an axe. He went into the woods and cut down an evergreen tree. He brought it home and set it up for all to see. On the tree he placed candles. When they were all lighted, it looked like the beauty of the starlit night. It became a tradition during the Christmas season.

Others in Germany decorated the tree with ornaments and this began the custom of the Christmas tree. Some years later, members of the British royal family married royalty from Germany. They brought the Christmas tree custom to Britain. For many years the custom was continued at the palace.

It was in the nineteenth century that Queen Victoria and Prince Albert placed a picture of their tree in one of the newspapers. People in Britain began to follow their example. Soon Christmas trees were traditional throughout England.

In America, Christmas trees were common among the German settlers. But they did not become popular until the middle of the nineteenth century. The popularity in England and the travels of persons to Germany caused many to start thinking of the tradition. Magazines began to publish pictures of the new custom, and the custom grew rapidly.

The Nativity Scene

The nativity scene is popular in Italy, France, and Spain. It is known as *presepio* in Italy, *crèche* in France, and *nacimiento* in Spain. In many places it is as popular as the Christmas tree. In America the nativity scene is also popular. Many churches have nativity scenes as part of their service on Christmas Eve. It was Francis of Assisi in Italy, who was responsible for our nativity scenes on Christmas Eve.

St. Francis of Assisi (1182–1226) loved the story of Christmas. He wanted to let all of the people in Greccio, Italy, know about the wonder of the birth of Jesus. He called one of his wealthy friends to come and help him set up a scene outdoors that would recall the beauty and mystery of the birth of Jesus.

His friend was happy to help St. Francis. Together they built a crib for the animals. They placed fresh hay in the manger. Then they brought animals such as oxen, donkeys, cows, and sheep. Finally, they enlisted people for the human parts in the story.

On Christmas Eve the people of the town came out to the manger. They brought torches to light their way. The other friars sang Christmas songs. Then Mary came riding on a donkey with Joseph alongside. In the manger they placed a small wax figure of the Christ child. Then the shepherds came to the scene. Finally, the wise men came riding on horseback.

When they were all assembled, St. Francis preached to the people about the Child of Bethlehem. All of the people went away rejoicing about what they had seen and heard. It was very much like that first Christmas night.

Manger scenes very quickly became popular throughout Italy. In Rome in the church of Santa Maria Maggiore, one of the first manger scenes is still on display. It dates back to the 1200s. The idea of the manger scene was taken by the Franciscan friars to other countries, such as France.

Charles of Bourbon, a Spanish prince, became Charles IV, king of Naples, in 1734. He became so interested in the idea of the nativity scene that he had many figures constructed for the manger scene. His wife, Queen Maria Amalia, and her servants created costumes for the figures. They used the finest lace and materials. They placed gold, silver, and precious jewels on the costumes.

It became fashionable for noble families to create very elaborate scenes. The families would visit one another and show off their treasures to their friends. Over 1,200 pieces are in the collection today at the Royal Palace of Caserta.

For a while the scenes lost popularity, but recently they have again become very popular. In Rivisondoli, a town in the Ambruzzi mountains in Italy, the whole town becomes involved in a live manger scene. Often there are more than six hundred actors. The manger is empty until Mary comes on Christmas Eve, riding on a donkey with Joseph alongside. Then the shepherds come. The scene continues until January 6, when the wise men come to participate in the nativity scene.

A Moravian Church tradition is the putz. Coming from the German word *putzen*, this word means "to decorate." Each year Moravians build a putz, which may be a simple manger scene. Others are much more elaborate. They begin with the prophecy from Isaiah and continue through the birth of Jesus in Bethlehem. They may even continue to the coming of the wise men and the flight to Egypt. The purpose of the putz is not to entertain. Members invite neighbors to their homes and share the good news of the gospel that Jesus came into the world to save sinners.

OTHER CHRISTMAS TRADITIONS

The Star

From the early Christmas celebrations, the star has been a reminder of the star that led the wise men to the cradle where Jesus was born (see Matthew 2:2). The star is also a reminder that Jesus said, "I am the light of the world" (see John 8:12). Christmas brings the light of God to a dark and sinful world.

Coming from German boarding schools of the nineteenth century, the Moravian Church developed the Moravian star. It was first designed to teach geometry principles to the students. But it now proclaims the light of Christ at Christmas. For the Christian it is a star that tells of the prophecy long ago that a Son would be born. It is a star that tells of the coming of the Christ child. It is a star that gives hope for the future coming of Christ again in power and glory to welcome those who put their trust in Him.

Christmas Cards

Christmas cards were first sent in Great Britain in the nineteenth century. The origin was not necessarily religious. But Christmas cards give us an opportunity to share the good news that Jesus came into the world to save sinners. Christmas cards allow us to share the joy of Christmas with friends, business associates, and family. Often Christmas cards are the only means that we have to keep in contact with people whom we do not see during the rest of the year.

EASTER

Easter is the most important holiday of the Christian year. Easter represents the triumph of Jesus Christ over death and sin. Easter is the day on which Jesus arose from the dead. Because He arose from the dead, all those who put their trust in Him as Savior and Lord will also be resurrected and live in heaven with God for ever. That is the message of Easter. Like Christmas, Easter has its roots in the Gospels of the New Testament. If you divide each of the Gospels into three parts, one of those parts is given to the cross and resurrection. For John, he devoted about half of his Gospel to the death of Christ and His rising from the dead.

Unlike Christmas, which is all joyful, Easter follows a time of sadness in the betrayal and suffering of Jesus. It was not until Easter morning that the true joy of Easter shines forth. Easter is not marked with the giving of presents or the sending of Christmas greetings. For many Christians, Easter is marked with an Easter dawn service. This service recalls the early morning visit of the women and the disciples to the grave. In place of the gloom and sadness that had come from Jesus' death, there was a new joy and excitement that Jesus was no longer dead. He was now raised from the dead and alive.

EASTER

The Jewish day begins at sundown when the stars are visible. By our calendar the day begins at midnight. We see these events from the way the Romans saw them. The Jewish leaders wanted to get rid of Jesus before the Jewish Sabbath began at sundown on Friday.

The Easter Story (John 11:45–12:11)

Before Jesus went to Jerusalem, the chief priests had sent a notice out to find and arrest Jesus. The priests were very jealous of Jesus' popularity and power. They feared that a Messiah, like Jesus, would bring the Roman armies against them. They did not want Jesus around. John tells us that they also wanted to kill Lazarus, whom Jesus had raised from the dead. But they feared the many people who loved Jesus.

The time was in the early spring. It was at the end of March, before the Passover in AD 30 that Jesus came from Galilee with His disciples to Jerusalem. Jesus knew what would happen in Jerusalem. He tried to tell the disciples that He must die, but they did not understand. Many of the people thought that He would restore the throne of David and drive out the Romans. Among the disciples, Judas also thought that Jesus would bring a new glory to the people of Israel.

Jesus came to Bethany. Martha and Mary prepared a great feast in honor of Jesus. Lazarus, their brother whom Jesus had raised from the dead, was there also. Mary showed her special love for Jesus by anointing Him with expensive oils. Then she dried His feet with her long and beautiful hair. Judas complained about the waste of money, but Jesus said that the story of her love and preparing Him for burial would travel with the gospel around the world.

The stage was set for one of the greatest dramas of all history. Jesus appeared in Jerusalem on Sunday. The events of Sunday began the week that will lead to Easter. For Christians this week has become known as Holy Week. We will try to reconstruct the events of Holy Week from the Gospels.

The Sunday Triumphal Entry
(Matthew 21; Mark 11:1–11;
Luke 19:29–44; John 12:12–19)

The Easter story begins when Jesus sent two of His disciples ahead to bring a colt to Him. The colt was one on whom no one had yet ridden. The disciples told the owners that the Master had need of the colt. Apparently, Jesus had prearranged this and the owners let the colt go. The disciples brought

Palm branches are a symbol for hope and victory.

the colt to Jesus. They put their coats on the colt and helped Jesus to mount the colt.

Jesus rode down the road from the Mount of Olives. The people came out and shouted, "Hosanna! Blessed is He who comes in the name of the Lord—the King of Israel" (John 12:13b). The people threw palm branches in His path into the city of Jerusalem. The people rejoiced at the miracles that they had seen Jesus perform, especially the raising of Lazarus from the dead.

The Pharisees were very upset by the whole scene. They complained that the whole world had followed Jesus. They told Jesus to control His disciples and tell them to be quiet. Jesus said to them, "I tell you, if they were to keep silent, the stones would cry out!" (Luke 19:40). At that time the disciples did not understand the meaning of the prophecy of Zechariah. John recorded it: "Fear no more, daughter of Zion; look! your King is coming, sitting on a donkey's colt" (John 12:15).

Coming to Jerusalem, Jesus was sad. He cried. He told those who were with Him that Jerusalem would fall. The great stones that had been laid for the Temple would be torn down. And it was all because they refused to recognize their Lord when He came to them.

Jesus made His triumphal entry into Jerusalem. He probably entered through the Golden Gate. Both Jews and Christians believe that the Messiah would enter the city through the Golden Gate. The Golden Gate is now located next to the Dome of the Rock. The Moslems had it closed and walled.

Entering through the Golden Gate would have brought Jesus into the area close by the Temple. Many of the people who had witnessed the raising of Lazarus from the dead began to praise God. They spread the word that this was Jesus, who had performed many miracles. Many people in Jerusalem came to see this Prophet, who had come from Nazareth in Galilee. Next, Jesus entered the Temple. He looked around the Temple and then left. That night He again returned to Bethany at the end of the day.

Monday (Matthew 21:12–18; Mark 11:12–19; Luke 19:45–48; John 12:20–36)

Leaving Bethany on Monday morning, Jesus saw a fig tree. The tree had leaves. But as He drew close to the tree, there was no fruit on the tree. Jesus said to the tree, "May no fruit ever come from you again!" (Matthew 21:19). The disciples, who were with Him, heard Jesus say this.

Arriving in Jerusalem, Jesus went again to the Temple. He found the merchants buying and selling. They had constructed stalls for livestock and the selling of doves. There were also bankers, who would make change for foreign currency. The noise and the smell of the animals did not aid worshipers to come closer to God. But what angered Jesus most was the profit that these dealers made within the Temple. They were charging the people too much. He overturned the tables. He drove them out of the Temple area. He said to them, "It is written, 'My house will be called a house of prayer.' But you are making it 'a den of thieves'!" (Matt. 21:13).

Many came who were blind and lame. Jesus healed them all. The scribes and the Pharisees watched. The children came and blessed Jesus by saying, "Hosanna to the Son of David." The religious leaders complained to Jesus. But Jesus answered by quoting Scripture that said that children and infants were prepared to praise.

Some Greeks, who had come to Jerusalem for the Feast of the Passover, asked Philip to see Jesus. They wanted to hear what He had to say. Philip told Andrew. Together, they told Jesus. Jesus then began to tell of His coming crucifixion. A voice from heaven proclaimed that the Father would glorify His Son. Jesus said to the people that it was for their benefit, not His. Jesus promised that when He was lifted up, He would draw all men to Himself.

Jesus left the Temple and again returned to Bethany to spend the night.

Tuesday (Matthew 21:20–26:16; Mark 11:20–14:11; Luke 20:1–22:6)

On the way to the Temple on Tuesday morning, as the disciples went with Jesus into Jerusalem, they passed the same fig tree. It was the one they had seen the day before. Peter called their attention to the tree that was now withered. Jesus used the tree to teach a lesson about faith. He told them that if they had just a little faith, they could do greater miracles than destroying the fig tree.

Tuesday was a difficult day for Jesus. The religious leaders were very angry. They had seen how Jesus healed the sick and performed miracles for the people. They had heard Him teach in the Temple. Together, the scribes, Pharisees, and Sadducees all tried to trap Jesus into saying something that would cause Him to be condemned for blasphemy. Then they could get rid of Him by having Him stoned. If they could not do that, maybe they could make Him say something that would get Him in trouble with the Roman governor. Instead, Jesus answered them very effectively and often in parables.

Their first trap was to ask Jesus by what authority He did these things, like healing the lame. Jesus responded by asking them a question. He asked them to tell Him from whose authority John's baptism came. Was it from heaven or from men? They feared the people to say that it came from men. They realized that if they said that it was from heaven, He would have asked them why they did not believe. So they answered, "We do not know." Jesus then said that He would not tell them by whose authority He performed His miracles.

Jesus then told a series of parables. The parables were directed at the religious leaders. The first told of a father who had two sons. The father told both sons to go to work in his vineyard. The first son said he would not go to work but later changed his mind and went. The second son said that he would go but never went. The first son did what the father wanted him to do. Jesus then drew the application. It will be easier for sinners to go to heaven than for religious leaders who know the truth but do not do what God wants.

The second parable told a story about a man who planted a vineyard. The man rented the vineyard to some tenants. He went away on a trip. Harvest time came. The owner sent many servants to collect the fruit. In each case the persons who rented the vineyard beat the servants. Some they killed. Finally, the man sent his only son. They killed him. Jesus then said that the man would come and kill the evil tenants and give the vineyard to others.

The chief priests and the Pharisees became very angry. They knew that Jesus had them in mind. They began to plot how they might get rid of Him. But they feared the people. The people believed that Jesus was a prophet. They could not arrest Jesus at that time.

Jesus continued to teach and tell parables. Finally, the Pharisees saw that Jesus silenced the Sadducees. One of the Pharisees asked Jesus what was the Great Commandment of the Law. Jesus responded with the Great Commandment: Love God with all your heart, soul, and mind. Love your neighbor as yourself. This was the heart of what Jesus was trying to teach through His ministry. The Pharisee commended Jesus for His answer. Jesus told the Pharisee that he was not far from the kingdom of God.

Jesus continued to teach. Finally, He went over to the treasury where the people brought their contributions to the Temple. He saw many bring large donations. But a widow came and placed two tiny coins in the treasury. Jesus called His disciples and told them that this poor widow had done more than all the wealthy persons. They gave a little out of their wealth. She gave a lot out of her poverty.

Jesus finished His teaching in the Temple. He and the disciples left and went to the Mount of Olives. One of His disciples was impressed with the size of the stones in the Temple. Jesus then began to teach the disciples about the destruction of the Temple. He described its destruction in detail. About forty years later the Romans destroyed the Temple, just as Jesus had said.

His disciples wanted to know more about the end times. They questioned Him further. The disciples probably thought that when the Temple was destroyed then Jesus would reveal Himself as the Messiah and bring in the glory of Israel. Jesus would reign and they would reign with Him. But instead, Jesus told them to be watchful.

Finally, Jesus was alone with His disciples. He told them plainly that in two days He would be crucified. Even as Jesus was telling the disciples about His coming death, the religious leaders were in the home of the chief priest. They were deciding how they might capture Jesus and get rid of Him.

As they talked, one of Jesus' own disciples, Judas Iscariot, came to the chief priest. He promised that he would betray Jesus to the priests for a price. They offered Judas thirty pieces of silver. That was the price of a slave. Judas was both greedy and dishonest. Judas accepted the offer and promised to point out Jesus to the soldiers of the Temple.

Wednesday (No Record)

On Tuesday Jesus must have been exhausted. Jesus was constantly criticized by the religious leaders. Jesus knew that they were planning to kill Him. The time was coming quickly. It would be over before the coming Sabbath. Jesus would need all of His strength for the difficult hours that lay ahead.

Thursday and Friday
(Matthew 26:17–27:10; Mark 14:12–71; Luke 22:7–71; John 13:1–18:27)

THE PASSOVER MEAL

Jesus sent John and Peter into Jerusalem. They were to find the place and make preparations for Jesus and the disciples to celebrate the Passover meal. Jesus must have arranged with the owner in advance. There was a lot of work to be done to

Jesus shares a last supper with His disciples.

prepare for the Passover. All of the dishes had to be prepared. In addition, after noon, the Passover lamb had to be taken to the Temple, and a portion was sacrificed. The remainder was used in the Passover celebration.

That evening Jesus gathered with His disciples in the upper room. This would be their final meal together. Before they ate the meal, Jesus went from disciple to disciple and washed their feet. Since they wore sandals on the dusty streets, foot washing was a custom in Palestine. Upon entering the home, a good host usually had a servant wash the feet of the guests. This custom provided good hospitality and comfort for the guests. Jesus did the foot washing Himself. Jesus explained that He did the washing to show them that if they would follow Him, they too must serve others.

The Passover meal began with a cup of wine. Jesus gave that cup of wine new meaning. He raised His cup and told the disciples that this represented His blood that would be poured out on the cross for them. Next, He broke the bread and told them that this represented His body that was broken for them. He ended by telling the disciples that they would need to follow this custom until He came again. Today in the church we continue to follow Jesus' instructions and hold communion to show our Lord's death until He comes again.

In Jesus' day the Passover lamb was the center of the meal. Only the shank bone of the lamb is used

in Passover seder today. Since the Temple was destroyed about forty years after Christ, it is no longer possible to sacrifice the lamb. Still, the original meaning of the sacrifice of the lamb has great importance for Christians. The entire meaning of the Passover takes on a new meaning. Jesus became the sacrificial Lamb. As a result of His sacrifice, sin has no more power over those who trust Him. The blood of the sacrificial lamb was placed on the doorpost of the Hebrew home at the Passover. The angel of death passed over the home where the blood was on the doorpost. Jesus' blood that was shed on the cross makes it possible for the follower of Jesus to live eternally with God.

At this point in the meal, Jesus told the disciples that one of them would betray Him. The disciples were very sad. They kept asking Jesus, "Is it I?" Jesus said that it was the one who dipped in the bowl with Him. With that, Jesus dipped the bread and gave it to Judas. It seemed that Jesus was trying to persuade Judas not to do such a terrible deed. But Judas was determined on following his own course. He soon left the group and went into the night to find the group of soldiers that would come and arrest Jesus.

After Judas left, Jesus began to teach the disciples. He told them that He must go away. Then He gave the disciples the command to love each other. He told them that all people would know that they are His disciples by the love that they had for each other.

Peter asked why he could not follow Jesus. Jesus said that Peter could not follow now but would indeed follow later. Peter then promised Jesus that even if all the rest left, he would stay. Jesus told him that before the rooster crowed three times, Peter would deny that he even knew Jesus.

Then Jesus promised to prepare a place for His followers. In heaven there would be a home for all who follow Jesus. Jesus told the disciples, "I am the way, the truth and the life. No one comes to the Father, except through Me." Jesus continued to teach them that they would need to pray in His name. They would receive the Holy Spirit. He then told them that He would one day return. He told them not to fear or be afraid. His love for them was so great that He would lay down His life for them.

To the Mount of Olives

Jesus and the disciples then left. The disciples followed Jesus into the night as they walked toward the Mount of Olives. As they made their way through the dark streets of the city, Jesus continued His teaching. It must have been at the Temple gates that Jesus saw the vine and large clusters of grapes. The vine had been a symbol of Israel (see Psalm 80:8-19). Jesus used the vine to illustrate the relationship between God and the true disciple.

Jesus taught the disciples that in the world they would have trials and troubles. But they should not be afraid, because Jesus had overcome the world. Then Jesus picked up the teaching where He had left off before they left the upper room. He told them that there was no greater love than that a man should lay down His life for His friends. Jesus said that He willingly and gladly lay down His life for them. He told them that the world hated Him. The disciples would also be hated by the world. But He said that He would send a Comforter to minister to them after He was gone out of the world.

Finally, Jesus lifted His eyes toward heaven. He prayed to the Father to glorify the Son, so that the Son could glorify the Father. The disciples believed that the Father had sent His Son. So Jesus prayed that the Father would protect them. He was sending them out into the world. He wanted the Father to protect them from the evil one. Then Jesus prayed for those who would come to believe on Him after He was taken out of the world.

Soon they crossed the brook Kidron and ascended the Mount of Olives to a place called Gethsemene. It was probably named Gethsemene because there had been an olive press there in the past. Jesus had gone there before. This time He asked the disciples to wait for Him near the gate. He took Peter, James, and John farther into the garden. Jesus asked Peter, James, and John to wait and watch while He went farther into the garden to pray. Jesus was very upset. He knew what lay ahead for Him. He prayed three times, and each time He returned to find the disciples sleeping. After the third time, He told the disciples to wake up. He said to them, "Get up; let's go! See—my betrayer is near."

The Arrest and Trial Before the Chief Priest

As Jesus spoke, Judas appeared. By this time, it must have been close to midnight. Judas came to Jesus and in the traditional manner of approaching a rabbi, kissed Jesus . Behind Judas were the chief priests, the Temple guard, and a small detachment of Roman soldiers. The soldiers were there because the chief priest had warned that Jesus was a Messiah, who would try to escape. They had come with weapons and lanterns to search for this Messiah. With more than one hundred thousand pilgrims in Jerusalem for the Passover celebration, they did not want to allow any chance for riots to happen. Instead of finding one who resisted arrest, Jesus gave Himself willingly to the mob. He told them to let the disciples go, since He was the One they wanted.

Peter tried to show his loyalty to Jesus by cutting off the ear of the servant to the chief priest. But Jesus did not want violence. He restored the ear of the servant. Jesus asked the mob why they came out to arrest Him. He asked them why they came in secret, when every day He had been in the Temple teaching and healing. It was clear that they had feared the people and did not want to arrest Him where it might cause a riot. They bound Jesus and took Him away. Out of fear, all of the disciples fled.

The soldiers took Jesus first to the home of Annas. Annas had been the high priest, but the Romans were not happy with him and replaced him. But Annas still had power in the Sanhedrin. Annas tried to get Jesus to testify. Jesus did not answer, except to say that He taught in the synagogues and in the Temple and did nothing in secret. He told Annas to ask those who heard Him. At that response, one of the guards struck Jesus. Jesus turned to them and said, "If I have said something wrong, give evidence of the wrong. But if I have spoken truth, then why did you strike Me?"

Annas asked no more questions, but sent Jesus bound to his son-in-law, Caiaphas. Caiaphas was the high priest. It was still night in the early morning hours. Caiaphas had gathered members of the Sanhedrin together in his house for the trial of Jesus. They were looking for an excuse to put Jesus to death. But they could not find any reason. They brought witnesses, but the witnesses disagreed. They even hired false witnesses.

THE SANHEDRIN

The Sanhedrin was the ruling court in Israel. There were seventy-one men from the Pharisees, Sadducees, and scribes. It was sometimes called the Council. They were responsible for the laws of Israel. According to their laws, a person was supposed to be tried during the daylight hours, not at night. It is not likely that the Romans allowed them to pronounce the death penalty. They wanted Jesus to be put to death, but they went to the Roman governor to pronounce judgment.

Jesus did not answer the charges of the false witnesses. The high priest wanted to charge Jesus with blasphemy. In order to do this he had to get Jesus to say that He was the Son of God. He asked Jesus, "Are you the Messiah, the Son of the Blessed One?" "I am," said Jesus, "and all of you will see 'the Son of Man seated at the right hand' of the Power and 'coming with the clouds of heaven'" (Mark 14:61–62).

With that the high priest tore his robes. That was a sign that blasphemy had been spoken. He told the Sanhedrin that no more witnesses were needed. Jesus had condemned Himself. They blindfolded Him and began to spit on Him and mock Him.

Meanwhile, Peter had been warming himself outside the judgment hall. He wanted to hear what happened to Jesus. As he was standing there, three times he was accused of being a follower of Jesus. Each time Peter denied that he even knew Jesus. On the third time, the rooster crowed. Peter remembered what Jesus had told him. He went away from the group and cried for his denial of Jesus.

By this time Judas learned that Jesus had been condemned to die. He too was sorry for what he had done to Jesus. Judas went out and hanged himself.

Friday (Matthew 27:11–61; Mark 15:1–47; Luke 23:1–56; John 18:28–19:42)

The Trial Before Pilate

By this time morning had come. The Sanhedrin sent Jesus bound to the Roman governor, Pilate. Very little is known about Pilate. In 1961 a group of archaeologists discovered a stone in Caesarea that described Pilate as the prefect in Judea.

At the trial before the Jewish religious leaders, Jesus said very little. Now the members of the Sanhedrin went to the gate of Pilate's palace. They would not go into the palace, since that would have caused them to be unclean under Jewish law. Pilate asked them what charge they were bringing against Jesus. They knew that Pilate would not be interested in their charge of blasphemy against Jesus. So they told Pilate that they had condemned Him. That should be enough. But they also said that Jesus did not believe in paying taxes to Caesar and that He claimed to be the King of the Jews.

Pilate took Jesus into the palace and questioned Him further. He must have already heard reports about Jesus' preaching and teaching. He could find no fault in Jesus. So Pilate returned to the chief priests and said that he could find nothing wrong with Jesus that deserved the death penalty. In the conversation he learned that Jesus came from Galilee. Pilate thought that this was a way out of his problem of what to do with Jesus. Herod Antipas ruled Galilee. He was in Jerusalem for the Passover. Pilate sent Jesus to Herod.

Jesus Before Herod

Herod was very interested, especially since Jesus was sent from the Roman ruler. He may have feared that John the Baptist had come back to life and wanted to see him. Or he may have heard that Jesus performed miracles. Herod told Jesus that he wanted to see a miracle. Jesus did not say anything to Herod. When Jesus did not say anything, Herod became very angry. He placed a royal robe on Jesus and, with the soldiers, began to make fun of Jesus. Herod would not do anything with Jesus. He finally sent Jesus back to Pilate.

Jesus Returns to Pilate

While Jesus was in front of Herod, Pilate's wife had a dream about Jesus. She sent a message to her husband. She told him not to have anything to do with Jesus. She urged him to let Jesus go. Pilate then held his court in front of the palace, where the crowd could watch. Pilate told the chief priests that neither he nor Herod had found anything worthy of death in the prisoner. Pilate wanted to have Jesus punished and released.

It was customary for the Roman governor to release a prisoner at Passover. Pilate thought that he could release Jesus. The chief priests had moved the crowd to demand the execution of Jesus. When Pilate wanted to release Jesus, the crowd demanded that Pilate release Barabbas instead. Barabbas had killed Romans and wanted all of Palestine to rebel. But the crowd insisted that Barabbas be released.

Pilate asked what he should do with Jesus. The mob said, "Crucify Him!" They continued to shout. Pilate had Jesus taken by the soldiers and beaten. On His head they placed a crown of thorns and put a robe of purple on His bleeding back. They mocked Him. They cried, "Hail, King of the Jews!" Then they spit on Him and struck Jesus in the face. When they finally tired of making fun of Jesus, they brought Him back to Pilate.

Pilate brought Jesus back in front of the crowd. He told them that he found nothing against Jesus to crucify Him. But the people shouted louder to crucify Jesus. He told them to crucify Jesus themselves. The priests did not have that power. When the priests said that He claimed to be the Son of God, Pilate became even more afraid.

Pilate again questioned Jesus. But Pilate could find no cause for crucifixion. The chief priests were afraid that they would lose. They tried another way to convince Pilate. They told Pilate that if he did not crucify Jesus, he was no friend of Caesar. This was a threat that they would inform Caesar that Jesus was guilty of the charges they brought to Pilate. It might end Pilate's career. Pilate gave in.

Pilate brought a bowl of water. In front of the people he washed his hands. He was telling them that it was not his fault that Jesus was crucified. Jesus' blood was upon the people. They said, "His blood be upon us and our children!"

With that, Pilate released Barabbas and sent Jesus for crucifixion. They tore off the royal robe and put Jesus' own clothes back on Him. The wounds from the beating were torn open again. Jesus was forced to carry the crossbeam of His cross to Mount Calvary, where they would crucify Him. But Jesus had become very weak, and fell. The soldiers forced Simon from Cyrene to carry the crossbeam to the hill. Many people followed. Some were making fun of Jesus. Others were crying.

Jesus' Crucifixion

By law the crucifixion had to be outside the walls of the city. It was about nine o'clock in the morning. They took Jesus to Golgotha, which in Hebrew means "the place of the Skull." They tried to give Jesus wine, mingled with myrrh to lessen Jesus' suffering. This is a reminder of the myrrh that the wise men brought to Jesus at His birth. It foretold the suffering that Jesus would experience on the cross.

At Golgotha they set up the crosses. There were two thieves who were also crucified on either side of Jesus. In each case, the prisoner was nailed through his wrists and feet to the cross. Then they dropped the cross into the hole that they had dug in the ground.

Pilate had the soldiers place an inscription over the cross of Jesus. It read, "THIS IS JESUS, THE

The death of Jesus on the cross.

Holy of Holies from the rest of the Temple was torn from top to bottom. There was an earthquake and many of the graves were opened. Persons who had died were resurrected. The rocks split. The jeering crowd was silenced and struck with awe. The centurion who stood and watched Jesus breathe His last breath exclaimed, "This man really was God's Son!"

JESUS' SEVEN LAST WORDS ON THE CROSS

1. To the soldiers—*"Father, forgive them, because they do not know what they are doing."* (Luke 23:34)

2. To His mother, Mary—*"Woman, here is your son."* To John the apostle—*"Here is your mother."* (John 19:26–27)

3. To the thief on the cross, who repented—*"I assure you: Today you will be with Me in Paradise."* (Luke 23:43)

4. To the crowd—*"I'm thirsty!"* (John 19:28)

5. To God—*"My God, My God, why have You forsaken Me?"* (Matthew 27:46)

6. To all in front of the cross—*"It is finished!"* (John 19:30)

7. To God—*"Father, 'into Your hands I entrust My spirit.'"* (Luke 23:46)

KING OF THE JEWS." It was written in several languages. The chief priests wanted that changed, but Pilate refused.

The soldiers cast lots for the clothes of Jesus. Many of the soldiers and others in the crowd began to make fun of Jesus. They told Him to come down from the cross and they would believe that He was the Son of God. One of the thieves also laughed at Jesus. But the other begged Jesus' forgiveness. Jesus told the thief that he would join Jesus in Paradise that day.

From noon to about three o'clock in the afternoon, the land was covered with darkness. At Jesus' death, the curtain in the Temple that separated the

Crucifixion was one of the cruelest deaths that a person could suffer. The chief priests wanted to get the bodies off the cross before the Sabbath. Since the Sabbath started at sundown, they had to work quickly. The soldiers broke the legs of the two thieves on either side of Jesus. When they came to Jesus, they discovered that He was already dead. Instead, they pierced the side of Jesus with a spear. Not breaking any of Jesus' bones and piercing His side had been foretold in the Old Testament.

The Burial of Jesus

Even the story of Jesus' burial is special. Joseph of Arimathea went to Pilate and asked for the body of Jesus. Joseph wanted to bury Jesus in his own new tomb. It is amazing that anyone would ask for the body of Jesus after the chief priests wanted Jesus put to death. It is even more amazing that Joseph was a member of the Council. It was the Sanhedrin, you will remember, that condemned Jesus to death. Joseph had become a believer.

Along with Joseph came Nicodemus. Early in Jesus' ministry Nicodemus, a religious leader of the Jews, had come to Jesus by night. He wanted to know how to become a follower of Jesus. He told Nicodemus, "For God loved the world in this way: He gave His One and Only Son, so that everyone who believes in Him will not perish but have eternal life" (John 3:16). Nicodemus saw this happen and believed. He now came with Joseph to help bury the body of Jesus.

Pilate asked the centurion if Jesus was already dead. They answered that He was. Pilate was surprised that Jesus had died so quickly. He gave them permission to bury Jesus. The two men took the body of Jesus from the cross to the tomb. There they wrapped it tightly in strips of linen. Nicodemus brought a mixture of myrrh and aloes. The spices weighed about seventy-five pounds. They wrapped these with Jesus' body. Remember the myrrh from the gifts of the wise men.

Joseph rolled a great stone in front of the tomb. He and Nicodemus left. The women from Galilee, who had been at the cross, followed the men to the tomb. They planned to prepare spices and perfumes to also anoint Jesus' body after the Sabbath.

Saturday (Matthew 27:62–66)

On Saturday the chief priests and the Pharisees went back to Pilate. They told Pilate that Jesus had said that He would rise again the third day. The religious leaders feared that the disciples would come and steal the body. They would then say that Jesus had risen from the dead. To prevent this, they asked Pilate to place a guard in front of the tomb.

Pilate agreed and gave them permission to take two soldiers and make the tomb secure. He told them to place a seal across the stone. This was probably a rope that was secured across the large stone and fastened with something like clay. It would show that the tomb had not been opened. The soldiers secured the tomb and sat through the night watch.

Sunday (Matthew 28:1–15; Mark 16:1–14; Luke 24:1–35; John 20:1–25)

At dawn on Sunday there was a great earthquake. An angel of the Lord rolled back the stone and sat upon it. The guards were frightened! The Gospel writer says that they appeared as dead men.

The Women Come to the Tomb

Mary Magdalene, Mary, the mother of James, and Salome came with the spices and perfumes that they had prepared to anoint Jesus' body. Instead, they found the angel sitting on the stone. He told them not to fear but to look at the grave clothes that were there. Then he told them to go and tell the disciples to meet Jesus in Galilee. Jesus had risen from the dead, just as He had promised. The women were filled with joy.

The women did not know what to think. They were excited but fearful. They returned to the disciples. Mary Magdalene met Peter and John, who were also coming to the tomb. Mary was confused and thought that someone had taken the body of Jesus. Peter and John went on to the tomb and found the grave clothes just as they had been told.

Meanwhile, Mary Magdalene was crying. She turned and saw a man standing in front of her. She thought it was the gardener and that he had taken the body of Jesus away. He said, "Why are you crying?" She explained what she thought. Jesus said, "Mary." Then she knew that it was Jesus!

The other women were also in the garden. Jesus met them. "Greetings," He said. They worshiped Him. Jesus sent Mary Magdalene back to tell the other disciples. He told them that He would meet the disciples in Galilee.

The Disciples on the Road to Emmaus

Cleopas and another disciple were headed toward their home in Emmaus. The town was about seven miles from Jerusalem. They were talking about the many things that had happened to Jesus. Jesus came alongside them. He acted as if He did not know what they were discussing. They did not recognize Jesus.

Jesus began to tell them about the many prophecies that were set forth in the Old Testament about Himself. The two disciples saw that the stranger was going on further. They asked Him to come to their home and have dinner with them. He stopped at their home.

It was not until Jesus broke bread with them and blessed the bread that they realized who He was. They were so excited. They had met with Jesus. They ran all the way back to Jerusalem to tell the eleven disciples. When they arrived, they found that Jesus had already met Peter.

Jesus Meets the Ten Apostles

That Easter Sunday evening ten of the apostles were gathered together. The doors were locked. They feared the Jews. As they were meeting, Jesus appeared to them. He said, "Peace to you!" Jesus tried to take away their fear. He ate food to show that He was not a ghost.

Then Jesus commissioned the disciples. He breathed on them and told them to receive the Holy Spirit. Then He told them that He was sending them out.

Thomas was not with the other disciples when they met Jesus. He said that he would not believe unless he could put his finger in the nail prints and in the pierced side of Jesus. One week passed and Thomas was with the ten disciples. Jesus appeared to all of them and told Thomas to come and put his finger in Jesus' nail prints and in His pierced side. Thomas believed. Jesus said, "Blessed are those who believe without seeing."

Jesus made other appearances to many of His disciples. After forty days Jesus ascended to the Father. But Easter is special. It was the day of resurrection.

EARLY CHURCH PRACTICES

Unlike Christmas, Easter has been celebrated since the time of the New Testament church.

For the early church, Easter was the most important holiday of the Christian year. On that day sin and death were conquered by Jesus' death and resurrection. Jesus became the Passover Lamb. Easter was also celebrated each week on the Lord's Day—the first day of the week. All Christians celebrate Easter. But not all Christians celebrate Lent, the period of forty days before Easter. Not all Christians celebrate Ash Wednesday either.

Passover celebrated the sacrifice of the lamb. The blood of the lamb placed on the doorpost meant protection from death for the Hebrew home. The family ate the Passover meal together. Easter celebrated the sacrifice of Jesus the Lamb of God. Jesus' blood meant release from sin and protection for the follower of Jesus. Christians participated in the Lord's Supper together each time they met.

For Christians, Easter became the traditional time for baptism. Baptism was also related to the Passover and escape from Egypt. Remember that the Hebrew people passed through the waters of the Red Sea on their escape from Egypt. They went through safely because God cared for them. The Egyptians, who chased the Hebrews to harm them, were drowned.

Baptism for new believers came at the end of a two-year period when they would learn about their new faith in Christ. During that time they were taught and helped by their "godparents." On Easter eve they would prepare for baptism by spending all night in prayer. When the rooster crowed at dawn on Easter morning, the new believers were baptized. They were buried in the water of baptism like Jesus in His death and burial in the tomb. They were raised to a new life of love and obedience to their new Lord and Master, Jesus Christ.

Following Jesus' practice with the disciples, foot washing was practiced on Thursday before Easter in the early church. But foot washing soon disappeared.

Fasting during Holy Week, the week before Easter, became common in the early church. Fasting was seen as preparing a Christian for being open to God's Spirit. Fasting was seen as a way to fight the devil. Fasting had the added benefit of saving money for food. The money saved could be used to help the poor and needy.

The origin of the name *Easter* is still a mystery. Most of the European countries have a name for Jesus' resurrection that is close to the name of Passover or Pasch. English is different. In English the term is *Easter*. One of the early Christian missionaries to England wrote that it came from Eostre. Eostre was a Saxon goddess of spring. More likely, Easter is derived from a German word that meant "resurrection". Easter celebration begins with Palm Sunday and continues through the day of resurrection.

The date of Easter was a problem for the early church. Passover fell on the 14th day of the Jewish month of Nissan. It did not matter on which day of the week it happened to fall. For Christians, Easter had to fall on a Sunday in order to remember Jesus' resurrection. The solution was not easy. Easter became the first Sunday after the full moon from March 22 to April 25. We still celebrate Easter, using the same method to find the date. As a result, Easter and Passover are usually close but no longer the same date.

As a means for punishment, crucifixion was practiced from the sixth century BC. It remained for the Romans to bring it to its most painful and powerful use. They tried to use crucifixion to keep people, who were not Roman citizens, to fear it as a punishment. When Constantine became the Roman emperor, he outlawed crucifixion permanently. He did it because it was the cruel death by which Jesus died.

Palm Sunday

Observance of Palm Sunday dates from the fifth century. It started in Jerusalem. The bishop of Jerusalem would play the role of Jesus. The people would place palm branches in the path of the procession. It would start at the Mount of Olives and go to the Church of the Resurrection. They sang hymns and psalms. They carried palm and olive branches.

Soon other Christian churches from other parts of the world also celebrated Palm Sunday.

Palm branches became known as a symbol for hope and victory. In other parts of the world where palm branches were not available, other branches were substituted. In Germany, willows or other branches were substituted for the palm branches. In Germany during the Middle Ages, a wooden statue of Jesus riding on a wooden donkey with wheels was drawn along the parade route. This was called a *palmesel*.

Lent

Lent represented the forty days before Easter. There is record of Lent by the fourth century. It was a time of preparation for new Christians who were about to be baptized. Eventually Lent did not include the Sunday observances, adding six days to the period of Lent. Later in the fourth century, the keeping of Lent was observed for all Christians. Fasting was an important part of the observance of Lent.

Lent recalled the forty days from Jesus' baptism through the temptation in the wilderness. During that time Jesus prayed. He prepared Himself for His ministry. The forty days were also a reminder of the wandering of the children of Israel in the wilderness and the relation to Passover. During that time Moses was on Mount Sinai for forty days. In addition, Elijah fasted for forty days on his way to Mount Horeb. All of these experiences are tied to the children of Israel or to the ministry of Jesus.

In the fourth century, Ash Wednesday came to be the start of the period of Lent. It was the seventh Wednesday before Easter. Christians had to wear sackcloth, a coarse cloth made of goat's hair. Wearing sackcloth and ashes was a sign of repentance in the Old Testament. The ashes were gathered from palm leaves. The palm leaves from the celebration of Palm Sunday were saved until the next year. They were burned to make ashes for the observance of Ash Wednesday. The ashes were placed on the forehead of the Christian.

Symbols of Resurrection

Many symbols have been used over the centuries to represent the death and resurrection of Jesus. In the early church these symbols were found on the walls of the catacombs—the burial places for early Christians who died in the Roman persecutions. Much of our early Christian art was found on these walls.

The Cross

Perhaps there is no better symbol of the resurrection than that of the cross. The cross represents the victory of Christ over sin and death. The early Christians used the cross to indicate that they were Christians. Crosses are found on the walls of the catacombs in Rome. Today, many churches use the cross behind the altar or the pulpit. It may also be placed on top of the steeple of the church. Some churches are built in the shape of a cross.

The Easter Lily

The Easter lily is a large white flower. Lilies grow all over the world. They symbolize the resurrection.

Lilies have also been a symbol of the purity of Eve when she left the Garden of Eden. As such, they have also represented the Virgin Mary.

The Phoenix

Originally, the phoenix was a pagan symbol. It came from ancient Greek mythology. The phoenix was a bird, like an eagle. It lived in Arabia and had colors of gold and red. There was only one of these birds alive at any one time. Every five hundred years it would burn itself on an altar. Then a new, young phoenix would arise out of the flames and live for another five hundred years. The early Christians took over the symbol and made it a symbol of eternal life. They saw the resurrection of Christ symbolized in the phoenix.

The Butterfly

The butterfly quickly became a symbol of the resurrection of Christ. The caterpillar enters the cocoon. Then it comes out of its cocoon

as a beautiful butterfly. Jesus came out of the tomb like the butterfly comes out of the cocoon.

Jonah

One of the favorite illustrations of the resurrection is the picture of Jonah. Since this is a biblical story, it was very popular. Jonah was in the belly of the great fish for a period of three days. On the third day Jonah came out of the fish on dry land. Jonah came back to life in a way similar to the way Jesus came out of the tomb.

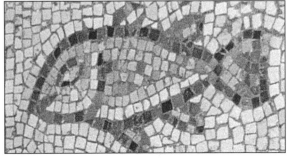

Ichthys

Ichthys was also a very early symbol of the risen Christ. In Greek, *ichthys* meant fish. The early

Christians used the sign of a fish to represent their Lord. The term included the first letters of the words, "Jesus Christ, Son of God, Savior." The symbol is still used by Christians today as a sign that they belong to Christ. It is often seen on cars.

Easter Eggs

The most common custom associated with Easter is the Easter egg. Eggs were a symbol of new life even in times before Christ. Christians adopted the symbol. In the Middle Ages eggs were not allowed to be eaten during Lent. That made the eggs more desirable at Easter. They were often colored and covered with beautiful designs. Then they were given as gifts.

Easter egg rolls became one way to celebrate Easter time. The roll of the egg symbolized the rolling back of the stone in front of the tomb where Jesus was buried. In 1878 President Rutherford Hayes started the practice of an Easter egg roll on the lawn of the White House in Washington DC. That practice has continued to the present. There was a period, between the years of 1942 to 1953, when the practice was briefly stopped.

THE PENTECOST

Pentecost (Acts 1–2)

Forty days after the resurrection, Jesus ascended to Heaven. Jesus gave the disciples their final instructions. They were to go into the world and teach the gospel. Jesus promised to give them the Holy Spirit, who would guide them to preach the gospel boldly.

Then Jesus rose into a cloud out of their sight. For the disciples that must have meant that He went into the cloud, which was the glory of God. Remember when God was with the people of Israel during the wandering in the wilderness. He appeared to them in a cloud that led them through the wilderness. The disciples would have known that and understood that Jesus had gone to be with God.

Certainly, the eleven apostles would have been there. In place of Judas, the disciples chose a man named Matthias. He would have been part of the small group. Along with them would have been the seventy described in Luke 10:1. Jesus' relatives also came to believe in Him. They would have been there. Altogether there were probably about 120 followers. They all gathered regularly to pray in the upper room. It may have been the same upper room in which they had eaten their last Passover meal with Jesus before the crucifixion.

Recall that before the Temple was destroyed in 70 AD, there were three great festivals in Jerusalem. Jewish people were required to attend all three. They were the Passover, Pentecost (or Feast of Weeks), and Tabernacles. Passover and Pentecost were celebrated in the spring. Pentecost came fifty days after Passover. The Feast of Tabernacles was celebrated in the fall. Both Pentecost and Tabernacles were harvest festivals to give thanks to God for the abundance of crops. To these festivals, the people brought their gifts and sacrifices to the Temple.

Pentecost (Acts 2:1–13)

During the Passover festival that year, Jesus had been crucified. Many of the one hundred thousand pilgrims returned to Jerusalem again for the festival of Pentecost. Pentecost came only ten days after Passover. In the Temple that morning the high priest, Caiaphas, would have waved two loaves of bread in front of the altar before the Lord. On the altar, he would have sacrificed two lambs that were without blemish. Then the Jewish men would have sung and danced before the Lord. This was the custom.

Meanwhile, the little band of disciples met together. They were engaged in prayer. Suddenly, there was a sound of rushing wind. Along with the wind came tongues of fire, which hovered over the heads of the disciples. It must have been an awesome sight!

Remember that in the Old Testament, when God appeared, there was usually fire. For example, Moses met God at the burning bush. The bush burned, but it was not consumed by the fire. Now, God's Spirit rested upon this little band of followers of Jesus. In that moment they changed from a group who feared the chief priests and the Pharisees to a bold group of witnesses for Jesus Christ.

With all of the people in Jerusalem for the festival, a crowd quickly gathered. Immediately, these disciples of Jesus began to tell the great works that God was doing. Their teaching and preaching was done in the languages of the foreigners who had come for the festival. The people were amazed! They could not understand how these plain Galileans could speak the languages of the many people who came from foreign countries. The Spirit of God gave the disciples boldness and the ability to speak in another language. Some of the people were not sure about this strange turn of events. They began to say that these people had drunk too much wine.

Peter's Sermon (Acts 2:14–47)

Then the apostle Peter stepped out and began to talk to the people who had gathered there. He told them that these people were not drunk with wine. It was only nine o'clock in the morning. Peter then began to witness to those things that the prophets had said long ago. He told them about the things that the prophet Joel had said. He showed them how evil men had taken Jesus and had crucified Him.

Next, Peter told about David's experience. He tied the death of Christ to the words of the great King David. He told them, "Therefore let all the house of Israel know with certainty that God has made this Jesus, whom you crucified, both Lord and Messiah!"

Many of the listeners were shaken. They realized that they had been guilty of missing the Messiah. They asked Peter and the rest of the apostles, "Brothers, what must we do?"

Peter replied, "Repent and be baptized each of you, in the name of Jesus the Messiah for the forgiveness of your sins, and you will receive the gift of the Holy Spirit." He continued to preach the message of repentance. Finally, Peter said, "Be saved from this corrupt generation!"

The writer Luke tells us that on that day three thousand persons accepted the message of Peter. They were baptized and joined the church in Jerusalem. They continued to study the Word of God and pray. They participated in the Lord's Supper.

Remember that many of these people had been in Jerusalem at the time that Jesus was crucified. Many of them had probably gone out to the tomb of Joseph of Arimathea. They saw with their own eyes the grave clothes from which Jesus had been resurrected. But it required Peter's explanation to convince them that they needed to repent and become part of the church in Jerusalem.

Pentecost still stands in the Christian church year but not as a feast of thanksgiving for the harvest. Pentecost is the birth of the New Testament church. Today each local church is part of that great company of believers who have become part of God's family, the Christian church in the world.

In the early church, Pentecost was celebrated as the close of the Easter season. The fifty days from Easter to Pentecost became known as the Great Fifty. The fifty days allowed a period of rejoicing at the resurrection of Jesus Christ from the dead and the birth of the church of Jesus Christ. When we become part of the church, we become part of that great company of believers down through the ages that love God, love each other, and witness of the saving faith in Jesus Christ.

Bible Geography

When we read the Bible, the stories come from very different lands and have very different custom from ours. As you read the Bible, you will want to look at the maps and read the text that tells about the maps. If you know where the stories happened, it will help you to better understand the stories. This section will help you to discover where the stories of the Bible took place.

The story of the Bible probably began somewhere in the Mesopotamian Valley. Bible scholars believe the Garden of Eden was located somewhere in that area. Mesopotamia is the land between the Tigris and Euphrates Rivers. If you look at the first map in this section, you can discover where the Mesopotamian Valley is located. It is also likely that the Tower of Babel was built somewhere on the plains in Mesopotamia. That was long ago, and we only have a very sketchy account in the Bible.

You may want to look at a globe or an encyclopedia and find where the Middle East is located on a world map. This area of the world is just as important today as it was in Bible times. The Middle East is the place where our Christian faith began. It is also the part of the world where Judaism and the religion of Islam began. Today Arabs, Jews, and Christians all claim parts of this very important area. The United Nations and the United States have tried to bring peace to this part of the world. So far they have not been very successful. You will want to understand the importance of this geographic area not only to better understand the Bible but also because so much of today's world news comes from this part of the world.

It is important for you to learn the names and places from the ancient world. What you learn in these elementary school years will be important for the rest of your life. To understand the Bible, you will need to have these geographic places in mind. Jewish faith and Christian faith are both related to Palestine. Jesus lived almost His entire life within the country of Palestine. We are called upon to take the message of the gospel to every country on earth. We will look at some other countries across the globe when we look at the missionary section in this volume.

In this section we will examine unique geographical features for some of the places that appear on the maps. The places we observe will be places that have some relation to the stories that are in the Bible.

Old Testament Geography
THE TRAVELS OF ABRAHAM

Before you begin reading this section about the travels of Abraham, you may want to reread the account of Abraham in the Bible section, Genesis 13–23.

Ur of the Chaldeans

Abraham grew up in the region of Mesopotamia (means "land between the rivers"). If you use a world map, this would be in present-day Iraq. Abraham was likely born and raised in the city of Ur of the Chaldeans. Look at the map. You will find Ur located near the Persian Gulf on the Euphrates River. In the surrounding area crops were grown. Farming was a primary occupation for many of the people of Ur. But Ur was no ordinary city. By the time of Abraham, Ur had become a big city. The streets of the city were twisted and turned without seeming to have a plan.

The homes of the people of Ur did have a plan. They were usually constructed of mud brick. There were two floors. The lower floor was used for entertaining and business functions. You would enter the house through the only door from the street. Inside was a room to welcome guests. The family lived on the upper floor. You would reach the family rooms by stairs. A courtyard was located in the middle of the house. It allowed the home adequate light during the daylight hours. Rainwater was collected, since water was scarce in that part of the world. At night, oil lamps served to light the home. Such houses were attractive and livable. There were some dangers, however. Snakes or scorpions often entered the homes. The size of the house varied according to the wealth of the family.

Religion was important to the people of Ur. The center of the city had a large ziggurat, or temple tower. The people of Ur worshiped over four thousand gods. In addition, they feared the demons and other evil gods they believed were intending to hurt them. The people had statues they would place in the entrances of their houses to ward off the demons and other evil gods. Their religion was one of fear. Everything was done to try to prevent the gods from hurting them. One of the main gods worshiped in Ur was Sin, the moon god. With all the gods, there was a very large group of priests who served the gods. Joshua wrote (Joshua 24:2) that Abraham's father Terah worshiped the many gods of Ur. But Abraham was called by the true God, Jehovah, to worship Jehovah God alone. Abraham obeyed God.

ZIGGURATS

Ziggurats were buildings that were built on a large base. Additional platforms were then built on top of the base to form a kind of pyramid. At the top of the ziggurat a temple was built to the god. In Ur, the god was Marduk.

The City of Haran

From what we can learn from the ancient writings, the city of Ur went through a period of political unrest. There were battles fought by local leaders and other battles fought by persons outside the area. It may have been this political unrest that caused Terah to decide to take his family away from Ur. They traveled north along the Euphrates River. They were headed for Canaan, according to Genesis 11:31. Canaan is present-day Palestine. But as they traveled north, they decided to settle in Haran instead. (Find Haran on the map located on page 112.)

The name *Haran* suggests that it was a "caravan route." That means that the caravans of camels and traders would come from lower Mesopotamia through Haran. Other caravans of traders would come from the north and some from Palestine and Egypt. This was an important place for traders from all directions. It was located on the trade routes that crossed the "Fertile Crescent." (A crescent is a half-moon, between the full and new moon phases. It carries the idea of a half circle with both concave and convex edges). Look at the map and with your finger trace the area from Ur, north to Haran, and then south along the Mediterranean coast to Egypt. The Fertile Crescent is not desert area but land that is watered and on which crops may be raised. It is also an area through which traders take their caravans and sell their goods in the cities of Egypt or to the cities of Mesopotamia.

Haran is an ancient city, like Ur. Haran is located on the edge of the Mesopotamian civilization. The chief god of Haran was Sin, the moon god. This god would have been familiar to Terah and may have been one of the reasons why he decided to settle in Haran. Recall that Laban and his family continued to live in Haran. Later, Abraham sent his servant to Haran to the home of Laban. Jacob married Rebekah, sister of Laban. Rebekah left Haran and came back to Palestine with the servant to marry Isaac. Years later, Rebekah helped Jacob deceive his

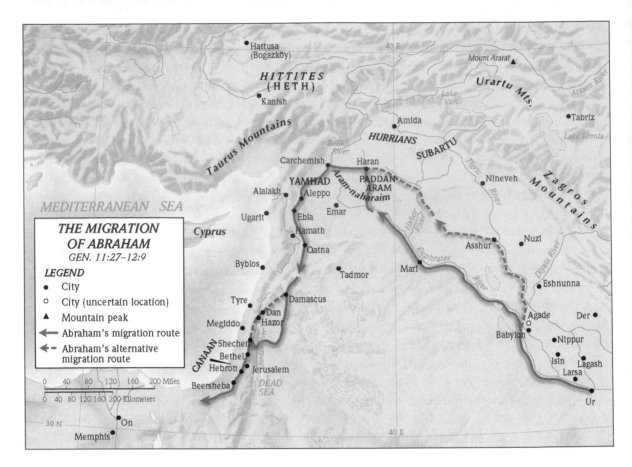

THE MIGRATION
OF ABRAHAM
GEN. 11:27–12:9

LEGEND

- City
- ○ City (uncertain location)
- ▲ Mountain peak
- ← Abraham's migration route
- ←– Abraham's alternative migration route

father and give the blessing for the oldest son to Jacob instead of Esau. Esau was so angry that Rebekah sent Jacob away to Laban's home. Jacob fell in love with Rachel. Laban made him work fourteen years to receive her as his bride.

Abraham in Egypt

God called Abraham to the Promised Land. Soon after arriving in the Promised Land of Palestine, the crops failed. There was famine in the land. Abraham gathered his family and went to Egypt. Recall in the biblical accounts that Sarah was beautiful. Pharaoh tried to take her into his palace. But God intervened and prevented that from happening. Pharaoh sent Abraham away with greater riches than what Abraham had brought. Upon his return to Palestine, Abraham built an altar to God at Bethel. Find Bethel on the map. Abraham settled near there.

Sodom and Gomorrah

You may recall this event from Genesis 13. Abraham and Lot came to a point where their flocks were too large, so they had to separate. Abraham told Lot to choose whatever land area he would like. Abraham agreed to go in another direction. Lot chose the best land along the plain of Jordan. He settled near the cities of Sodom and Gomorrah. Sodom was located at the southern tip of the Dead Sea. Gomorrah was located slightly to the east of Sodom.

There is an account in Genesis 14 of several kings from Mesopotamia coming south along the Fertile Crescent to conquer Sodom. It is likely they came south to Sodom because there are no metal deposits in Mesopotamia. Copper is found in the Dead Sea and is mined there. Copper was used during this time to make weapons for war. Copper was also used for farm equipment. If the kings could defeat Sodom, they would be able to supply their need for copper. Lot was in serious danger. Abraham came to Lot's rescue, and the kings were defeated and had to return to their homeland.

Then in Genesis 18–19 we find that the people of Sodom and Gomorrah were very wicked. They did not follow God's rules. God did not believe they would change their sinful ways. Therefore, God decided to destroy both cities. When the angels of the Lord came to warn Lot and his family, men from the city wanted to harm them. God struck the men of the city with blindness. Then destruction rained down from heaven. Fire destroyed the two cities. Unfortunately, Lot's wife looked back at the city even though she was warned not to by the angels. She was turned into a pillar of salt. Lot and his two daughters escaped.

THE PROMISE TO ABRAHAM

Abraham and his wife, Sarah, were growing older. They did not have any children. But God promised to provide Abraham and Sarah with a family. As the years passed, nothing happened. Sarah was beyond the age of bearing children. God's promise did not seem as if it would come to pass.

Abraham wanted to leave his vast wealth to a son. Since he did not have a son, he followed the laws of the land. He planned to take one of his servants, Eliezer, and make him his heir. God stopped Abraham.

Years passed and there was no sign of Sarah having a baby. Sarah gave her maid Hagar to Abraham. Hagar had a son, Ishmael. Ishmael became the father of a large group of nomads (wanderers). The Bible does not give us many details about the family of Ishmael.

God finally showed His power, and Sarah had her own son, Isaac. Isaac became the father of Jacob and Esau. Jacob took the birthright from Esau. Later, with the help of his mother, Jacob also took the blessing away from Esau. Jacob had to flee

for his life. Years later Jacob and Esau again cared for each other as brothers.

The line of the family was now set. Abraham was the father of the Hebrew people. Isaac was also blessed by God. He lived in the land of Palestine. His son Jacob became the next in line. Jacob lived in Palestine until there was famine in the land. His son Joseph had become second to Pharaoh in Egypt. Jacob and his family migrated to Egypt and settled in the land of Goshen. For the next four hundred years, the people of Israel lived in Goshen. In the next map we will watch their Exodus from Egypt to return to the Promised Land of Palestine and settle there.

TENT OF A NOMAD
Abraham lived in a tent like this illustration. The tent was portable. Abraham could move from place to place and take his home with him.

MOSES, JOSHUA, AND THE EXODUS

Before you study the map and read the text in this section, you may want to return to the Children's Bible section in this handbook and read the sections from the Book of Exodus.

Life in Egypt

Egypt is an ancient land with a long and powerful history. Egypt is a land that is about the combined size of the states of Connecticut and Massachusetts. It depends upon the Nile River for its livelihood. The Nile is one of the longest rivers in the world. It flows from within Africa and brings rich soil from the south. Life in Egypt lies along the Nile. Each year the Nile overflows its banks, which brings rich soil to the banks along the river. The Nile also waters the land for farming. Villages grew up along the river. People would leave their homes in the villages each morning to care for the barley or other crops that grew along the river.

Only a united country with a central government could gain control over the flow of the river. There were many such groups who ruled the country during its long history. Pharaoh was successful in uniting Egypt. From the time of Joseph, Pharaoh owned all the land. But the people paid their taxes and were able to continue to farm their land. The Egyptians did not like the cattle and sheepherding of the nomads to the east. They tried to keep the bedouin tribes out of Egypt. Since many came from the east, in times of strength, the Egyptians kept them out. At other times the sheepherders would come and settle in the Delta region at the northern part of Egypt, where the Nile flowed into the Mediterranean Sea.

The Egyptians worshiped many gods. Among those gods were the pharaohs, whom the people believed were also gods. Much effort went into the preparation of tombs for the pharaohs. The Egyptians believed they would live after death in a way similar to the way they had lived on earth. For the pharaoh, that meant that he had to be buried with his wives and a food supply. For that reason the pyramids were built. The Egyptians would wrap the bodies to create what was called mummies. Many of those mummies have been found in the pyramids and may be seen in museums today.

Many of the Hebrew people were shepherds. The Egyptians did not want them to raise their sheep and live along the river where the Egyptians lived. The Hebrew people were kept in the land of Goshen. Goshen is located in the Delta region. (Find Goshen on the map.) Over the four hundred years that passed since the people of Israel came to Egypt, several different pharaohs came to the throne. By the time of Moses, the pharaoh on the throne did not like the growth of the people of Israel. He made every effort to try to slow their growth, and he made them his slaves to build his pyramids. Life for the people of Israel was painful, so they cried out to God to help them.

THE LIFE OF MOSES

Pharaoh was still trying to stop the growth of the Israelites. He wanted all male babies to be killed. Moses was born, and when he was too old for his mother to conceal him, she had his older sister, Miriam, place him in a basket. Pharaoh's daughter found the baby and took him into the palace. Miriam asked Pharaoh's daughter if she would like her to find a nurse for the infant. Miriam brought the baby's mother to care for him. The princess adopted the child, and she called him Moses, meaning "drawn out of the water."

Moses learned about the Israelites from his mother. Moses also learned the arts of the Egyptians. He had the best education a child could have in Egypt. But when he became an adult, he saw one of the Egyptians beating an Israelite. Moses killed the Egyptian. Moses was afraid Pharaoh would hear about what he had done, so Moses had to flee for his life. He went to the desert and there met and married Zipporah. Her father accepted him into their home, and Moses tended the flocks of Jethro. Moses learned the desert region.

God called Moses from a burning bush on Mount Sinai. At first Moses did not want to take the leadership of the people of Israel to bring them out of Egypt. However, God persuaded Moses to obey Him. God sent Moses and Aaron, Moses' brother, to Pharaoh. Ten plagues were brought upon the people of Egypt. Each of the plagues opposed one of the gods of Egypt. Jehovah God showed the Egyptians that their gods were powerless against Him. Finally, the angel of death came upon the people of Egypt, and all the firstborn of children and animals died. Then Pharaoh let the people of Israel go.

THE TEN PLAGUES

1. Water to blood—*Exodus 7:14–25*
2. Frogs—*Exodus 8:1–15*
3. Gnats—*Exodus 8:16–19*
4. Flies—*Exodus 8:20–22*
5. Plague on the cattle—*Exodus 9:1–7*
6. Boils—*Exodus 9:8–12*
7. Hail—*Exodus 9:13–25*
8. Locusts—*Exodus 10:1–20*
9. Darkness—*Exodus 10:21–29*
10. Death of the first born—*Exodus 11:1–12:30*

THE EXODUS

The people of Israel left Egypt quickly. They were not organized, so when the trip became difficult, they complained. (Look at the map to see the route they took as they left Egypt.) After they had been gone for a period of time, Pharaoh decided that he wanted the slaves to return. He gathered troops and rode against the people of Israel. The people soon had reports that Pharaoh was chasing them. They complained even more and feared that they would be destroyed. Moses told them not to fear, but to trust the Lord. He waved his rod over the sea, and the waters parted. The Israelites passed over on dry land. Finally, Pharaoh and his men came to the sea and started across. Moses waved his rod again, and the waters returned. All of the Egyptians were killed.

Several weeks passed and the people again complained to Moses and Aaron because of a lack of food. They went to God, and He provided manna (which means, "What is it?") from heaven. God gave the people clear instructions about how they were to gather the manna. They were not allowed to take too much. Nor were they allowed to gather manna on the Sabbath Day. For the next forty years manna provided food for the people of Israel.

At Rephidim, the Amalekites fought against the people of Israel. Joshua led the battle for the Israelites. Moses extended his arms toward heaven. When he lowered his arms, the Amalekites were successful. When he raised his arms, the Israelites were defeating the Amalekites. God was teaching the people of Israel that they needed to depend totally on Him. When they did, they were able to defeat the enemy.

Finally, the people of Israel reached Mount Sinai. Reread the account of their appearance before God in Exodus 19 and 20. God made His covenant with the people. They agreed to obey God. At Mount Sinai the people of Israel became a nation. But as soon as the people left Sinai, they began to complain about the lack of meat in their diet. God provided quail, which are small birds, for them to eat.

Kadesh Barnea

The cloud of God's presence guided the people of Israel away from Mount Sinai. They traveled through wilderness of Paran for the next eleven days. At the northern end of this wilderness they came to a city, Kadesh Barnea. The people set up their tents and camped there.

Moses sent spies out to look at the land. When the spies returned, they had good news and bad news. The good news was that the land was as special as they had been told. It was a land that was flowing with "milk and honey." This meant that there was good land for them to raise their crops. The bad news was that the people who lived in the land were very powerful. Their cities were walled

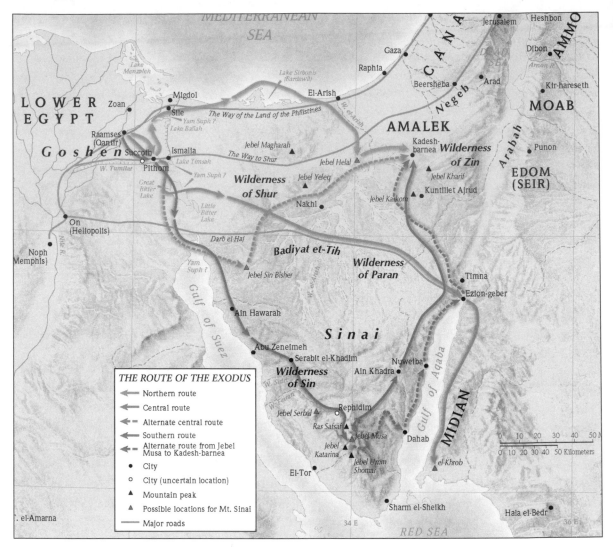

THE ROUTE OF THE EXODUS

⟵ Northern route
⟵ Central route
⟵ – Alternate central route
⟵ Southern route
⟵ – Alternate route from Jebel Musa to Kadesh-barnea
• City
○ City (uncertain location)
▲ Mountain peak
▲ Possible locations for Mt. Sinai
— Major roads

and well defended. Only Joshua and Caleb wanted to trust God to lead the people into the land and claim it for Israel.

God had delivered the people of Israel from the Egyptians. Why could God not deliver them from these people? They did not believe they could trust God. They even thought of choosing a new leader and did not even trust Moses.

God became angry with the people. He punished the spies, and many died. Moses prayed for the people, and the rest were spared. God said that none of the people over age twenty would enter the Promised Land except Joshua and Caleb.

Since they had failed to obey God, a group of Israelites set out to fight. But God was not with the Israelites. The Canaanites came out and defeated the Israelites.

For the next thirty-eight years the people of Israel camped at Kadesh Barnea. A group of Israelites, led by Korah, tried to take the leadership away from Moses and Aaron. God told Moses to place twelve rods in the Tabernacle for each of the twelve tribes of Israel. The one that budded would identify God's choice. Only Aaron's rod budded. This rod was placed in the Tabernacle, meaning the priests would come from the family of Aaron. The Levites would assist the priests. Korah and his followers died along with all who wanted to follow him.

Entering the Land of Palestine

After the many years encamped at Kadesh Barnea, the day finally came to move. Imagine how excited the people must have been. At last they were going to enter the Promised Land. Most of these people had not been alive when the Lord brought the people out of Egypt. Remember that Joshua and Caleb were spared and would enter the Promised Land.

There was a water shortage. Moses was so angry at these people for their disobedience to God, he struck the rock that God had told him to strike. But his anger at the people caused him to strike the rock too hard. Water poured out of the rock. God told Moses that he could not enter the Promised Land because of his anger.

During this time, Moses' sister Miriam and brother Aaron both died of old age. God led the people down to Ezion-geber. (Find it on the map. It is at the northern end of the Gulf of Aqaba.) God wanted the people to avoid a fight with the peoples of Edom and Moab. The Israelites became angry with Moses, and many were killed by serpents. Moses prayed for the people. God told Moses to raise a brass serpent on a pole. All who looked on the serpent were spared death.

As they traveled north, two Canaanite kings refused to allow the people of Israel to pass through their land. The Israelite army defeated them and then camped south of the Dead Sea.

The Moabites were another group who wanted to get rid of the Israelites. Balak, king of Moab, sent for Balaam. Balaam was known for placing a curse on people. When Balaam got to the mountaintop and looked down on the people of Israel, God would only let Balaam bless the people of Israel. When Balaam could not curse the people, he told Balak to trap some of the people of Israel to sin against God. Balak did this. God became angry, and many of the Israelites died in a plague.

From there the people went around Moab and camped on the east side of the Jordan River. Moses knew that his time was soon to end. God told Moses to set Joshua apart to lead the people into the Promised Land. Then God allowed Moses to go to a mountain and look across the Jordan River at the Promised Land before he died.

Crossing the River Jordan

Some of the tribes of Israel wanted to settle on the east side of the Jordan. But most of the people wanted to settle on the west side. To do that, Jericho was the first city that the people had to conquer. Jericho was the gateway to the hills on the west side of the Jordan River.

Two spies were sent to look at the city of Jericho. The people of Jericho began looking for the spies. Rahab hid the spies in her house and asked the men to promise to keep her and her family safe when the Israelites came to overtake the city. She sent the men of Jericho along the river to find the spies. Meanwhile, Rahab helped the spies to get away and hide in the mountains. The Israelites kept their promise. Rehab and her family were spared and joined the people of Israel.

Joshua led the people across the Jordan River. God allowed the river to be stopped temporarily. However it happened, the people were able to cross the river on dry land. They built a pile of stones on the west bank, one for each of the twelve tribes of Israel.

God wanted the people of Israel to know that He was the Conqueror. He had the people of Israel march around the walls of Jericho once each day for seven days. On the seventh day they marched seven times. At the end they blew the ram's horn and shouted. The walls of the city fell. The people of Israel defeated Jericho.

This brought fear to the other Canaanite peoples. Joshua led the people of Israel to conquer most of the remaining areas of Palestine. Joshua helped each of the tribes find a place to settle. Only a few places, like Jerusalem, were held by the people of the land.

For the next several hundred years the judges ruled Israel.

SAUL, THE FIRST KING OF ISRAEL

Before you begin this study of David, Solomon, and the later kingdom, you may want to read the section from Samuel through Solomon mentioned earlier in the Children's Bible section of this handbook.

The people of Israel were no longer satisfied with the judges to rule over them. They wanted a king. It was difficult for the twelve tribes of Israel to fight against the threat of the Philistines. (Philistia is located along the Mediterranean Sea. Find it on the map.) Samuel was God's prophet. Samuel prayed to God. God said that Samuel should anoint Saul as king of Israel. Samuel anointed Saul as king in secret.

Saul's first test came when the men of Jabesh Gilead sent out cries for help. They were being attacked by the Ammonite king and his army. Saul and many from the tribes of Israel answered the call. They saved the men of Jabesh Gilead, and Saul was easily installed as king.

Saul set up his palace at Gibeah. (Find Jabesh Gilead (on the western bank of the Jordan River) and Gibeah (located north of the city of Jerusalem) on the map. Notice that the country of Ammon is located very near Jabesh Gilead.) Saul's early years were good because he obeyed the Lord.

Saul was not interested in making the borders of Israel bigger. He only wanted to protect the country as it was. Saul reigned for forty years. Later in his reign, Saul stopped listening to the Lord or to Samuel, God's prophet. He began to do things the way he wanted to do them, not the way God wanted Saul to do them. God became angry with Saul and told Samuel that Saul would not remain as king.

DAVID ANOINTED TO BE KING

Time passed, and God told Samuel to go to the home of Jesse in Bethlehem. (Find Bethlehem on the map. It is near Jerusalem.) God told Samuel

that he was to anoint one of Jesse's sons to be king over Israel. Samuel called for all the sons of Jesse to appear before him. God told Samuel that these were not the ones. Samuel asked Jesse if he had any other sons. David was out tending the sheep. Jesse called him home. God told Samuel to anoint David king.

That must have angered his brothers, because they treated him badly. Some time later, Saul was on the battlefield. A giant from the Philistines named Goliath was threatening the armies of the Lord. Goliath stood more than nine feet tall. He promised to kill anyone who came out to face him. None of the Israelites wanted to fight Goliath.

David came to the battle to bring his brothers some food. When he saw the armies facing each other and Goliath threatening the army of Israel, David decided to go and fight the giant himself. Saul must have been tired of the days of waiting and agreed to let David fight.

David went to battle with Goliath not with amor and a spear but with his sling and stones. He had used the sling many times to protect the sheep, killing both lions and bears. Goliath made fun of this boy coming out against him. But David bravely told Goliath that he came in the name of the Lord. David aimed the stone in his sling for the forehead of the giant. Goliath fell dead on the spot. David cut off his head. The armies of Israel chased the Philistines and won the day.

David became popular with the people of Israel. Saul was not happy that David was so popular with his people. He soon wanted to get rid of David, so David had to flee for his life. He went down to the city of Gath among the Philistines. David fought for their king against the Amalekites who were also enemies of Israel.

Meanwhile, Saul and his armies fought against the Philistines. They lost the battle, and Saul died that day.

DAVID BECOMES KING

Saul's son, Ishbosheth became king in Mahanaim in Gilead. You can find Gilead and the city of Mahanaim on the east bank of Jordan, above the River Jabbok, in the northern part of Israel. David became king of Judah in the city of Hebron. (Hebron is located south of Jerusalem on the map.) What had been a unified Israel was now in civil war. After several years, Ishbosheth was killed. David moved quickly to strengthen his position. He was proclaimed king over all Israel.

It was important for David to find a capital for the whole country. He did not want to settle in the areas that had been controlled by Saul. David sent his general, Joab, to conquer Jerusalem. Jerusalem was controlled by Canaanite people, the Jebusites. A long siege of the city was needed. Finally, Joab and his men went in to the city at night. They entered the city through a water shaft. Then they opened the gates, and David's army took over the city. Jerusalem became the new capital for Israel.

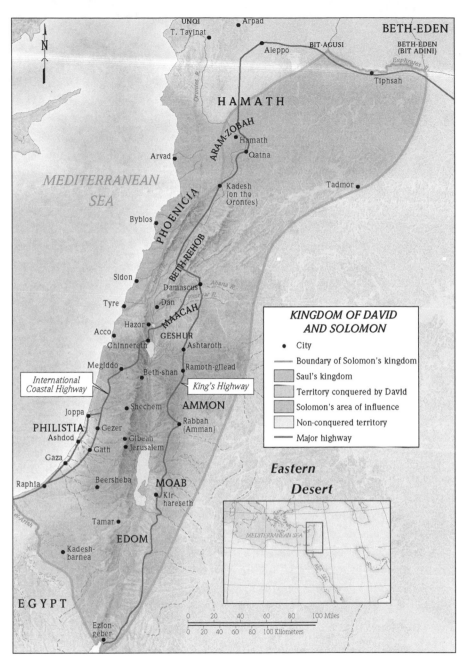

KINGDOM OF DAVID AND SOLOMON

- • City
- —— Boundary of Solomon's kingdom
- Saul's kingdom
- Territory conquered by David
- Solomon's area of influence
- Non-conquered territory
- —— Major highway

David built his palace there. David wanted to build a temple to the Lord to place the Ark of the Covenant. God told David he had fought too much. The king who followed David, his son Solomon, would build the House of the Lord.

David started with a small kingdom and gradually expanded it. David brought all of the twelve tribes together. His armies defeated the Philistines,

119

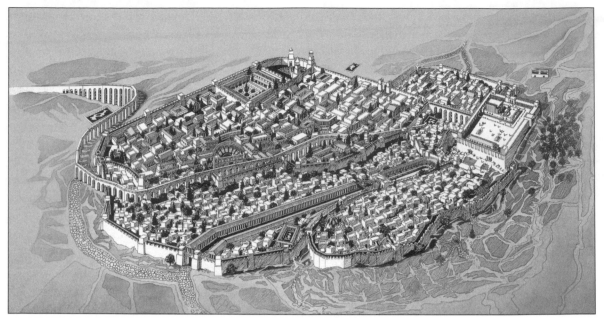

View of Jerusalem from the southwest during the time of David (1000 to 962 BC). This view shows the Tabernacle in the upper right section. David's palace overlooks the Tabernacle. The fortress is in the center.

who had to pay money to David. He was able to bring the Edomites, Ammonites, Moabites, and Arameans into his kingdom. David made treaties with the Phoenicians. His kingdom stretched from Ezion Geber on the Gulf of Aqaba in the south to Lebo Hamath in the north.

You will recall from reading the Bible passages about David that he sinned against God. As much as David loved God, he made some bad choices. Eventually, David repented of his sin. His family struggled with serious problems. For example, David's son Absalom tried to take the kingdom away from his father.

David grew old and had to give up his kingdom. His wife Bathsheba kept after David until he agreed to let their son Solomon become king after he died. David gave his son a much larger kingdom than he received. After David's death there was peace in the kingdom. During David and Solomon's reigns, this was a most important time in the life of Israel.

SOLOMON BECOMES KING

Solomon started his reign by asking the Lord for wisdom. With wisdom, God also gave Solomon wealth. In the first part of his reign, Solomon was a good king. He made agreements with other countries, such as Egypt. Solomon even married the daughter of Pharaoh to keep peace with Egypt.

Solomon established trade with distant countries. From the north, he received horses, grain, wine, oils, and timber. Some of the other countries were forced to pay Solomon large sums of money each year. From the south, Solomon received monkeys, parrots, gold, ivory, special woods, jewels, perfumes, and spices. From Egypt, he received chariots. Solomon was able to make Israel a prosperous nation. To his own people, though, he was hard. The people had to pay heavy taxes that were often too heavy to bear. This caused Solomon to have some enemies.

Solomon built a large palace for himself. He also built a palace for the daughter of Pharaoh. Then he built the Temple to the Lord. The Temple would house the Ark of the Covenant. The Ark no longer was moved from place to place. Remember that the Ark of the Covenant originally contained the Ten Commandments, Aaron's budding rod, and a golden pot of manna. It is believed that the rod and manna were lost when the Ark was taken captive by the Philistines. The tablets of stone, however, of the Ten Commandments were the symbol of the Jewish faith. They were the agreement that God made with the Israelites that they would be His people. Wherever the Ark was, the presence of God was there also.

Solomon's Temple was magnificent and large. It was built of white limestone with two large bronze pillars at the door. At the opening of the Temple was an outer room. In the main sanctuary, the floor, walls, and ceilings were covered with cypress wood. In the sanctuary were the table of shewbread, an incense altar, and stairs that led to the most sacred room in the Temple—the Holy of Holies. This part of the Temple was only entered once a year by the high priest. He brought a sacrifice for the sins of the people on the Day of Atonement. Outside the sanctuary was the large altar of sacrifice and the laver, or basin of water, for the cleansing of the priests.

Toward the end of Solomon's long forty-year reign, he did not continue to follow the Lord God. Instead, Solomon married many wives from other lands. They worshiped the gods from their homelands. They urged Solomon to worship their gods too. The Lord God became angry with Solomon, but God promised not to take the kingdom away from him because of David. After Solomon died, the kingdom would be taken from Solomon's family.

THE DIVIDED KINGDOM

Solomon's son, Rehoboam, came to the throne. He became king in Judah. When he traveled to the north to Shechem, he told the elders of the northern tribes that he would be meaner than Solomon.

The elders from the northern kingdom refused to accept Rehoboam as king. They turned to Jeroboam. Jeroboam had opposed Solomon and lived in Egypt until Solomon died. Shechem became the capital of the northern kingdom, which was known as Samaria.

The northern kingdom made up the ten tribes of Israel located in the north. In the northern kingdom there was no family line on the throne. All of the kings were evil. They set up worship of the god Baal. There were prophets to the people of Samaria. Prophets were godly men who received a message from God. But the kingdom only became worse. God finally allowed the Assyrians to take the people of Samaria into captivity about seven hundred years before Jesus. The people from the northern ten tribes married foreigners in the strange land where they were taken. As a group, they never returned to Samaria.

The southern kingdom of Judah was different. It was made up of two tribes, Judah and Benjamin. The family line of David stayed on the throne. Some of the kings were evil and followed other gods. Others worshiped the Lord Jehovah. The southern kingdom also had prophets who warned of destruction if the people did not follow God. The southern kingdom was finally taken captive by the nation of Babylon one hundred twenty years after Samaria fell.

The people of Judah repented of their sin. They lived in Babylon, but they hoped to return to Judah. Seventy years later some of the people did return. Many stayed in their new home, but many others returned to Jerusalem and Judah. They followed God's commands. They did not marry outside of the people of Judah. Because they came from Judah, they became known as Jews.

The people of Judah rebuilt the Temple. They established a new life in Judah. They longed to be rid of foreign rulers, like the Syrians. For a while they were able to be free. But it did not last long, as the Romans took over Palestine.

New Testament Geography

THE PUBLIC MINISTRY OF JESUS

Before you begin this study of the public ministry of Jesus, you may want to read the sections of the Children's Bible from the Gospels on the life and ministry of Jesus. We will not examine the birth and crucifixion narratives in this section. They were covered under "Christmas" in the section on the church year. We cannot cover all of the experiences of Jesus. We will select some examples from each period of His ministry.

The Early Ministry of Jesus

Jesus was about thirty when He began His public ministry. John the Baptist was already preaching about repentance. He was baptizing all who wanted to repent and follow the Lord.

The Baptism (Matthew 3:13–17)

Jesus traveled from Galilee to meet John the Baptist at the River Jordan. The location was probably just north of the Dead Sea. Jesus came to John to be baptized. John did not want to baptize Jesus, but Jesus said, "Allow it for now, because this is the way for us to fulfill all righteousness" (Matthew 3:15). After He was baptized a voice from heaven declared,

"This is My beloved Son.
I take delight in Him!" (Matthew 3:17)

From there Jesus was led by the Spirit into the wilderness. The wilderness was located in the desert to the east of the Jordan River and just north of the Dead Sea. For forty days Jesus was in the wilderness. The devil tempted Jesus.

The Temptation (Matthew 4:1–11)

Satan saw that Jesus was hungry. He said to Jesus if you are the Son of God, you should turn the stones into bread. Jesus quoted Scripture, "It is written: Man must not live on bread alone, but on every word that comes from the mouth of God" (Matthew 4:4). This temptation was similar to the one for Adam and Eve. Jesus did not fall to the evil one.

Next, the devil took Jesus to the top of the Temple. Again, he said to Jesus, if You are the Son of God, You could cast yourself down, and the angels will come to Your rescue. Jesus answered with, "It is also written: You just not tempt the Lord Your God." (Matthew 4:7). Jesus refused to show His power foolishly.

In the last temptation Satan took Jesus to see all the kingdoms of the world. He told Jesus that he would give all those to Jesus if Jesus would bow down and worship him. Jesus told him, "Go away, Satan! For it is written: You must worship the Lord Your God, and you must serve Him only" (Matthew 4:10). Satan was telling Jesus that he could give all the kingdoms of the world to Jesus. Jesus could avoid the cross and the suffering. It would be an easy way out. But if Jesus had followed Satan, we would not have salvation and hope.

THE MOUNT OF TEMPTATION OF JESUS
This view shows the Mount of Temptation, photographed from the Old Testament city of Jericho.

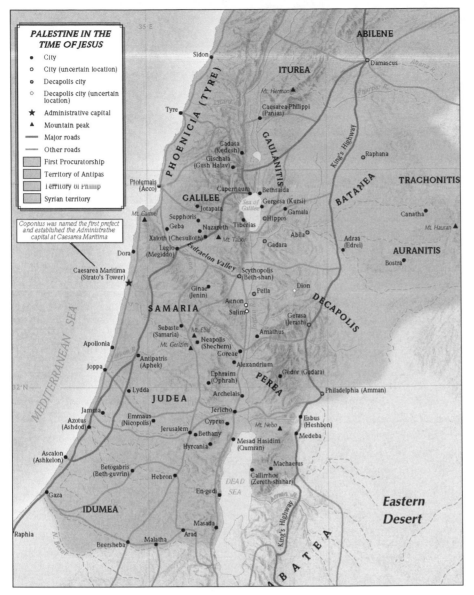

The map legend reads:

PALESTINE IN THE TIME OF JESUS

- • City
- ○ City (uncertain location)
- ▣ Decapolis city
- ○ Decapolis city (uncertain location)
- ★ Administrative capital
- ▲ Mountain peak
- — Major roads
- — Other roads
- First Procuratorship
- Territory of Antipas
- Territory of Philip
- Syrian territory

Coponius was named the first prefect and established the Administrative capital at Caesarea Maritima

Cleansing the Temple (John 2:13–22)

Jesus went to Jerusalem to celebrate the first Passover of His ministry. He walked through the Temple, where people were selling animals for sacrifice. There were also money changers in the Temple. Jesus became angry and threw over their tables. He told them that they would not make His Father's house a marketplace. He drove them out of the Temple.

Witness to Nicodemus (John 3:1–21)

Many people saw the miracles that Jesus performed. They believed in Him, though Jesus was not yet well-known.

While Jesus was still in Jerusalem, Nicodemus came to Jesus secretly. Nicodemus was one of the ruling group, the Sanhedrin. Jesus told Nicodemus that to find the kingdom of God, he must be born again. Nicodemus did not fully understand. He thought that Jesus was talking about physical birth. Jesus used the illustration of the serpent that was raised by Moses in the wilderness to save the people from the serpent bites. He was comparing it to Himself; He must be lifted up for people to have eternal life.

The Wedding at Cana (John 2:1–11)

Jesus began to call some of His disciples. Then He left Judea to travel north back to Galilee. When He got back home, His mother asked Him to come to a wedding at Cana. Find Cana in Galilee on the map. Perhaps it was a relative of the family since she asked Jesus to go too. The host of the feast discovered there was not more wine. Mary asked Jesus to help and he performed His first miracle. He turned the water in the large jugs to wine. By doing His first miracle at a wedding feast, Jesus blessed the home.

Witness to the Woman of Samaria (John 4:1–42)

On His way back to Galilee, Jesus went through Samaria. Recall that the Samaritans did not obey God and married persons who were not Israelites. The Jews and the Samaritans did not have much relationship with each other. Look at the map. Many times the Jews would go from Jerusalem to Perea and north to Decapolis on the east side of the Jordan River. They would avoid going through Samaria on their way to Galilee.

But Jesus went straight through Samaria. He stopped at Sychar. (Find the town on the map. It is on the west side of the Jordan River in Samaria.) The disciples went to the town to buy food. Jesus met a woman at the well and began talking to her. She understood Jesus to be the Messiah. She went to the town and brought other persons to Jesus. They wanted Him to stay with them, so He stayed two days and preached to them.

THE GALILEAN MINISTRY

The popularity of Jesus grew. During this year of His ministry, all of Palestine came to know about Jesus. We cannot recount all of the events of this period. Some examples will suggest why Jesus became so popular.

Healing the Nobleman's Son (John 4:46–54)

Jesus went back to Cana. Remember the town where Jesus performed His first miracle of turning the water into wine. This time there was a royal official whose son was very sick. He came to Jesus and begged Jesus to come to his home and heal his son. Jesus told him to go home. His boy would live and recover. This miracle showed those who were watching that Jesus had power over life. He could answer the man's request even at a distance.

Capernaum (Mark 1:16–45)

Capernaum became the home of Jesus for the rest of His Galilean ministry. Capernaum was a busy center for trade. (Find Capernaum on the map. It is along the western shore of Lake Galilee.) Jesus had been rejected in His hometown of Nazareth. But in Capernaum, He preached in the synagogue, and His message was accepted. He also was able to heal the sick. Along the shore, Jesus found four of His disciples. They were Peter, James, Andrew, and John. They left their fishing business on the lake and followed Jesus. The Galilean ministry was very successful. Jesus' popularity grew as people heard about the miracles that He performed and heard His preaching.

The Sermon on the Mount (Matthew 5–7)

Jesus spent His time carefully preparing His disciples and a large group of people who joined Him along the shore of Galilee. The Sermon on the Mount gave those who followed Him an understanding of the kingdom of God. In the sermon Jesus began by telling what kind of person God wants in His kingdom. Then Jesus went on to teach about the Law of Moses. God expects more than just outward behavior. He is interested in our hearts. If a follower of Jesus holds anger, hatred, or jealousy, that is not pleasing to God.

Jesus concluded the Sermon on the Mount by comparing two kinds of persons. One was like the house built on sand. When the storm came, the house could not stand. The other person built his house on the rock. When the storm came, the house stood firm. Those who follow Jesus should

THE MOUNT OF THE BEATITUDES
This view shows the Mount of the Beatitudes, where Jesus delivered the Sermon on the Mount.

build firmly on the foundation of being the kind of person who pleases God. The only way we can become such a person is if we know, understand, and practice God's Word.

THE SEA OF GALILEE
This view shows the Sea of Galilee from the northwest.

Jesus Calms the Storm (Mark 4:35–41)
Jesus had ministered to the people for long hours. He was very tired. The disciples got into a boat on the Sea of Galilee. Jesus fell asleep in the boat. A great storm gathered and overtook the little boat. The disciples woke Jesus up. They asked Him whether He cared that they were about to die in the storm. Jesus told the sea to become calm. The disciples were amazed when the sea did just as He said.

Jesus Sent the Disciples Out Two by Two (Mark 6:6–13)
Jesus wanted to teach the disciples to minister in His name. He also had compassion on the people who seemed to be sheep without a shepherd. He prepared the disciples; then He sent them out to teach in the villages and towns. They were able to heal persons who had diseases, and they preached about the kingdom of God. Jesus wanted to give the disciples experience in ministering in His name. One day they would need to have this kind of experience to teach, preach, and heal.

The Feeding of the Five Thousand (John 6:1–14)
The disciples came back from their experiences preaching to the people. They told Jesus what had happened. Jesus was so busy and did not have time to eat. He told the disciples that together they should put out onto the lake and head for a place to rest. Crowds had gathered. They saw where Jesus was going, and they followed along the shore.

Jesus had compassion on the crowds. He healed the sick persons among them. He taught them, but the time passed quickly. The dinner hour had come, but there was nothing to eat. Jesus told the disciples to go to the city and buy bread. But the disciples said they could not buy that much food. Then Jesus asked them to find anyone who had food. The disciples found a boy who had five loaves and three fishes and brought him to Jesus.

Jesus asked for the boy's lunch. When He received it, Jesus blessed it and gave it to the disciples to give to the hungry people. All were fed, and the disciples picked up what was left. There were twelve baskets of food left over. Jesus had performed one of His great miracles for the people because He had compassion on them.

Confession of Peter (Mark 8:27–38)
The disciples had seen Jesus heal the sick. They had seen Jesus preach and teach about the kingdom of God. The disciples had seen Jesus control the wind and the waves. Then Jesus asked the disciples, "Who do people say I am?" The disciples answered that some believed He was John the Baptist, who had come back to life. Others said that Jesus was Elijah or one of the other prophets.

Jesus asked who the disciples thought He was. Peter answered for the group. He said, "You are the Christ!" Jesus told them not to tell that to others.

Jesus was not yet finished with His ministry. Surely that would make the religious leaders angry, and they would try to get rid of Him before He had finished teaching His disciples.

Then Jesus began to teach the disciples that He must die. He told them that the religious leaders would kill Him. But in three days He would rise again. He said that to follow Him was not an easy path. But it was—and is—in the best interest of all who follow Him to give up some other things that make their lives comfortable.

Jesus did many other things during this time in Galilee. Now, He felt that the disciples were ready.

Many of the religious leaders already disliked Jesus. They disturbed His teaching by interrupting Him. They were discourteous, offensive, and they tried to embarrass Him. They did not want the people to follow Him.

It was time to head toward Jerusalem and the events that would happen there.

Later Ministry in Judea, Perea, and Jerusalem

It might have been in the month of October that Jesus arrived in Jerusalem. (See Judea and Jerusalem on the map.) It was about six months before the Passover and the crucifixion. The people were all amazed at the teaching of Jesus. They were asking, "Could Jesus be the Messiah?"

Many people were gathered in Jerusalem for the Feast of Tabernacles. They wanted to see Jesus. At first, Jesus did not appear.

During the feast, there were two rituals or ceremonies that were popular with the people. The priests poured water in the Pool of Siloam. They recited Isaiah 12:3: "You will joyfully draw water from the springs of salvation."

On the last and most important day of the festival, Jesus stood up and cried out, "If anyone is thirsty, he should come to Me and drink! The one who believes in Me, as the Scripture has said, will have streams of living water flow from deep within him" (John 7:37–38).

The second ceremony was the lighting of the candelabra in the Temple. Then Jesus spoke to them again: "I am the light of the world. Anyone who follows Me will never walk in the darkness, but will have the light of life" (John 8:12).

After the Feast was over, Jesus was aware that His time was running out. He had so much that He wanted to finish, but there was little time left for Jesus.

Jesus sent out the seventy-two followers to preach about the kingdom of God. They went to many towns. This is described in Luke 10:1–24. Jesus Himself told the parable of the good samaritan. (For the story, see the *Children's Bible*.)

As Jesus told about His relationship with the heavenly Father, the religious leaders became angrier with Jesus. They wanted to destroy Him.

Jesus went to Perea. (See its location on the map.) While He was there, word came from His friends that Lazarus was sick. Jesus did not leave Perea right away. He stayed another two days. Meanwhile, Lazarus died and was buried.

Jesus traveled to Bethany, where Lazarus lived with his sisters, Mary and Martha. (Notice on the map that Bethany is very near Jerusalem.) The family group was very sad. Martha went out to meet Jesus. He talked with Martha about the power of God. But when Mary came out to meet Jesus, she cried about her brother's death. Jesus cried with her.

Then Jesus went to the tomb. He told them to roll back the stone. There He raised Lazarus from the dead. Some of the people believed in Jesus, but others went quickly and told the Pharisees. The religious leaders decided they would get rid of Jesus.

Jesus returned to Perea. The end of Jesus' ministry was coming quickly.

Soon the Passover would come. Jesus wanted to take the Passover meal in Jerusalem, so He made His way back there. The people in Jerusalem thought He would bring the kingdom of God. They were excited. When He arrived in Jerusalem, they thought He would bring back the glory of

THE ROMAN EMPIRE IN
THE AGE OF AUGUSTUS
- • City
- Territory under Roman control
- Senatorial provinces
- Imperial provinces
- Principal client states
- Unconquered territory
- Provincial boundaries

Israel by being an earthly king. The stage was set for the events of the final week.

The rest of the events happened in Jerusalem. We looked at these events in the section on the Easter celebration found in the section on the Christian year.

THE ROMAN EMPIRE AND JUDAISM

Remember that four hundred years passed between the close of the Old Testament and the beginning of the New Testament. During that time, Rome became the most powerful city in the world. The Roman armies conquered and controlled the lands around the Mediterranean Sea. Roman ships controlled the seas.

Palestine was no different. More than sixty years before Jesus was born, the Roman army and its general, Pompey, marched into Jerusalem. They took all of Palestine for Rome. From that point on, the history of both the Jewish peoples

and the Christians were connected with Rome.

On the map find the city of Rome. It is located in Italy. Then, with your finger trace all of the countries that Rome conquered. See if you can name some of the countries that were under Roman control. You may need to look at maps of Europe, Africa, and the Middle East to find the names of the countries or parts of countries today. To get you started, consider Britain, Spain, France, southern Germany, etc.

The City of Rome

Rome is an ancient city. It was established in 753 BC and is located on the Tiber River. Rome grew in size to include the seven hills. At first a king ruled it. Then the people revolted against the taxes and the evils of the king. The rule of the king came to an end in 510 BC.

The people took control of the government, and Rome became a republic. Consuls, who were elected, ruled it. They formed the Roman Senate. This Senate ruled for almost five hundred years. During these years, the Roman army conquered all of Italy and began to enlarge the territory that it ruled. The Roman legions (the army) conquered other lands. The Roman Senate sent a governor to rule the new provinces. Rome then taxed the conquered lands.

Many of the conquered people were taken as slaves. Some were taken back to Rome. Some slaves worked for the large landowners to farm the lands. Others helped to build the public buildings and new homes for their owners. A few of the educated slaves served the Roman families by caring for the education of the children.

At least a million people lived in the city of Rome. Some of these people lived in beautiful homes. But most of the people lived in crowded apartment houses. The streets of Rome were crowded, noisy, and dirty.

Rome provided the people with free food. They could obtain grain from the great state warehouses. Wine was cheap and easily obtained by the people. The state also provided games for entertainment.

The religion of Rome brought several religions together. When Rome conquered a new territory, the gods of the conquered lands were often taken into the group of Roman gods. For example, the Greek god, Zeus, became the Roman god, Jupiter. The Greek gods were given Roman names and worshiped. One of the purposes of worship was to not offend the gods. The Romans thought that would bring evil. So they often worshiped many gods to avoid evil consequences. They also practiced magic. Many temples and buildings were constructed to honor the gods.

The Roman Empire

The Republic finally came to an end. In 27 BC, the Roman Senate declared Augustus Caesar to be emperor of Rome. Augustus reigned for more than forty years to AD 14. Augustus was a powerful ruler. He kept the people of Rome happy by giving them grain from his large warehouses to make bread.

He provided for the people's entertainment. The people could watch the chariot races in the Circus. The Circus was not a place for clowns and high wire acts, as we think of the circus today. *Circus* meant circle. One can see the remains of the Circus even today in Rome. It was actually an oval, around which the chariots would race. Caesar also provided the gladiators for the people's entertainment. A gladiator would fight another gladiator or a wild animal, such as a lion. They would fight to the death. Gladiators were slaves from other countries who were trained to fight. If they won enough contests, they might be given their freedom.

Caesar built buildings and established peace in the Empire. He built roads throughout the Empire. These roads were used for trade. They also allowed the armies of Rome to travel to the large conquered territories and report back to the emperor.

Jesus was born during the reign of Augustus Caesar. Remember that Caesar called all persons to return to their place of birth. There they would be counted in the census and put on the tax rolls. Mary and Joseph went back to Bethlehem, since they came from the line of King David. (David's family came from Bethlehem).

The next emperor was Tiberius. He was ruler during the time Jesus was ministering in Palestine. During the early years of Christianity, the emperors did not pay much attention to Christians. Christians were considered to be a branch of Judaism. But as more and more converts became Christians, the emperor could no longer ignore them.

During the rule of Nero, there was a change in attitude of the government. A great fire burned much of the city of Rome in AD 64. Many people lived in large apartment houses that were destroyed. The fire caused a great tragedy and many people lost their lives and homes. Many people believed that Nero, himself, set the fire.

To take the blame away from himself, Nero had to find someone to blame. Nero blamed the Christians for the great fire in Rome. He began to search out the Christians and to send many to the gladiators to be killed. Others were killed by wild animals. Peter and Paul were both killed in Rome by Nero. For almost all of the next three hundred years, the Christians were persecuted, and many thousands died.

The Empire grew quite large. It reached its largest extent around AD 150. But Rome was becoming an evil society. The people liked the killing. The taxes were very high, and society was beginning to have problems from within.

At first, the relations between the Jews and the Romans were mostly good. Later some of the emperors forced Jews to leave Rome. In Palestine, the story was very different. The Roman general Titus marched on Jerusalem in AD 70. He destroyed the Temple of Herod. Back home in Rome a monument was built in honor of Titus's victory over the Jews. In Rome today, one can still see on the monument the soldiers carrying the menorah and other Jewish articles away from Jerusalem.

The Emperor Hadrian tried to get rid of Judaism. He passed a law that prohibited the Jews from performing the rite of circumcision. The emperor had a pagan temple built in the place of the Jewish Temple. He wanted to make Jerusalem a Roman city and to practice pagan Roman religion there. Simon bar Kochba led a revolt. He and his followers often came down and attacked the Roman soldiers from the Judean hills. They would strike quickly. Then these brave fighters would retreat to the hills for safety. They held off the Romans for several years. But in the end the Romans conquered. They killed half a million Jews and enslaved many more. Jerusalem remained a conquered city until 1948, when many Jews again populated it. These people returned from all over the world to Jerusalem.

The Christians were also badly persecuted until the rule of Constantine. On the night before Constantine went to do battle with Maxentius to gain control of the Empire, Constantine was with his troops at the Milvian Bridge in Rome. During the night, Constantine had a vision. In the sky he saw the Greek letters X (Chi) and P (Rho). These are the first two letters for the name of Christ. Constantine believed that he should conquer in the name of Christ. His army was baptized, and on their shields were placed the Christian symbols.

The next day Constantine was victorious. His Edict of Milan in AD 313 gave Christians the right to practice their beliefs. Constantine restored to Christians many of the properties that had been taken by the Romans. He rebuilt churches and participated in helping Christianity to become the religion of the Empire.

By AD 325 Constantine saw the Empire beginning to fall apart. He moved the capital from Rome to Constantinople (present-day Istanbul) in Turkey. This was in the East. Rome was still ruled by several other emperors until its final destruction.

Rome continued as the capital city in the West until AD 476. Romulus Augustulus was still only a teenager when he became the Roman emperor in AD 475. The German tribes of the Goths, Visigoths, Vandals, Burgundians, and Franks overran the city of Rome and many of the principal cities in the Empire. The great Roman farms were destroyed. The word *vandalism* taken from the German tribe, means to destroy both public and private property. On September 4, the sixteen-year-old Romulus Augustulus gave up his title as Roman Emperor. In his place, Odoacer, leader of the German fighters, took over Rome. Rome was finally destroyed.

Herod the Great

Recall Herod the Great from the story of the wise men at the birth of Jesus. Herod the Great occupied a unique position among the governors who served Rome. He was not a governor but a local king. The Romans rewarded his loyalty by allowing him to remain as a king in Palestine. Herod's father had sent his army to help the Romans when they needed help. When his father died, the Romans allowed Herod to continue to rule in Palestine. Herod was very successful. Even though he was not

This view shows the Heriodian, the great palace of Herod the Great. It has fallen into disrepair and piles of stones. At one time it was very beautiful.

a Jew, he understood some of their desires, such as keeping the Roman soldiers out of the Temple. Nevertheless, Herod was greatly disliked by the Jews.

Herod's family came from Idumea. (Refer to the map and you will find Idumea located south of Judea and to the west of the Dead Sea.) Idumea was the land where the descendents of Esau had settled.

Herod ruled in Palestine from 37 BC to 4 BC. In the first few years of his reign, Herod secured his position as king. He did this by being cruel to the people he ruled. Then Herod began a building program. To build large buildings was expensive, so Herod taxed the people very heavily. His cruelty and heavy taxation added to the reasons why the people of Palestine hated him.

First, he built huge palaces for himself in Jerusalem and Jericho. He constructed fortresses in Jerusalem and Masada. (Masada is along the western shore of the Dead Sea.) He built a city in honor of Caesar and named it Caesarea. (Caesarea is located along the Mediterranean seacoast in Samaria.) Caesarea had a sheltered harbor to protect ships from the storms on the Mediterranean. There was no safe harbor along the Mediterranean, so Herod had one built.

Perhaps his most ambitious building project was the reconstruction of the Temple. This was the project that pleased the Jews the most. The Temple was beautiful. It had gardens, fountains, and many courts, as well as the Temple itself. The Fortress of Antonia that Herod had constructed, stood just outside the wall of the Temple. If a disturbance happened in the Temple, the Roman soldiers were close enough to the Temple to keep order.

In the later years of his reign, Herod became a jealous ruler. He believed that his favorite wife, Mariamne, had been unfaithful to him. As a result he had her killed. Herod had ten marriages and fifteen children, and there was a lot of fighting within his family.

Herod feared two of his sons and had them killed. Augustus Caesar is reported to have said, "It would be better to be one of Herod's pigs than a son." Recall that at the birth of Jesus, it was necessary for Mary and Joseph and the baby Jesus to flee to Egypt. The wise men had told Herod about the new King of the Jews. Herod was so jealous that he had babies in the area of Bethlehem killed.

Herod became very ill. Again, he had a third son killed. Then Herod died. His son Archelaus had a great funeral for his father. There were troops in full battle dress. They carried his body into the Judean wilderness, where he was buried.

Herod's will was brought to Rome before Caesar. Caesar decided that three of Herod's sons would rule in Palestine. But the Roman governor Pontius Pilate was also appointed to govern part of Palestine. Recall that Pilate was the ruler who had Jesus executed.

Little is said in the Bible about the rest of Herod's family line. Agrippa I helped Emperor Claudius gain control of the Roman Empire after the murder of Caligula. Agrippa was rewarded with rule over Palestine that equaled that of Herod the Great. He is mentioned in Acts 12. He won favor with the Jews by opposing the Christians. His son Agrippa II ruled from AD 50 to 100. He was only given part of his father's territory. His death brought an end to Herod's family of rulers.

THE TRAVELS OF PAUL

The First Missionary Journey: Galatia in Asia Minor

The apostle Paul and Baranbas spent time at the church at Antioch in Syria. The local church there prayed for Paul and Barnabas and sent them to tell the good news of the gospel. The gospel is still good news! God sent His Son, Jesus Christ, to save us from sin and open heaven to all who will believe.

The missionaries set sail for the island of Cyprus (see Acts 13–14). They crossed Cyprus and sailed north on the Mediterranean Sea to Attalia. Then they traveled overland to Antioch (in Asia Minor), Iconium, Lystra, and Derbe. Each place they went, they preached the gospel in the synagogue. They received a hearing from the Jews and the "God-fearers," (Gentiles who were interested in becoming Jews). Some of the Jews and the "God-fearers" believed in Jesus. That was the start of a local church. John Mark, who had come to help them, deserted them. Then there was trouble among the Jews. Many did not like the message of Paul and Barnabas. The Jews stirred up trouble and forced them to retreat back the way they came.

On the map trace the first missionary journey of Paul and Barnabas. Try to remember the names of the places they visited. Look for Antioch (in Syria), the island of Cyprus, Attalia, Antioch (in Asia Minor), Iconium, Derbe, and Lystra.

The Second Missionary Journey: Across Asia Minor and through Greece

The story of this journey is told in Acts 15:40–18:22. Barnabas wanted to take John Mark again on the second journey. Paul refused. The two parted. Paul took Silas. They left Antioch in Syria and went overland to the same cities they visited in Asia Minor. Then they went on to Troas on the coast. Paul had a vision. He saw the man from Macedonia calling them to come across the Aegean Sea to Macedonia.

They set sail and traveled over the Roman roads to Philippi, Thessalonica, and Berea. They had more trouble with the Jews, and Paul had to leave and go south to Greece. He brought the gospel to the great city of Athens. When his companions caught up with him, they went on to Corinth. He stayed in Corinth and established a church there. Priscilla and Aquila became believers and helped Paul with the church there. Leaving Corinth, Paul traveled to Ephesus in Asia Minor. From there he and Silas sailed for Jerusalem. Then he returned to Antioch in Syria to tell all that God had done in starting and establishing the churches.

The Third Missionary Journey: Return to the Churches in Asia Minor and Greece

The third missionary journey began again from Antioch in Syria. This journey is described in Acts 18:23–20:38. Paul wrote letters to some of the churches that had been established on previous trips. Paul was excited about the opportunity to bring Christ to the people of Asia Minor and Greece.

Paul and his companions went back through the areas in Asia Minor where they had been several times before. They strengthened the churches there. Then they went to Ephesus and stayed for three years. From Ephesus they went back to the churches in Macedonia and Greece. From there they retraced their steps back across the Aegean Sea to Troas and Miletus. Then they sailed to Jerusalem. Paul was told that he would be taken prisoner. That did not stop him.

The Journey to Rome: Cyprus, Shipwreck at Malta and on to Rome

Paul was in Jerusalem at the time of festival of Pentecost. The story is told in Acts 21:38–28. He was accused of taking a Gentile into the inner court of the Temple. That was forbidden. Even the Romans respected the right of the Jews to keep the inner Temple holy. A riot broke out. Paul had to be rescued by the Roman troops. Paul told them that he was a Roman citizen. He was put in jail.

He stayed in jail for two years. Then he had to appear before the Roman governor. Paul believed that the trial would lead to his death. Since he was a Roman citizen, he appealed to Caesar. The governor agreed to see him.

Paul was taken under guard to the coast, and they set sail for Rome. They stopped in Crete. Then they set sail again and were shipwrecked. All during this time Paul preached Christ to the soldiers who guarded him. They were able to get to the island of Malta. From there they sailed up the coast of Italy to Puteoli. From there they went by foot into Rome. Paul remained in Rome for the next two years. He preached Christ to all who would listen. Many people became Christians as a result.

Trace Paul's travels to Rome. What cities did he visit on the way to Rome?

We do not know what happened to Paul after he was released. There are many who believe that he went on to Spain. The emperor summoned him back to Rome where he died as a martyr for his faith in Christ. Paul is buried there today.

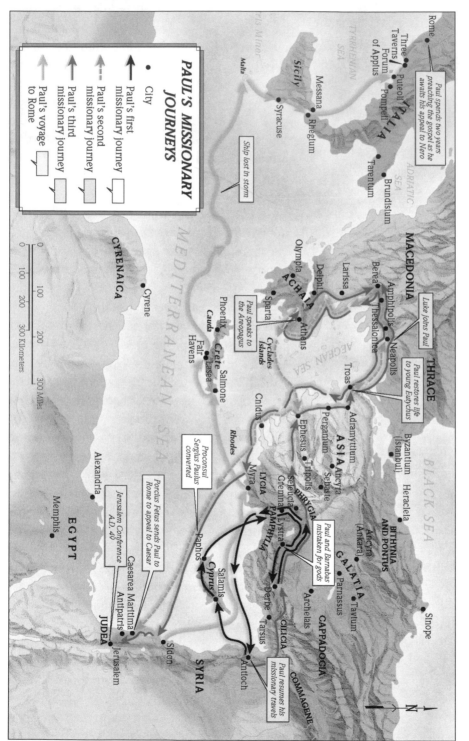

PAUL'S MISSIONARY JOURNEYS

- City
- Paul's first missionary journey
- Paul's second missionary journey
- Paul's third missionary journey
- Paul's voyage to Rome

Ship lost in storm

Paul spends two years preaching the gospel as he awaits his appeal to Nero

Luke joins Paul

Paul restores life to young Eutychus

Paul speaks to the Areopagus

Proconsul Sergius Paulus converted

Porcius Festus sends Paul to Rome to appeal to Caesar

Jerusalem Conference A.D. 49

Paul and Barnabas mistaken for gods

Paul resumes his missionary travels

132

Lesson Plans

INTRODUCTION

The most important book that we have is the Bible. It tells us how the world was formed. It tells us how we were created. It tells us how sin entered the world. It tells us how to find peace with God and forgiveness of sin. It tells us about our future

Children need to be introduced to the Bible early in life. They need more than just listening to isolated Bible stories. The Bible writers, under the inspiration of the Holy Spirit, gave us the entire story of God's redemption in Christ. Children need to learn the significance of stories like Daniel in the Lion's Den, but as part of the entire story of God's history of redeeming man from sin.

Programs like the Core Knowledge Foundation series have clearly shown that children are capable of learning good comprehensive material. This material will provide them with a solid foundation for their future. If we do not develop this foundation in the elementary school years, they are unlikely to learn it during the teenage years. Their interests turn elsewhere during adolescence.

Significant advances have been made in the last two decades in the science of learning and how the mind works. It is clear from what we know about the mind today that prior knowledge is essential to further learning. This prior knowledge base must be built during the elementary years.

This handbook is designed to introduce children to God's redemptive relationship to mankind. It is important to help children gain this understanding and appreciation early in life. The book and its activities can be used for several years. There are a variety of activities that can be used at different age levels.

As children get beyond second grade, they can begin to deal with the concepts of time and place more easily. Before that time, you will need to help them see how the specific Bible stories relate to their own time and place. The world we live is secular and postmodern. We must run against the tide and not capitulate to the postmodern point of view. If we do not, we will lose the next generation.

Children need to learn basic content. Their knowledge of God's Word will stay with them throughout their lives, if they learn it now. They need to learn the major themes of the Bible— God's creation, sin and the fall, God's chosen people, salvation in Jesus Christ, God's new humanity in the church, and God's Word—the Bible. This book will help your child explore these great issues.

COURSE OVERVIEW

We have tried to provide all that you will need to teach your children the Bible.

The course is divided into 15 lessons. Lessons 1–7 guide you through the Old Testament. Of those, lesson 1 is an introduction to the Bible.

Lessons 8–14 will lead you through the New Testament. Lesson 8 reviews the Old Testament and introduces the New Testament.

Lesson 15 is a lesson on Bible geography. If you wish to cut down on the number of lessons, you might consider integrating lesson 15 into the other parts of the total study of the Bible, lessons 1–14.

For each lesson a variety of activities are presented. (Activity sheets are after each lesson and may be enlarged and duplicated. The answers for these sheets are found in the back of the book.) You will need to pick and choose those activities that will stretch each child. Remember that if they are going to go deeper later, they will need to learn the content now. The curriculum should spiral back on itself as the child grows older. It is not a problem to return to the material in this volume as the child moves a year ahead. You can recycle through this material again as your child grows and use activities that will appeal to the older child.

It is important to allow children to memorize Scripture. Research has shown that children have an amazing facility to memorize. We lose that ability as we grow older. Children understand much of what they are memorizing at their level, even if the full import of the Scripture is not gained until later. But if they do not memorize the Scripture when they are young, they will not be able to more fully appreciate the meaning later.

SUGGESTIONS FOR PREPARATION

1. Study the handbook in advance. Read the material that you need to cover from the Handbook with your child. Read the passages of Scripture from a modern translation, such as the Holman Christian Standard Bible.

2. Read the objectives for the lesson you plan to teach. Examine the identifications so that you will be able to help your child understand new concepts, persons, or geographical locations.

3. With the objectives in mind, read through the learning activities. Think about what activities will best suit your child at his or her level of learning. Star those activities that you want to include in the lesson. Prepare a simple lesson plan that will include objectives, Scripture to be studied, identifications, content, and the particular activities that you will use. You need only a sentence or phrase to identify what you will do. Most of the work is already done for you. The lesson plan is important, since it becomes a road map for where you have been. You will want to refer back to it when you are ready to take your child to the next phase.

4. Locate any additional resources that you might need. Let me emphasize that you do not need to go beyond the materials that are available at a stationary store or that you may already have at home. Still you may want to look in your church library, public library, or on Web sites and supplement what is suggested. A word of caution is in order concerning videos and other media. Make sure that the content maintains fidelity with the biblical account. Some videos take liberties with the text and can change the meaning, giving your child a false understanding of the biblical revelation as God gave it.

5. Do background studies where appropriate. Study background information for Egypt, Babylonia, Palestine, Persia, Rome, and Greece. Your child will benefit in his or her studies at school as well. Take field trips. Expose your children to as many good experiences as possible. This will help them have interest and develop a love for God's Word and His people.

6. Keep records of what you have covered and test the children periodically. Suggested activities have test-related items, such as crossword puzzles, fill-in-the-blanks, etc. Find out what they are learning and emphasize or re-teach (if necessary) concepts, persons, or places as necessary. Keep records of progress. You will also want to keep samples of the children's work for good examples.

7. Stress the whole. Do not get caught up in minutiae. An analogy that is significant here is the difference between the individual trees versus the forest. It is all too easy to see the individual tree and miss the forest. For example, if you teach the story of David and Goliath, it is easy to perceive this as a superhero story. Your child may miss the essential concept that this was God's way of dealing with the Philistine, who was defying the armies of God. He or she may also miss the role that story plays in the rise of David to become accepted by the people as God's anointed king over Israel.

8. Try to select activities that are age appropriate. First and second graders need extra help with understanding time and place. They can see time and place as related to the place where they are today. By third grade they have basic understanding of time and place, so time lines and maps become even more important.

9. Have fun with your children! Learning should be fun. Keep in mind that your own attitude is important. You can inspire your children to enjoy their learning experiences.

You have a special opportunity to teach and lead your children to love and understand God's Word! Don't miss the opportunity. Sometimes it is easy to become discouraged and allow the child to do something else, rather than engage them with the Bible and Christian experiences.

When you are tempted to discouragement, recall the experience of Moses.

> By faith Moses, when he had grown up, refused to be called the son of Pharaoh's daughter and chose to suffer with the people of God rather than to enjoy the short-lived pleasure of sin. For he considered the reproach for the sake of the Messiah to be greater wealth than the treasures of Egypt, since his attention was on the reward. (Hebrews 11:24–26)

Remember where Moses learned about the people of God? It was not through being chosen by Pharaoh's daughter to live in the palace. It was through the instruction that he received from his mother as a child. As a parent, you can make a difference in the life of your child as well.

Read to your child. Treasure the opportunities when you can hold your child on your lap and read aloud to him or her from God's Word. Talk about your faith in Christ. Learn along with your child. Select learning activities that you can do by simply modifying them to use with your child. If you are homeschooling, you might want to invite other children who are being homeschooled to join you and your family for the study of the Bible.

We are praying for you!

TO TEACHERS

You have a God-given opportunity to make a difference in the lives of the children whom God has entrusted to your care. It is essential to teach the school subjects, but you have a particular opportunity to teach them the eternal truth of God's Word. It is clear from the history of Israel that teachers were an essential part of the early teaching of the faith for children. Even today, Jewish children attend Hebrew school to learn not only the language but their Hebrew faith.

They memorize large portions of Scripture. Jesus, Himself, went through this kind of preparation. It is not surprising that He was prepared by age twelve to talk with the religious teachers in the Temple. He amazed them! When we next see Jesus in the Gospels, He is baptized and moves directly to the wilderness and the temptation experiences. Remember how He responded to Satan? In each case, Jesus quoted from the Word of God. Can we do any less for our children?

While this passage comes from a period when teaching was more primitive, the principle still holds. One of the unique opportunities for the Christian school is to teach in the light of God's revelation.

> Listen Israel: The LORD your God, the LORD is One. Love the LORD your God with all your heart, with all your soul, and with all your strength. These words that I am giving you today are to be in your heart. Repeat them to your children. Talk about them when you sit in your house and when you walk along the road, when you lie down and when you get up. Bind them as a sign on your hand and let them be a symbol on your forehead. Write them on the doorposts of your house and on your gates. (Deuteronomy 6:4–9)

There are a number of activities from which to choose. You should have enough to design your curriculum as you choose.

May God grant you wisdom and guidance as you minister to the precious lives of your children.

We are praying for you!

Unit One: The Old Testament: Lessons 1–7

UNIT SUMMARY

This set of lessons will provide the learner with background in the Old Testament through chronological Bible teaching; help the learner gain an understanding of the dealings of God with humanity from the beginning of time to the end of the Old Testament; and help the learner develop a lifelong love for God's Word to us through the Bible.

OVERVIEW

Objectives

By the end of this unit, the learner should be able to

- recall the significant persons, who are identified and described in the Old Testament and be able to describe their contribution to the fulfillment of God's purposes,

- understand and appreciate the significant events that occurred in the Old Testament in the chronological development of God's dealing with humankind from Adam to the end of the Old Testament,

- develop an understanding of sin and the seriousness of its consequences and appreciate how God responded to sin in the Old Testament era,

- understand how God dealt with sin in the Old Testament and appreciate God's redemptive activity in the Old Testament and His continuing redemptive activity in the New Testament and today, and

- develop a lifelong love and appreciation for God's Word—the Bible.

Content Summary and Rationale

There is a wealth of content in the Old Testament that is often ignored or overlooked. Yet God's redemptive activity in the New Testament cannot be fully understood without a clear understanding of His activity in the Old Testament.

The Book of Genesis gives us insight into the origin of humankind, the origin of sin, and the human dilemma that sin caused. The Book of Genesis also shows us how God extended His love, even to a sinful and stubborn humanity, in order to win a fallen humanity back to Himself. God's redemptive activity comes to full realization in the New Testament, when God sent His only Son, Jesus, to die on the cross to bring all who would accept the free gift of salvation back to Himself.

Genesis also shows how humanity sank in its sinfulness, until it almost appeared hopeless. But God called Abraham and his heirs to a new and covenant relationship with Himself. The remainder of the Old Testament is a continuing history of the covenant relationship with the Israelite people. At times they obeyed and served God, and at other times they turned aside. But God continued to love this people and continued to call out those who would love and obey Him.

The content of this Old Testament unit leads the learner to see the hand of a loving God in history. When God calls one to faith in Himself and the achievement of His purposes in history, we are not called to blindly believe. There is a long history of God's relationship with humankind and a clear picture is presented. Failure to believe and trust God leads to disastrous consequences and ultimately death. But for all those who believed and trusted God, there were long-term positive consequences. Those who followed God experienced His blessing and, ultimately life.

We approach this unit chronologically, focusing upon the historical circumstances of God's dealing with humans throughout the Old Testament era. We are not ignoring the important wisdom and poetic literature of the Old Testament. But as children begin to formulate their understanding of who God is, we want them to have a clear understanding of the ways God dealt with humanity from the beginning of time. God may have appeared to be cruel at times, but His hatred for sin caused Him to destroy and eliminate evil persons and cities. We stand in awe of the ways by which God entered history and sought after humankind. This is the narrative that we will examine in this unit. We will look at the other parts of the Old Testament in a future volume.

Key Concept

God created the universe and authored all life. God created humans, and He loves them and wants all humankind to come to Himself. But God is also holy and just. He cannot tolerate sin. For humans to come back to God, they must follow His prescription for redemption and fellowship with Him. That prescription is found in the Word of God—the Bible—and each child needs to develop a love and appreciation for the Bible.

Prior Knowledge Needed

For most children, the kindergarten and preschool years will provide them with a few stories from the Old Testament. The story of David and Goliath is one of those stories. If the child is left with only a limited knowledge of the story, the child may be tempted to view David as one of the "superheroes," like Superman or Spiderman.

This unit does not presuppose that the child has any more than a superficial knowledge of the Old

Testament and some of the more prominent stories, like David and Goliath. Because the child's understanding is in the process of developing, future learning will be built upon what the child learns during these years. Therefore, it is essential to guide the child's understanding of God and the Old Testament in ways that will provide opportunities for the child to grow toward a comprehensive and healthy understanding of who God is and what God requires of all who will love and serve Him. This unit will help to develop the child's understanding of God and His purposes, as found in His revelation of Himself in the Old Testament.

RESOURCES FOR TEACHERS AND STUDENTS

- Buchanan, Edward, *Parent/Teacher Handbook The Bible, Vol. 1* (Nashville, Tenn.: Broadman & Holman, 2003).
- Butler, Trent, ed., *Holman Illustrated Bible Dictionary* (Nashville, Tenn: Holman Bible Publishers, 2003).
- Dockery, David, ed., *Holman Bible Handbook* (Nashville, Tenn.: Holman Bible Publishers, 1992).
- An encyclopedia—*World Book, Funk and Wagnalls, Britannica*, etc. (may use CD-ROM)

LESSON 1: INTRODUCTION TO THE BIBLE

Readings from the Parent/Teacher Handbook: The Bible, Vol. 1: "Discovering God"

OBJECTIVES
By the end of lesson, the learner should be able to
- identify the books of the Bible,
- name the members of the Trinity,
- develop a reverence and love for the Bible as God's Word, and
- compare and contrast God and Satan.

IDENTIFICATIONS
Concepts
- *Trinity is God*—Father, Son, and Holy Spirit
- *Love*—a characteristic of God

- *Angels*—heavenly beings who surround God
- *God's Word*—the Bible—has been given to us to instruct us in how to find God and how He wants us to live

People
- *God:* Creator of the universe and the One who cares about us enough to send His son to die on the cross, so that we may find God and salvation through Him
- *Lucifer:* An angel who rebelled against God and causes trouble for humans today

MATERIALS NEEDED
- *Parent/Teacher Handbook: The Bible, Vol. 1*
- Activity Sheets for Lesson 1
  (*Note: Activity sheets are located at the end of each lesson.*)
- Crayons and/or markers
- Blank sheets of white paper for drawing
- Roll of shelf paper or butcher paper for Activity 2
- Masking tape and plastic tape
- Reusable adhesive
- 3x5-inch index cards for Activity 3
- Lined paper for writing
- Stickers of animals, happy faces, people, etc. (optional)

LEARNING ACTIVITIES FOR LESSON 1

Activity 1—Books of the Bible

Adults today do not know the books of the Bible and have difficulty finding their way around the Scriptures. In order to read and study the Bible, it is important to know the names of the books and be able to put them in the correct category and order.

Help your children learn that the Bible is really a library of 66 books—39 in the Old Testament and 27 in the New Testament. The first task for this lesson is to learn where the books of the Bible fit into the total library.

After your children are familiar with the books of the Old Testament, take the blank sheet of books (Activity Sheet 1) and help your children write the names for each of the books in the appropriate section of the Old Testament. Ask the children not to look at the correct answers until they cannot remember any more of the names. Work at this process until the children are able to get all the names correct. You will need to work on this task for several weeks, but the results will be worth the effort.

(*Note: The New Testament books will be learned in unit 2.*)

After the children are thoroughly familiar with the books of the Old Testament, the final task will be to assist them in memorizing the names of all of the books of the Old Testament in the correct order.

If you know a song for the books of the Bible, you will want to sing it with your class. This is an excellent way to help the children memorize the names of each of the books.

Activity 2—Time Line for Bible History

Develop a time line for the history of the time periods covered by the Bible. Activity Sheet 2 provides a list of approximate dates.

Use a sheet of shelf paper or butcher paper 3 to 6 feet in length, and write significant dates along the lower margin. Allow enough space for your children to draw pictures of the biblical events as you come to them in your readings in the handbook. For example, for the section on the period before history begins. The children could draw pictures showing Creation, the creation of Adam and Eve, the Fall, Adam and Eve driven from the Garden of Eden, Cain and Abel, Noah and the Flood, and the Tower of Babel. Later, you will want to add the period of the Patriarchs—Abraham to Joseph. You may attach the new material to the prehistory, or you may keep them as separate sets of events. If you place them on the wall, use masking tape or plastic adhesive (obtainable at a stationary store) that will hold the paper to the wall but not leave marks on the surface.

This activity will be ongoing as you move through the material in the handbook.

Activity 3—Characteristics of God and Satan

Use Activity Sheet 3. Talk about the characteristics of God with the members of your class at the conclusion of this exercise. God is the Creator of the universe, perfect (without sin), holy (perfect goodness), omniscient (all-knowing), omnipotent (all-powerful), omnipresent (present everywhere), and love (expresses complete devotion and acceptance for all mankind).

Activity 4—Understanding the Trinity

Use Activity Sheet 4. Help your children to understand that the Trinity is a difficult concept, even for adults to comprehend. But the Bible is very clear that we worship one God, who is in three persons—Father, Son, and Holy Spirit. We have illustrated these two concepts using the triangle to represent the three persons of the Trinity and the circle to represent the unity and oneness of God. Recall that Jesus said, "The Father and I are one" (John 10:30). Also, in John 15:26 Jesus identified the Holy Spirit as the Counselor, the One who came from the Father and the Son.

Activity 5—Purposes of Angels

The Bible does not tell us a lot about angels. But from what it does tell us, they are important beings in the service of God.

After your children are familiar with the material in the handbook about angels, have them use Activity Sheet 5 to explore the purposes of angels. The sheet is in the form of agree/disagree statements. Read the statement and ask the children whether they agree or disagree with it.

When you have completed the exercise, compare the children's answers to the answers provided in the back of the book. Talk about angels and their roles, as we understand it from the Bible.

Activity 6—Memorize Scripture: 1 John 4:16 (for younger children) or John 3:16 (for older children)

"God is love." Help the younger children know what this short verse means. It is simple on the surface but profound in meaning. Because God is love, we can face trials in life and not be beaten down. God is ever before us and behind us with His tender loving care.

Write each of the words on a 3x5-inch index card. Mix them up and have your children place them in the right order. You will need to review this verse again for several days until the class members have learned it by heart.

For third grade and above, you may want to use John 3:16: *"For God loved the world in this way: He gave His only Son, so that everyone who believes in Him will not perish but have eternal life."*

Activity 7—Bible Verse Memory Book

Make a Bible Verse Memory Book to keep all of the verses that the children memorize.

Cut a sheet of 12x18-inch construction paper in half for the cover.

Fold 8 sheets of plain white paper in half and staple them inside the construction paper to form a booklet. You may want to cut pieces of lined paper at the bottom of each page in the booklet. Your class members may print each memory verse on the lined paper. At the top of the page have your children illustrate the Bible verse, using crayons, markers, or stickers.

Begin the booklet with the first verse to memorize for this lesson—1 John 4:16 or John 3:16. Continue to use the booklet throughout the entire set of lessons in this unit.

ACTIVITY SHEET 1: BOOKS OF THE BIBLE/THE OLD TESTAMENT

Books of the Law
1.
2.
3.
4.
5.

Books of Poetry and Wisdom
1.
2.
3.
4.
5.

Books of Minor Prophets
1.
2.
3.
4.
5.
6.
7.
8.
9.
10.
11.
12.

Books of History
1.	7.
2.	8.
3.	9.
4.	10.
5.	11.
6.	12.

Books of Major Prophets
1.
2.
3.
4.

ACTIVITY SHEET 2: TIME LINE FOR BIBLE EVENTS

(dates are approximate)

Before History	Creation, the Fall of Man, the Flood, and the Tower of Babel
2100–1900 BC	The Patriarchs—Abraham, Isaac, Jacob, and Joseph
1800–1500 BC	Egyptian slavery for the people of Israel
1500–1450 BC	The Exodus and the wilderness wandering
1400–1100 BC	The Period of the Judges
1000–900 BC	The United Kingdom of Israel under Kings Saul, David, and Solomon
900–587 BC	The Divided Kingdom to the fall of Jerusalem
587–525 BC	The Exile—Babylonian Captivity
525–400 BC	The Restoration to Israel by King Cyrus of Persia
400–4 BC	The Period between Old and New Testaments—Malachi to Matthew
4 BC	Jesus' birth in Bethlehem
4 BC–AD 30	Jesus' life and ministry to His Crucifixion, Resurrection, and Ascension
AD 33	The Conversion of the apostle Paul on the road to Damascus
AD 47–61	Paul's missionary journeys and trip to Rome
AD 67	Paul's death at the hand of Emperor Nero
AD 100	The end of the Apostolic Era
AD 100–1999	Christian Era
AD 2000+	Our life today

ACTIVITY SHEET 3: CHARACTERISTICS OF GOD AND SATAN

Directions: Choose the characteristics at the right that describe God and the characteristics that describe Satan, and write them in the appropriate column. You may want to add some characteristics not on the list.

Characteristics:
Enemy of mankind
Keeps promises
Is love
Protects believers
Morning star
Has some power
Perfect
Hates sin
All-powerful
Is Holy
Intelligent
Sovereign
Present everywhere
Tries to hurt believers
Rebelled against God
Created everything
Knows everything
Made some angels sin

GOD	SATAN

ACTIVITY SHEET 4: THE TRINITY

How does this illustration describe the Trinity?

_____

_____

_____

God the Father

Jesus Christ, Son   Holy Spirit

ACTIVITY SHEET 5: PURPOSES OF ANGELS

Directions: In the space provided, write **A** for statements with which you agree and **D** for statements with which you disagree.

___1. God created the angels.

___2. Angels were created to serve human beings.

___3. Angels are less important than human beings.

___4. Angels provide a good example for us.

___5. Angels take joy in doing God's will.

___6. Angels are not aware of what happens here on earth.

___7. *Angel* means "one who is a companion."

___8. Angels were created without sin.

___9. Angels are very intelligent.

___10. Angels worship God continuously.

Lesson 2: Creation to the Tower of Babel

Readings from the Parent/Teacher Handbook: The Bible, Vol. 1: "God Creates," "Sin Enters the World," "Noah and the Flood," and "The Tower of Babel"

Objectives

By the end of this lesson, the learner should be able to

- identify each of the seven days of Creation and express thanksgiving to God for His creation and promises
- develop an understanding of and explanation for the sin of Adam and Eve in the Garden of Eden
- compare and contrast the sacrifices and actions of Cain and Abel,
- order the events of Noah and the Flood, and
- describe the significance of the Tower of Babel.

Identifications
Concepts

- *Flood*—brought upon humanity to destroy their sinfulness
- *Ark*—ship constructed by Noah to house animals and Noah and his family
- *Rainbow* and its relationship to no future floods
- *Promise*—looking forward to a Redeemer
- *Babel*—tower constructed in opposition to God

People

- *God:* Creator and Sustainer of all life
- *Adam and Eve:* first parents of all humanity
- *Serpent:* the Devil seeking to tempt Eve
- *Noah:* godly man whom God chose to build an ark and keep his family safe from the rising waters
- *Cain and Abel:* first sons of Adam and Eve who brought sacrifices; Cain's wasn't accepted by God, resulting in his murder of Abel.

Materials Needed

- *Parent/Teacher Handbook: The Bible, Vol. 1*
- Activity Sheets for Lesson 2
- Potting soil
- Blank paper, lined paper, drawing paper
- Jug of water
- A roll of shelf or butcher paper
- Paper plates
- Prism
- Stapler
- Animal crackers
- Crayons and markers
- Plastic or wooden floatable boat
- Large plastic tub
- Paper or wooden blocks

Learning Activities for Lesson 2

Activity 1—Mural of the Days of Creation

Read the section, "God Creates," from the handbook. Help your children visualize what a great act God did when He created everything and everyone.

Design a mural to express the feelings involved. Use a sheet of shelf paper or butcher paper to give your class members enough space to draw each of the seven days of Creation. Label each of the days and draw pictures to illustrate the events. Write captions under each of the pictures to describe what it must have been like. Here are the days of creation:

- Day 1—God first created the heavens and the earth and then He created light.
- Day 2—God separated the water from the sky.
- Day 3—Dry land was separated from the sea, and plants and trees were created.
- Day 4—The sun and moon appeared to cause day and night, seasons and years.

- Day 5—Sea life (fish) and birds to fly in the air were created.
- Day 6—Animal life and human beings were created. Humans were different. They were created in the image of God and told to rule over the animal kingdom.
- Day 7—God rested from His creation.

Attach the mural to the wall and talk about what the children drew for each of the days of Creation.

Activity 2—Looking at God's Creation

Take your class outside the house and look for something that God created on each day of Creation.

Day 1—God created the heavens and the earth, and then He created light. Look at the heavens and think about the stars that are far above the earth. Observe the light of day and the artificial light at night. (Do not look directly at the sun.)

Day 2—God separated the water from the sky. Go to a lake or the sea and look at the water. Imagine what it must have been like to have a vast sea without land.

Day 3—Dry land was separated from the sea and created plants and trees. Find a lake or sea and imagine what it must have been like to separate the sea from the land. Look at plants and trees. Imagine what the land would be like without the trees and plants that God created.

Day 4—Sun and moon appeared to create day and night and seasons and years. Notice the sun. (Do not look directly at the sun.) Look at the moon at night. Imagine what the world would be like without the sun and moon.

Day 5—Sea life (fish) and birds to fly in the air were created. Go to an aquarium to see the sea life, both freshwater and seawater. You might go to a pet shop and look at the fish.

Day 6—Animal life and human beings were created. Humans were different. Humans were created in the image of God and told to rule over the animal kingdom. Visit a zoo and talk about how God made each of these animals special. Go to a local mall and sit and observe the people coming and going. Think about how each person is different and has different hopes and dreams. What do you think they are thinking? Do they seem happy or sad? Are they persons whom you think you might like?

Day 7—God rested from His creation. Go to a church and sit quietly and reflect on what God did in creating everything special. Think about how God loves every person whom He created. Think about how God loves you.

You may want to sit quietly in church and do the next activity as well.

Activity 3—Prayer of Thanksgiving to God for Some Part of Creation

On lined paper, have each child write a prayer of thanksgiving for a part of creation for which you are particularly thankful.

To get you started, here is a way that you might begin:

Dear God, Thank You for your creation of trees, grass, and animals. Thank You most of all for people. Thank You for Moms and Dads and children, like me.

I also want to thank You for . . . Amen.

Activity 4—Fill in the Blanks for Adam and Eve

Use Activity Sheet 4 and have the children fill in the blanks to complete the story of Adam and Eve from Genesis 3. Words are found to the right of the activity and some are used more than once.

Activity 5—Compare the Sacrifices of Cain and Abel
Use Activity Sheet 5 to compare the facts about Cain and Abel from the story in Genesis 4.

Activity 6—Recreate the Flood in Miniature
Provide a large tub for this activity. Have the children use the tub to make the earth. Use material that will be destroyed when the water washes over it. Potting soil would be a good choice for this purpose. Encourage each child to be as creative as possible, using twigs for trees, and build houses and other buildings with leaves.

Place a plastic or wooden floatable boat on top of the soil in the tub. This will represent Noah's ark.

Reread the story of the Flood. Take a jug of water and pour the water over the earth, as if the rains were descending on the earth (be careful not to pour water into the boat).

Watch as the water covers the earth and the buildings. Use just enough water to cover everything that was placed in the tub. Observe the boat/ark floating in the water.

If you can do this activity outdoors and can allow the water to evaporate, have the children watch the drying process. Recount how the floodwaters receded and it took many days for the land to dry out.

Be sure to talk about the sinfulness of the people and why God destroyed them with the floodwaters.

Activity 7—The Rainbow
Follow the previous activity with a discussion of the rainbow. Read Genesis 9:13–16. God made a promise to humans that He would never destroy humanity again through the rising flood-waters. To show His promise God placed a rainbow in the sky, whenever it rains and the sun is shining.

You can demonstrate the rainbow with a prism. Show the children how the white light is divided into the different colors of the rainbow. Use sunlight or a strong white light and shine it through the prism. The prism will separate the light into the colors of the rainbow. If you do not have a prism, have your class members color a rainbow with varied colored crayons or markers.

Activity 8—Create a Boat to Represent the Ark
Retell the story of Noah and the ark. Stop retelling the story at the point where Noah is commanded to build the ark. Have your class members make a boat to represent the ark. Cut two paper plates in half. Staple the halves together and decorate it to make a boat.

Continue to tell the story. God spared animals and had them enter the ark two by two. He wanted them to replenish the earth after the floodwaters receded. Have your children place different animals (crackers) two by two in his/her ark. Then continue to tell the story to its conclusion.

Activity 9—Field Trip to a Zoo
This is an excellent time to take your class to the zoo. Take a pad of paper and have the children and an accompanying parent help list all the animals that the children see. Talk about how God created each animal differently.

Younger children may want to draw some of the animals they saw at the zoo.

Have older children do a report on one or more of the animals. Use the encyclopedia and discuss the habitat and eating habits of the animals observed.

Activity 10—Construct a Tower for the Tower of Babel

Have your class build a tower. Use paper or wooden blocks. Try to build the tower as tall as possible.

Now, read the story of the Tower of Babel.

Ask the following questions:

- Why did the people build the Tower of Babel?
- Why was God angry with the people for building the Tower of Babel?
- What did God do to the people as a result of the Tower of Babel?

After you have helped them to understand that the people were trying to reach God and act as if they were as powerful as He was, help the children understand that this is sin and God will not allow it. God wants His people to trust Him and not themselves. God caused them to speak different languages and they had to move to different parts of the earth.

If possible, bring in a person who speaks another language. Have the children try to communicate with the person using the other language. This will help your children see how difficult it is to communicate with a person who speaks another language.

Activity 11—Memorize Genesis 1:1

Commit Genesis 1:1 to memory: *"In the beginning God created the heavens and the earth."* Write each of the words on a 3x5-inch index card and keep practicing the verse. Put each word in order.

Eventually have each child recite the entire verse from memory, with the reference. Have them write Genesis 1:1 in their Bible Verse Memory Books. They may want to illustrate the verse as well.

Also, review the verse they learned in the last lesson.

WORKSHEETS FOR LESSON 2

ACTIVITY SHEET 4: STORY OF ADAM AND EVE AND THEIR SIN

Directions: Fill in the blanks with the appropriate answer.

_____ and _____ lived in the Garden of _____. They were very happy there. Each day they _____ with God. God told them that they could eat of the _____ of the Garden, except for _____ tree in the center of the Garden. One day a _____ came to Eve and asked why she did not eat of that one tree. She said that _____ told them that they would _____ if they ate from it. But _____, who was disguised as a serpent, put _____ in her mind and said that they would become like _____ They would know _____ from evil, if they ate from it. So_____ ate of the fruit and gave it to _____ also. As soon as they ate of the fruit, they knew that they had disobeyed. They were embarrassed that they did not have _____ to cover themselves. They sewed _____ leaves together to wear. Then, they _____ from God. Because of their _____ they had to leave the beautiful Garden and work _____to provide for their family. But God promised to send a _____ one day, who would make _____ between God and man.

WORDS:
Adam
Eve
good
one
sin
peace
God
Eden
die
doubt
clothes
fruit
Redeemer
walked
hard
serpent
fig
hid
Satan
die

ACTIVITY SHEET 5: COMPARISON OF CAIN AND ABEL

Directions: Consider the facts about Cain and Abel from the ones listed below. Write the facts that are appropriate for Cain and the ones that are appropriate for Abel in the correct columns. Read the passage "Sin Enters the World" in the handbook. Also read Genesis 4 in the Bible.

Cain	Abel

FACTS

Son of Adam and Eve

He brought sacrifices of fruits from his land to God.

Younger son

Older son

He brought a lamb sacrifice to God.

He was a farmer.

God was pleased with his sacrifice.

He was a sheepherder.

God was not pleased with his sacrifice.

He killed his brother.

LESSON 3: THE PATRIARCHS—ABRAHAM TO JOSEPH

Readings from the Parent/Teacher Handbook: The Bible, Vol. 1: "Abraham, the Man of Faith," "Isaac Marries Rebekah," "Jacob Learns to Trust God," and "God Cares for Joseph"

OBJECTIVES

By the end of this lesson, the learner should be able to

- describe the life of Abraham and define faith as exhibited by Abraham,
- explain the life of Isaac as the son of Abraham,
- explain how God blessed Jacob and compare Jacob and his brother Esau, and
- describe how God worked in Joseph's life to bring him to Egypt and become second in command to the Pharaoh.

IDENTIFICATIONS

Concepts

- *Faith*—the acceptance of God's guidance in life
- *Choosing a wife for Isaac*—returning to kinfolk to find a godly wife
- *Birthright*—special privileges belonging to the firstborn male child in a family
- *Blessing*—conferring something good upon the firstborn son

People

- *Abraham:* patriarch of the Israelites
- *Terah:* father of Abraham

- *Lot:* son of Haran, Abraham's brother
- *Sarah:* wife of Abraham
- *Hagar:* handmaid of Sarah
- *Ishmael:* son of Abraham and Hagar, but not the son of promise
- *Isaac:* son of Abraham who was the son of promise
- *Rebekah:* wife of Isaac
- *Esau:* firstborn son of the twins born to Isaac and Rebekah
- *Jacob:* second son of the twins born to Isaac and Rebekah; he was the son of promise
- *Laban:* brother of Rebekah and father of Leah and Rachel
- *Rachel:* second wife of Jacob. He worked fourteen years to obtain her hand in marriage
- *Leah:* first wife of Jacob whom he received after seven years of working for Laban

MATERIALS NEEDED

- *Parent/Teacher Handbook: The Bible, Vol. 1*
- Activity Sheets for Lesson 3
- Crayons and markers
- Blank sheets of white paper for drawing
- Lined paper for writing
- Clothes and props for the role-play scenes

LEARNING ACTIVITIES FOR LESSON 3

Activity 1—Arrange the Events of Abraham's Life

Read the section from the handbook called "Abraham, the Man of Faith." Then, have the children arrange the events of Abraham's life, using Activity Sheet 1.

Activity 2—Compare Adam and Abraham

To compare Adam and Abraham, use Activity Sheet 2. This is a Venn diagram, which focuses upon the similarities and differences between two persons or items. In this case, the two people are Adam and Abraham. In the left circle, write the numbers of the characteristics that are given that apply only to Adam. In the right circle, write the characteristics that are appropriate for Abraham. In the center where the circles intersect, write the numbers of the characteristics that apply to both Adam and Abraham.

Discuss with your children the differences and similarities between Adam and Abraham. What can we learn about ourselves and about God from these two Bible characters?

Activity 3—Define Faith
After you have read "Abraham, the Man of Faith" in the hanbook, use Activity Sheet 3 for this lesson. Have the children complete the answers to the questions.

Activity 4—Crossword Puzzle for Abraham Through Jacob
Using Activity Sheet 4, help your class members complete the crossword puzzle.

Activity 5—Draw a Picture of Jacob as He Slept and Dreamed of the Staircase to Heaven
Reread the story of Jacob sleeping on the stone. He was escaping from the anger of his brother Esau, after taking away Esau's inheritance. Jacob was on his way to his uncle's home in Haran.

He was very tired and fell into a deep sleep. While he was asleep, Jacob had a dream. He saw a staircase leading to heaven, and angels were going up and down the staircase to heaven. Then God spoke to him. God said, "I am the God of Abraham and your father Isaac. I will bless you. I will make your family great. Through your family all the peoples of the world will be blessed."

Have the children draw a picture of Jacob sleeping on the rock and illustrate what he saw in the dream that he had that night in Bethel.

Activity 6—Unscramble the Names of Jacob's Children
The names of Jacob's sons are very important to the history of Israel. From Jacob's twelve sons came the twelve tribes of Israel, with two exceptions. Levi became the tribe of priests. The priests served all of Israel, so they were not allotted a geographical place in Israel. That left eleven sons. Of the eleven sons, Joseph went to Egypt and became the second in command to Pharaoh. Joseph himself did not father a tribe. To make up for Levi becoming the tribe of priests for all Israel and for Joseph, who did not father a tribe, Joseph's two sons became the fathers of tribes of Israel. They were Ephraim and Manessah.

In Activity Sheet 6 you will find the names of Jacob's twelve sons and one daughter, plus the names of Joseph's sons. On this sheet the letters of the names are scrambled. The names of the children of Jacob and Joseph are listed. Have your class members unscramble the letters and discover the correct name.

Remind the class that these include the names of the twelve tribes of Israel. They also include Jacob's daughter, Dinah, as well as Levi, and Joseph.

Activity 7—Fill in the Blanks in the Story of Joseph's Life
On Activity Sheet 7, have the children fill in the blanks from the life of Joseph. The words are found at the right of the activity.

Activity 8—Role-Play Joseph's Brothers Coming to Egypt to Buy Food
Reread the section "Jacob's Sons Go to Egypt" (Genesis 42). You may also want to read Genesis 43–47. This is a long section, so you will need to summarize this for your class. You may want to have some dress-up clothes that will add authenticity to the scenes. Fill pillow cases with clothes or something to resemble the bags of grain. You will need a silver-colored cup to represent the one from Joseph. (You can use a cup that has been wrapped with aluminum foil).

Using the following scenes, role-play the brothers coming to Joseph:

Scene 1: The brothers come to Egypt to buy grain. Joseph accuses them of being spies. He has them put in jail for three days. He tells them not to return unless they bring their younger brother, Benjamin. He keeps Simeon in prison.

Scene 2: The brothers are desperate for food. Jacob allows Benjamin to return with them. Joseph gives them a big dinner. Later, he accuses them of stealing his cup. Joseph keeps Benjamin because the cup was found in his sack.

Scene 3: The brothers come back a third time. Joseph cannot hold back. He shows them who he is and forgives them for what they did to him years ago.

Scene 4: The brothers go home, and Jacob and his family return to Egypt. They are all reunited.

After you have played the scenes, talk about love and forgiveness. How did Joseph show godly courage and forgiveness? How does God want us to act to those who treat us badly?

Activity 9—Field Trip to a Local Museum to Look at Egyptian Antiquities
Take your children on a field trip to a museum to examine Egyptian antiquities. If you cannot find a museum, you can look up material in an encyclopedia or on the Internet.

Help the children find answers to questions like the following: What was life like in ancient Egypt? How did the pharaohs treat their subjects? Why were the pyramids and sphinx built? Why was the Nile River so important to life in Egypt? What was the religious life like in Egypt? Write down the answers.

Activity 10—Memorize Hebrews 11:8
Have your class memorize Hebrews 11:8 and include the verse and a drawing in their Bible Verse Memory Booklets.

"By faith Abraham, when he was called, obeyed and went out to a place he was going to receive as an inheritance; he went out, not knowing where he was going."

WORKSHEETS FOR LESSON 3

ACTIVITY SHEET 1: EVENTS OF ABRAHAM'S LIFE

Directions: Number the events from 1 (for the first event) to 8 (for the last event) in the order in which they occurred in Abraham's life.

___a. God blessed Abraham with lots of grandchildren.

___b. Abraham was willing to obey, but God provided a lamb for sacrifice.

___c. Isaac, the son of promise, was born to Abraham and Sarah in old age.

___d. God promised Abraham that He would make of Abraham a great nation.

___e. Abraham moved from Ur to Canaan.

___f. God tested Abraham's faith by asking Abraham to sacrifice his only son, Isaac.

___g. Abraham became rich with flocks and herds.

___h. Abraham and his nephew Lot separated.

Directions: A Venn diagram will help you compare Abraham and Adam. From the characteristics below the Venn diagram, select those characteristics that are only present in Adam and write those numbers in the circle for Adam. Do the same for Abraham on the right. Write the numbers for the characteristics that are true for both in the ellipse that intersects both circles.

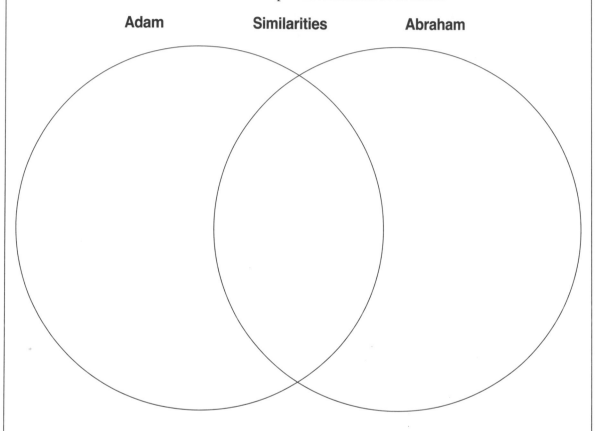

Adam　　　**Similarities**　　　**Abraham**

Characteristics:

1. Obeyed God
2. Blessed by God at the end
3. Trusted God
4. Disobeyed God
5. Father of Israel
6. Blessed by God at the beginning
7. Married to a wife
8. Loved by God

9. Demonstrated faith in God
10. Created directly by God
11. Failed to trust God
12. Father of all mankind
13. Father of a son
14. Named the animals
15. Given God's covenant

ACTIVITY SHEET 3: DEFINITION OF FAITH

1. What does the word *faith* mean?

_____

2. Who had *faith* in this story?

_____

3. Because he had *faith*, what did God promise him?

_____

4. How can you have *faith* today?

_____

5. If you have *faith*, will that please God?

_____

ACTIVITY SHEET 4: CROSSWORD PUZZLE FOR ABRAHAM THROUGH JACOB

The promised son of **3 Down** and **6 Across** was Isaac. God led Abraham's servant to go back to Sarah's homeland to find a wife for **10 Down**. The wife the servant found for Isaac was **7 Down**. Years later, Isaac and Rebekah had twin boys, **8 Across** and **13 Down**.

When Isaac was very old, he wanted to bless Esau, his oldest son, and give him his **9 Across**. But Rebekah prepared a meat dish with two **5 Down**. Jacob took the dish to his father. He was pretending to be Esau. When Esau came with his own meat dish to his father, his father told Esau that he

had already given the **1 Down** to Jacob. Esau was very **14 Across** with his brother.

Because Esau wanted to kill his brother, Jacob left and traveled to **2 Across**. On the way he had a **11 Down**, where God promised to bless him. Jacob went to stay with **15 Across**, Rebekah's brother.

While Jacob was there, he fell in love with **4 Down**. Jacob agreed to work seven years for Laban in exchange for his daughter. But on Jacob's wedding night, Laban gave his firstborn daughter **12 Across** to Jacob for his wife. Jacob had to work another seven years to marry Rachel.

God blessed Jacob, his flocks, and his family. From Jacob came the twelve tribes of Israel.

ACTIVITY SHEET 6: SCRAMBLED NAMES OF JACOB'S SONS, DAUGHTER, AND JOSEPH'S SONS

DJAUH _____

HSIRCAAS _____

AND _____

PEJHOS _____

ANBINJEM _____

BREENU _____

BZIUNEU _____

ILVE _____

THIAPANAL _____

SERAH _____

HINAD _____

DAG _____

NSEIOM _____

NSESAMHA _____

HRMEAIP _____

Names of the twelve Sons of Jacob, the Daughter of Jacob, and the Sons of Joseph:

REUBEN—tribal name
DAN—tribal name
NAPHTALI—tribal name
GAD—tribal name
ASHER—tribal name
ISSACHAR—tribal name
ZEBULUN—tribal name
DINAH (daughter of Jacob)
JOSEPH
   EPHRAIM (son of Joseph)—tribal name
   MANESSAH (son of Joseph)—tribal name
SIMEON—tribal name
LEVI (father of the line of priests)
JUDAH—tribal name
BENJAMIN—tribal name

ACTIVITY SHEET 7: EVENTS IN THE LIFE OF JOSEPH

Directions: From the words at the right, fill in the blanks for the life of Joseph.

1. Joseph was the son of _____.
2. Jacob gave Joseph a beautiful _____ of many colors.
3. Joseph had two _____ that his brothers would bow down to him.
4. The brothers of Joseph _____ him and planned to kill him.
5. Reuben suggested putting Joseph into an empty _____ so that he could save him later.
6. The brothers decided to _____ Joseph as a slave to some traders.
7. The brothers dipped his coat in the _____ of an animal and took it back to show Jacob.
8. Jacob believed his son had been killed and was very _____.
9. Joseph was sold to _____, one of Pharaoh's officers, and became head over his household.
10. Because Joseph would not stay alone with Potiphar's wife, he was arrested and thrown into _____.
11. In prison, Joseph interpreted dreams for Pharaoh's _____ and cupbearer.
12. When Pharaoh had a dream that no one could interpret, the _____ remembered Joseph. Joseph interpreted the dream for Pharaoh.
13. Pharaoh was so pleased that he made Joseph _____ in command for all of Egypt.
14. Joseph's family suffered greatly with a _____ that came upon the land of Palestine.
15. When the brothers came to _____ to buy food, Joseph recognized his brothers. They did not recognize him.
16. When Joseph told them who he was, they were very _____.
17. Joseph believed that God had _____ him and helped him save his family from famine.
18. Their family was _____ when Jacob came to Egypt with the rest of his family.

WORDS:
baker
sad
hated
second
blood
cupbearer
Egypt
famine
reunited
prison
well
Jacob
frightened
coat
protected
Potiphar
sell
dreams

LESSON 4: MOSES, THE LAWGIVER

Readings from the Parent/Teacher Handbook: The Bible, Vol. 1: "Moses' Birth and Call," "Moses Delivers Israel from Egypt," "Moses and the Ten Commandments," and "Worship and the Tabernacle"

OBJECTIVES

By the end of this lesson, the learner should be able to
- identify the major events in the life of Moses,
- explain how God led the people of Israel to be released from the land of Egypt through the plagues on the people of Egypt,
- recount God's leadership for His people in the wilderness, and
- describe the Law of Moses and the Ten Commandments.

IDENTIFICATIONS

Concepts
- *Plagues*—deep distress brought upon the Egyptians to cause Pharaoh to let the people of Israel go from Egypt
- *Ten Commandments*—the two tablets of stone on which God wrote His moral code
- *Law of God*—God's requirements for His people
- *Golden Calf*—the golden calf that Aaron and the people of Israel made to worship in place of God while Moses was on Mount Sinai
- *Tabernacle*—the tent of meeting, where God met with the people of Israel in the wilderness and later in the Promised Land

People
- *Moses:* God's choice to lead the people of Israel from captivity; name means "pulled from the water"
- *Pharaoh's daughter:* discovered the baby Moses floating in the basket on the river and pulled him from the water to be brought up in her house
- *Jethro:* Moses' father-in-law
- *Zipporah:* Moses' wife
- *Aaron:* Moses' brother
- *Miriam:* Moses' sister
- *Pharaoh:* the ruler of Egypt who refused to let the people of Israel go to the Promised Land

MATERIALS NEEDED
- *Parent/Teacher Handbook: The Bible, Vol. 1*
- Activity Sheets for Lesson 4
- Crayons and markers
- Blank sheets of white paper for drawing
- 3x5-inch index cards
- Glue and tape
- Lined paper for writing
- Stapler
- Modeling clay or dough recipe for Activity 6

LEARNING ACTIVITIES FOR LESSON 4

Activity 1—Biographical Sketch of Moses

On 3x5-inch index cards, draw events from the life of Moses. Be sure to label each picture. Arrange the cards in the order in which the events occurred. Fasten the cards in the right sequence to a strip of tape. Use the story sequence of cards to retell the story of Moses' life.

Events include:
- Moses being placed in the basket lined with pitch and set afloat in the bulrushes of the River Nile
- Moses growing up in the palace of Pharaoh
- Moses killing the Egyptian who was beating the Israelite person
- Moses fleeing to the land of Midian in the desert

- Moses caring for the flocks of his father-in-law, Jethro
- Moses meeting God at the burning bush in the desert
- Moses standing before Pharaoh and bringing on the plagues
- Moses guiding the people out of Egypt into the wilderness
- Moses on Mt. Sinai receiving the Law of God
- Moses looking across the Jordan River to see the Promised Land

Activity 2—The Burning Bush

Draw a picture of the burning bush where God met Moses in the desert when Moses was tending the flocks of his father-in-law, Jethro. What would a burning bush look like that was burned but not consumed by the fire? Encourage the children to use the reds and yellows that would have been present in the bush that was not consumed. After your children have completed their drawings of the burning bush, talk about the following questions:

- How would you feel if you saw a burning bush and it began to talk to you?
- How do you suppose Moses felt about the bush and about God who spoke to him out of the bush?
- What did God say to Moses? What did God want Moses to do? What did God give Moses to help him do what God commanded him to do?

Activity 3—Graphic Organizer Chart

Create a graphic organizer chart by taking a piece of paper and dividing it into three columns containing the following headings: What I Know; What I Would Like to Know; and What I Learned. Duplicate a copy for each child. Help the children think about what he or she knows about the Egyptians. If your children are younger, you will need to guide the search for information by asking questions about what he or she knows already. List these items in the first column of the chart.

Then talk about what the children do not know, but would like to know, about the Egyptians. You may have to help the children discover ideas about which to raise questions. It will help you to read an article about the Egyptians in the *Holman Bible Dictionary* or in one of the encyclopedias that were listed in the resources. If you have an encyclopedia CD-ROM, look at the information and pictures together with your students to stimulate their questions.

After you have written the children's questions in the second column, write what they discover in the third column. Use the resources listed above to help the younger children find answers.

For older children, encourage self-exploration of the resources. With your supervision, have the children write the questions to be researched. Then let them explore the resources to find the answers. Again, you may need to provide help and encouragement so that your children do not become fatigued or burned out.

Activity 4—Draw Pictures of Each of the Ten Plagues

Review the list of the ten plagues that were brought upon the people of Egypt. The plauges are provided on page 115 of the handbook.

Have the children draw a picture for each of the ten plagues. It was not until the last plague—when the firstborn of every Egyptian died—that Pharaoh let the people of Israel go into the wilderness to worship God.

Activity 5—Diary of the Red Sea Experience

Make a diary about the experience of the Israelites at the crossing of the Red Sea. Have each class member imagine they are a child among the people of Israel as the Egyptians are pursuing them to bring them back to Egypt. Use wide-lined paper to enable the children to write easily. You may need to help younger children write their diary of the experience.

Help them visualize what it must have been like to be in that situation and to see the hand of God miraculously open the sea. Since this happened over three days, label the days Day 1, Day 2, and Day 3 and write "Dear Diary" on the next line of each page.

Along with each diary entry, the children can draw a picture on white construction paper to illustrate what is happening.

Upon completion, staple the pages together to form a booklet of the experience.

Activity 6—Clay Model of the Ten Commandments

Make a model of the tablets of stone on which were written the Ten Commandments. In order to make a model of the Ten Commandments, you will need to assemble items that are common in most kitchens. These include: flour, salt, alum, and vegetable oil. Pour 2 cups of water into a saucepan and bring it to a boil on the stove. Add food coloring to make a light brown or gray dough. In a mixing bowl, mix 2 cups of flour with 1/2 cup of salt. Pour in 1 tablespoon of powdered alum and 3 tablespoons of vegetable oil. Add the colored water to the other ingredients in the mixing bowl. Knead the dough until it is sold and pliable. Place the dough in a plastic bag to keep out the air. You can now form the tablets of stone. With a toothpick, form the numbers 1 to 10, representing the Ten Commandments. Allow the tablets to dry until hard. After you have made the model, then complete the next activity, which will name each of the Ten Commandments.

Activity 7—Ten Commandments—Missing Words Exercise

Read "The Ten Commandments" in the handbook. Then turn to Activity Sheet 7 to complete the worksheet.

After your children have completed the worksheet, discuss the meaning of each commandment. Are the commandments still helpful today? Tell your children that God has given the Ten Commandments as a moral compass to keep us from making sinful choices. The Ten Commandments are important for today. Many people do not follow the Ten Commandments, but they suffer the consequences. Help your children to see how important they are. You may have to explain some of the words to them.

Activity 8—Worship in the Tabernacle

Worship in the Tabernacle was very important to the people of Israel. Read the section "Worship and the Tabernacle" in the handbook. Talk with your class about the importance of worship of God in the Tabernacle.

You can set up your own version of the Tabernacle so that your children have the experience of worship today. Arrange the room so that there are chairs in a small circle for times of prayer. Place the Bible in a prominent position. The Word of God is important today, just as it was in Bible times.

The Hebrew people also used musical instruments to sing praise to God. If you have a piano and/or other instruments in the room, use them to play songs and hymns. Decorate your room with colored pictures that the children have created over the past several weeks.

In the Tabernacle that you have created, spend some time together in worship. Read Psalm 100—a psalm of praise—from the Bible. Sing gospel songs, such as "Jesus Loves Me." Pray together. Make this a special time of worship together.

Activity 9—Memorize Mathew 22:37

To help your children understand what God desires of those who follow Him, have your children memorize the Great Commandment of the Law. Jesus summarized how we are to be responsible to God.

"He said to him: 'You shall love the Lord your God with all your heart, with all your soul, and with all your mind.'"

Have the children place this Scripture in their Memory Bible Verse Book and illustrate it.

WORKSHEET FOR LESSON 4

ACTIVITY SHEET 7: THE TEN COMMANDMENTS

Directions: After checking the material in the handbook, fill in the blanks in the exercise below.

1. You shall not have any other _____ before me.

2. You shall not make any _____ to serve or worship.

3. You shall not take the name of the _____ carelessly but with reverence.

4. You shall keep the _____ day holy.

5. Show respect for your _____ and _____ that you may live long on the earth.

6. You shall not _____.

7. You shall not be _____ to your husband or wife.

8. You shall not _____.

9. You shall not speak _____ against your neighbor.

10. You must not _____ another person's possessions.

Readings from the Parent/Teacher Handbook: The Bible, Vol. 1: "Joshua Leads the People to the Promised Land," "Samson and the Judges," and "Samuel, and the Last of the Prophets"

OBJECTIVES

By the end of this lesson, the learner should be able to

- explain the work of Joshua as he replaced Moses and describe his military leadership at the Battle of Jericho,
- order the events in Samson's life and explain how Samson missed God's best for his life's work, and
- show how Samuel was the last of the judges and the first of the prophets.

IDENTIFICATIONS

Concepts

- *Dependence upon God*—led to the destruction of the wall around Jericho
- *Twelve tribes of Israel*—each of the sons of Jacob and Joseph established a tribe for the nation of Israel
- *Judges*—men called of God to oversee Israel
- *Kings*—men called of God to rule over Israel

People

- *Joshua:* God's chosen leader for Israel after Moses
- *Rahab:* protected the spies of Israel and was adopted into the family of Israel
- *Samson:* born with a vow before God not to shave his head and in turn he received great strength
- *Delilah:* woman whom Samson loved; she betrayed him to the Philistines
- *Eli:* priest whose sons were evil; he was replaced by Samuel
- *Samuel:* the last of the judges and the first of the prophets; annointed Saul, and later David, to become king over Israel

MATERIALS NEEDED

- *Parent/Teacher Handbook: The Bible, Vol. 1*
- Activity Sheets for Lesson 5
- Crayons and markers
- Blank sheets of white paper for drawing
- 3x5-inch index cards
- Lined paper for writing
- Words to the hymn "Trust and Obey"
- *Josh and the Big Wall* VeggieTales video
- Chairs

LEARNING ACTIVITIES FOR LESSON 5

Activity 1—Joshua's Instructions from God

For this activity read "Joshua Becomes Leader" in the handbook. Then read Joshua 1:1–9 in the Bible. God spoke to Joshua after the death of Moses. Moses had had a special relationship with God, but now Moses was dead. It remained for Joshua to lead the people of Israel into the Promised Land. That was a very difficult task. When Moses had been alive, Joshua could turn to Moses because he talked with God. Now Joshua was alone. But God assured Joshua that he was not alone. God would be with Joshua!

First, God told Joshua that He would be with Joshua. Joshua did not need to fear. The task that God gave Joshua was a large task. Joshua was to bring the people of Israel into the land that God had promised to Abraham several hundred years before. God said, "I will be with you every step of the way!" What more could one ask?

Second, God told Joshua, "Be strong and courageous!" Joshua was not to be either fearful or discouraged. God would be with him.

Third, God told Joshua not to turn aside from the Law of God that he had received from Moses.

Now talk with the children about the difficult task Joshua had with with taking the people of Israel into the Promised Land. There were giants and valiant fighting men in the land. God promised to guide His servant Joshua, but he had to keep close to God in the Word of God that had been given to Moses. Today we face many problems in our own lives. But God is still there. He wants to guide us just as He led Joshua. We must depend upon Him. We must continually read God's Word. There is no other way that we can please God and receive God's blessing.

The principles set forth in this chapter of Joshua are ones that adults need to share with the younger generation. Children need to learn early that the only way to please God and receive God's blessing is to follow the same instruction that God gave Joshua: trust and obey.

If you have the words to the hymn "Trust and Obey," you can conclude your discussion with your children by reading or singing that old familiar hymn.

Activity 2—God's Promises to Joshua

An alternate activity or a reinforcing activity uses Activity Sheet 2. Read Joshua 1:1–9 in the Scriptures. Paraphrase the story for your class.

Then help the children fill in the blanks in the activity sheet. Discuss the promises of God.

Activity 3—The Scarlet Cord

One of the great stories in the Bible is the story of Rahab. She was a woman who lived on the wall of the city of Jericho. Rahab saw the hand of God helping the people of Israel. She wisely defended the spies, who came to look at the city. In exchange, she received the promise that she and her family would be protected from the war that would come. She would become part of the people of Israel.

Read "Joshua Sends Spies to Jericho" in the handbook. Then work through the puzzle on Activity Sheet 3.

Activity 4—Josh and the Big Wall *Video*

The VeggieTales video, *Josh and the Big Wall* is a good activity for your class to watch. Like any video, you will want to watch it first and then with your class. The video will capture the attention of the children. Be sure to discuss what happens in the video with the children.

This video may leave the false impression that the people chose whether or not they would obey God in marching around the city. The Bible text, Joshua 6, is very clear that the people of Israel strictly obeyed the Lord and did everything that God commanded. Aside from this possible misinterpretation, the video gives the children a good look at what was done.

Activity 5—Drama of the Wall of Jericho

Children love to dramatize situations. Have your class gather to dramatize the story of the wall of Jericho. Place some chairs around a circle to suggest the wall of the city. Have the children bring horns and march around the chairs seven times as the people of Israel did around Jericho. On the seventh time have them make noise and have the chairs fall down. This is the way that it happened in Jericho. The wall collapsed, and the people of Israel got the victory for God.

Why did God command the people to march around the wall of the city? Who received the honor for the defeat of the city of Jericho? Were the people in a position to be proud of themselves for defeating Jericho?

Activity 6—Litany at Entering the Promised Land

A litany is a prayer of praise. A line of praise is interspersed with a line of response from the congregation. To help children become familiar with a litany, read Psalm 136. This psalm is a good example of a litany. The repeated line is, "For His love is eternal." The key is that one of the lines must be repeated throughout.

Reflect on the feelings of the people of Israel. They were poised for a new venture into the land of Palestine. What had God done for them? What were some of their fears about the future? Could they trust God to protect them as He had in the past?

Have the children sit in a circle around you. Tell them to imagine they are children of Israelite families back in Joshua's time. What would their feelings have been like? Use the material in the next several paragraphs to rehearse for them what God had done. Tell them to sit quietly in an attitude of prayer as you guide their thinking.

God had led them safely out of the land of Egypt. While forty years had passed and the adults had not been there at the time, they had been told by their parents about the deliverance of God.

These adults had experienced the care of God for them in the wilderness. The cloud of God's presence led them by day and the pillar of fire led them by night. They had manna and quail to eat. God has been with them.

Now, they were coming into the land that had been promised to Abraham, Isaac, and Jacob. The time had come to go across the Jordan River and go into the land to possess it.

As they were camped on the east side of the Jordan, they must have been a little anxious about what they would face on the other side. But God had cared for them to this point. They believed that He would care for them as they entered the land, that would become their new home.

Ask the children how they might express their feelings to God in this situation. Tell them that it would not be surprising for the people of Israel to break into a litany of praise to God for all that He had done for them. The litany would allow them to recall all the good things that God had done. The litany would give them an opportunity to thank God for His care. The litany would express their longing for God to bless them in this new adventure.

Try putting together your own litany of praise and thanksgiving to God for His guidance and protective care. Below is a model that you might use to construct a litany of praise and thanksgiving to God to express gratitude for His care:

- When we were in Egypt, He _____ us.
  Give thanks to the God of Israel, for His love endures forever.
- When we were in the wilderness, He _____ us.
  Give thanks to the God of Israel, for His love endures forever.
- God was with us in the _____ by day and the _____ by night.
  Give thanks to the God of Israel, for His love endures forever.
- God has given us _____
  Give thanks to the God of Israel, for His love endures forever.
- God alone is _____
  Give thanks to the God of Israel, for His love endures forever.
- God's love is with us and _____
  Give thanks to the God of Israel, for His love endures forever.

159

Read the litany as a prayer. The leader will read the lines of praise and the children will read the response lines.

Activity 7—Character Feeling Chart of the Events from Samson's life

When he started out, Samson had such great potential. God was with Samson. In the middle of his life, he wasted his blessing from God. To be sure, Samson killed some of the Philistines and did some things to make the lives of the Israelites better. But he used God's blessings for his own benefit, not for the benefit of God's people. He made very poor choices.

At the end of his life, Samson lost his eyesight. He was put in prison. He worked at hard labor. He was brought to the temple of Dagon, the Philistine god. The people made fun of Samson. He was miserable! But by then his hair had regrown and he was again mighty. This time he was able to break down the temple of Dagon. But he lost his life in the process.

Consider the life of Samson. Turn to Activity Sheet 7. It is a Character Feeling Chart. Together with your class, think about the life of Samson. In the first part of this chart, write a sentence about how you think Samson would have felt growing up as a young boy with such awesome physical power. Draw a picture of Samson's face at that stage of his life. Help the children think about ways such strength would be used today by a young man growing up in our world.

Next, write a sentence about how Samson would have felt in the middle of his life. Again, draw a picture of his face as it might have looked in the middle of his life. Do you think Samson was happy? Why or why not?

Finally, at the end of his life, Samson must have had strong feelings about his life. Write a sentence that would express those feelings. Draw a picture illustrating Samson destroying the temple of Dagon. How did he feel at this time in his life?

Discuss with the children: What does this chart tell you about the life of Samson?

Activity 8—An Epitaph for Samson

An epitaph is a short statement about a person that reflects that person's life. For Samson that would have been difficult. Samson's great potential was not realized in his lifetime. It was in his death that he achieved what God had wanted him to do.

Have the children draw a tombstone and think about an appropriate epitaph for Samson. In one short sentence write a fitting description of Samson's life. They could start with: Here Lies Samson Who . . .

Use the epitaph as a springboard for discussion of a person's life. How important is the way we live each day? By staying close to God, it is possible to be what God wants us to be. We not only please God, but we have the best life that is possible.

Activity 9—The Life of Samuel—a Wordfind

Read "Samuel, the Last of the Prophets" in the handbook. Duplicate copies of Activity Sheet 9 and give to the children. Have them complete the wordfind by circling the words on the puzzle sheet.

Talk about the life of Samuel and his importance in doing what God desired for His people, Israel. Why did the people want a king? Why did God tell Samuel to anoint David as a new king in place of Saul?

Activity 10—Memorize Joshua 24:15b
At the end of his ministry to the people of Israel, Joshua gave them his parting words. During his lifetime, the people followed God. In his speech, Joshua told the people to stay true to God. He told them not to follow the false gods of the peoples around them. One of his great statements comes in that speech in chapter 24, at the end of verse 15. He said,

"As for me and my family, we will worship the LORD."

Have the children write this verse in their Bible Verse Memory Books. Have them draw a picture of Joshua giving this speech to the people of Israel. Ask them to memorize this verse.

WORKSHEETS FOR LESSON 5

ACTIVITY SHEET 2: GOD PROMISES JOSHUA . . .

Directions: Complete this worksheet by writing the right word in the space provided.

1. God told Joshua that _____ His servant was dead.

2. God called Joshua to lead the people into the _____.

3. God promised to give Joshua every place that Joshua set his _____.

4. The country from Lebanon to the Euphrates River to the _____ to the west

   would belong to the people of Israel.

5. God said, "Be _____ and courageous."

6. God said, "Be careful to _____ the Law."

7. "Do not let the _____ of the Law leave you. Think about it constantly."

8. "Be careful to _____ everything written in it."

9. "Then you will be _____."

10. "Do not be _____ or discouraged, because the Lord will be with you."

Directions: Fill in the blanks.

```
1. S
2. ___ C
3. ___ A ___
4. ___ R ___
5. ___ L
6. ___ E ___
7. ___ T ___
8. ___ C ___
9. ___ O ___
10. ___ R ___
11. ___ D
```

Questions from "Joshua Sends Spies to Jericho"

1. Joshua sent two _____ to look at the city.

2. The name of the city was _____.

3. It had to be _____ before they could enter Palestine.

4. The home of _____ was on the wall of Jericho.

5. She knew that God had protected the _____.

6. The Israelites had come from _____.

7. Rahab hid the spies under _____ of flax.

8. When the king's men came, Rahab _____ the spies.

9. Then she let them down by a _____.

10. She told them to wait _____ days before returning to camp.

11. The same scarlet _____ protected Rahab when the Israelites destroyed the city.

ACTIVITY SHEET 7: CHARACTER FEELING CHART: EVENTS FROM SAMSON'S LIFE

Directions: Draw a picture of Samson's face in the picture frame at each stage of his life, and write a sentence to describe his feelings on the lines to the right of the picture.

Beginning of Samson's Life

End of Samson's Life

ACTIVITY SHEET 9: THE LIFE OF SAMUEL

Directions: Complete the wordfind, using the words in all caps. The words may go up and down, across, or on an angle. They may go backwards. Retell the story of Samuel from the wordfind.

1. Eli was the PRIEST. Eli's sons took bribes and were dishonest. God did not want Eli's sons to continue as priests.

2. HANNAH was the wife of Elkanah. She did not have a child. She prayed for a son. She promised to dedicate her son to the Lord.

3. God answered her prayer. Samuel was born. He grew up serving God with Eli and became a judge for God and a PROPHET.

4. Samuel lived in the city of RAMAH. Samuel's sons did not follow God either. They were also dishonest.

5. The people of Israel wanted a king, like their neighbors around them. God told Samuel to select SAUL to be their king.

O	J	V	J	O	P	G	O	T	X	X	C	N	Z	P
H	W	Y	K	O	G	E	S	L	U	A	S	T	R	Z
P	E	A	O	P	X	E	R	P	T	J	H	B	N	J
W	Z	D	P	V	I	U	I	J	B	W	W	X	Y	U
A	Q	W	L	R	H	A	M	A	R	Y	S	Y	L	D
T	N	W	P	T	E	H	P	O	R	P	A	M	R	G
P	Z	H	F	Q	X	U	Z	S	A	F	D	O	N	E
B	Z	W	V	P	S	B	A	M	U	V	Y	W	X	J
P	Q	N	O	K	U	B	C	O	U	J	F	Z	B	G
L	F	Y	O	D	Y	X	U	F	M	N	I	F	L	J
Z	D	I	I	Q	M	T	K	X	X	H	G	X	D	K
K	C	V	C	E	I	H	L	M	N	M	P	R	J	D
C	A	O	E	H	A	N	N	A	H	I	A	A	T	M
D	H	E	C	U	O	E	M	C	J	D	B	V	W	I
W	O	M	W	X	A	O	P	I	W	F	Z	Q	T	S

6. Saul disobeyed God and later was rejected by God. God told Samuel to anoint a new king. His name was DAVID. David was a good king and followed God.

Readings from the Parent/Teacher Handbook: The Bible, Vol. 1: "God Chooses David," "David Becomes King," "Solomon Builds the Temple," "Elijah, the Prophet to Israel," "Jonah's Story," and "Young Josiah Becomes King"

OBJECTIVES

By the end of this lesson, the learner should be able to

- identify the major events in the life of King David,
- show how Solomon started his life well, but because he failed to stay close to God, he ended his life poorly,
- describe the purposes for and the effects of the divided kingdom of the northern ten tribes of Israel and the southern two tribes of Judah,
- contrast Elijah, the prophet of God, with the false prophets of Baal and the wicked King Ahab and Queen Jezebel,
- retell the story of Jonah, the prophet to the Assyrians of Nineveh, and Jonah's disobedience to God and its consequences, and
- explain the recovery of God's Word by King Josiah and the people's response.

IDENTIFICATIONS

Concepts

- *Sacrifice*—offering given to God, usually a burnt offering of an animal
- *Ark of the Covenant*—box that became the dwelling place for God among His people, Israel
- *Sin*—disobeying the law of God
- *Punishment*—result of disobeying God
- *Repentance*—expressing sorrow for sin
- *Temple*—built by Solomon for worship of God
- *Mercy*—given by God to Nineveh for repentance

People

- *Saul:* first king over Israel
- *David:* king of Israel after Saul and a man after God's own heart

- *Goliath:* giant from among the Philistines, who fought with David and was killed
- *Jonathan:* son of Saul; good friend of David
- *Bathsheba:* beautiful woman with whom David sinned
- *Uriah:* husband of Bathsheba
- *Nathan:* God's prophet who confronted David about his sin
- *Absalom:* David's son who revolted against his father and lost his life fighting David's army
- *Solomon:* son of Bathsheba and David and heir to the throne of Israel after David; greatest king of Israel
- *Queen of Sheba:* visiting queen, who visited King Solomon
- *Rehoboam:* son of Solomon and his unwise actions led to a split in the kingdoms of Israel and Judah
- *Jereboam:* son of one of the king's servants, and became king of the northern ten tribes of Israel
- *Ahijah:* prophet of God, who confronted Jereboam for his sin
- *Elijah:* God's prophet, who confronted the prophets of Baal and King Ahab
- *Ahab:* King of Judah, whose wicked wife, Jezebel, led the people into idol worship
- *Prophets of Baal:* leaders in worship of the idol Baal
- *Naboth:* owned a vineyard that Ahab wanted; Jezebel had him killed and Elijah confronted Ahab
- *Jonah:* God's prophet who was sent to Assyria to preach repentance; Jonah disobeyed and ended up in the belly of a great fish
- *Josiah:* boy king of Judah, who rediscovered the Word of God in the Temple and restored worship and obedience to God

MATERIALS NEEDED

- *Parent/Teacher Handbook: The Bible, Vol. 1*
- *Holman Bible Dictionary*
- Activity Sheets for Lesson 6
- Crayons and markers
- Blank sheets of white paper for drawing
- Stapler
- Lined paper for writing
- Glue
- Paper plates and tongue depressors

- Glitter, sequins, plastic eyes, felt, etc. (optional)
- Posterboard
- 4x6-inch cards
- 4 plastic bottles (do not use glass bottles)
- Chenille wire (may be found in a craft store)
- Shoe boxes
- Construction paper
- Starch
- Yarn
- Balloons

LEARNING ACTIVITIES FOR LESSON 6

Activity 1—Nine Scenes from the Life of David

Introduce this unit by reading "God Chooses David" and "David Becomes King" from the handbook. We probably have one of the most complete descriptions of David's life from a teenager to his death of anyone in the Bible. God's hand was on David. David loved God with all of his heart. The psalms are a good example of how David praised God and pleased Him. But David was not perfect. He sinned against God, and it hurt the rest of his reign as king. It is important to note that David repented and God forgave him of his sin.

Provide each child with a sheet of white drawing paper. Ask them to draw scenes from each of the main events in David's life. At the conclusion of this exercise, staple the scenes into a booklet showing the life of David. You may want to encourage them to use symbols (given below) to describe each of these scenes. Read the appropriate Scripture as background before the children begin each scene. Have in mind the scenes you want them to include, but allow the children to brainstorm what should be included.

Scene 1: David as a shepherd. (1 Samuel 16)

Have the children draw a young lad in his late teens as he is out with the sheep on the grazing land. They might include David wrestling with a bear to protect his sheep. The symbol for this scene would be a sheep.

Scene 2: David is anointed to be king by Samuel. (1 Samuel 16)

David kneels before Samuel. Samuel pours oil on David's head. This was part of the ceremony showing whom God had chosen to become king over His people. Saul was still king, so Samuel and David had to be careful that word of this anointing did not reach the ears of the king. A symbol for this scene would be the flask of oil.

Scene 3: David plays the harp for Saul. (1 Samuel 16)

In this scene the children should include David sitting before King Saul in the throne room. Saul is on his throne. David is sitting next to the king with his harp. David is playing and soothing the king. The most appropriate symbol would be David's harp.

Scene 4: David kills the giant, Goliath. (1 Samuel 17)

David goes to the front lines of the battle in order to bring his brothers food. He discovers that the giant, Goliath, is defying the people of God. Goliath dared anyone to come and fight with him. None of the Israelites would go. The Philistines were waiting for Goliath to kill an opponent from Israel. The Philistines would make slaves of the Israelites. But David called upon God and went to meet Goliath. David hit Goliath in the forehead with a stone from his sling. Goliath fell dead and David cut off Goliath's head. The scene is the victory for David. The symbol is David's sling.

Scene 5: David flees from Saul. (1 Samuel 18–31)

Saul became very jealous of David. Saul hunted for David and tried to kill him. David had to flee for his life. A symbol would be a cave in which David hid from Saul.

Scene 6: David's rise to power. (2 Samuel 1–10)

Saul died in battle with the Philistines. David became king over Judah and then over all of Israel. David conquered Jerusalem and made it his new capital. David brought the worship of God to Jerusalem and God made a covenant with him. David continued to enlarge his kingdom. David as king on his throne would represent this period of his life. The symbol would be a crown.

Scene 7: Sin with Bathsheba. (2 Samuel 11–12)

At a time when kings go to war, David stayed home. He sinned against God. Then he tried to bring Bathsheba's husband, Uriah, back home. He failed at that and had him placed in the front lines, where Uriah was killed. David was confronted by Nathan the prophet. David acknowledged his sin and repented. God forgave him. David married Bathsheba. A symbol might be the palace.

Scene 8: Absalom revolts against his father. (2 Samuel 14–18)

Absalom was David's favorite son and the one he wanted to replace him. But when Absalom was sent away from the court of David for killing his half brother, Absalom began to plot against his father. Absalom raised a large army to fight. David had to flee. Eventually, Absalom was killed and David was restored. A symbol might be a sword.

Scene 9: The end of David's life. (1 Kings 1–2)

Eventually, David became old. Before his death, Bathsheba entreated David to make her son, Solomon, the new king. David called Solomon to his side and told him that he would become king. David instructed him to keep the Law of the Lord and walk in God's commandments. David died. Solomon was chosen to become the new king. A symbol for this scene might be a scroll for the Law of the Lord.

After the children have completed all of their drawings, staple the pages together into a booklet. You may want to show these booklets at the next gathering of parents.

Activity 2—Opposites Exercise: David and Goliath

Turn to Activity Sheet 2. Duplicate copies of the sheet for the children to complete. Reread the story of David and Goliath from the handbook.

Ask the children to write the appropriate answers for David and the appropriate answers for Goliath. Use the completed activity sheet as a springboard for discussion of the battle between David and Goliath. Why did David and Goliath fight? Was David a superhero or was he following God? How was David successful? Was it because of David's own strength, or how would you explain it?

Activity 3—The Meaning of Repent

For this activity, you will need to use Activity Sheet 3. Use the numbers that stand for letters to spell out the meaning of the word *repent*. After the children have decoded the message, read about the word and David's repentance on page 34 of the handbook. Stress the importance of this word. When we sin against God, we must repent in order to restored our relationship with God. What does it mean to "feel sorry for my sin?" How can I show God that I am truly sorry for my sin? Talk about the answers to these questions.

Activity 4—The Wisdom of Solomon (1 Kings 2–3)

The new king, Solomon, met God in a dream. God promised to give Solomon anything that he desired. Try to have the boys and girls think about something that they would ask for if they had the opportunity to ask for anything they desired. To help them appreciate what Solomon experienced, have them do the activity that follows.

Ask the students to stand in a circle. Tell them to think of anything that they would like to ask for. Select one child to stand in the middle of the group. Without words, have the child act out what he or she would ask for. Have the other members of the group try to guess what the child in the middle is asking for. Once someone guesses correctly, the next child in the circle moves into the middle. Keep playing until all members of the group have had a turn to be in the middle.

Next tell the children that you are now going to look at what Solomon asked for. Turn to "The Wisdom of Solomon," in the handbook. Read the selection. How did Solomon show his wisdom?

Now hand out Activity Sheet 4. Complete the exercise in small groups of two or three.

After completing the activity, talk about how Solomon started well, but he did not continue doing what was right. He did the things that he wanted to do. When he was old, Solomon did evil in God's sight. How can we avoid falling into sin as Solomon did? Conclude this activity in prayer that God will help us not only to start well but also to end well.

Activity 5—Solomon Builds the Temple (1 Kings 6–8)

Read about Solomon's Temple in the *Holman Illustrated Bible Dictionary* under "Temple of Jerusalem." The sacrificial system is very important. When we read in the New Testament: "By this will, we have been sacrificed through the offering of the body of Jesus Christ once and for all" (Hebrews 10:10). We cannot fully understand that unless we are familiar with the sacrificial system in the Temple. Sacrifice of animals on the altar of burnt offerings was necessary to atone for the sin of the people. Ever since Adam and Eve were expelled from the Garden of Eden, God required death to atone for sin. Jesus died once for all. Through our trust in Him, we can enter the presence of God.

In the Old Testament, however, Jesus' death had not yet occurred. Death of an animal was necessary to atone for sin. Under Moses' Law, it was clearly specified what sacrifices had to be made to atone for sin. As a result, the sacrificial system was defined with the Tabernacle in the wilderness. It grew to its peak in the Temple in Jerusalem under Solomon.

Help the children identify the pieces of furniture that were placed in the Temple. You might share the picture of the Temple and the arrangement of the furniture from the *Holman Illustrated Bible Dictionary*. It is not necessary to identify all of the courts and other areas of the Temple. Concentrate on the furniture inside the Temple and the two pieces that are in front of the Temple.

In front of the Temple was the altar of burnt offerings. On this altar the animal sacrifices took place. Behind the altar was the laver, containing water for the ceremonial washing of the priests.

Inside the Holy Place, the outer room of the Temple, were most of the pieces of furniture. Only the priests entered the Holy Place. It contained the altar of incense. On the altar of incense the priests burned the sweet-smelling incense. The table of shewbread contained fresh loaves of bread. The great menorah or seven-branched lampstand stood inside the Holy Place. The candles shed light inside the Holy Place.

Next, in line toward the back of the Temple came the veil. This was a very thickly woven curtain, that separated the Holy Place from the Holy of Holies. This was the furthest place from the door of the Temple. Only the high priest was allowed to enter the Holy of Holies once a year to place the blood of the sacrifice for the atonement of the people on the Ark of the Covenant. The Ark of the Covenant was a gold-covered box or chest. On top of the Ark were two cherubim or angels with their wings folded toward each other. It was considered to be the throne of the invisible God. You may also want to read the "Ark of the Covenant" in the *Holman Illustrated Bible Dictionary*. Between the angels was the place where the high priest placed the blood on the Day of Atonement.

Duplicate copies of Activity Sheet 5. Discuss the elements of the Temple with the children. Then have them fill in the blanks on the activity sheet.

Activity 6—Elijah Puppet Presentation (1 Kings 17–2 Kings 2)

Divide the group into three groups for one of each of the following scenes: (1) the woman and the cruse of oil, (2) the contest on Mount Carmel, (3) Elijah taken into heaven.

Reread the story of the woman with the cruse of oil in the handbook, "Elijah, Prophet in the Wilderness," and in 1 Kings 17. For the first scene, have this group make puppets for the prophet Elijah, the woman, and her son. To do this, draw the face of each person in the story on separate paper plates. Attach each paper plate with glue and staple to a tongue depressor.

Next, prepare a backdrop for the story. This might consist of a large sheet of posterboard on which the children have painted or colored the house where the prophet stayed. On another sheet, draw the bedroom where the child lay sick. Be sure to include the cruse of oil and the container for flour. Assist the children to become thoroughly familiar with the story and to prepare to retell the story to the entire class using their paper plate puppets and backdrops they have prepared.

For the second scene, reread the story in the handbook, "Elijah and the Prophets of Baal," and in 1 Kings 18. Follow the same procedure as for the first scene for each of the characters in this story. You will have more characters since Elijah, the prophets of Baal, and the people, who are bystanders need to be included.

Prepare a backdrop for this scene on posterboard. Draw two altars with sacrifices on the altars. On a second sheet of posterboard, draw a black cloud in the sky and the lightning from heaven that set fire to the sacrifice. Including the water and stones around the altar. Help this group to become thoroughly familiar with the story. Have them prepare to retell the story to the entire class using the paper plate puppets and the backdrops they have prepared.

For the third scene, reread the story in the handbook, "Elijah Is Taken to Heaven," and 2 Kings 2. Follow the same procedure for making paper plate puppets for each of the characters of this story. You will need Elijah and Elisha.

Prepare a backdrop sheet on posterboard. Draw the chariot of fire that is going to heaven. Also, draw the cloak that Elijah left for Elisha as he flew toward heaven. Help this group to understand the story completely and prepare to retell the story to the entire class using the puppets and prepared backdrop.

After all the groups have completed their work making the puppets and the backgrounds, have each group retell their stories to the entire class. Ask the children to explain what each of these scenes tells about Elijah and his relationship to God.

Activity 7—Naboth's Vineyard (1 Kings 21)

Read the story of Naboth's vineyard in the handbook and in 1 Kings 21. Depending on the size of your class, you may need to divide the class into smaller groups. If you have a very large class, have each smaller group work with the entire story. If you have a small class, have each group work on one scene in this story.

Provide each group with 6 4x6-inch cards to retell the story of Naboth's vineyard. On the lined side of the first card, write the following segment of the story: *Naboth owns a large vineyard. It was given to his ancestors. God told the people to pass their property to the next generation. The vineyard was next to King Ahab's palace. Ahab wanted the vineyard.* On the blank side of the card, have the children draw a picture to illustrate this segment of the story.

On the lined side of the second card, write the following segment of the story: *King Ahab asked Naboth if he could buy the vineyard. Naboth told the king that his ancestors had passed the vineyard to him, and he could not sell the vineyard even to the king.* On the blank side of the card, have the children draw a picture to illustrate this segment of the story.

On the lined side of the third card, write this segment of the story: *King Ahab went back to the palace and sulked. He was very angry with Naboth. He wanted that vineyard. He did not know what to do to get the vineyard.* On the blank side of the card, have the children draw a picture to illustrate this segment of the story.

On the lined side of the fourth card, write this part of the story: *Queen Jezebel, Ahab's wife, held a feast. Jezebel promised to get the vineyard for the king. Naboth was invited to the feast. During the feast, the queen accused him of saying things against God. This crime was punished by stoning.* On the blank side of the card, have the children draw a picture to illustrate this segment of the story.

On the lined side of the fifth card, write this part of the story: *Naboth was stoned. The king was now free to take Naboth's property for his own.* On the other side of the card, have the children draw a picture to illustrate this segment of the story.

Conclude the story by writing this segment of the story on the lined side of the card: *Elijah confronted King Ahab. Elijah told Ahab that he would be punished. But Ahab repented. He wore sackcloth and ashes to show that he was sorry for what he had done. God forgave Ahab.* On the other side of the card, have the children draw a picture to illustrate this part of the story.

After all of the students have completed their parts of the story, have members of the groups retell the story using the descriptions and the pictures.

Ask the children to tell what they learned from this story about God, about people, and about God's love and mercy.

Activity 8—Jonah and the Great Fish (Jonah 1:17–2:10)

This activity will help the children focus on what Jonah must have experienced when he disobeyed God and ended up in the belly of the great fish.

For each child, cut two figures of a large fish with its mouth open. Cut out a small figure of Jonah or make one out of chenille wire. Staple and paste the edges of two halves of the fish together leaving the mouth edge open. Stuff the two halves of the fish with cotton balls to make it appear three-dimensional. Place the figure of Jonah inside the mouth of the fish. Children may take the fish home and hang it in their room as a reminder that we must obey God.

Talk about the feelings Jonah felt when he was in the belly of the fish. Why did he run away from God? [Jonah did not want God to show mercy on the people of Ninevah]. Did Jonah believe that God would find him in Spain? [Jonah probably believed that God was back in Israel and would not find him in Spain]. What can we learn from this story? [We must obey God when He tells us to do something].

Activity 9—King Josiah's Reforms (2 Kings 22–23)

Divide the class in pairs to write a newspaper article for the *Jerusalem Gazette* on the finding of the Book of the Law. Have the children pretend that they are newspaper reporters and the Book of the Law has just been rediscovered as repairs are being done on the Temple. The children should tell what King Josiah did and how the people responded. Reread the section in the handbook, "Young King Josiah Becomes King," and 2 Kings 22–23.

The following facts should be included in the article:

- Workmen were repairing the Temple during the reign of King Josiah.
- The high priest, Hilkiah, opened the cornerstone of the Temple and found the Book of the Law.
- The Book of the Law had been lost because the evil kings and priests did not want God's Law to be taught in the kingdom.
- The Book of the Law was taken to King Josiah, and the king's messenger read from the Book of the Law.
- King Josiah was very upset because he knew that he and his people had not been following God's Laws.
- King Josiah read the laws to the people and they promised to obey the law.
- The false priests to the idols were removed from the land.
- The priests destroyed all of the altars and idols that were dedicated to the false gods.
- The Passover was again celebrated as God had directed in the Law of Moses.

Activity 10—Who Am I? Review

For this activity, make copies of Activity Sheet 10, one for each child. Have each child write the appropriate name for the person described in the blank provided. A list of names is provided for the children to choose from at the right of the page.

Activity 11—Memorize Psalm 119:9–11

To help your children understand what God desires of those who follow Him, have your students memorize Psalm 119:9–11. This is an important text for children to learn and keep for future reference, when temptation comes. For younger children, just have them memorize verse 11.

Below is the complete text for these verses—

How can a young man keep his way pure?
    By keeping Your word.
I have sought You with all my heart;
    don't let me wander from Your commands.
I have treasured Your word in my heart
    so that I may not sin against You.

Place a copy of these verses in each child's Bible Verse Memory Book and have them illustrate it.

WORKSHEETS FOR LESSON 6

ACTIVITY SHEET 2: DAVID AND GOLIATH

Directions: At the bottom of the sheet you will find word or phrase opposites. Write the correct word or phrase opposites to describe David and Goliath.

DAVID	GOLIATH

Word or Phrase Opposites:

Slingshot	Heavy armor	Big	Lost his life
Faith in himself	No armor	Faith in God	Small
Sword and shield	Won the fight		

ACTIVITY SHEET 3: THE MEANING OF REPENT

Directions: Fill in the letters assigned to the numbers to tell what the word *repent* means.

Repent means to ___ ___ ___ ___ ___ ___ ___ that ___ ___ ___
               20 5 12 12 7 15 4   25 15 21

are ___ ___ ___ ___ ___ ___ ___ ___ ___ ___ ___ and ___ ___
   19 15 18 18 25 6 15 18 19 9 14   20 15

___ ___ ___ ___ ___ ___ ___ ___ from that ___ ___ ___.
20 21 18 14 1 23 1 25   19 9 14

Key:		
A=1	B=2	C=3
D=4	E=5	F=6
G=7	H=8	I=9
J=10	K=11	L=12
M=13	N=14	O=15
P=16	Q=17	R=18
S=19	T=20	U=21
V=22	W=23	X=24
Y=25	Z=26	

ACTIVITY SHEET 4: SOLOMON'S LIFE

Directions: Take your Bible, and in groups of two or three find the following references:

1 Kings 2:7; 3:3, 6, 12, 28; 4:29; 11:1, 4, 6

What do these verses tell us about Solomon? Did he change in later life from the direction of his life in the early days of his reign? In the appropriate column, write the characteristics of Solomon in his early days and in his last days.

EARLY DAYS	LAST DAYS

ACTIVITY SHEET 5: SOLOMON'S TEMPLE

Directions: Fill in each of the blanks with the appropriate word from the list below:

veil   laver   incense   throne   Jerusalem   Holy of Holies   altar of burnt offerings
sacrifice   shewbread   Ark of the Covenant   menorah   Holy Place

1. The Temple built by King Solomon stood in _____.

2. On the outside of the Temple stood the _____ where the great sacrifices took place.

3. Also on the outside stood the _____, where the priests washed their hands and feet before entering the Temple.

4. Walking through the great doors to the Temple led to the _____ inside the Temple.

5. This room was lighted by the great _____, which had seven branches with seven candles.

6. Also in this room was the altar of _____, which made the inside smell very sweet.

7. The table of _____ contained freshly baked bread.

8. Moving further toward the back of the Temple was the thickly woven _____ that separated the front room, where the priests served, from the back room.

9. The back room was called the _____ of _____.

10. Only the high priest entered the back room once each year to place the _____ of blood before the Lord.

11. The back room contained the _____ of the _____.

12. This was the _____ room of the invisible God.

ACTIVITY SHEET 10: WHO AM I?

Directions: Write the name of the person who is described.

Names:
Jonathan, Nathan, Goliath, Josiah, Uriah, Saul, Jonah, Jereboam, Elijah, Naboth, King Ahab

1. I was the first king of Israel. _____

2. I was a giant from Philistia, fighting against Israel. _____

3. I was a prophet of God who defeated the prophets of Baal. _____

4. I was the king of Judah who rediscovered God's Word in the Temple. _____

5. I was the Queen of _____, who came to visit King Solomon.

6. I was a wicked king of Judah and my wife was Jezebel. _____

7. I was the husband of Bathsheba and a soldier in the army of King David. _____

8. I owned a vineyard that the king wanted. He had me killed to take my vineyard. _____

9. I was a close friend of David and the son of a king. _____

10. I was a servant in the household of King Solomon and chosen by the people of Israel to be a king of the northern ten tribes. _____

11. I was the prophet who had to tell King David that he had sinned against God. _____

12. I was a prophet, who disobeyed God and had to spend three nights in the inside of a great fish, before I did what God told me to do. _____

Readings from the Parent/Teacher Handbook: The Bible, Vol. 1: "Jeremiah and the Fall of Jerusalem," "Daniel and the Princes of Israel," Esther Saves the Jewish People," and "The Return to Jerusalem"

OBJECTIVES

By the end of this lesson, the learner should be able to

- describe the work of Jeremiah, God's prophet, to call the people of Judah to repent for their sin,
- explain the faithfulness to God of Daniel, Shadrach, Meshach, and Abednego in spite of their captivity in Babylon and the consequences of their actions,
- show how Esther—a young woman who was faithful to God—saved her people from disaster, and
- examine the faithfulness of Nehemiah to the God of Israel through prayer, which led to the rebuilding of the wall in Jerusalem to protect the Holy City and the worship of God.

IDENTIFICATIONS

Concepts

- *Prophet*—one who speaks God's message to the people
- *Idols*—an object of worship other than the living God
- *Captive*—one who is taken or held as a prisoner
- *Cupbearer of the king*—person who drank before the king to protect the king
- *Walls of Jerusalem*—walls around the city to protect it from invaders
- *Jewish feasts*—prescribed festivals for celebration in the annual calendar

People

- *Jeremiah:* known as the weeping prophet because his obedience to God led him into difficulty with others
- *Zedekiah:* last king of Judah, who was taken into captivity in Babylon
- *Nebuchadnezzar:* Babylonian king who took the people of Judah into captivity

- *Daniel:* godly young man and prophet of God to the people of Judah in captivity in Babylon, interpreted dreams of the king
- *Shadrach, Meshach, and Abednego:* three young men who were protected by God from the evil Babylonian king
- *Belshazzar:* last Babylonian king, who was defeated by the Persians
- *Darius:* king of Persia who defeated Belshazzar
- *Ahasuerus (Xerxes):* Persian king who was on the throne when Esther became his queen
- *Haman:* evil Persian who tried to destroy the people of Judah
- *Mordecai:* uncle of Esther, who pled with her to help save her people
- *Esther:* Jewish girl who became queen of Persia; she helped save her people from the wicked Haman
- *Zerubbabel:* grandson of King Jehoiachin, who was taken into captivity; Zerubbabel returned to Israel during the first year of King Cyrus' reign
- *Ezra:* priest and scribe who returned from captivity during the reign of Artaxerxes and led the fight to restore the Law of God to Israel
- *Nehemiah:* cupbearer of the Persian King Cyrus, who went back to Jerusalem to rebuild the walls

MATERIALS NEEDED

- *Parent/Teacher Handbook: The Bible, Vol. 1*
- Activity Sheets for Lesson 7
- Crayons and markers
- Pencils
- Blank sheets of white paper for drawing
- Lined paper for writing
- Construction paper
- Paper bags, the size for lunches

Activity 1—Jeremiah, the Prophet (Jeremiah 1, 5, 9, 37–38)

This activity might begin like a telephone call—"Jeremiah, you have a call on line one." Place your students in a circle around the room. To the first child in your circle, whisper the words of God to Jeremiah (Jeremiah 1:7): *"Do not say: I am only a youth, for you will go to everyone I send you to and speak whatever I tell you."*

The first child will whisper what he/she heard to the second child and so on around the circle. NO REPEATING is allowed. The student can only say the verse ONCE to the next child. Have the last student repeat what he/she heard. Compare the last statement with the first statement. Most likely the verse became completely distorted.

Tell the children that such distortion comes from passing the message from one person to the next. For that reason, God did not allow His message to be distorted. Rather, He gave it to one man—Jeremiah. (Later, we will memorize this verse and the one that follows).

Duplicate copies of Activity Sheet 1 for your students. Have the children complete the puzzle. Note that the puzzle is built around the word *prophet*.

After they have completed the puzzle, talk about the word *prophet*. What does this word mean? Why was Jeremiah called a prophet? How did Jeremiah receive God's message for the people? Are there prophets today? (Note that God still speaks to us today through pastors and teachers in our churches.)

Activity 2—Daniel and the Princes of Israel (Daniel 1–12)

Duplicate Activity Sheet 2. This is a graphic organizer to help the children think about consequences that come from actions we take. Daniel is a good example of the kind of man that God chooses and blesses. Daniel and his friends Shadrach, Meshach, and Abednego refused to do anything against God. They were placed in several difficult circumstances. They did not know that God would protect them. But they did know that they would not disobey God. God did protect them.

Have the children complete the activity sheet. For younger children, this exercise may be too difficult. For them, you talk about each situation and have them draw pictures of each situation: (1) eating at the king's table, (2) Shadrach, Meshach, and Abednego in the fiery furnace, but with another man from God to protect them, and (3) Daniel in the lion's den.

Activity 3—A Food Test for Daniel and His Friends (Daniel 1)

Provide the students with two baskets. In the one basket place fruit and vegetables that are appetizing and good to eat. In the other basket place candy, chips, cookies, and things that are not healthy to eat. Ask the students from which basket they would like to eat. (Most likely, they will choose the "junk" food). Then ask them which food is better for them. Talk about the importance of not eating "junk" food as a steady diet. This was the same dilemma the Hebrew princes faced.

On sheets of lined paper at their seats and/or on the chalkboard, have the children write adjectives that represent each basket of food. Discuss these adjectives and what the children liked or disliked about each basket of food. Talk about the results for the Hebrew princes and why they obeyed God and not the king.

Activity 4—*Captivity for the Children of Israel (2 Kings 25; Jeremiah 39)*

This activity is designed to help children understand the difficulty of being captured by the Babylonians under King Nebuchadnezzar. While they do not need to understand the full horror of the captivity, they can gain some understanding of the discomfort.

For this activity, choose two students to serve as the keepers of the dog pound. They are dog catchers. Their goal is to catch as many dogs as they can. The rest of the students in the class are dogs. Each dog catcher has a pound—an area of the room that is set aside for the captured dogs. You might use chairs arranged in a circle to contain the dogs.

The dog catcher tags the dogs, and the dogs must go to the pound. While they are in the pound, the children may not talk or do anything. When all of the children are caught, the dog catcher who has the most dogs wins.

After all the children have been caught, talk about how they felt as they were captured and placed in the pound. Then discuss how the people of Judah must have felt when they were taken captive and forced to go to a new land. They longed for home in Palestine. They felt abandoned by God. But that is why God sent His prophets to the people, to assure them that He had not forgotten them. Though they were being punished for their disobedience, but God would again bring them back to their homeland and to the Temple, where they could worship Him.

Activity 5—*Nebuchadnezzar's Dream (Daniel 2)*

King Nebuchadnezzar had a dream. He did not remember what happened in the dream. None of his wise men or astrologers could tell Nebuchadnezzar what the dream was about. They could not tell him the meaning. He decided to have all these men killed.

Daniel heard of the threat. Daniel asked for some time to find out what the dream was and what it meant. He went home and prayed. God revealed the dream and the meaning to Daniel. Daniel returned to the king and told him the dream and its interpretation.

Reread "Nebuchadnezzar's Dream" in the handbook. Have each child write out the interpretation of Nebuchadnezzar's dream. (The interpretation is also found in the handbook.)

After the children have finished the exercise, have them talk about what the dream was and what it meant. Why was Daniel able to remember the dream? Why did Daniel interpret the dream for the king? Stress the point that when we are walking close to God, he helps us to do things that we cannot do for ourselves.

Activity 6—*The Writing on the Wall (Daniel 5)*

Belshazzar became king at the death of his father, Nebuchadnezzar. He was profane and decided to host a feast for his princes of the realm. They drank to the idol gods. Belshazzar called for the vessels that had been captured in the raid of the Temple at Jerusalem. He wanted to drink from them and make sport. Suddenly, a hand appeared on the wall and it wrote these words: *Mene, Mene, Tekel, Parsin.*

Belshazzar was frightened. He could not find any men who could interpret the writing. The queen suggested that Belshazzar call Daniel, who had worked for his father. Daniel was called. Daniel told the king that his reign would end. He had taken the holy goblets from the Temple in Jerusalem and had not honored them.

The meaning of the words is as follows:
- MENE means that God has judged your reign and it is over!
- TEKEL means that God has weighed your life in the balance and He is not pleased with you.
- PARSIN means that your kingdom will be given to the Medes and the Persians.

That night the kingdom was destroyed and Belshazzar was killed.

Discuss with the children the fear that must have swept over Belshazzar when he saw the hand writing on the wall. Take a peice of construction paper and fold in half. On the outside of the paper, have the children write the words that were written on the wall. Inside the children may write the interpretation of the mysterious handwriting on the wall.

Retell the story. Focus attention on the importance of God's judgment of those who fail to obey Him. We cannot be careless about the things of God.

Activity 7—Daniel in the Lion's Den (Daniel 6)

The story of Daniel in the lion's den is important for children to understand because it demonstrates the protective and providential care of God. It is not a story of a superhero. Rather, it is the story of a man who obeyed God, and God protected him. Daniel did not know that God would protect him. He obeyed God no matter what the consequences were to him personally.

Have the children make paper bag puppets. Use brown sandwich bags. Use the bottom of the bag for the face. Your children can use construction paper to make faces and glue them to the bottom of the bag.

Make one bag to represent the Persian king, King Darius. Make another bag to represent Daniel. Make four or five bags to represent the king's advisors, who were jealous of Daniel and wanted to get rid of him. Have the rest of your children make puppets of the lions.

Optionally, you might want to have several of the students make a background depicting a den in a cave. While Daniel is in the den with the lions, their mouths are closed. But when the jealous advisors are thrown to the lions, the lions devoured them.

After you have finished retelling the story with the puppets, talk about God's protective care for Daniel. Also talk about the need for prayer, as Daniel demonstrated each day. Finally talk about the importance of obeying God, regardless of the consequences.

Activity 8—Esther Saves the Jewish People (Esther)

The story of Esther is a beautiful story of the way in which a young girl became queen of Persia. She went to the king and pled with the king to save her people from the scheming of the wicked Haman. Read the story in the handbook.

Duplicate and cut out the cube that is found on Activity Sheet 8. Next, have the children draw the scenes as described in the instructions on the activity sheet. Allow the children to complete the scenes before you fold the cube and paste the tabs.

Work in small groups and have one person in each group share the story in sequence, using his/her cube.

Have others in the group share ways by which God has protected their family.

Activity 9—Story Pyramid—The Return to Jerusalem (Nehemiah 1–13)

Duplicate the graphic organizer on Activity Sheet 9, which works through the story of Nehemiah. Read "The Return to Jerusalem" in the handbook. Also read Nehemiah 1–13. The wall around Jerusalem was very important to protect Jerusalem from the outside kings and others who wanted to keep the people of God from worshiping and carrying out their responsibilities before God.

Nehemiah is a good example of a person who was close to God. His prayer led to the pilgrimage back to Jerusalem to rebuild the walls. He had to meet many obstacles in the search for carrying out God's will.

Using the story, have the children complete the Story Pyramid. Then have the children tell the story of Nehemiah and Ezra. Talk with the children about the importance of prayer as shown by Nehemiah. Tell them also about the protective care of God in meeting the obstacles that were in the way of Nehemiah completing the task for God.

Activity 10—Crossword Puzzle Review

Review the section beginning with "Jeremiah and the Fall of Jerusalem" and ending with "The Return to Jerusalem" in the handbook. Duplicate copies of the Crossword Puzzle Review on Activity Sheet 10. Give the Crossword Puzzle and the explanatory sentences to the children. Have them complete the Crossword Puzzle by writing the words in the appropriate places on the puzzle sheet. For younger children, you might list the names of the persons on the puzzle sheet.

Talk about the challenges faced by the different persons discussed in these passages. Check the understanding of your children across this unit.

Activity 11—Memorize Jeremiah 1:7–8

To help your children understand what God desires of those who follow Him, have them memorize Jeremiah 1:6–8. These are good verses because they show that it does not matter what the age of an individual person is, God wants us to help do His work now. (For younger children, you may want them to memorize only verse 6).

"But I protested, 'Oh no, LORD GOD! Look, I don't know how to speak, since I am only a youth.' Then the LORD said to me: 'Do not say: I am only a youth, for you will go to everyone I will send you to and speak whatever I tell you. Do not be aftrai of anyone, for I will be with you to deliever you.'"

You will want to find a place in your booklet for Scripture memory. Have the children write the verse, illustrate it, and put in their Bible Verse Memory Books.

WORKSHEETS FOR LESSON 7

ACTIVITY SHEET 1: PROPHET PUZZLE

Directions: Fill in the blanks.

Jeremiah the Prophet

1. P
2. R
3. O
4. P
5. H
6. E
7. T

Questions:

1. There were many _____ that God sent to His people to give His message.
2. God called _____ to be His prophet to the people of Judah.
3. The message that the prophet gave came from _____.
4. The message called on the people _____.
5. God was going to judge the people because they were _____ and wicked.
6. The people continued to burn _____ to the idols.
7. Because they did not listen and obey, God had to bring _____ upon them.

ACTIVITY SHEET 2: DANIEL AND THE PRINCES OF ISRAEL

Situation 1—Daniel and his friends ordered to eat at the king's table.

CAUSE		EFFECT
In captivity, Daniel and his three friends were told to eat the king's food. This was against what God told them.		_____ _____ _____

Situation 2—Daniel's three friends are forced to bow down to an Idol.

CAUSE		EFFECT
King Nebuchadnezzar of Babylonia ordered everyone to bow down to the statue, that he said was a god.		_____ _____ _____

Situation 3—Daniel is ordered not to pray to any other than Darius.

CAUSE		EFFECT
The new King Darius of Persia, ordered an edict that no one could make any requests to any god, but to him, the king.		_____ _____ _____

ACTIVITY 8: ESTHER SAVES THE JEWISH PEOPLE

Story Cube:

1. Duplicate the blank story cube (can be enlarged).
2. In block 1, write the name of the story.
3. In block 3, draw a picture of Esther.
4. In block 2, draw a picture of Mordechi telling the king about the plot against his life.
5. In block 4, draw the king signing the death warrant against the Jews because Haman tricked the king.
6. In block 5, draw the Jewish people praying for Esther.
7. In block 6, draw the dinner for the king and Haman and the expo sure of the plot, which led to Haman's death.

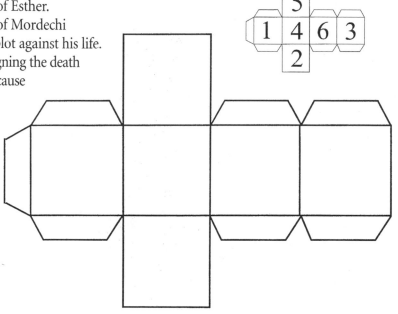

ACTIVITY SHEET 9: THE RETURN TO JERUSALEM

Story Pyramid

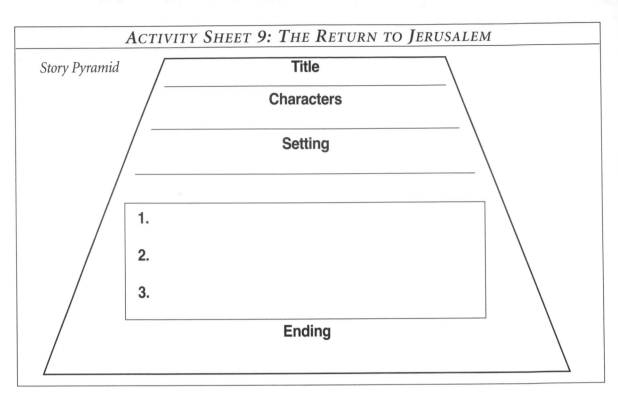

Title

Characters

Setting

1.

2.

3.

Ending

ACTIVITY SHEET 10: CROSSWORD PUZZLE REVIEW

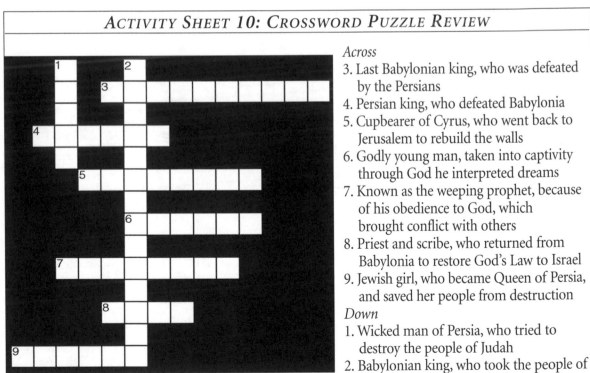

Across

3. Last Babylonian king, who was defeated by the Persians
4. Persian king, who defeated Babylonia
5. Cupbearer of Cyrus, who went back to Jerusalem to rebuild the walls
6. Godly young man, taken into captivity through God he interpreted dreams
7. Known as the weeping prophet, because of his obedience to God, which brought conflict with others
8. Priest and scribe, who returned from Babylonia to restore God's Law to Israel
9. Jewish girl, who became Queen of Persia, and saved her people from destruction

Down

1. Wicked man of Persia, who tried to destroy the people of Judah
2. Babylonian king, who took the people of Judah into captivity

Unit Two: The New Testament: Lessons 8–14

UNIT SUMMARY

This set of lessons will provide the learner with background in the New Testament through chronological Bible teaching. The learner will gain an understanding of the life and ministry of Jesus and the birth and growth of the early church of the New Testament. The learner will also develop a lifelong love for God's Word to us through the Bible.

OVERVIEW

Objectives

By the end of this unit, the learner should be able to

- review the Old Testament study from the previous 7 lessons,
- understand significant persons who are identified and described in the New Testament and be able to describe their contributions to the fulfillment of God's purposes,
- understand and appreciate the significant events that occured in the New Testament in the chronological development of God's dealing with humankind from the life and ministry of Jesus to the end of the New Testament,
- understand how God dealt with sin in the New Testament and appreciate God's redemptive activity through Jesus' sacrificial death and resurrection and His continuing redemptive activity during the New Testament times and today, and
- develop a lifelong love and appreciation for God's Word in the New Testament.

Content Summary and Rationale

After four hundred years passed between Malachi and Matthew, God's redemptive activity in the world continued with the birth of John the Baptist and reached its zenith in the life, ministry, death, and resurrection of God's own Son, Jesus Christ.

The Gospel writers tell us about the miraculous birth and sinless life of Jesus. But Jesus did not stop with a good life and ministry. He went to the cross of Calvary in order to redeem us from sin. No longer were sacrifices of animals necessary. God's Son, Jesus, died once and for all. God raised Him from the dead and demonstrated that God desires that all men should come to Him for salvation from sin here and now and have eternal life in the hereafter. The prophecy of Jeremiah in the Old Testament came true. The Law of God was no longer only written on tablets of stone but now upon the hearts of all who believe. Through Christ, a person could come to know God and become part of God's family.

The New Testament account continues in the Book of the Acts. The church is born. Acts provides us with understanding of the struggles of the early church to become what God desired. Before He ascended to the Father, Jesus taught His disciples that they would become His witnesses in Jerusalem, Judea, Samaria, and to the uttermost parts of the world.

The apostle Paul became the first missionary to the Gentiles (those persons in other parts of the Roman Empire who were not Jews). Paul planted churches across the Roman world. He wrote letters to the churches to correct their failures and strengthen their ministry. Since we are dealing only with the chronological Bible message historically, we will not cover the letters in this volume. We may refer to specific passages for study, however.

Finally, we come to the end of time and the Book of the Revelation. John's ecstatic vision helps us see the conclusion of life as we know it today. We will look briefly at the New Jerusalem and the new heaven and new earth.

Key Concept

God came to earth in the person of Jesus to bring sinful man back to Himself. What Adam and Eve lost at the Fall—when the relationship with God was severed—was now restored by God Himself coming to earth, living a sinless life of sacrifice and ministry, dying on the cross as a sacrifice for us, and being resurrected to a new life. This relationship with God will one day be our experience also if we accept the new life that Jesus provides.

Prior Knowledge Needed

Similar to the Old Testament stories, most children who have attended church through the kindergarten and preschool years have heard many stories about Jesus. However, their knowledge is very limited. Most do not understand the importance of Jesus' life and death on the cross for our sin even though they have been exposed to the Christian holidays of Christmas and Easter.

You can use the limited knowledge that they have to enlarge their understanding. Help them develop a more comprehensive view of the life and ministry of Jesus. Help them integrate the stories that they have heard about Jesus into a more holistic understanding of Jesus.

RESOURCES FOR TEACHERS AND STUDENTS

- Buchanan, Edward, *Parent/Teacher Handbook: The Bible, Vol. 1* (Nashville, Tenn.: Broadman & Holman, 2003).
- Butler, Trent, ed., *Holman Illustrated Bible Dictionary* (Nashville, Tenn.: Holman Bible Publishers, 2003).
- Dockery, David, ed., *Holman Bible Handbook* (Nashville, Tenn.: Holman Bible Publishers, 1992).
- *Holman Bible Atlas* (Nashville, Tenn.: Holman Bible Publishers, 1998).
- An encyclopedia—*World Book, Funk and Wagnalls, Britannica,* etc. (may use CD-ROM)

SUPPLEMENTARY RESOURCES FOR TEACHERS

- Sims, Lesley, *A Visitor's Guide to Ancient Rome* (London, England: Usborne Publishing, 1999). Available from Barnes and Noble and other bookstores online.
- *The Visual Bible—Matthew* is a dramatization using the actual Scriptures. Visual Bible—Matthew may be used throughout the life and ministry of Jesus, lessons 8–10.
- *The Visual Bible—Acts* may also be used for the missionary journeys of Paul in lesson 13. Both series are available in VHS or DVD format at your local Christian bookstore. The DVD version provides access to the specific events that you may wish to show. The VHS version will have to be cued for the event that you wish to show.

LESSON 8: INTRODUCTION TO THE NEW TESTAMENT AND THE BIRTH OF JESUS

Readings from the Parent/Teacher Handbook: The Bible, Vol. 1: "The New Testament: Jewish Life at the Beginning of the New Testament" to "The Birth of Jesus"

OBJECTIVES

By the end of this lesson, the learner should be able to
- review the Old Testament study from the previous seven lessons,
- differentiate among several religious and political groups—the Pharisees, Sadducees, Zealots, etc.,
- identify the essential parts of the story of the miraculous birth of Jesus in Bethlehem,
- show how Jesus grew through childhood and continued to please God, and
- demonstrate how important it is to memorize Scripture at any age, but especially as a child.

IDENTIFICATIONS

Concepts
- *Common language*—Greek spread along with Greek culture through the Mediterranean world
- *Birth of Jesus*—miraculous birth through the Holy Spirit
- *Baptism*—buried in the water and raised to new life
- *Temptation*—Satan's pull to sin against God

People
- *Alexander the Great:* military genius who conquered lands from Greece to the northern part of India
- *Zealots:* group that opposed Rome and took every opportunity to kill Romans
- *Cyrus:* king of Persia who sent many of the people of Judah back to Palestine
- *Pharisees:* Jewish religious group that tried to maintain purity of the Jewish religion
- *Sadducees:* Jewish political group that was part of the ruling class in Judah
- *John the Baptist:* last of the prophets
- *Zechariah:* priest in the Temple and father of John the Baptist

- *Elizabeth:* mother of John the Baptist
- *Angel Gabriel:* angel sent by God to announce the birth of Jesus
- *Augustus Caesar:* emperor in Rome who was on the throne when Jesus was born
- *Jesus:* Son of God who was given birth through Mary
- *Mary:* mother of Jesus
- *Joseph:* earthly father of Jesus, who was told in a dream about the miraculous virgin birth by the Holy Spirit
- *Shepherds:* men who were in the fields when the angels announced the birth of Jesus
- *Wise Men:* men from the East who came to Bethlehem, following the star
- *Simeon:* devout old man who lived to see the Christ
- *Anna:* prophetess who was in the Temple when Jesus was brought

MATERIALS NEEDED
- *Parent/Teacher Handbook: The Bible, Vol. 1*
- Activity Sheets for Lesson 8
- Crayons and markers
- Blank sheets of white paper for drawing
- Roll of shelf paper or butcher paper
- Masking tape and plastic tape
- Reusable adhesive
- 3x5-inch index cards
- Lined paper for writing
- Plaster of Paris or a dough recipe
- Push pins
- Tempera paints
- Mixing bowl
- Construction paper
- Toothpicks
- Posterboard
- Plastic Ziplock Bags
- *The Visual Bible—Matthew* (optional)

Activity 1—Review of the Old Testament

This is a very important activity in the study of the Bible. If children are to gain a comprehensive understanding of the Bible, they need to see the complete history of God's redeeming love toward sinful men and women. They need to see more than just the individual stories of how God acted in the life of Abraham or the life of Moses or the life of David. Children (and adults) need to see an overview of God's activity through the centuries. This activity is designed to help them gain "the big picture."

Duplicate Activity Sheet 1. Divide your class into seven smaller groups of students. Note that there are seven segments to the chart of the "Review the Old Testament." Have each of the groups take one of the segments of the chart and prepare that portion for a mural.

When your students have completed the mural, you should talk about the meaning of the Old Testament in the drama of God's redemption of mankind. Begin by discussing the God of Creation and the way sin entered the world. Mankind became increasingly wicked as time passed. God destroyed the world with the Flood. It appeared that the situation was hopeless.

Then God found Abraham. Abraham obeyed God. God then made a covenant with Abraham and promised to redeem humankind through the line of Abraham. (See also the chart on Activity Sheet 2.) Continue through the Old Testament, which now follows the line of Abraham and prepares the way for the coming of the Messiah, Jesus Christ.

Discuss the meaning of sacrifice in the Old Testament. Find a picture of an altar and use to talk about sacrifice. God's righteous Law demands the life of an animal to be sacrificed in order to redeem the life of a person who has sinned against God. It is important to note here that all people have sinned and will die if they do not repent. Knowing about sacrifies in the Old Testament is essential since it prepares the way for the sacrifice of Jesus, once and for all, on the cross in the New Testament. It is better not to discuss the death of Jesus at this point but to prepare your students to understand the meaning of the sacrifice of a lamb and that the sacrifice of a lamb was not fully adequate. There had to be a better sacrifice that would occur once and for all. But what would it be?

Activity 2—Charts of the Old Testament Review

Either duplicate or enlarge Activity Sheet 2. Use this chart to show the steps of sin by Adam and Eve that led to death, and the steps of faith that led to life for Abraham.

Talk about the sin of *covetousness*. Covetousness is at the root of sin. The word comes from a Hebrew word that means to "delight in," "desire," or "be pleasant." When Eve ate of the fruit of the tree of the knowledge of good and evil, she went through the process of imaging being like God. Satan beguiled her into believing that God was depriving her of something that would be good for her. He led her to stop trusting God. It was her attitude of not believing God that led her to disobey God's command. The disobedience led to sin and death.

By contrast, Abraham believed God. When God called him, Abraham listened and believed that God would work in his best interest. Abraham obeyed God. Recall the memory verse from Hebrews 11:8: *"By faith Abraham, when he was called, obeyed and went out to a place he was going to receive as an inheritance; he went out, not knowing where he was going."* This led to the covenant and to God's blessing. It also led to life everlasting for Abraham in the next life after death in this life.

Our sin follows a similar pattern. We doubt God. Then we distrust Him. Then we disobey. Then we must repent and ask God's forgiveness. It is much better if we have faith in God, believe God, trust God, and obey God. We are much happier as a result.

Activity 3—Books of the Bible: New Testament

Have the students continue their memorization of the books of the Bible by learning the books of the New Testament. Before you begin this task, review the books of the Old Testament. Remind your students that the four hundred silent years passed—more than twice as many years as the United States has been a nation—before God moved among His people again. This time God sent Jesus. The New Testament is about Jesus and how He became our Savior.

Memorize the names of the twenty-seven New Testament books of the Bible. The first task is to learn where these books of the Bible fit into the total library. Read over Activity Sheet 3 to help your children categorize the various books of the Bible.

After your children are familiar with the books of the New Testament, take the blank sheet of books on Activity Sheet 3. Help your children write the names for each of the books in each section of the New Testament. Ask the children not to look at the correct answers until he cannot remember any more of the names. Work at this process until the children are able to get the names correct. You will need to work on this task for several weeks, but the results will be worth the effort.

After the children are thoroughly familiar with the books of the New Testament, the final task will be to assist them to memorize the names of all of the books of the New Testament in the correct order.

If you know the song for the books of the Bible, you will want to sing it with your class. This is an excellent way to help the children memorize the names of each of the books.

Activity 4—Time Line for Bible History

Use the time line to help your students discover the main events in the New Testament. Remember that a time line is going to be best understood by children in the third grade or above. You may still do the activity at lower grades, but their perception of time is very limited. The pictures will provide younger children with a sequence task, however. That can be a helpful process.

Develop a time line for the history of the time periods covered by the New Testament. Activity Sheet 4 gives a list of approximate dates.

Use a sheet of shelf paper or butcher paper that will stretch 3 to 6 feet in length, and write significant dates along the lower margin. Allow enough space for your children to draw pictures of the events as you come to them in your readings in the handbook.

To assist you with this project, you may find pictures in a Bible coloring book or online.

You can attach the new material to your past time lines, or you can keep them as separate sets of events. If you place them on the wall, use masking tape or plastic adhesive (obtainable at a stationary store) that will hold the paper to the wall but not leave marks on the surface.

This activity will be ongoing as you move through the material in the handbook.

Activity 5—Fill in the Blanks

Duplicate enough copies of Activity Sheet 5 for each of the members of your class. Have them complete the worksheet.

Activity 6—Field Trip to the Holy Land Experience™

It would be ideal to take your children across the ocean to the Holy Land. Assuming that is not possible, there is an alternative in the United States. It is the Holy Land Experience™ in Orlando, Florida. The Holy Land Experience™ is a Christ-honoring experience of the Holy Land from three thousand miles away and as much as seven thousand years ago. It is an educational experience, with reproductions of the Tabernacle, Herod's Temple, the tomb of Jesus, a bazaar, and the Quamran caves (where the Dead Sea Scrolls were discovered).

One exceptional exhibit is the authentic reproduction of Jerusalem as it was in the first century. This is the largest indoor recreation of Jerusalem of its kind in the world. A little further along is The Scriptorium: Center for Biblical Antiquities. Housed in this unique eighteen thousand-square-foot museum are copies of many of the rarest manuscripts from biblical times. They are presented in a way that will excite even the dourest museum visitor. In addition, there are many dramatizations performed during a typical day at the Holy Land Experience.™

This field trip would be an excellent way to summarize many of the studies the children have worked on through the volumes in this series. You can learn more about the Holy Land Experience™ by visiting their Web site, www.holylandexperience.com.

Activity 7—Show The Visual Bible—Matthew (Matthew 1–2)

To illustrate the background of the events of the birth of Jesus, you may want to show the children *The Visual Bible—Matthew* as an introduction to the events of this lesson. Remember that this is the version given in Matthew and does not portray the angels singing in chorus to the shepherds. It does give the narrative of the coming of the magi or wise men, as well as the escape to Egypt. For this lesson, view the biblical material through chapter 2. If you are using the DVD version, the place to begin is marked, but you will still have to observe carefully where to stop at the end of chapter 2.

Next, read aloud "The Birth of John the Baptist"and "The Birth and Early Life of Jesus" in the handbook. Note the differences from the account of Luke. Talk about the things that the children saw in the video before you begin to work on the activities for this lesson. Briefly talk about how our understanding of the events is affected by watching the events as opposed to using our imaginations when we read about the events.

Activity 8—Mary with Elizabeth Jigsaw Puzzles (Luke 1)

The teacher should read the story of Mary and Joseph in the handbook. Do not read this story to the children until you have finished this activity.

Use a permanent black marker to draw puzzle pieces on posterboard. Use the template found on Activity Sheet 8. You can enlarge and duplicate the template and paste it on the posterboard, or you can use the template as a guide and draw the puzzles freehand. You will need five puzzles in all. Do not cut the puzzles apart.

Using a different colored marker, in large letters write one of the following verses on one of the puzzles that you have created:

Luke 1:30b–3: *"Do not be afraid, Mary, for you have found favor with God. Now listen: You will conceive and give birth to a son, and you will call His name Jesus."*

Luke 1:37: *"For nothing will be impossible with God."*

Luke 1:49–50: *"Because the Mighty One has done great things for me, and holy is his name. His mercy is from generation to generation on those who fear him."*

Luke 1:46–48: *"My soul proclaims the greatness of the Lord and my spirit has rejoiced in God my Savior, because He has looked with favor of the humble condition of His slave."*

Luke 1:54–55: *"He has helped His servant Israel, mindful of His mercy, just as He spoke to our forefathers, to Abraham and his descendents forever."*

Cut each puzzle apart and put it in a separate Ziplock bag. Have the children work in groups of two to three persons per group. Ask each group to put the puzzle together. Ask them to tell what the verse means. Circulate the puzzles through all the groups so that all the children will read all of the verses. When all have finished, read the material from the book and the verses from Scripture. Talk about Mary's feelings in these experiences.

Activity 9—Simeon and Anna See Jesus (Luke 2:21–38)

After eight days, Mary and Joseph took Jesus to the Temple to carry out the rites that were necessary for a Jewish male child. In the Temple they met two persons who were looking for the birth of the Messiah. They were Simeon and Anna. Simeon was an old, devout man whom God had spared to see the Lord's Messiah. Anna was a prophetess. She also wanted to see the Christ child.

Read the story carefully. Allow the students to interview you and ask you questions about what Simeon and Anna said about Jesus. Have them ask questions like the following:

Simeon: 1. Who was Simeon?
2. Why did Simeon come to the Temple on this day?
3. Why did Simeon bless Jesus?
4. What did Simeon's prayer of praise mean? (vv. 29–32)
5. What was the meaning of what Simeon said to Mary? (vv. 34–35)

Anna: 1. Who was Anna?
2. Why was Anna in the Temple?
3. What did Anna do in the Temple?
4. What did she do with Jesus?

After the interviews are completed, talk with the children about the meaning of these encounters with Simeon and Anna.

Activity 10—Map of the Travels Surrounding the Birth of Jesus

Before this session, duplicate enough copies for each child to have a copy of Activity Sheet 10—the map of Palestine. Have the children draw, with different colored markers, the following routes:
1. The route taken by Mary to her cousin, Elizabeth. She went from Nazareth south through Samaria to Ain Karim.
2. The route Mary and Joseph took to Bethlehem before the birth of Jesus. Since the Samaritans and the Jews disliked each other, Mary and Joseph had to cross the Jordan River into Perea and then back across the river above the Jabbock River to Jericho and on to Jerusalem and then to Bethlehem.
3. The route Mary and Joseph took to go from Bethlehem to the Temple in Jerusalem.
4. The route the wise men took to visit Jesus. They came from the East, down from Damascus through Decapolis, then through Perea to Jericho and on to Jerusalem and then Bethlehem.
5. The route Mary, Joseph, and the baby Jesus followed to go to Egypt. They traveled to Hebron and on to Gaza and on to Egypt.
6. The route Mary, Joseph, and Jesus took when they returned to Nazareth. They avoided going through the territories of Herod's son. They traveled north through Gaza, along the coast and through Samaria to Nazareth.

Talk with your class about the various journeys that Jesus' family took in order to care for Him and protect Him.

Activity 11—Memorize Luke 2:10–11

Have each child commit to memory:

"But the angel said to them, 'Do not be afraid for you see, I announce to you good news of great joy that will be for all people: because today in the city of David was born for you a Savior, who is Christ the LORD."

They can write each of the words on a 3x5-inch index card and use these to practice the verse by putting the words in order.

Have each child try to recite the entire verse from memory, with the reference. Then have them write Luke 2:10–11 in their Bible Verse Memory Books. They can illustrate the verse as well.

You may also want to review the verse that you learned in the last lesson.

WORKSHEETS FOR LESSON 8

(Sheet for Activity 1 on page 189)

ACTIVITY SHEET 2: REVIEW OF THE OLD TESTAMENT—SIN AND ITS CONSEQUENCES

Sin of Adam and Eve
The Steps of Sin That Lead Down to Death

Doubt

Distrust of God

Sin of Covetousness— wanting to be like God

Disobedience to God

Death!

Sin of Adam and Eve
The Steps of Sin That Lead Down to Life

Faith of Abraham

Abraham believed God

Abraham trusted God

Abraham obeyed

Faith—believing and trusting God

Life!

ACTIVITY SHEET 1: REVIEW OF THE OLD TESTAMENT

Review of God's Redeeming Grace—Old Testament

1. God **creates** the heavens, the world, seas and fish, the animal kingdom, and man.
2. Adam and Eve—the first parents—**sin** against God; sin enters the world.
3. The world grows more **evil**—Cain murders Abel, Noah is saved from the Flood, and the people build the Tower of Babel.

---

4. God calls out Abraham and **redeems** a new people through the **covenant**, and He makes a **promise** to Abraham.
5. Isaac is heir to **God's promise**.
6. Jacob is heir to **God's promise**, and Jacob's sons become the fathers of the twelve tribes of Israel.
5. Joseph becomes vice regent of Egypt, and the family of Israel goes to Egypt. This ends the **Period of the Patriarchs**.
6. The Israelites spend four hundred years in Egypt; they grow as a people, but suffer during the reigns of new pharaohs.

---

7. Moses is born and grows up in the household of Pharaoh; this begins the **Period of the Exodus**.
8. God **redeems** Israel from slavery through Moses.
9. Moses leads the people of Israel into the wilderness to worship God.
10. God makes a new **covenant** with the people of Israel at Mount Sinai and gives the Law and the Ten Commandments.
11. For forty years the people wander in the wilderness; God leads them with a cloud by day and a pillar of fire by night.
12. Moses dies; God calls Joshua to lead the people into the **Promised Land**; this is the fulfillment of **God's promise**.

---

13. The people live in the **Promised Land** and are ruled by the **Judges**.
14. The Judges fail to unify the people, as in the case of Samson.
15. **Samuel** is both a **prophet** and a judge; God told him to anoint Saul king and the **Period of the Judges** ends; later Samuel anointed David to replace Saul.

---

16. Saul begins the **Period of the Monarchy**, or kings of Israel; Saul did not obey God, and his family was removed from power and replaced by David.
17. **David** reigns as king of Israel about 1000 BC; David conquers **Jerusalem**; **worship** is now centered in Jerusalem—the City of David.
18. **Solomon** becomes king at David's death; Solomon builds the **Temple** in Jerusalem.
19. **Sacrifices** in the Temple show God's demand of death for the **redemption** of man.
20. After Solomon, the northern ten tribes of Israel break away from the two tribes to the south in Judah; the country is divided between **Israel** to the north and **Judah** to the south.
21. Israel's kings do evil in God's sight; Israel is taken into captivity by **Assyria** as God's **punishment** in 722 BC.
22. God raises up **prophets**, such as Jeremiah, to proclaim His Word in Israel and calls the people to **repentance**; but the people will not listen.
23. Judah has good kings and bad kings; they survive as a nation until God brings punishment on them by having them taken into captivity by **Babylonia** in 587 BC; captivity ends the **Period of the Monarchy**.

---

24. Captivity in Babylonia, under the Babylonian king Nebuchadnezzar begins the **Period of Exile**.
25. In the **Period of the Exile**, the people of Judah remain true to God; they repent; God gives them prophets—like Daniel in captivity—to keep them true to God.
26. In captivity, **Esther** becomes queen of Persia and helps to keep the Israelites from being destroyed by the wicked Haman.

---

27. Under Ezra and Nehemiah, many of the people return to the land of Judah; this is the **Return to the Promised Land**.
28. The **Temple** is rebuilt and completed in 515 BC; **worship of God** is restored in Jerusalem.
29. The **Old Testament** ends with the Prophet Malachi.

• The next four hundred years are the **Silent Years**.
• God is still at work with His people, even during these **Silent Years**.
• **When** will God speak again?

ACTIVITY SHEET 3: THE BOOKS OF THE BIBLE—NEW TESTAMENT

Gospels
1.
2.
3.
4.

The Book of History
1.

The Letters of Paul
1.
2.
3.
4.
5.
6,
7.
8.
9.
10.
11.
12.
13.

The General Letters
1.
2.
3.
4.
5.
6.
7.
8.

The Book of Prophesy

ACTIVITY SHEET 4: TIME LINE FOR NEW TESTAMENT EVENTS

400–4 BC	Period between Old and New Testaments—Malachi to Matthew
4 BC	Birth of Jesus*
AD 24	Baptism of Jesus
AD 25–27	Ministry of Jesus
1st year	Early ministry and relative obscurity
2nd year	Year of popularity
3rd year	Year of conflict and opposition
AD 27 AD	Crucifixion of Jesus
AD 33 AD	Conversion of Paul
AD 47-48	Paul's first missionary journey
AD 49–52	Paul's second missionary journey
AD 52–56	Paul's third missionary journey
AD 56	Arrest of Paul in Jerusalem
AD 56–58	Appearances of Paul before Felix and Festus
AD 58-61	Paul travels to Rome
AD 62	Release from prison
AD 64	Burning of Rome; Emperor Nero blames Christians
AD 67	Second imprisonment in Rome
AD 67	Paul is executed by Emperor Nero
AD 70	Destruction of Jerusalem under the Roman general Titus (later Emperor)
AD 100	Death of John the apostle
AD 2000+	Our life today

*(Note: During the Middle Ages there was a mistake in calculating the date for the birth of Jesus)

ACTIVITY SHEET 5: FILL IN THE BLANKS

Directions: Fill in the blanks as a review of this lesson.

1. Name the first four books of the New Testament.

_____, _____, _____, _____

2. What are these books called? _____

3. What book tells about the beginning of the church? _____

4. Who wrote many letters to the churches across the Roman world? _____

5. What are the other letters of the New Testament called? _____ _____

6. What book of the New Testament tells about the future? _____

7. There are _____ books in the New Testament.

ACTIVITY SHEET 8: JIGSAW PUZZLE— RETELL THE STORY OF MARY WITH ELIZABETH

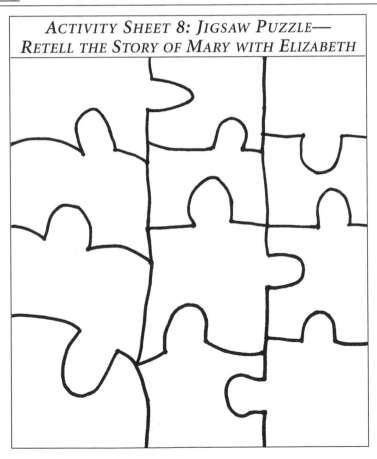

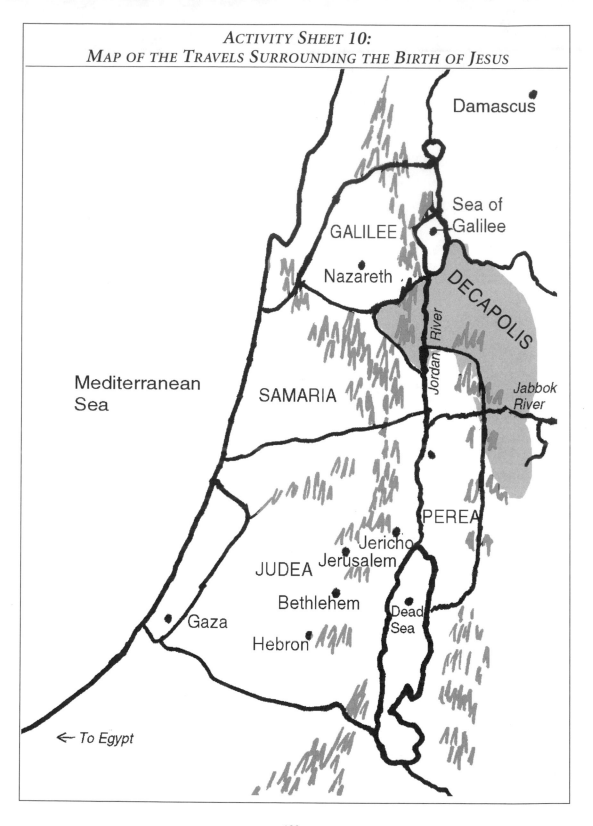

ACTIVITY SHEET 10:
MAP OF THE TRAVELS SURROUNDING THE BIRTH OF JESUS

Damascus

Sea of
Galilee

GALILEE

Nazareth

DECAPOLIS

Jordan River

Mediterranean
Sea

SAMARIA

Jabbok
River

PEREA

Jericho

Jerusalem

JUDEA

Bethlehem

Dead
Sea

Gaza

Hebron

← To Egypt

Readings from the Parent/Teacher Handbook: The Bible, Vol. 1: "John the Baptist," to "Jesus Raises Lazarus from the Dead"

OBJECTIVES

By the end of this lesson, the learner should be able to
- describe Jesus' teaching and miracles,
- describe the miracle of Jesus feeding the five thousand,
- recount the parable of the good Samaritan and explain its meaning,
- tell the story of the lost son and give its meaning,
- interpret the relationship that Jesus had with children, and
- sequence the events in the resurrection of Lazarus and interpret the meaning of this event.

IDENTIFICATIONS

Concepts

- *Teaching*—helping people understand the meaning of the gospel or good news
- *Preaching*—delivering a sermon to the people
- *Healing*—causing people to get well from diseases
- *Miracles*—extraordinary event that was caused by God's intervention
- *Beatitudes*—declarations from the Sermon on the Mount
- *Lord's Prayer*— prayer given to the disciples by Jesus as a model prayer
- *Parable*—story that contains a moral principle

- *Samaritan*—person from Samaria after the repopulation of the northern kingdom

People

- *Jesus:* grown to manhood, Jesus was both fully man and fully God
- *Disciples:* called ones to minister on behalf of Jesus
- *Mary:* friend of Jesus from Bethany
- *Martha:* sister of Mary
- *Lazarus:* brother of Mary and Martha
- *Boy* with loaves and fishes in the feeding of the five thousand

MATERIALS NEEDED

- *Parent/Teacher Handbook: The Bible, Vol. 1*
- Activity Sheets for Lesson 9
- Crayons and markers
- Blank sheets of white paper for drawing
- Roll of shelf paper or butcher paper
- Masking tape and plastic tape
- Reusable adhesive
- 3x5-inch index cards
- Lined paper for writing
- Red Kool-Aid
- An opaque pitcher
- A clear pitcher
- 5 loaves of bread
- 2 life-sized fishes made of cloth or cardboard
- *The Visual Bible—Matthew* (optional)

LEARNING ACTIVITIES FOR LESSON 9

Activity 1—The Visual Bible—Matthew

View *The Visual Bible—Matthew* in advance of this session. You will need to choose appropriate scenes for the children to view. Begin with "John the Baptist Prepares the Way" and continue through "The Little Children with Jesus." You should note that the parables of the good Samaritan and the lost son are not included in Matthew's gospel. Be selective on the events that you will choose. In the DVD format, you can easily choose those events that are appropriate.

In the handbook, read the appropriate events. After the children have viewed the events that you have chosen, ask them what these events tell us about Jesus. Discuss the answers to this question with the children.

Activity 2—The Life of Jesus (The Gospels)

One of the many lasting contributions that you can make to the lives of the children you teach is to provide a foundational understanding of the life and ministry of Jesus Christ. To assist you in that process, we have prepared a chart of the life, ministry, death, and resurrection of Jesus. See Activity Sheet 2.

In advance of this session duplicate copies of the chart and the questions. Guide the children as they look at the chart. Have them work in pairs and answer the questions about the chart. Help them to get firmly in mind the segments of Jesus' life: Period of Preparation; Period of Ministry in which He was Unknown; Period of Ministry in which He achieved Fame; Period of Ministry in Conflict with the Pharisees and Sadducees; and the Period of Sacrifice, which included His triumphal entry into Jerusalem, His death on the cross, His resurrection from the dead, and His ascension into heaven.

Activity 3—Jesus Attends the Wedding at Cana (John 2)

Jesus' mother, Mary, asked her son to attend a wedding feast with her. The bride or groom may have been a relative of Mary's. The family ran out of wine for the guests. This would have been an embarrassment to the groom. Mary asked her son to help. Jesus responded by telling the men to get water that was stored in the giant water pots. The water, stored in the pots, normally was used for washing the feet of the guests. While this seemed like a strange request, Mary told the host to do what Jesus asked.

Jesus turned the water into wine. In this first miracle Jesus met the need and also placed His blessing on that wedding. Jesus was also blessing marriage as God's way to establish a home and family.

Before the session, pour a package of Kool-Aid into an opaque pitcher. Fill a clear pitcher with tap water. Retell the story of the wedding at Cana from the handbook, "The Wedding in Cana." When you have finished telling the story, pour the tap water into the opaque pitcher. Stir the contents. Pour the red Kool-Aid into cups and distribute to the children. Be sure to remind them that this is Kool-Aid. What Jesus did was a true miracle in that He turned the water into wine.

Remind the children that God met a need in this miracle. He blessed that marriage, and He blesses marriages today. Family is God's plan to care for boys and girls in a loving home.

Activity 4—Jesus and His Twelve Disciples (Matthew 10:1–4)

Learning the names of the twelve disciples can be facilitated by Activity Sheet 4. (The names are given in Matthew 10:1–4.) In advance of this session, duplicate both the question sheet and the Wordfind. Have the children complete the question sheet first. Then have them complete the Wordfind.

Be sure to spend some time with the children discussing the importance of the disciples who carried the gospel to the world. For younger children, you may want to help them write the names of the apostles on the question sheet.

Activity 5—Demonstration of the Feeding of the Five Thousand

Be sure to acquaint the children with the story of "The Feeding of the Five Thousand" from the handbook. Tell them that this activity will help them understand the meaning of this miracle.

In advance of this session, place a piece of masking tape down the center of the room. On one side place the five loaves of bread and the two fishes. On the other side of the tape, place the stack of one hundred sheets of paper. Enlarge and duplicate the fish and bread patterns on Activity Sheet 5, enough for each child.

Before you begin this exercise, have the children cut out the fish and loaf of bread. Then have the children write "50" on each of the 100 sheets of paper. Tell the children that each of the sheets of paper represents 50 people. It would be helpful for the children to understand how many people that is by counting the number of children in your class and determining how many more it would take to make fifty children in the class.

Then, ask them to think about how much bread and fish they might eat if that was their diet for the day. Perhaps they could each eat one fish and loaf of bread. Have each child take one piece of paper, marked "50" and on each sheet of paper place a loaf of bread and 1 fish. Tell them that if this were the situation in which Jesus fed the five thousand, each of the sheets of paper marked "50" would have one loaf of bread and one fish. That is a total of 100 loaves of bread and 50 fishes for each child.

Now have the children look on the other side of the tape and see what Jesus had to work with. He only had five loaves and two fishes. Yet He fed all five thousand persons and there were twelve baskets left over. Ask, "Could you have fed that many people with only five loaves and two fishes?" When they say "No," tell them, "That is right, but Jesus could and did." Have the children also think about the boy who gave to Jesus all the lunch that he had. Ask, "Would you like to have been that boy who gave Jesus his lunch? Why or why not?" Discuss.

Activity 6—Create a Storyboard of the Good Samaritan

A storyboard is used by film makers to script a story and to present the visuals. You will need one 4x6-inch card for each scene in the story.

Have the children work in groups of three and create a storyboard for the Parable of the Good Samaritan. Students will need ten cards for each group to draw the following scenes: (1) Merchant leaves his wife and family, (2) Merchant starts down the road to Jericho, (3) Merchant is beaten by robbers, (4) Priest passes by, (5) Levite passes by, (6) Samaritan comes to help, (7) Samaritan takes the merchant on his donkey, (8) Merchant is taken to the inn, (9) Merchant is given care, and (10) Samaritan leaves the inn the next morning.

Mix up the cards and have the students sequence them in the correct order for the story. You can also glue them in the correct order to a large sheet of posterboard for display.

When you have finished the exercise, ask the children what the parable means? Encourage them to find ways that they can help other people who are in need.

From the script created by the storyboard, choose students to act out the story. You will need the following characters: merchant, merchant's wife, three robbers, Levite, priest, Samaritan, and innkeeper. Have the children act out the story from the scenes presented in the storyboard.

Activity 7—Retelling the Parable of the Lost Son with Paper Plate Puppets

Divide the class into three groups. Reread the story of the "The Parable of the Lost Son" in the handbook and in Luke 15:11–32. For the first scene, have a group make puppets for the older son, younger son, and the father. Draw the face of each person in the story on one of the paper plates. Attach each paper plate with glue and staple to a tongue depressor.

Next, prepare a background for the story. This might consist of a large sheet of posterboard on which the children have painted or colored a house where the family lived. Help the children become thoroughly familiar with the story so they can retell their part of the story to the entire class using the paper plate puppets and the backgrounds they prepared.

For the second scene, follow the same procedure for each of the characters in the story. You will need more characters for this scene. The young son has gone to the far country and is partying with many of his friends. For the second scene you will also need puppets of the pigs.

Prepare a background for this scene on posterboard. On the first sheet prepare for a large gathering having fun together. On a second sheet of posterboard, prepare a pigpen for the prodigal son to eat and sleep with the pigs. Help this second group to become thoroughly familiar with the story also. Have them prepare to retell their part of the story to the entire class using the paper plate puppets and the backgrounds they have prepared.

For the third scene, follow the same procedure for each of the characters of this story. You will need servants, the father, the younger brother, and the older brother.

Prepare a background sheet on posterboard. Draw the home of the family. Help this group to understand their part of the story completely and prepare to retell the story to the entire class using the puppets and prepared background.

After all of the groups have completed their work with the puppets and the backgrounds, have each group in correct sequence retell their stories to the entire class. Ask the children to explain what each of these scenes tells about the parable of the lost son.

Activity 8—Jesus with the Children (Matthew 19:13–15)
In the handbook read "Jesus with the Children." Also read through Matthew 19:13–15. Talk with your class about the ways Jesus loved children. How was He concerned for them? How did Jesus feel about children?

Sing the well-known, well-loved song "Jesus Loves Me." The music and words can be found in a hymnal.

Activity 9—Lazarus (John 11)
In the handbook read "Jesus Raises Lazarus from the Dead." Also read through John 11.

In advance of this session, duplicate copies of Activity Sheet 9 for your students. Review the story of Mary, Martha, and Lazarus for your children. Then ask the students to circle the names of Mary, Martha, and/or Lazarus as they are appropriate for each of the statements. Go over the correct answers to each statement.

Activity 10—Memorize John 14:6
To help your children understand what Jesus gave to His followers, have your children memorize John 14:6. This verse shows us who Jesus is. It tells us that God wants us to come to Him.

"Jesus told him, 'I am the way, the truth, and the life. No one comes to the Father, except through Me."

Have the children write the verse in their Bible Verse Memory Books and illustrate it.

ACTIVITY SHEET 2: QUESTIONS ABOUT THE LIFE OF JESUS FROM THE CHART

1. In what period of Jesus' life did the baptism and temptation experiences occur?_____

2. In what period of His ministry did Jesus call the disciples?____ _____

3. In what period of Jesus' ministry did He come into conflict with the Pharisees and the Sadducees?
_____

4. In what period did the trial and crucifixion take place? _____

5. In which year of Jesus' ministry did the first cleansing of the Temple occur? _____

6. At what point did the ascension take place? _____

7. In what year of Jesus' ministry did the early Judean ministry take place? _____

8. The period of Jesus' fame happened in which year of His ministry? _____

9. Jesus' later Judean ministry happened in which year of His ministry? _____

Life of Jesus

Childhood	Jesus' Public Ministry							Sacrifice	
	Unknown		Fame		Conflict				
	Early Life	Early Ministry	Galilean Ministry		Later Galilean Ministry	Judean Ministry	Perean Ministry	Triumphal Entry	Resurrection
Birth - 4 B.C.	John baptizes Jesus	Jesus Cleanses Temple	Jesus Returns to Galilee	Jesus calls the 12 Disciples		Jesus conflicts with Pharisees and Sadducees		Death ✝	Ascension ⬆
Jesus in the Temple - 12 years old	Temptation of Jesus	Judean Ministry		Jesus teaches the Disciples					
	First Year		Second Year		Third Year				

Directions: Read the description of the disciple and then find the name. Write it in the blanks.

1. I am a son of Zebedee, and I came along with my brother. I wrote one of the four Gospels. My name is J _ _ _. (See Matthew 4:21)

2. My father's name was Alphaeus and my name is the same as one of the sons of Zebedee. My name is J _ _ _ _. (See Luke 6:15)

3. I did not come from Galilee. I kept money for the disciples, but I will be remembered for the evil deed that I committed. My name is J _ _ _ _. (See Luke 6:16)

4. I brought my brother to Jesus. I also helped Jesus find the boy to feed the multitude of people. My name is A _ _ _ _ _. (See Luke 6:14)

5. Nathaniel heard about Jesus from me. I also brought some Greeks to see Jesus. My name is P _ _ _ _ _. (See John 1:43–45)

6. Jesus told me that I would be a rock. My name is P _ _ _ _. (See Matthew 16:18)

7. I was a tax collector before I met Jesus. I wrote one of the Gospels about the life of Jesus. My name is M _ _ _ _ _ _. (See Matthew 10:3).

8. My name was also Didymus. At the tomb of Jesus, I would not believe, unless I could see the nail prints in Jesus' hands and feet. My name is T _ _ _ _ _. (John 20:24–28)

9. I was known as a Zealot. These were men who worked hard to get rid of the Romans from Palestine. My name is S _ _ _ _. (See Luke 6:15)

10. I also had the same name as another disciple. With my brother and another disciple, we were close to Jesus. My name is J _ _ _ _. (See Matthew 4:21)

11. I once asked Jesus why He showed Himself to us and not to others. My name does not appear much in the Gospels. My name is T _ _ _ _ _ _ _ _. (See Matthew 10:3)

12. Philip told me about Jesus. My name is B _ _ _ _ _ _ _ _ _ _.
(See Mark 3:18)

Directions: Find the names of the disciples from above and then circle them on the wordfind. Names may be found, written up and down, across, backwards, or on a diagonal.

X	L	E	L	S	I	G	L	G	C	C	A	N	Y	E
X	S	B	O	R	T	H	P	W	A	N	D	R	E	W
Z	U	L	N	C	C	J	J	E	P	Q	B	S	W	S
U	E	J	T	V	J	R	R	G	X	U	N	A	I	M
G	A	W	A	L	F	U	M	K	R	D	T	M	G	Z
T	D	P	E	Z	E	T	D	E	Z	Q	O	O	Z	N
M	D	K	V	M	Q	B	T	A	F	N	S	H	C	X
A	A	M	O	W	O	E	P	Z	S	S	V	T	R	H
P	H	Q	L	E	P	L	X	P	G	J	O	H	N	J
O	T	M	B	H	P	E	O	J	Y	S	T	A	S	A
J	E	U	H	T	I	P	H	H	S	V	E	Y	U	M
Q	R	M	Y	T	L	L	B	J	T	P	I	M	M	E
F	Q	P	C	A	I	Y	A	I	D	R	U	J	A	S
Q	V	Q	W	M	H	N	T	X	N	F	A	D	M	J
W	X	E	Z	Z	P	K	K	A	Q	Y	D	B	M	B

ACTIVITY SHEET 5: THE FEEDING OF THE FIVE THOUSAND

Pattern: Loaf of Bread and One Fish

Directions: Cut out as many loaves of bread and fishes as you need. Check the learning activity instructions.

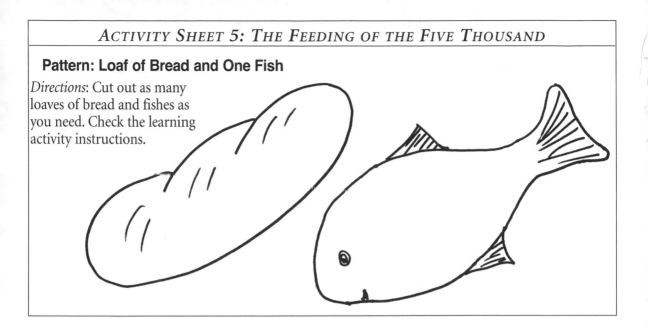

ACTIVITY SHEET 9: CHARACTERISTICS CHART FROM THE STORY OF LAZARUS

Directions: Circle the appropriate names of Mary, Martha, and/or Lazarus as they relate to each of the statements to the left of the names. There may be more than one answer for each statement.

1. Loved by Jesus.   Mary   Martha   Lazarus

2. Prepared a meal
   for Jesus   Mary   Martha   Lazarus

3. Became very ill
   and died.   Mary   Martha   Lazarus

4. Poured perfume on
   Jesus' feet.   Mary   Martha   Lazarus

5. Very sad when their
   brother died   Mary   Martha   Lazarus.

6. Was raised from the
   dead by Jesus.   Mary   Martha   Lazarus

7. Became upset when
   her sister would not
   help her.   Mary   Martha   Lazarus

Readings from the Parent/Teacher Handbook: The Bible, Vol. 1: "Jesus Enters Jerusalem," to "The Resurrection Appearances of Jesus"

OBJECTIVES

By the end of this lesson, the learner should be able to

- recreate the story of Jesus' triumphal entry into Jerusalem,
- retell the events of the Last Supper
- describe the events in the Garden of Gethsemane,
- explain the meaning of the crucifixion and its meaning for us, as Jesus died for our sins,
- explain the importance of the resurrection and its significance for believers then and now,
- recount the postresurrection appearances of Jesus to the women, the disciples, the two disciples on the road to Emmaus, and Thomas,
- define and describe the Great Commission for disciples then and now, and
- explain the ascension of Jesus from earth to heaven and describe the promise given by the angels.

IDENTIFICATIONS

Concepts

- *Last Supper*—Jesus' last supper with the disciples at Passover in the upper room
- *Garden of Gethsemane*—garden where the disciples went with Jesus to pray the night He was betrayed
- *Mount Calvary*—the place of crucifixion
- *Crucifixion*—form of killing by nailing a person to a cross
- *Burial*—caring for the body of the deceased person
- *Tomb*—place where the body of Jesus was placed after death
- *Great Commission*—command in Matthew 28:19–20 to preach the gospel
- *Resurrection*—rising from the dead
- *Ascension*—Jesus going up to heaven

People

- *Jesus:* Savior and Lord
- *Judas:* disciple who betrayed Jesus for thirty pieces of silver
- *Peter:* disciple who was a leader among the group
- *James:* brother of John and close disciple of Jesus
- *John:* close disciple of Jesus who was given care of Mary at the cross
- *Pilate:* Roman governor who condemned Jesus to death
- *Caiaphas:* high priest who wanted Jesus killed
- *Barabbas:* robber and insurrectionist whom Pilate released in place of Jesus
- *Joseph of Arimathea:* wealthy nobleman who gave his tomb for Jesus' burial
- *Nicodemus:* a member of the Sanhedrin who followed Jesus
- *Mary:* one of the women who went to the tomb
- *Mary Magdalene:* woman whom Jesus healed and who went to the tomb
- *Salome:* woman who went to the tomb on Easter morning
- *Disciples on the road to Emmaus:* two followers of Jesus with whom He journeyed to Emmaus
- *Thomas:* disciple who refused to believe until he saw the nail prints in Jesus' hands

MATERIALS NEEDED

- *Parent/Teacher Handbook: The Bible, Vol. 1*
- Activity Sheets for Lesson 10
- Crayons and markers
- Blank sheets of white paper for drawing
- Roll of shelf paper or butcher paper
- Masking tape and plastic tape
- Reusable adhesive
- 3x5-inch index cards

- Lined paper for writing
- Scents (see Activity 2)
- Palm branches
- Construction paper
- Dowels
- Rough sandpaper
- Sticks of cinnamon
- Yarn
- Paper plates
- Paper punch
- Scissors
- Rocks about 2 to 3 inches in size
- Chenille wire
- Toy horse (with a head attached to a dowel)
- Glue
- Cotton
- Shoe boxes
- Posterboard
- Magazines or catalogs for cutting out pictures
- *The Visual Bible—Matthew* (optional)

LEARNING ACTIVITIES FOR LESSON 10

Activity 1—The Visual Bible—Matthew *(Matthew 21–22, 26–27)*

Before the session, view the scenes for the above chapters from *The Visual Bible—Matthew*. Begin with "The Triumphal Entry" and continue through "The Great Commission." Use this as background for the remaining activities that you will achieve in completing this unit. Help the children to understand the meaning of these great events for the people of Jesus' time and ours.

Activity 2—Mary's Love for Jesus *(John 12:1–11)*

Before you teach this lesson, gather a variety of perfumes and lotions. You may find porous cards at the perfume counter in a department store for smelling different perfumes. Take the different perfumes and lotions you gathered and pour a little of each of them on separate cards. You will also want to read the story of Mary's love for Jesus expressed by anointing His feet with fine perfume (John 12:1–11). Note that the pure nard that Mary used was worth a year's wages. This story provides a good transition from the last lesson that ended with the raising of Lazarus and the beginning of the events that will lead to Jesus' crucifixion.

To begin the lesson, pass the cards around to your students. Ask them to smell the perfume or lotion. Ask the students to try to guess what the particular scent would be used for, such as dressing up, smelling good, etc. Ask them to determine which of the scents was the most expensive. Ask them if they would like to have their feet washed with any of the perfumes. Finally, take the cards away and ask them if they can still smell one of the perfumes. You might even spray some perfume in the room to simulate what the disciples smelled in the home of Mary, Martha, and Lazarus.

After you have written their responses on the chalkboard, briefly describe each of the scents and what it is designed to be used for. Tell the students you are going to tell them a story about someone who used perfume and strong scent. Tell them the story of Mary's act of love and devotion toward Jesus when she bathed his feet with expensive perfume and dried his feet with her hair. Note that the smell filled the house. Also emphasize these facts: (1) this is the beginning of the events that will lead to Jesus' crucifixion, (2) Judas was evil, stealing from the money kept by the disciples to care for the poor, and (3) there is a link between the raising of Lazarus and the crucifixion of Jesus.

Activity 3—Act Out the Triumphal Entry into Jerusalem *(Matthew 21:1–17; Mark 11:1–19; Luke 19:28–48)*

Be sure to acquaint the children with the story "Jesus Enters Jerusalem" from the handbook. Read all of the biblical passages for this activity. Then help the children become familiar with the events of these passages. When they are well acquainted with these events, tell them that they will play-act these passages.

Before this session begins, have either branches that you have cut from a tree or prepare branches cut from green construction paper and glued to wooden dowels. You may want to help the children dress for the occasion with appropriate costumes. One child can ride a wooden horse (used here as a donkey) to portray Jesus astride the donkey, riding into Jerusalem. Other children can place the palm branches in the path and cry "Hosanna!" This will be the first scene.

When the procession comes to Jerusalem, they will pass through the gate into the Temple area. In the Temple area, the child will dismount the donkey and come to the tables. (These may be located in another room). On the tables will be toy animals (for sacrifice) and money, which the people have paid to purchase the animals. Have the child who rode the donkey do as Jesus did in overturning the tables and condemning the use of the Temple for buying and selling.

When all of this has taken place, return to the classroom. Discuss the meaning of the triumphal entry into Jerusalem and Jesus' condemnation of the commercialism in the Temple. Help the children understand the prophecy that was made in the Old Testament about the Messiah coming to Jerusalem on a donkey. He was the Prince of Peace, coming as a king but not as a warrior to conquer, just as Solomon had done (1 Kings 1:33) and Jehu after him (2 Kings 9:13). The reference to the Messiah is found in Zechariah 9:9. These activities are in keeping with Psalms 115–118. Jesus was jealous for the House of God, that it not be a place for buying and selling, but a place of prayer (Isaiah 56:7).

Activity 4—The Cross and Spices for Burial (John 19:38–42)

Read John 19:38–42, which describes the descent from the cross. To remind the children of this very sad scene, cut large crosses from large sheets of rough sandpaper. Make the crosses approximately 4 inches wide and 6 inches tall. Have the children rub cinnamon sticks all over the sandpaper. This scent will serve as a reminder of the sweet-smelling spices that were used to prepare Jesus' body for burial. Punch a hole in the top of the cross and place a loop of yarn through the hole. The children can take the crosses home and hang them in their rooms.

Activity 5—Tomb (John 19:38–42 and John 20:1–20)

Get the following supplies: yarn, paper plates, markers, scissors, and a paper punch. Create the tomb out of two halves of a paper plate. Put them back to back and punch holes at $3/4$-inch intervals around the outer edge. Use yarn to lace the two halves together. Cut a half circle for the entrance to the tomb on the front half.

Place a rock or piece of cardboard in front of the opening to prevent the disciples from stealing Jesus' body away at night. You might also place two soldiers in front of the tomb. The soldiers can be made from chenille wire. You can also place a figure of Jesus inside the tomb.

Discuss the meaning of the tomb with the class.

Remove the figure of Jesus from the tomb. Talk with students about what happened there. Read the material from the handbook. The tomb was empty! Jesus arose from the dead. Emphasize the wonder of this event. What do these events tell us about what Jesus did for us at Calvary?

On the front of the tomb the children may want to draw an angel and decorate the tomb with flowers. They may also want to add figures of the women who came to the tomb. That was a joyous day!

Sing the chorus of the hymn, "He Lives." Words can be found in a hymnal.

Activity 6—The Great Commandment and the Great Commission

Both the Great Commandment and the Great Commission were given to all Christians. Divide the class in half. Have one-half work on a post of the Great Commandment:

> *"You shall love the Lord your God with all your heart, with all your soul, and with all your mind. . . . You shall love your neighbor as yourself."* (Matthew 22:37–39)

Have the other half work on a poster of the Great Commission:

> *"Go, therefore, and make disciples of all nations, baptizing them in the name of the Father and of the Son and of the Holy Spirit, teaching them to observe everything I have commanded you. And remember, I am with you always, to the end of the age."* (Matthew 28:19 20)

Have the students spend time decorating the poster with appropriate symbols or pictures to show the love of God to each of us, to the church, and to the world. Provide them with old magazines so the children can cut out pictures.

Activity 7—Pictures of Thomas (John 20:24–29)

Read carefully the words of Thomas and the words of Jesus from John 20:24–29. Review the material in the handbook for "Disciples on the Road to Emmaus" that tells the story of Thomas. Describe the scene to the children in your class. Provide each child with a sheet of white construction paper. Ask the children to fold the sheet in half.

On the left side, have them draw a picture of Thomas with the other disciples before he met the resurrected Jesus. Illustrate with a call out that says, "I will not believe unless I can see the nail prints in His hands."

On the right half, have them picture Thomas prostrate before Jesus. Illustrate with a call out that says, "My Lord and My God!" Have Jesus say, "Blessed are those who have not seen, yet believe!"

Activity 8—Ascension Diorama (Matthew 28:16–17; Mark 16:19–20; Luke 24:50; Acts 1:9–11)

Read the subsection "Jesus in Galilee" from the handbook. Read the passages of Scripture for this event, listed above.

You will need shoe boxes for each of your children, cotton, markers or crayons, and construction paper. Line the shoe box with blue construction paper to represent the sky. Line the bottom with brown construction paper to symbolize the earth on which the disciples were standing.

Have the children glue the cotton to the inside of the top of the shoe box. Cut out feet from construction paper. These will show Jesus ascension into the cloud. The children can also make little figures of the disciples to place around the inside of the shoe box. These will be looking up at Jesus ascending into heaven. Have the children make two angels, dressed in white, and place these near the disciples. The angels tell the disciples that Jesus will come again.

Activity 9—Wordfind

To review this lesson, use Activity Sheet 9. Duplicate copies of the wordfind for each member of your class. Have them read the sentences and find the underlined words in the puzzle.

Activity 10—Memorize John 11:25–26a

To help the children understand the meaning of the resurrection, have them memorize the following verses. These verses describe for us that Jesus is alive! He has provided a way for us to live eternally in His presence.

"I am the resurrection and the life. The one who believes in Me, even if he dies, will live. Everyone who lives and believes in Me will never die—ever."

Have each child write the verses in their Bible Verse Memory Books and illustrate them.

WORKSHEET FOR LESSON 10

ACTIVITY SHEET 9: WORDFIND REVIEW

Directions: Circle the capitalized words that are found on the next page to complete the puzzle. You may find the words across, up and down, backwards, or diagonally.

Words for the wordfind:

1. ANGELS stood at the empty tomb.

2. Jesus' ASCENSION came forty days after the resurrection.

3. Before Jesus went to heaven, He gave the Great COMMISSION.

4. Two disciples were on the road to EMMAUS when they met the resurrected Christ.

5. Mary MAGDALENE was one of the first women to come to the tomb on Sunday.

6. Another woman who went to the tomb was MARY.

7. The RESURRECTION of Jesus took place three days after His crucifixion.

8. Jesus' death and resurrection provide SALVATION to all persons who believe in Jesus.

9. When Jesus was resurrected, the SOLDIERS were afraid and fell, like dead men.

10. THOMAS doubted the resurrection until Jesus showed Himself to the doubting disciple.

```
W J W K R W O T D W M A R Y M
N F G A S C E N S I O N M A V
M N L A F N N X D C O C G S M
F V R Q L O O C C J K D J O X
K L E H N I M I Q T A Z V L K
O S S I Z S L O T L O W K D V
Q G U S M S F E E A L G C I N
Z C R X A I U N E R V F G E M
H K R T U M E A N G E L S R E
A M E K T M O Z M O J Z A S J
R P C S R O K H J M P T N S Z
Z V T Q K C S Q T I E D R E U
C F I Y J Q P M N X O J J C F
I I O J J O B E X C R V E Z L
C T N I U D Q B T E D X F N G
```

LESSON 11: BIRTH OF THE CHURCH, MISSIONARY JOURNEYS OF PAUL, AND THE REVELATION

Readings from the Parent/Teacher Handbook: The Bible, Vol. 1: "The Day of Pentecost," "The Birth of the Church," "Conversion of Saul," "Peter and Cornelius," "The Travels of Paul," and "The Book of the Revelation"

OBJECTIVES

By the end of this lesson, the learner should be able to

- explain the birth of the church at Pentecost,
- describe the Gospel to the Gentiles through Cornelius,
- describe the events of Paul's conversion,
- explain the missionary journeys of Paul,
- explain the importance of Paul's appeal to Caesar and the journey to Rome,
- define the concepts of grace, missionary, and salvation to the Gentiles, and
- explore the spiritual effectiveness of the churches in the Book of the Revelation.

IDENTIFICATIONS

Concepts

- *Pentecost*—Jewish feast day that also became the birth of the church with the coming of the Holy Spirit
- *Grace*—God's gift of unmerited favor bestowed on humanity
- *Missionary*—one who proclaims the gospel
- *Salvation*—God's gift to all who believe through the death and resurrection of Jesus
- *Conversion*—being born again to new life in Christ
- *Appeal to Caesar*—formal petition by a Roman citizen for Caesar to hear his case
- *Prophecy*—declaration of divine will

People

- *Peter:* Jewish disciple who became the leader of the church
- *Paul:* Pharisee who was converted to Christ, became a missionary to the Gentiles, and wrote many of the letters of the New Testament
- *Barnabas:* companion of Paul on his first missionary journey
- *James:* brother of Jesus who became a leader in the church at Jerusalem (Galatians 1:19)

- *John Mark:* young man who turned back from the missionary journey but later became an important witness
- *Lydia:* seller of purple dye for royal clothing who was converted to Christ (Acts 16:12–15, 50)
- *Silas:* companion of Paul on his later missionary journeys
- *Gallio:* Roman proconsul of Achaia, headquartered in Corinth (Acts 18:12–17)
- *Felix:* Roman procurator of Judea at the time Paul was arrested in Jerusalem; hoped for a bribe from Paul for Paul's release (Acts 24:26)
- *Festus:* successor of Felix as Roman procurator of Judea (Acts 24:27)
- *John the Apostle:* later became bishop of Ephesus; suffered for his faith in Christ; wrote a Gospel, letters, and Revelation
- *Philippian jailor:* keeper of the jail in which Paul was incarcerated and who later became a Christian (Acts 16:35–36)
- *Silversmiths:* from Ephesus; started a riot over their lost business because Paul preached that Diana of the Ephesians was an idol (Acts 19:23–41)

MATERIALS NEEDED

- *Parent/Teacher Handbook: The Bible, Vol. 1*
- Activity Sheets for Lesson 11
- Crayons and markers
- Blank sheets of white paper for drawing
- Roll of shelf paper or butcher paper
- Masking tape, plastic tape, glue
- Reusable adhesive
- 3x5-index cards
- Lined paper for writing
- Swatches of cloth cut from an old sheet or something similar
- Old magazines from which to cut pictures
- Posterboard
- *The Visual Bible—Acts* (optional)

Activity 1—The Visual Bible—Acts

Before you begin this session, view *The Visual Bible—Acts*. On the first disc view scenes from "Receiving the Promised Gift," "Ministry of Peter and John," "The Story of Stephen," "The Story of Saul," and "Peter and the Gentiles." On the second disc, you will need to be selective from Paul's missionary journeys. From the first missionary journey, you might choose "Barnabas and Saul Sent from Antioch." From the second journey, you might select "Paul's Vision of the Man from Macedonia," "Lydia's Conversion in Philippi," "Paul in Corinth," and "Gallio Will Not Try Paul." From the third journey, you might select "The Riot in Ephesus." From Paul's Trip to Rome, you might select "Paul Is Arrested," "Paul Sails for Rome," "The Shipwreck," "Paul Preaching in Rome Under Guard," and "Epilogue."

Then review the material in the handbook including "The Day of Pentecost," "The Birth of the Church," "Conversion of Saul," "Peter and Cornelius," "The Travels of Paul," and "The Book of Revelation."

The birth and growth of the early church is an exciting story. Your students should be enthralled with these developments. Help them to see that these developments are an extension of the resurrection of Jesus Christ, as the church expands from Jerusalem to the entire world.

Activity 2—Pentecost (Acts 2:1–41)

Pentecost was a major Jewish holiday. It celebrated the grain harvest. It also celebrated the giving of the Torah (Law of Moses) to the people of Israel. The festival came seven weeks and one day after Passover. Like most Jewish holidays, it was desirable for a faithful Jewish person to go to Jerusalem to celebrate the festival. Hence, on this Pentecost there were many Jewish persons from all over the Roman Empire who had returned to Jerusalem to celebrate the feast.

Review "The Day of Pentecost" and "The Birth of the Church" in the handbook. However, on this particular Pentecost, something very different happened. In the Old Testament, God's Spirit came to rest upon an individual for a period of time. Jesus promised that the Comforter would come and dwell with the believer. On Pentecost after that first Easter, the Holy Spirit came upon the disciples as they were gathered to pray. He descended upon them, and tongues of fire appeared above their heads. They spoke in many different languages. For many of the visitors to Jerusalem, the disciples spoke in their native tongue.

This event afforded Peter the opportunity to proclaim the gospel. Many people had been in Jerusalem fifty days earlier at Passover and were aware of the events surrounding the crucifixion of Jesus. For many there, Peter's message was all they needed to hear to accept the gospel and believe. On that day about three thousand persons were added to the church.

Retell the story to your class. Then have them draw pictures of the event of Pentecost. Be sure that they include the disciples in the upper room with the tongues of fire over their heads.

Activity 3—The Gospel to the Gentiles (Acts 10:1–11:18)

This is the story of Peter and the centurion Cornelius. Cornelius was a godly man, but he was from the Italian band, probably a Roman and a Gentile. He was known as one who "feared God." This probably meant that he was becoming a proselyte to Judaism. During this time, Judaism was very evangelistic, and many persons from outside the Jewish faith were in the process of becoming Jewish. Cornelius had not gone through circumcision, which was required. Cornelius saw a vision. God allowed him to see beyond his immediate circumstances and toward the coming of the gospel. Cornelius was instructed to send for Peter to come and tell him and his household about the gospel.

The next day the attendants to Cornelius were on their way to Joppa. The apostle Peter was on the rooftop. He fell into a trance and saw a large sheet descending from heaven. On the sheet were many different types of animals. All of the animals were ceremonially unclean according to the Law of Moses. (See Leviticus 11 for a list of the clean and unclean animals.) The voice from heaven said, "Get up, Peter; kill and eat!" Peter refused. The voice said, "What God has made clean, you must not call common." All his life Peter had kept the Law and did not want to change now. But the same vision came a second and a third time. Finally, while Peter was confused about what the vision meant, a knock on the gate heralded the emissaries from Cornelius.

Peter went with them and preached the message of salvation through Jesus Christ to Cornelius and the others of his household. While he was speaking, the Holy Spirit came upon these people. Peter and the other Jewish Christians were astounded. Peter said they should be baptized. These were the first Gentiles to come into the church. Peter's attitude toward the Gentiles changed because God intervened.

Tell this great story to the children in your class. While Pentecost is the birthday of the church, the conversion of Cornelius and others who feared God with him marks the coming of the church to the Gentiles. For those of us who aren't Jewish, this opened the door for us to come to Christ.

In advance of this session, cut small swatches of cloth. Bring old magazines for the children to cut out pictures. Glue pictures of animals to the swatch of cloth. Have one child in each group tell the story of the unclean animals to his/her small group.

Now, ask the students to retell the story of Peter and Cornelius using the swatch of cloth and mounted animals on the cloth. How did Peter interpret the dream and why?

Activity 4—The Meaning of the Gospel
In the Sermon on the Mount, Jesus said,

"Enter through the narrow gate; because the gate is wide and the road is broad that leads to destruction, and there are many who go through it. How narrow is the gate and difficult the road that leads to life; and few find it" (Matthew 7:13–14).

Have the children work in teams. Give them a sheet of posterboard and have them draw two roads—one wide and the other narrow. On each of the roads, write what makes it desirable. Tell what characteristics the people show when they follow one road or the other.

Activity 5—The Missionary Journeys of Paul (Acts 9:1–38:31)
Read "The Travels of Paul" from the handbook. You will probably need to supplement that reading with your own study of the references following each of the items chosen as symbols from the list below. This activity will help you briefly describe the various incidents of Paul's missionary journeys. Choose symbols that will help you describe some of the incidents in Paul's missionary experience and place them on a table in front of the class. Then give a quick summary of what happened as it relates to each of the symbols on the table.

1. Basket—After Paul's conversion, there was a plot among the Jews in Damascus to kill Paul. The Christians lowered Paul over the city wall in a basket to protect him (Acts 9:23–25).

2. Stone—There was a plot among the Jews and the Gentiles to stone Paul and Barnabas on the first missionary journey in the cities of Lystra and Derbe (Acts 14:1–7).

3. Toy boat—Paul and his companions traveled by ship on several of his journeys, but on the third missionary journey, they sailed to Assos to preach the gospel (Acts 20:13–16).

4. Picture of a Roman building—Paul was beaten and later claimed his rights as a Roman citizen, who had not been found guilty of a crime against Rome, when he was assaulted in the Temple (Acts 22:1–30).

5. Letter and envelope—Paul wrote many letters to the churches to which he ministered. See the Letters of Paul throughout the New Testament.

6. Idol—Artemis was the idol goddess of the Ephesians. The silversmiths complained that Paul and his companions destroyed their business by converting people to Christianity. They started a riot (Acts 19:23–41).

7. Piece of purple velvet—Lydia was a seller of purple dye for cloth that was sold to the aristocratic persons; she was wealthy. Lydia became a convert of Paul (Acts 16:13–15).

8. Candlestick—The candle is symbolic of Paul's Jewish heritage. He described his background and education at the feet of Gamaliel (Acts 22:2–5).

9. Tent—Paul had a trade as a tent maker, and he plied this trade while he was on his missionary journeys (Acts 18:2–4).

10. Plastic snake—Paul was bitten by a viper on the island of Malta, but God protected him and he did not have any ill effects (Acts 28:1–6).

11. Creme or ointment—In Philippi, as in some other cities, Paul and Silas were beaten. They had to apply salve to the wounds (Acts 16:22–24).

12. Chain—In several places, Paul was placed in irons and chains. While he was in Rome, Paul was chained to the guard. It afforded him a great opportunity to preach the gospel to the guards (Acts 28:17–20).

13. Broken boat—Paul was shipwrecked in the Mediterranean Sea while he was on his way to Rome (Acts 27:42–44).

14. Sheet of music—Paul and his companions were in jail, but they did not cease to sing and express their joy toward God. Circumstances did not change their inner peace. The Philippian jailor became a Christian when the earthquake disrupted the jail and he feared that the singing prisoners would escape (Acts 16:25–34).

15. Walking staff—Many of the trips that Paul took were done on foot. Trace some of these journeys on a map.

Activity 6—God's Grace Puzzle (See Romans 5:6–8 for the Concept of Grace)

Read the sidebar on "Grace" in the handbook under the section entitled "The Travels of Paul." Make sure that your children are familiar with the idea of grace. Then, prepare copies of the Grace Puzzle on Activity Sheet 6. Have the children complete this activity.

Activity 7—Diary of Paul's Trip to Rome (Acts 27:1–28:16)

Read "Paul's Journey to Rome" in the section "The Travels of Paul" in the handbook. You will need to supplement that with Acts 27:1–28:16. Use the scriptural account to expand the children's understanding of the perilous trip to Rome. Look at a map of Paul's Journey to Rome in the back of your Bible, a Bible dictionary, or a Bible atlas.

Have each child pretend to be Paul and write a diary about the experiences of Paul's trip to Rome. Include this perspective as he boarded the ship and sailed toward Rome. Consider the shipwreck and his experiences in safely getting to land. He landed in Italy at Three Taverns, on the West coast. Find it on the map. Then Paul traveled north on the Old Appian Way to the colossal city of Rome. Use wide-lined paper for your children to write easily. You may need to help younger children write their diary of the experience.

Help them visualize what it must have been like to be in that situation and to see the hand of God protecting Paul at sea. Continue for each of Paul's experiences. Imagine the whole experience. Along with each diary entry, your children may draw a picture on white construction paper to illustrate what is happening. Upon completion, staple the pages together to form a booklet of the experience.

Activity 8—Crossword Puzzle Review of Acts

To review the activities of the early church and Paul, use Activity Sheet 8. Duplicate the activity and have the members of your class complete the puzzle.

Activity 9—Matching the Churches in Revelation (Revelation 2–3)

Read the subsection "The Seven Churches" in the handbook. In advance of this session, make multiple copies of Activity Sheet 9.

Be sure that the children are aware of the seven churches and the problems that they had. The children will find the answers in the description in the above reading. Give each child a copy of the activity sheet and ask them to complete the matching exercise.

Activity 10—Memorize Acts 1:8

To help your children grapple with what it means to be a missionary, have them memorize this verse. It describes the task that Jesus left for His followers. Jesus commissioned us to witness to His saving power and love for all mankind. We begin at home, as did the Jewish believers in Judea and Samaria. Then our witnessing extends to the ends of the earth.

But you will receive power when the Holy Spirit has come upon you, and you will be My witnesses in Jerusalem, in all Judea and Samaria, and to the ends of the earth.

Have the children write the verses in their Bible Verse Memory Books and illustrate them.

WORKSHEETS FOR LESSON 11

ACTIVITY SHEET 6: GOD'S GRACE

Directions: From the paragraph below, find the words that will complete the puzzle for the word "Grace." Fill in the blanks.

Paragraph:

G _ _ _ _ _ of God's free gift

through the _ _ _ _ R of God to bring

_ _ _ _ A _ _ _ _ to all who believe.

Grace is C _ _ _ _ _ _ _ _ _ _

upon the human _ E _ _ _ _ _ _

of accepting or rejecting God's grace.

G _ _ _ _ _

_ _ _ _ R

_ _ _ A _ _ _ _

C _ _ _ _ _ _ _ _ _ _ _

_ E _ _ _ _ _ _

ACTIVITY SHEET 8: CROSSWORD PUZZLE REVIEW

Directions: From the sentences below, complete the crossword puzzle.

Across

7. Paul was strongly opposed in this city by the silversmiths.
8. The Holy Spirit came on the disciples on this day.
9. Paul's first European convert was a seller of purple.

Down

1. Paul made his appeal to this Roman ruler.
2. Paul preached in this Greek city and established a church.
3. Paul was converted on the road to this city.
4. Peter and _____ offered the crippled man the ability to walk.
5. Paul was assaulted in this city on the first missionary journey.
6. Paul caused a riot in the Temple in this city.

ACTIVITY SHEET 9: MATCHING THE CHURCHES IN REVELATION

Directions: Match the churches on the left with the description of their spiritual condition on the right.

Churches	Description
___ 1. Ephesus	a. You remained true to My name.
___ 2. Smyrna	b. You are dead! Wake up!
___ 3. Pergamum	c. You are neither hot nor cold!
___ 4. Thyatira	d. You have lost your first love!
___ 5. Sardis	e. You have remained true!
___ 6. Philadelphia	f. Some of you have been put in prison for your faith.
___ 7. Laodicea	g. You have been faithful!

LESSON 12: RELIGIOUS PRACTICE OF CHRISTIANS AND CHRISTIAN SYMBOLS

Readings from the Parent/Teacher Handbook: The Bible, Vol. 1:"Religious Practices," subsections "The Lord's Day" and "Christian Church." If you have Parent/Teacher Handbook, Vol. 2, read the section "Christianity and the Fine Arts." Read only the subsection entitled, "Christian Symbolism Found in the Catacombs."

OBJECTIVES

By the end of this lesson, the learner should be able to
- discover how the Lord's Day originated,
- examine the celebration of the Lord's Day in today's world,
- discover the meaning of the Christian church building, and
- iIdentify the religious symbolism in the Catacombs.

IDENTIFICATIONS

Concepts

Lord's Day—the first day of the week, when Christ arose from the dead;, for the church it took the place of the Jewish (Saturday) Sabbath

Church—believers in Jesus Christ who have banded together to preach, teach, and minister for Christ

Church building—building that replaces the synagogue for Christians in which to worship and teach

Martyr—a person who voluntarily suffers death for witnessing to his faith or who refuses to renounce his religion

Chi Rho—first two letters in Greek for Christ, often used as a monogram

Dove and olive branch—symbol of peace that the Spirit of God brings

Fish—in Greek, the word *ichthus* means "fish" and was used by early Christians as an acrostic for "Jesus/Christ/of God/the Son/Savior"

Anchor—early Christian symbol of hope from Hebrews 6:18–19

Good Shepherd—Jesus is pictured as the Good Shepherd and the symbol taken from Jesus' parables in Luke 15:3–7 and John 10:1–18

Places

Your hometown

Catacombs, Rome, Italy: subterranean gallery of tombs for the dead where Christians buried other believers, especially during the persecutions; contained early Christian symbols

MATERIALS NEEDED

Parent/Teacher Handbook: The Bible, Vol. 1
Activity Sheets for Lesson 12
Crayons and markers
Blank sheets of white paper for drawing
Masking tape and plastic tape
3x5-inch index cards
Lined paper for writing
12x18-inch construction paper
8½x11-inch construction paper
Posterboard
Wooden placques
Decoupage
Acrylic paint

LEARNING ACTIVITIES FOR LESSON 12

Activity 1—Origin of the Lord's Day

Read "The Lord's Day" in the handbook. Talk to your students about the origin of the Lord's Day and how it is different from the Sabbath observance of Jewish people.

In advance of this session, duplicate copies of "Questions About the Lord's Day" found on Activity Sheet 1. Have the children in your class complete the activity sheet.

Activity 2—Prepare a Booklet of My Home Church

Read "The Christian Church" in the handbook.

Provide the members of your class with a sheet of white 12x18-inch construction paper. Fold the sheet in half, so that it may be used as a cover for a booklet. Using crayons or markers, have each child draw a picture of his/her home church. Use this for the cover of the booklet. Entitle the booklet "My Church." Have each child write his name at the bottom of the page under the drawing.

Provide each child with two sheets of large lined paper. Ask each student to write a title on the sheet:"Purposes of the Church." Then on the next line write "Great Commandment—Love the Lord with all your heart, soul, and mind." Below that write "Great Commission—Go into all the world and preach the gospel."

On the next page write "What a Church Does." List the following: Worship, Teach, Witness, Fellowship, Minister.

Place these two sheets inside the "My Church" booklet.

Activity 3—Finding the Ministries of Your Church

In advance of this session, have the members of your class bring a bulletin or newsletter from their church to class. Examine the worship bulletin or church newsletter to find all of the five tasks that the church does—Worship, Teach, Witness, Fellowship, and Minister. You may have to provide help in finding the five tasks in each church. How many of these tasks can each child find in the worship bulletin or the church newsletter? What tasks are left out? What tasks are present several times?

You might also have the children look for evidence of the Great Commandment and the Great Commission in the worship bulletin or church newsletter.

Talk about the importance of each of these tasks, the Great Commandment, and the Great Commission.

Activity 4—Diary Entry: What We Did on Sunday

Have each child think about what they did on Sunday. Then on a sheet of large lined paper, have them list all of the activities that they did on the Lord's Day. They might list "I ate breakfast," "I went to Sunday school," "We studied the life of Jesus in Sunday school," "I went to children's church," "The minister talked about loving God," "My family went out for dinner," etc.

Place this sheet inside the cover of the booklet, "My Church."

Activity 5—Questions About My Home Church

Continue the study of the Lord's Day by having the children write the answers for the "Questions About My Home Church" on Activity Sheet 5. Place the completed questions and answers inside the cover of the booklet, "My Church."

Activity 6—The Catacombs, Rome, Italy

To teach the remaining activities in this section, turn to "Christianity and the Fine Arts" in the handbook and read the subsection "Christian Symbolism in the Catacombs." (Note: This section does not follow sequentially from "Religious Practices of Christians." We will return to "Religious Practices of Christians" in the next lesson and continue sequentially through the book).

A brief information sheet on the catacombs is provided on Activity Sheet 6. You will want to describe the catacombs to your class.

The official Web site for the catacombs is www.catacombe.roma.it.

Activity 7—Signs and Symbols

Help the children distinguish between a sign and a symbol. A sign is a device that gives direction. For example, we use a "Stop" sign to indicate that an automobile is required to stop at an intersection. A symbol is something that stands for something else. For example, ever since the early Church, the fish has stood for "being a Christian." Talk with the children about the differences between signs and symbols.

Duplicate Activity Sheet 7 for the members of your class. Have them color the signs and symbols. The "Stop" sign should be colored red. The "School: Children Crossing" sign should be colored yellow. The symbol of the cross might be colored yellow. The *chi rho* symbol might be colored red. The symbol of the fish might be colored blue. The dove might be colored light blue. The Good Shepherd might be colored tan. The anchor might be colored black. Have the children label each sign and symbol.

Add this page to the "My Church" booklet. Staple the pages inside the complete booklet.

Activity 8—Decoupage the Student's Favorite Christian Symbol

Have each of your students select the symbol that he or she likes best. Copy and cut out the symbol of the child's choice from Activity Sheet 7.

In advance of your session, obtain wooden plaques for class members from a craft store. You will also need fine sandpaper, sponge brushes, a base coat acrylic paint, and decoupage finish.

Have the children sand the wood smooth. Apply several coats of acrylic paint, lightly sanding between each coat. Cut the Christian symbol from the activity sheet. Carefully cut around the symbol. Apply a coat of decoupage finish to the back of the symbol. Then place the symbol on the plaque and apply decoupage to the front of the picture and plaque. Let dry overnight.

Activity 9—Wall Hanging

Copy the fish symbol and have the children use it to make a wall hanging. Use 8½x11-inch construction paper. Using markers, write a phrase to go with the fish symbol. Such phrases as the following might be used:

"Jesus Christ, the Son of God, is my Savior."

"Jesus Christ is Lord."

"I am a Christian because Jesus is my Savior."

"Jesus loves you and me."

Cut a frame for the wall hanging from a contrasting color of construction paper and glue the picture to the frame.

Activity 10—Memorize Psalm 122:1

To remind your children what the church means to us, have them memorize Psalm 122:1.

I rejoiced with those who said to me, Let us go to the house of the LORD.

Have the children write this Scripture in their Bible Verse Memory Books and illustrate it.

ACTIVITY SHEET 1: QUESTIONS ABOUT THE LORD'S DAY

Directions: Fill in the blanks with answers from the material on the Lord's Day in the handbook.

1. What day of the week is designated as the Lord's Day? _____

2. Why is this day called the Lord's Day? _____ __

3. What did God create on the first day of the week? _____

4. Jesus appeared to His disciples on the _____ day of the week.

5. Thomas was not with the disciples the first time Jesus appeared to the disciples. On the next _____ Jesus came again.

6. The early followers of Jesus continued to meet on the _____ day of the week.

7. Worship on the "eighth" day of the week meant that Jesus made a _____ creation.

8. Constantine made a law that all work should stop on _____.

ACTIVITY SHEET 5: QUESTIONS ABOUT MY HOME CHURCH

Directions: Answer each of the following questions.

1. The name of my church is___ _____.

2. The pastor of my church is _____ __.

3. The thing I like best about my church is _____.

4. I wish my church had _____.

5. When I go to church, I feel _____.

6. During the worship service, I enjoy most _____.

ACTIVITY SHEET 6: THE CATACOMBS

During the first three hundred years of the Church, many Christians suffered from persecution by the Romans. Many died as martyrs. A martyr is one who voluntarily allows himself or herself to die for the Christian faith. (We will discuss this in detail in a later unit).

Ancient Rome had a law preventing burial within the limits of the city. Most Romans who died were cremated. Christians wanted their bodies to be buried so they would be raised in the resurrection. Outside the walls of Rome there were underground burial places. They were dug out of the walls of a lava rock called *tuffa*. The walls did not need additional support but allowed passageways and burial crypts to be built into the tuffa.

The catacombs were built during the second century. After AD 313, when Christianity became an established religion in the Empire, use of the catacombs declined. The openings in the walls were approximately 24 inches high by 56 inches long. The bodies were wrapped with linen cloth and covered with ointments and spices to overcome the odors. The name of the deceased person, date of death, and a Christian symbol were placed on the slab that closed the opening in the wall.

At the ends of the hallways that contained the crypts were located chapels. These allowed the relatives and other Christians to hold communion and services for their Christian friends and family. Primitive Christian symbols were also placed on the walls of these chapels.

From these early Christian symbols we can learn a lot about the Church. Let us examine some of the symbols.

ACTIVITY SHEET 7: SIGNS AND SYMBOLS

Traffic signs:

Christian symbols:

Readings from the Parent/Teacher Handbook: The Bible, Vol. 1: "The Christian Church Year," "Christmas," "The Christmas Story," "Early Church Practices," and "Christmas Traditions"

OBJECTIVES

By the end of this lesson, the learner should be able to

- identify and describe the Christian church year,
- define the components of the church year,
- examine the Christmas story in greater detail,
- identify the early church practices related to the celebration of Christmas, and
- identify the origin and background of selected Christmas traditions.

IDENTIFICATIONS

Concepts

Church year—celebration of annual events that teach us about our Christian faith

Christmas—day commemorating the birth of Jesus; December 25

Epiphany—means "to make manifest"; January 6, the day on which Jesus was manifest to the wise men and the day of His baptism, some years later

Advent—season preceding Christmas, including the four Sundays before Christmas

Christmas tree—an evergreen fir tree decorated with lights and ornaments for Christmas

Nativity scene—a manger scene with the Baby Jesus and attending figures of Mary, Joseph, animals, shepherds, and wise men

Bethlehem star—star that led the wise men to Jerusalem and then to Bethlehem

Christmas cards—cards sent at Christmas to friends to commemorate the season

People

Holy family: Mary, Joseph, and the Baby Jesus

Herod the Great: Idumean ruler under Caesar, who ruled Israel

St. Nicholas: Christian man who loved people and did good deeds; forerunner of Santa Claus

Places

Bethlehem: means "House of Bread"; town in which Jesus was born

Nazareth: town in which Jesus lived as He was growing up

Egypt: country to which Mary and Joseph fled to protect Jesus from Herod's cruelty of slaughtering the innocent children

MATERIALS NEEDED

Parent/Teacher Handbook: The Bible, Vol. 1

Activity Sheets for Lesson 13

Crayons and markers

White paper for drawing

Lined paper for writing

Construction paper and posterboard

Glue

Old Christmas cards

Gingerbread mix

Masking tape and plastic tape

Aluminum or gold foil

Scissors, X-ACTO knife (not for child use)

Cutting board

3x5-index cards

8¹/₂x11-inch green, red, and white card stock

LEARNING ACTIVITIES FOR LESSON 13

Activity 1—Define the Events of the Christian Church Year

Read the material included in the section "Religious Practice of Christians" and the subsection "The Christian Church Year" in the handbook.

There are two cycles in the Christian church year. They are Christmas and Easter.

Cycle of Christmas—Advent to Epiphany

Advent begins the Christmas season. Advent includes the four Sundays before Christmas. Advent allows Christians to prepare for the incarnation of Jesus in human form. It may be celebrated with the Advent candle. The Advent candle often is a wreath that has four candles. One candle is lit on each of the four Sundays before Christmas.

Christmas always comes on December 25 in the Christian calendar. Christmas is a reminder of the coming of the Christ Child. The shepherds were an important part of that celebration. We normally celebrate by sending cards and giving gifts, as the wise men did to the Christ Child. It is easy to get caught up in the commercialism of the season, so it is important for Christians to set aside part of Christmas Eve or Christmas Day to commemorate the birth of Christ. We need to focus upon what God did that day two thousand years ago.

Christmas celebration in many churches includes Epiphany. *Epiphany* means "manifestation." It is celebrated at the time when the wise men were guided by the star and came to see Jesus. It is also traditionally the date when Jesus was baptized by John the Baptist in the River Jordan and became manifest to the world as the Son of God.

Cycle of Easter—Lent to Pentecost

Many churches do not celebrate Lent; if you come from a church tradition that does not celebrate Lent, you may choose to disregard this discussion of Lent. For those churches who do celebrate Lent, it is the forty-day period before Easter. It is a period of preparation for the coming of Easter. It can be a time of repentance and looking back over the past year, as well as looking forward to the death and resurrection of Jesus.

Holy Week refers to the time of Jesus' last week here on earth. Included are the events of Jesus' triumphal entry into Jerusalem, cleansing the Temple, disputing with the Pharisees and Sadducees, the Last Supper, the trials, the crucifixion, Jesus' death, and the burial of Jesus.

Easter is the holiest day of the Christian church year. On this day Jesus arose from the dead. He was triumphant over death. He purchased our salvation by His death on the cross and now was victorious over death in resurrection to new life. One day all who have put their trust in the Lord Jesus will be resurrected with Christ and live eternally with Him.

Pentecost comes fifty days after Easter. It commemorates the coming of the Holy Spirit and the birth of the church. The Holy Spirit comes to live within believers in Jesus Christ and gives them power to live for Christ by fulfilling the Great Commandment and carrying out the Great Commission.

The church had finalized the church year around these two cycles by about the fourth century AD. But why is the church year important? The church year is important to the Christian church for the same reasons that the Jewish year is important to Judaism. It is an annual reminder of God's goodness in providing salvation for His people through the death, burial, and resurrection of His only Son, Jesus Christ. The church year serves an educational purpose—to teach children and remind adults that our salvation has been purchased at an awesome price. It teaches in the same sense that God taught the Hebrew people, described in Deuteronomy 6:4–9. We ignore or carelessly teach the events of the Christian church year to our peril for both our generation and the next.

Talk about the two cycles of the church year and their significance for our Christian faith. You may want to consider Activity 2 as part of your discussion of the church year.

Activity 2—Calendar of the Christian Church Year

How does one picture the church year? Turn to Activity Sheet 2. Make copies of the "Calendar of the Church Year" for each of the members of your classroom. Discuss the church year. You may want to take a calendar and mark the days for this year. Be sure to tell the children that the other parts of the church year are important also. The Sundays after Pentecost and prior to Advent provide time for us to grow in our faith and trust in Jesus. They give us time to teach about our faith.

Activity 3—The Hope of Christmas (Luke 2:1–40; Matthew 2:1–23)

Read the material included in "Religious Practice of Christians" and the subsection "Christmas" in the handbook and the Christmas story as told in Luke 2:1–40 and Matthew 2:1–23.

The birth of the Christ Child resulted in the coming of the long-awaited Messiah. He brought hope to all humanity. Christmas is a very special holiday in the Christian year. In this lesson, you will want to examine not only the Christmas story but some of the traditions that have grown up around the celebration of Christmas over these two millennia.

For this activity, you need to duplicate on green card stock the Christmas tree found on Activity Sheet 3-A. Also duplicate the tree ornament pattern (Activity Sheet 3-B) on red and white card stock duplicating paper. Cut out strips of construction paper to frame the Christmas tree. Have these materials in readiness for the students for this activity.

On each of the Christmas balls have the children write one of the gifts that Christ gave to us through His birth, ministry, death, and resurrection. You may use the following gifts with Scripture passages to accompany the gift, or write your own gifts along with Scripture. They are the following: Hope—Hebrews 6:19–20, Peace—Luke 2:14, Joy—Romans 15:13, Eternal life—John 3:16, Faith—Galatians 2:15–16, Salvation—2 Corinthians 6:2, Goodwill—Luke 2:14, Mercy—Titus 3:4–7, Holy Spirit—John 14:25–27, and Love—1 Corinthians 13.

Activity 4—Retelling the Christmas Story with a Crèche (Luke 2:1–40; Matthew 2:1–23)

If you have access to *The Visual Bible—Matthew*, you may want to display the background for the events of the birth of Jesus. It will provide an excellent introduction to the events of this lesson. View the following scenes: "The Genealogy of Jesus," "The Birth of Jesus," "The Visit of the Magi," and "The Escape to Egypt, The Return to Nazareth."

Locate a Christmas crèche and bring it to the classroom. If possible, find one that is not a family treasure so that the children may help you retell the story of Jesus' birth using the pieces of the crèche. As you study this lesson, have the crèche in view for the class members to see. Read the material on the birth of Jesus in "The Christmas Story" section of the handbook and as told in Luke 2:1–40 and Matthew 2:1–23. Pay particular attention to the subsection "The Nativity Scene" in the "Christmas Traditions" section.

The nativity scene has been popular from its beginning with Francis of Assisi in Italy, France, and Spain. The scenes used live people and animals to portray the characters of this event. In America, many people in their homes and churches also have manger scenes that are displayed during the Christmas season. Some of the church scenes still use live people and animals. But most commonly, the crèche contains china, wood, or plastic figures.

You may want to retell the story of Christmas by first telling how the crèche came to be associated with the Christmas story. Then allow the children from your class to volunteer to help you retell the story. You might even have members of your class tell the story for another class in the building.

Have each child take one of the crèche pieces and describe what happened. You can even expand the story to tell of the Annunciation to Mary and the dream that Joseph had back in Nazareth. You can recount the story about Mary's journey to visit Elizabeth. You can discuss the arduous journey to Bethlehem and how they could find no room in the inn. Then recall the events at the birth of Jesus in the cow stall. Don't forget the animals, as well. Remember the shepherds on the hillside, watching their flocks of sheep, when suddenly the hillside was ablaze with light and the heavenly host called their attention to the birth of the Messiah. They left their sheep and went to Bethlehem to see this event. You can describe the visit to the Temple and the prophecies of Simeon and Anna. Recall the visit of the wise men and the anger of Herod, that caused Mary, Joseph, and Jesus to flee to Egypt. Finally, help them remember the return to Nazareth.

You may want to finish the story with the singing of some traditional Christmas carols such as "Away in a Manger." The words to the song are as follows:

Away in a manger, no crib for his bed, the little Lord Jesus laid down his sweet head.
The stars in the sky looked down where he lay, the little Lord Jesus asleep on the hay.

The cattle are lowing, the poor baby wakes, but little Lord Jesus, no crying he makes.
I love thee, Lord Jesus, look down from the sky, and stay by my cradle til morning is nigh.

Be near me, Lord Jesus; I ask Thee to stay, close by me forever and love me, I pray.
Bless all the dear children in Thy tender care, and fit us for heaven to live with Thee there.

Activity 5—Make a Christmas Card for Parents

With the story of Christmas freshly in mind, have the children make a Christmas card for their parents. This affords a good opportunity for the children to think about the Christian significance of the Christmas season and avoid the commercialism that is so attached to Christmas celebration in our communities.

Take an 8½x11-inch piece of construction paper and fold it in half. On the front of the card, have the child either draw or paste a picture of the nativity scene with Mary, Joseph, and the Baby Jesus in the manger. Have the children write a greeting inside the card. Tell them to make the greeting very special to express their love for their parents. Help them make the connection between their love for their parents and the tranquility of the scene with Mary, Joseph, and Jesus. Remind the children that Jesus came to earth to bring peace, joy, and love. This card presents an opportunity for them to be emissaries of Jesus in returning their love to their parents. It is a tangible expression of that love.

Activity 6—Giving a Gift to Others in a Children's Home

Remind the children, with the memory of the story of the birth of Jesus still fresh in mind, the reason why we give gifts at Christmas. We give gifts because we recall that the Magi brought gifts of gold, frankincense, and myrrh to Jesus and because Jesus gave so much to us.

This is a wonderful opportunity for the children to express that kind of love and appreciation for others. Whether the study of this unit is near Christmas or far away from Christmas, it does not matter. Ask the children to either purchase a gift or make something that will express the same attitude of giving, because Christ gave to us. Collect the toys or other gifts and have them given to the children in a children's home. They should be children who are about the same age as your students. These children may not receive many gifts during the year.

Activity 7—Make an Advent Calendar

Advent calendars are always good to have at home as the anticipation of Christmas draws near. You will need to either find or create a large picture of something associated with Christmas. The picture that the child creates can be cut from construction paper of various colors and the parts glued to the picture sheet. You can use either 12x18-inch construction paper or a smaller version 8½x11-inches. Affix the picture that you have selected to a desk with masking tape. Draw twenty-four 1x1-inch squares using a ruler and pencil. Do not draw the left side of the square because that will be the hinge for the window. The squares should not be any closer than 1½ inches to one another.

After the squares have been drawn, take the sheet to a cutting board. The teacher will cut out each of the three sides of the squares using an X-ACTO knife. The child can then carefully fold each square and crease the hinge on the left side. Each square should be numbered sequentially from 1 to 24.

With masking tape, affix the sheet with the squares to another sheet of construction paper. The new sheet will be underneath the picture sheet. Have the child lightly mark an X under every window.

Now either create with markers or find small pictures that relate to the Christmas story. Try to have the children use Christian symbols or pictures to stress the religious nature of Christmas. Old Christmas cards can be a good source for small pictures. Place a picture on top of each X on the under sheet and glue them down. When the child has finished with the under sheet, place the picture sheet on top of the under sheet and secure the outer border with glue and tape. You may want to use a different colored sheet of construction paper to create a border or frame for the picture sheet. Glue the strips of construction paper to the outside of the picture sheet.

Close the hinged windows and store until the first of December. Then open one square a day until Christmas Day.

Activity 8—Make a Bethlehem Star

Have the children make a Bethlehem star that they can hang in their room at home. Use the star pattern on Activity Sheet 8. Duplicate the star on card stock paper. Cover the star with aluminum foil or gold foil. You can add glitter to the surface of the star. Punch a hole in the top point of the star. Use a piece of yarn to hang the star.

You can make this a three-dimensional star by cutting two identical stars from the card stock paper and cutting a slit half way down from the point in the one and up from the bottom in the other. Then push the two stars together and lightly glue them to permanently hold them together. Decorate and hang with yarn.

Activity 9—Chrismon Ornaments

Chrismon is a word that combines *Christ* and *monogram*. Many times the entire green evergreen tree is decorated with the Chrismon ornaments. These ornaments are usually white and gold. Students can make the ornaments and take them home to place on their Christmas tree at the appropriate time.

Make the Chrismon ornaments from felt or cardboard. Some of the Chrismon ornaments may be made from the patterns given as symbols on Activity Sheet 7 in Lesson 12. They include the fish, cross, *chi rho*, dove, shepherd, and anchor. You can also use the star pattern from Activity Sheet 8. In addition, you may want to construct a triangle to represent the Trinity, a circle to represent eternity, a lamb to represent Christ as the sacrificial lamb, and a crown for the victorious Lord of glory.

First, trace the patterns and cut out the shapes. Paint the shapes with white or gold acrylic paint. You can then add gold or silver glitter. Allow them to dry and talk about the symbols.

Activity 10—Advent Wreath

Have each child make an Advent wreath. The wreath is used during the four Sundays preceding Christmas. Advent wreaths may be purchased or made. Evergreen branches or ivy may be twisted around and inserted into a Styrofoam circle base. Evergreen branches are symbolic of eternal life. Four purple candles are set in the circular base. (White candles may be substituted, if necessary). One candle represents each of the four Sundays prior to Christmas. A fifth white candle is placed in the center of the wreath and is lighted on Christmas day.

Write and duplicate instructions for parents about the meaning and use of the Advent wreath. When they light the first candle on the first Sunday, the parents should read Isaiah 60:2–3. The theme of this Sunday is hope. Gather as a family and sing Christmas carols and pray together. On the second Sunday, light the previous candle and a new candle. The Scripture for this week is Mark 1:4 and the theme is love. Continue in the same manner for the third Sunday. Light the two previous candles and a new one. Read Isaiah 35:10, and the theme is joy. Sing carols and pray together. On the fourth Sunday, read Isaiah 9:6–7. The theme is peace. Sing and pray. Finally, light the candle in the center on Christmas Eve after sundown or on Christmas Day. Read Luke 1:68–79; Luke 2:1–20; and Matthew 2:1–23. Sing and pray.

Activity 11—Graham Cracker House

One of the traditions from Germany that surrounds Christmas is the construction of a gingerbread house. If the time for studying this lesson is around Christmas, you will find packages in the grocery store for constructing a gingerbread house. If the time is not around Christmas, you may want to construct your own. In place of the gingerbread, use graham crackers. Cut a milk carton and use it to form the walls of the house and provide support. You can cut out windows and doors and form the roof and chimney. You may hold the graham cracker walls to the house with white icing. Decorate the house with peppermint candies, pretzels, gumdrops, etc.

The temptation will be to eat the sweets off the house. Help your children resist that temptation.

Activity 12—Memorize Galatians 4:4–6

To help your children see that Jesus' coming to earth was no accident, have them memorize this verse. It provides insight into the heavenly Father's intent in sending His only Son to earth to teach, minister, and die for us. For younger children, you might want them to learn only verses 4 and 5.

But when the completion of the time came, God sent His Son, born of a woman, born under the law, to redeem those under the law, so that we might receive adoption as sons. And because you are sons, God has sent the Spirit of His Son into our hearts, crying "Abba, Father!"

Have the children write these verses in their Bible Verse Memory Books and then illustrate them.

ACTIVITY SHEET 2: CALENDAR OF THE CHURCH YEAR

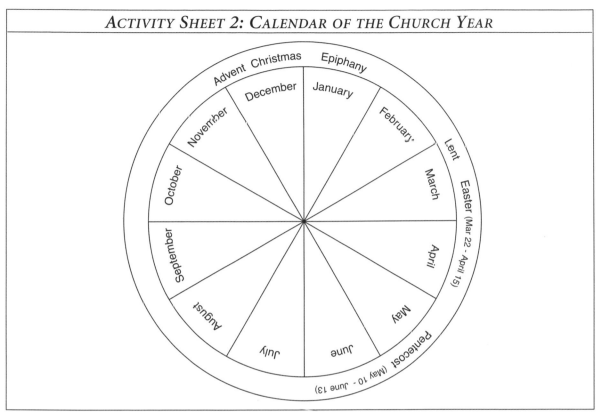

ACTIVITY SHEET 3-A: CHRISTMAS TREE PATTERN

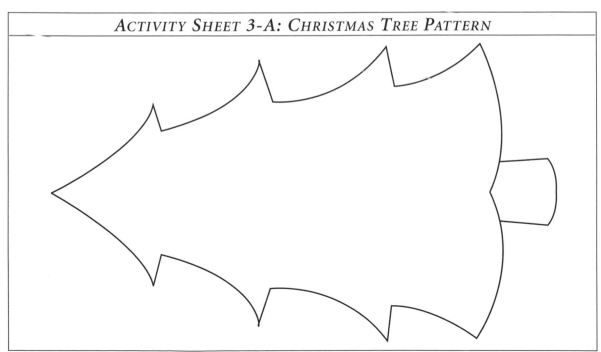

ACTIVITY SHEET 3-B: PATTERN FOR CHRISTMAS ORNAMENTS

ACTIVITY SHEET 8: BETHLEHEM STAR

LESSON 14: THE CHURCH YEAR FOR CHRISTIANS—EASTER

Readings from the Parent/Teacher Handbook: The Bible, Vol. 1: "The Christian Church Year," "Easter," "The Passover Meal," "Early Church Practices," and "Pentecost"

OBJECTIVES

By the end of this lesson, the learner should be able to

- describe the events of Passion week,
- discover the path that led Jesus to the cross,
- examine the trials and crucifixion of Jesus,
- explain the resurrection,
- describe the appearances of Jesus after the resurrection,
- demonstrate understanding of the ascension of Christ,
- examine early church practices that related to the crucifixion and resurrection, and
- discover the birth of the church at Pentecost.

IDENTIFICATIONS

Concepts

Arrest—in the Garden of Gethsemane, after the betrayal by Judas

Trials—religious and civil trials that led to crucifixion

Crucifixion—killing by hanging on a cross and eventually not being able to breathe

Burial of Jesus—in the new tomb of Joseph of Arimathea

Phoenix—mythical bird that had a rebirth every five hundred years; it would die in the flames and a new bird would emerge from the pyre; a symbol of resurrection

Butterfly—emerges from the cocoon as a butterfly and is a symbol of resurrection

Jonah—the prophet who disobeyed God, was swallowed by a great fish, and was saved to carry out his mission

Fish—in Greek the word *ichthus* means "fish" and was used by early Christians as an acrostic for "Jesus/Christ/of God/the Son/Savior"

Pentecost—Jewish feast day that became the day when the Holy Spirit came upon the disciples and the church was born

People

Pilate: Roman governor who condemned Jesus to death

Herod: one of the tetrarchs who ruled in Judea; son of Herod the Great

Caiaphas: high priest, who condemned Jesus to death

Judas: one of Jesus' disciple, who betrayed Him

Barabbas: a Zealot who had killed and was released by Pilate in place of Jesus

Mary Magdalene: follower of Jesus who had received His forgiveness for the sins of her past life

Peter: disciple who became a leader in the church

John: the beloved disciple, who also was a strong leader in the church

Places

Golgotha: "place of the skull" where Jesus was crucified

MATERIALS NEEDED

Parent/Teacher Handbook: The Bible, Vol. 1

Activity Sheets for Lesson 14

Crayons and markers

White paper for drawing

Lined paper for writing

Reusable adhesive, masking tape, and plastic tape

Construction paper and posterboard

3x5-inch index cards

1x1-inch wood in 7½x4-inch lengths

3x3-inch wood squares

Clay for making pottery, such as Fimo or Sculpey

Cardboard paper towel rolls

Wax paper	Toothbrush
Cookie sheet	Toothpicks
Rolling pin	Pencil with new eraser
Hard-boiled eggs	Paper plates

LEARNING ACTIVITIES FOR LESSON 14

Activity 1—Events of Holy Week (Matthew 21:1–28:15; Mark 11:1–16:14; Luke 19:29–24:35; John 12:12–20:25)

Review the events of the Easter cycle from the discussion in activity 1 of Lesson 13. In this lesson we will study the Easter cycle. The Easter cycle begins with preparation for Easter and continues with Holy Week. Holy Week culminates in the death and burial of Jesus in the tomb. Three days later Jesus arose from the dead. He ministered to His disciples for forty days. Then He ascended into heaven. He promised to send a Comforter, the Holy Spirit. While the little band of disciples was waiting for the Spirit, they were gathered for prayer on the Feast of Pentecost. Suddenly the Holy Spirit descended upon them, and the church was born.

Create a time line of the events of the last week of Jesus' life on earth, from Sunday to Sunday. If you have access to *The Visual Bible—Matthew*, you may want to show the appropriate scenes for the last week of Jesus' life. These include scenes from "The Triumphal Entry" to the "Great Commission." You will need to be selective, since this involves a great deal of material. You may want to focus on those scenes that are outlined below for the use of small groups. Events like the Last Supper will be helpful to the children as they think about what to draw for the time line.

Read the "Easter Story" in the handbook. The description by days of Holy Week will help your students to understand what happened to Jesus during Holy Week.

Have the students work in small groups. Provide each of the small groups with a sheet of construction paper. You will need to read the appropriate section from the Gospel of Matthew. Help the children in each group to summarize the activities that are appropriate for the days for which they are responsible.

Each small group will contribute to the entire time line by drawing a picture on construction paper that is most appropriate and most dominant for the set of events that occurred on their day(s). Divide the groups as follows:

Group 1—Sunday and Monday

Since this group has the first two days of Holy Week, they will need to produce two pictures—one for Sunday and the other for Monday. The dominant issue on Sunday is the triumphal entry into Jerusalem. The dominant item on Monday is the cleansing of the Temple. They might also include Jesus healing in the Temple as well.

Group 2—Tuesday and Wednesday

This group will need to produce two pictures also. Tuesday was a busy day of disputation with the scribes and the Pharisees. That should be reflected in their picture. They may also want to portray Mary anointing the feet of Jesus. Wednesday was a silent day. It can be shown as such. Jesus probably rested for what was to come.

Group 3—Thursday

This is the busiest day for Jesus. It started in the evening, about 6 p.m. The disciples met for the Passover meal. About 9 p.m., they went to the Garden of Gethsemane. Jesus was in prayer until about midnight, when the soldiers with Judas came out to find Jesus. Judas betrayed Jesus. Continuing through the night, there were trials before Caiaphas and ending with the trial before the Sanhedrin. This began about 6 a.m. Peter denied Jesus during the night as well.

Group 4—Friday

Pilate first heard the case against Jesus on Friday morning. Pilate did not want to rule on Jesus, so he had Jesus sent to Herod. Pilate got no help from Herod, and Jesus was sent back to Pilate. Pilate pronounced

Jesus "not guilty." But that did not satisfy the crowd. Pilate had Jesus beaten and sent Him to the cross. That evening Joseph of Arimathea and Nicodemus took the body of Jesus and buried it in Joseph's tomb.

Group 5—Saturday and Sunday

The women came to the tomb on Saturday. A stone was in front of the entrance. There was a guard set to make sure that His disciples did not take Him from the tomb. Sunday was the day of triumph. Jesus rose from the dead. He appeared to Mary Magdalene, the other women, the two disciples on the road to Emmaus, Peter, and to the other apostles.

After all of the drawings are completed, tape the various sheets together and, using reusable adhesive, fasten the time line to the wall for at least the duration of this lesson.

Activity 2—Wordfind Puzzle on the Last Supper

Duplicate copies of the wordfind puzzle on the Last Supper on Activity Sheet 2. Talk with the class about the meaning of the Last Supper and have them complete the Wordfind.

Activity 3—Chart of the Trials of Jesus (Matthew 25:47–27:30)

Read the story of the arrest and trials of Jesus in the "Easter" section of the handbook.

Turn to the chart on Activity Sheet 3. Duplicate copies for each of your students. Have the children or teacher read the passages and determine the decision that was made at each of the trials. Complete the chart.

Activity 4—Make a Wooden Cross

Read the story of the arrest and trials of Jesus in the "Jesus' Crucifixion" and "The Burial of Jesus" in the handbook.

The universal symbol of the Christian faith is the cross. Darkness filled the sky as Jesus hung on the cross and died for my sin and your sin. Hate, sin, and the devil appeared to have conquered. The hour for humanity was dark indeed. But through His death on the cross, God forgave all persons who place their trust in Jesus Christ as Savior and Lord. When everything seemed grim, His death brought the world's brightest hour. God's love was victorious. Jesus Christ bore our death so that we might one day live with Him for all eternity.

To recognize the accomplishment of Jesus on the cross, have the children make wooden crosses that they can keep as a reminder of the death of our Lord that day. You will need 1x1-inch wood for this project. Each cross will need to be $7^1/_2$ inches high. The arms of the cross should be cut in 4-inch lengths. For the greatest endurance, you may want to groove the vertical and horizontal pieces to fit together. Glue them in place. For the base, obtain 3-inch squares of wood from a craft store or a lumber company. Drill a small hole in the base and place a wood screw to secure the cross to the base. You can also glue the base.

Have the children sand the wood with fine-grained sandpaper. You may stain the crosses or leave them natural wood color. Spray paint the crosses with clear acrylic. When dry, gently sand. Coat with a second coat of clear acrylic and let dry.

Activity 5—Resurrection Appearances

Read the story of the arrest and trials of Jesus in the "Easter" section of the handbook.

How do we know that Jesus rose from the dead? There are extensive eyewitness accounts in the Gospels of the resurrection. Turn to Activity Sheet 5. You will find a chart of the resurrection appearances of Jesus with Scripture references. Read the Scripture passages and tell the students about the resurrection experience from the viewpoint of the eyewitness accounts.

Have the students complete the chart assignment and tell whose name needs to be placed into the appropriate block.

Activity 6—Make the Tomb in Which Jesus Body was Placed
We celebrate the empty tomb. The tomb of Joseph of Arimathea was recently hewn out of rock. You can create a model of the tomb with pottery clay. Clay can be obtained at a craft store. You will need a rolling pin. Roll out the clay and then mold it to the shape of a mound. Make sure the inside is hollow. Place an entryway in the front of the tomb. Fashion a stone to be placed alongside the tomb. After you have finished making the tomb, place the tomb and the stone on a cookie sheet that is covered with aluminum foil. Bake in the oven at 225° for 20 minutes.

Allow the newly made tomb to cool. Place soft cotton swatches of material or gauze inside the tomb to show that Jesus was not there. He had risen from the dead just as He had said. We celebrate the empty tomb every Lord's Day and especially on Easter.

Activity 7—Symbols of the Resurrection
There are many symbols for the resurrection. Some of those symbols are included on Activity Sheet 7. The descriptions of the symbols are also given on the activity sheet. Talk about the symbols. Then have the children match the symbols to the descriptions.

Activity 8—Easter Egg Coloring
Read the story of the arrest and trials of Jesus in the "Easter" section of the handbook.

Easter eggs are a symbol of the resurrection, as noted in the previous exercise. In advance of this session, hard-boil a number of eggs. Have them ready for class. Use rings cut from cardboard paper towel rolls to hold the eggs. Use tempera paints. Color the entire egg. When the egg is dry, paint designs with toothbrushes and toothpicks. You may use a pencil with a new eraser to paint as well.

Have the children use some of the Christian designs from the previous activity to decorate their eggs. The peacock, phoenix, etc., make excellent designs.

Activity 9—Easter Story Cookies
You will need:
1 cup pecan halves, broken
1 tsp. vinegar
3 egg whites
pinch of salt
Preheat oven to 350° and lightly grease a cookie sheet.

1. Place pecan halves in a plastic, resealable bag. Give children wooden spoons, and let them pound the pecans into small pieces. Set aside. Explain that after Jesus was arrested, He was beaten by soldiers. (Read John 19:1–3.)

2. Let each helper smell the vinegar. Then measure 1 teaspoon into the mixing bowl. Explain that while Jesus was on the cross, He was thirsty, and the soldiers gave Him vinegar to drink. (Read John 19:28–30.)

3. Separate the eggs. Add the whites to the vinegar. Explain that eggs represent life and that Jesus gave His life to give us life. (Read John 10:10–11.)

4. Sprinkle a little salt into each person's palm, and let each one brush it off into the mixture. Then they can taste their salty palm. Explain that this reminds us of the salty tears shed by those saddened by Jesus' death. (Read Luke 23:27.)

5. So far, the ingredients aren't very appetizing; but now sugar is added, and you must trust that it will have a pleasant result. Explain that the sweetest part of this story is that Jesus died because He loves us. He makes it possible to know Him and belong to Him. (Read Psalm 34:8 and John 3:16.)

6. Beat with electric mixer on highest speed for 12 to 15 minutes until stiff peaks form. Point out the pearly white color, the color of purity for those who have been cleansed from sin by Jesus' death. (Read Isaiah 1:18 and 1 John 3:1–3.)

7. Fold in nuts. Drop rounded teaspoons of the mixture on the cookie sheet. Explain that each mound resembles a rocky tomb like the one in which Jesus' body was placed. (Read Matthew 27:57–60.)

8. Put the cookie sheet in the preheated oven, close the door, and turn the oven completely off. Together, secure the oven door with tape. Explain that Jesus' tomb was sealed. (Read Matthew 27:65–66.)

9. Time for bed! Explain to the children that they may feel sad and disappointed to leave the cookies in the oven. Remind children that Jesus' followers were sad when His tomb was sealed. (Read John 16:20, 22.)

10. On Easter morning, open the oven door and give everyone a cookie. Ask everyone to take a bite. The cookies are hollow! On the first Easter morning, Jesus' followers were amazed to find His tomb opened and empty. He had risen! (Read Matthew 28:1–9.)   (April 1999 issue of *HomeLife.*)

Activity 10—Celebrating Easter
Turn to Activity Sheet 10. Duplicate the questionnaire for students to think about Easter as a holiday. Have them review their understanding of Easter and think about its significance. Then have them complete the questionnaire.

Activity 11—Memorize Philippians 3:10
Duplicate copies of the memory verse written in Secret Code on Activity Sheet 11.

My goal is to know Him and the power of His resurrection and the fellowship of His sufferings, being conformed to His death.

Have the children fill in the letters to complete the memory verse. Have them practice the verse until they know it. They should then write it in their Bible Verse Memory Books and illustrate it.

ACTIVITY SHEET 2: THE LAST SUPPER WORDFIND

Directions: Find the underlined words below in the wordfind puzzle.

1. <u>John</u> and <u>Peter</u> were sent to Jerusalem to make preparations for the Passover meal.
2. Jesus washed the feet of the <u>disciples</u>.
3. Jesus and the disciples ate the <u>Passover</u> meal.
4. Jesus told them the meaning of the cup of wine. It represented His blood shed on the <u>cross</u>.
5. Jesus said the <u>bread</u> represented His body that was broken for them.
6. Jesus told the disciples that one of them would <u>betray</u> Him.
7. Jesus said the one who will betray Me dips in the bowl with Me. Jesus gave the bread to <u>Judas</u>.
8. After Judas left, Jesus gave the disciples a command to <u>love</u> one another.
9. Jesus promised to prepare a place called <u>heaven</u> for His followers.

```
J C E U J J Z H B U N Y X I Y
F P Q B N B I D L S T W M I N
K S T J N P R E T E P X I B M
C W Z C E A K S X J J N W L B
G A S T V S E D W D G V D N L
V J U D A S J H K C W I V U Z
J H K R E O L V W C S Y S Y G
D H Y P H V O W F C V T V Q Y
Y A E N M E V P I U J C G O C
O M C B V R E P Y F C Z D Q O
S K W R A H L A Y C H R S Q J
D U B E W E R M P V D Z O N L
O Z C A S T U P T N C F R S J
G J O D E Q F Y D T Z S J Z S
E K W B S F F B T P A G V R G
```

ACTIVITY SHEET 3: THE TRIALS OF JESUS

Directions: Fill in the decisions that were made at the different trials of Jesus.

TRIAL	SCRIPTURE	JUDGE	DECISION
Religious Trials (Jewish)			
1st	John 18:12–14	Annas	
2nd	Matt. 26:57–68	Caiaphas	
3rd	Matt. 27:1–2	Sanhedrin	
Civil Trials (Roman)			
4th	John 18:28–38	Pilate	
5th	Luke 23:6–12	Herod	
6th	John 18:39–19:6	Pilate	

Appearances of Jesus after the resurrection:

Who saw the empty tomb?	Mary _____ and other women	Mark 16:1–5
	_____ and the other disciple (John)	John 20:2–10
	_____ at the tomb	Matthew 28:11–15
Who saw Jesus alive after the resurrection?	Mary Magdalene and other _____	Matthew 28:5–9
	Disciples at _____	Luke 24:13–2
	Simon _____	Luke 24:33–34
	The _____ disciples (not Thomas)	John 20:19–23
	The _____ disciples (including Thomas)	John 20:26–28
	_____ fishing	John 21:1–14
	Five _____ brothers	1 Corinthians 15:3–8
Who saw Jesus ascend into heaven?	The eleven _____	Matthew 28:16–20 Luke 24: 50–51

ACTIVITY SHEET 11: MEMORY VERSE IN SECRET CODE

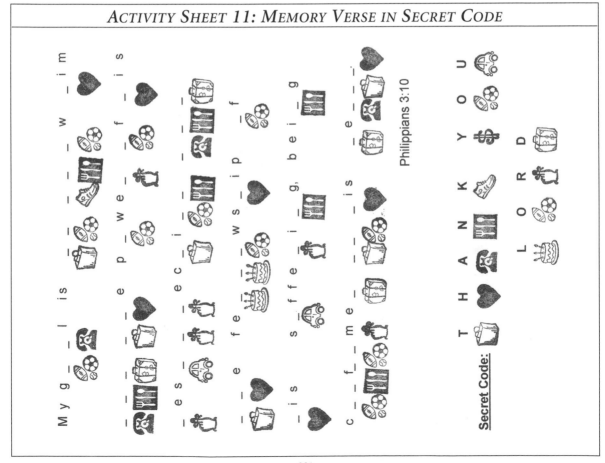

Philippians 3:10

My g___ ___ is ___ es ___ is

w ___ im ___ is

___ f ___ we ___ e p ___ we ___ e

ci ___ ws ___ ip ___ f

f ___ e ___ fe ___ g, bei ___ g

s ___ ffe ___ g, is

c ___ f ___ me ___ e

THANK YOU LORD

Secret Code: _____

Directions: Match the resurrection symbol with the description.

A. ____ 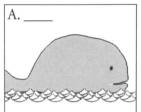　　B. ____ 　　C. ____ 　　D. ____

E. ____ 　　F. ____ 　　G. ____

1. Easter eggs—Chicken enclosed in the shell breaks forth to life.
2. Phoenix—Mythical bird; at death every five hundred years it bursts forth in flame and out of the flame emerges a new Phoenix.
3. Easter Lily—Spring flower that springs forth from a seemingly dead bulb to beautiful life.
4. Peacock—When the peacock sheds its feathers, it bursts forth with new and more brilliant colors.
5. Great fish of Jonah—Jonah was in the great fish for three days and three nights, similar to Jesus' entombment.
6. Lamb of God—Lamb of God is no longer wounded; stands with the banner of victory.
7. Butterfly—Caterpillar goes into the cocoon, similar to a tomb, and emerges as a beautiful butterfly.

ACTIVITY SHEET 10: CELEBRATING EASTER

Directions: Complete these questions.

1. What special things does your family do to celebrate Easter?

2. What is the Easter service like in your church?

3. Have you ever attended an Easter sunrise service? If you have, what did you think of it?

4. Have you ever attended a drama or musical presentation in your church that retold the Easter story?

5. Is Easter as important as Christmas? Why or why not?

6. What do you like best about Easter?

Unit Three: Bible Geography—Lesson 15

UNIT SUMMARY

This set of activities will focus upon the geography of the Holy Land and go back in time for several thousand years to the time of the patriarchs and come forward in time to the life and ministry of Christ, about two thousand years ago.

OVERVIEW

Objectives

By the end of this lesson, the student should be able to

- describe the lands in which Abraham lived and traveled,
- explain and describe the lands of the Exodus,
- discover the places Jesus visited in Israel, and
- identify the places where the apostle Paul visited on his missionary journeys.

Content Summary and Rationale

Through this set of activities, the student will be able to discover the places where Bible characters lived, traveled, taught, preached, and ministered. This set of activities will also help the student to discover the ancient time period in which these events occurred. For the student, the time dimension will go back in history several thousand years. The distance dimension will carry the student across several thousand miles from North America to the Holy Land in the Middle East.

This set of activities is important because learners will discover that the peoples of the Bible were very different from people who live in our community. Without moving across the time dimension and the space dimension, the student will not be able to grapple with the significant differences between then and now and between here and there. Both of these concerns will affect the way in which the learner is able to relate to Bible times and Bible people. The Bible lands, as we know them today, are still an area of heated tension for Jews, Christians, and Islamic peoples.

Key Concept

The key concept for this study is the importance of the physical location of the Holy Land in the Bible. God gave the covenant and promise for a specific land grant to Abraham and his descendants.

Prior Knowledge Needed

Basic understanding of time and distance are needed to fully appreciate this unit. First and second graders will have difficulty with this unit. You may still introduce them to the countries of Palestine, Babylonia, and Egypt. Everything must be referenced in relation to the child to the child's own location today. Children will also have difficulty understanding the meaning of "two thousand years ago." For third graders, you may call attention to the Middle East and its current place of prominence on the news each day.

RESOURCES FOR TEACHERS AND STUDENTS

- Buchanan, Edward, *Parent/Teacher Handbook: The Bible, Vol. 1* (Nashville, Tenn.: Broadman & Holman, 2003).
- Butler, Trent, ed., *Holman Illustrated Bible Dictionary* (Nashville, Tenn.: Holman Bible Publishers, 2003).
- Dockery, David, ed., *Holman Bible Handbook* (Nashville, Tenn.: Holman Bible Publishers, 1992).
- *Holman Bible Atlas* (Nashville, Tenn.: Holman Bible Publishers, 1998).
- An encyclopedia—*World Book, Funk and Wagnalls, Britannica*, etc. (may use CDROM)

Readings from the Parent/Teacher Handbook: The Bible, Vol. 1: "Bible Geography"

MATERIALS NEEDED
- *Parent/Teacher Handbook: The Bible, Vol. 1*
- *Holman Bible Dictionary*
- Activity Sheets for Lesson 15
- Crayons and markers
- Construction paper
- Blank sheets of white paper for drawing
- Roll of shelf paper or butcher paper

- Masking tape, plastic tape, reusable adhesive
- 3x5-inch index cards
- Lined paper for writing
- Travel brochures and posters, especially to the Holy Land
- Magazines with pictures to be cut out
- Maps
- Overhead projector

KEY VOCABULARY

Places

1. Jerusalem	9. Jordan River	18. Dead Sea	28. Magdala
2. Bethlehem	10. Haran	19. Judea	29. Tiberius
3. Nazareth	11. Ur	20. Galilee	30. Decapolis
4. Egypt	12. Shechem	21. Samaria	31. Capernaum
5. Sodom	13. Hebron	22. Edom	32. Cana
6. Gomorrah	14. Beer Sheba	23. Ammon	33. Idurnea
7. Dead Sea	15. Tyre	24. Jordan	34. Kadesh Barnea
8. Fertile Crescent	16. Gaza	25. Negev	
	17. Mediterranean	26. Sinai	
	Sea	27. Phoenicia	

LEARNING ACTIVITIES FOR LESSON 15

Activity 1—Trip to the Holy Land

Help your children develop a sense of the places where the Bible events took place. Prepare an imaginary trip from where you are presently located to New York City. From Kennedy Airport, take a jet plane to Tel Aviv, Israel. From Tel Aviv you will travel by bus to many of the interesting places where the Bible characters lived and traveled so many years ago.

Discuss the travel plans using the maps on Activity Sheet 1-A and 1-B. Duplicate the outline map for all members of your class. This is a map for Israel today. Have the children write the names of the cities they want to visit on their map using the map on Activity Sheet 1-B as a reference. These should include Tel Aviv, Jerusalem, Bethlehem, Nazareth, Beer Sheba, Hebron, Shechem, Tyre, and Gaza. Indicate the bodies of water, such as the Sea of Galilee, Jordan River, and Mediterranean Sea. Have them write the names of the political divisions, such as Judea, Galilee, Lebanon, Syria, Samaria, Jordan, Negev, and Sinai.

Next, create a travel itinerary. To help you with this activity, you can obtain travel brochures and posters from your local travel bureau. Try to obtain materials for the Holy Land. If the class is older, have them research in the library and on the encyclopedia CD-ROM for information about Israel. They can also discover many helpful items online. If the children are younger, you may need to prepare materials in advance.

When you have gathered the materials, brochures, and posters, have the children develop a classroom environment that shows the trip to Israel. Have groups of children working on different activities to prepare for this unit. One group could decorate your classroom with the materials that you have gathered.

Each child will need a passport. Cut the passports from construction paper and fold the 12x18-inch construction paper to form a booklet. Staple pages inside the passport. On the front, decorate the passport with an eagle and other markings. On the first page, place a picture of the child. On the next page, place a map of Israel. Each of the pages may be used to detail the activities in which the children engaged while on their trip to the Holy Land. Pictures may be cut from magazines or drawn by the children. Students can add to their passport as they study the various sections of the Bible geography section.

Your class may want to develop a travel brochure for the trip. What will they see on the trip? Find pictures in magazines, online, and in copies of old *National Geographic* magazines. See Activity Sheet 1-C for a form to help them plan their trip.

Also have each child make a list of the things that he/she will need to bring on a trip for several weeks in the Holy Land.

Activity 2—Time Line for Bible History

Develop a time line for the history of the time periods covered by the Bible.

Use a sheet of shelf paper or butcher paper that will stretch 3 to 6 feet in length and write significant dates along the lower margin. Allow enough space for the members of your class to draw pictures of the events as you come to them in reading in the book. You will want to chart the Period of the Patriarchs—Abraham to Joseph. If you place them on the wall, use masking tape or plastic adhesive (obtainable at a stationary store) that will hold the paper to the wall but will not leave marks on the surface.

This activity will be ongoing as you move through the material in the geography section of the book.

Activity 3—The Ziggurat

Normally, a ziggurat was a stepped building that rose on platforms to form a sort of pyramid. The ziggurat was usually capped with a temple to one of the gods of the ancient world. It is believed that the Tower of Babel was a ziggurat. Certainly Abraham would have seen several such buildings. Both Ur and Haron had ziggurats.

If you are working with young children, they can build a ziggurat from blocks. For older children, use modeling clay or plaster of Paris to construct a ziggurat.

Find a picture of a ziggurat in the *Holman Illustrated Bible Dictionary*, and use the picture as a model to help the children construct the ziggurat.

Activity 4—The Travels of Abraham and What Life Was Like in Abraham's Time

The travels of Abraham are very important. It was through faith that Abraham received the promise. His inheritance would be the Land of Promise, and his descendents would number as the sand of the sea or the stars in the heavens. Read the material in the handbook called "The Travels of Abraham" in the Bible geography section.

Duplicate Activity Sheet 4-A. Have the children trace the travels of Abraham and identify on the map the cities, countries, and bodies of water through which Abraham would have traveled. A complete map is provided in the answers section.

How was life different in Abraham's day from what it is today? From the material in your handbook, "The Travels of Abraham," use Activity Sheet 4-B for comparisons between his day and ours. Have the children fill in the charts. The areas for comparison include home, religion, transportation, and safety.

Complete the review of the patriarchs by completing the crossword puzzle for the travels of Abraham on Activity Sheet 4-C.

Activity 5—Moses and the Exodus

Read the material in the handbook "Moses, Joshua, and the Exodus," in the Bible geography section. Help your children to understand life in Egypt for the Israelites. Recall the miracles of God in raising up Moses and in sending the plagues upon the Egyptians. The result was the Exodus from Egypt by the Israelites. The Egyptians were drowned in the Red Sea when they tried to chase the people of Israel.

The Israelites then spent forty years in the wilderness of Sinai. During that time Moses received the Law of God for the people. Later, under the leadership of Joshua, the people of Israel conquered Palestine on the west side of the Jordan River. Refer to the *Holman Bible Atlas*, "Route of the Exodus," for a map of the Exodus. You may also refer to the *Holman Illustrated Bible Dictionary*, p. 525 for a map of the Exodus wanderings. Have your children trace the wanderings to Mt. Sinai and up to Kadesh Barnea. You can duplicate a fresh copy of the outline map of the Fertile Crescent from Activity Sheet 4-A for members of your class. Help them identify the significant places of the Exodus.

To help your class review the persons and places of this period of Jewish history, make copies of the Wordfind for the Exodus on Activity Sheet 5. Have the students work together in pairs until all have completed the exercise. The words are provided in the paragraphy to the left of the puzzle.

Activity 6—David, Solomon, and the Divided Kingdom

In the handbook read "Saul, the First King of Israel," "David Annointed to be King," "David Becomes King," "Solomon Becomes King," and "The Divided Kingdom" in the Bible geography section.

King Saul was the first king to reign over Israel. He set up his palace at Gibeah. He was not interested in enlarging the borders of Israel. He wanted to protect the country as it was. He reigned for forty years. He did not obey God, and God did not continue the house of Saul.

David was called by God to reign in Saul's place. David was a man of God. He enlarged the borders of Israel and united the tribes into a nation. David conquered Jerusalem and made Jerusalem his capital. His sin at midlife prevented him from being all that God desired. But David was a man who had a close walk with God.

His son, Solomon, started out his reign well. He asked God for wisdom. He received wealth and prestige throughout the world at that time. Unfortunately, he married many wives, and they caused him to sin against God. God promised not to remove Solomon for the sake of David. But when Solomon died, the kingdom split between the northern ten tribes in Samaria and the southern two tribes in Judah.

All of the kings of Samaria did evil before the Lord. The northern ten tribes were taken into captivity by the Assyrians in 722 BC. For Judah, there were bad kings but also good kings. God spared Judah until 587 BC. In that year Jerusalem and Judah were taken captive by Nebuchadnezzar, the king of Babylon.

Many of the people of Samaria married outside of Israel in the countries where they were taken captive. The Samaritans who returned to Palestine were not pure Israelites. By contrast, many of the people of Judah who remained outside of Palestine set up synagogues and remained Jewish. Others came back after 538 BC to Palestine and Judah. The Temple was rebuilt in 515 BC.

The end of the Old Testament occurred about 400 BC. During the period known as the Intertestamental Period, the time period between the Old and the New Testaments, the people of Judah were subjugated and later won their freedom under the Maccabees. Rome conquered Syria and

Palestine under Pompey in 64–63 BC. Judah was then ruled by the family of Herod the Great. He rebuilt the Temple again. Judah remained as a conquered nation until the Romans, under Titus, finally destroyed Jerusalem and the Temple in AD 70.

To help your children understand the split in the kingdoms north and south, look at a map in a Bible atlas to identify the locations. Have each child identify the locations that are listed on the map.

Make another segment of the time line to include "David, Solomon, and the Divided Kingdom." Continue with your butcher paper or shelf paper to expand the timeline.

Activity 7—The Public Ministry of Jesus and The Galilean Ministry

Read "The Public Ministry of Jesus"and "The Galilean Ministry" in the handbook. As you read this section, turn to Plate V in *Holman Illustrated Bible Dictionary*, in the color plate section, after page 1450. As you read, try to follow Jesus' travels around Palestine.

Locate these places, rivers, and cities from His early ministry: Jordan River (just north of the Dead Sea) where Jesus was baptized; Dead Sea; Cana, where Jesus turned the water into wine; the Temple in Jerusalem; Samaria, where Jesus witnessed to the woman at the well. List also the political geographical boundaries: Judea, Idumea, Samaria, Galilee, Syria, Decapolis, Perea, and the Nabataeans.

Find these places from His Galilean ministry: Cana (again); Capernaum; the Sea of Galilee, where Jesus delivered the Sermon on the Mount; and the Sea of Galilee that Jesus calmed.

For the later ministry, Jesus was back in Perea, Judea, and the city of Jerusalem.

You may also want to find these additional places: Phoenicia, Bethlehem, Shechem, Sychar, Joppa, Caesarea, Tyre, Sidon, Nazareth, Magdala, and Tiberius.

When you have completed this task yourself, help your students find the places. A large map on a map stand or a projected map using an overhead projector will help the children locate the geographical places. As you come to each place, talk about how that place fit into the life and ministry of Jesus. Note that Jesus lived and ministered in the confines of the area shown on the map.

Activity 8—The Roman Empire and Judaism

Read "The Roman Empire and Judaism" in the Bible geography section. Use it as the basis for the study of life in Rome and Palestine during the first century. This activity can be used with younger children, but the teacher will need to do more of the research. Send older children to an encyclopedia, especially one on a CD-ROM. This will greatly help them in their quest.

Have one group of children research ancient Rome in the first century AD. What was it like to be a Roman citizen? What did they do for entertainment? What were their homes like? What was their religion? What kind of food did they eat? What was the political situation like? Who was Augustus Caesar? Who were Emperor Claudius and Emperor Nero?

Have a second group research what it must have been like to be a Jewish boy or girl in Palestine during this period of the first century AD. Ask the same kinds of questions about the people of Palestine. What was life like in Palestine?

Have the children in each group write their findings on an overhead transparency or on newsprint with markers. Have each group display the findings and discuss life in the two different places.

Activity 9—Memorize Hebrews 11:8

To help your children understand the importance of obedience as God desires, have them memorize Hebrews 11:8–10. These are good verses because they show what Abraham was called upon to do. For younger children, have them memorize only verse 8.

By faith Abraham, when he was called, obeyed and went out to a place he was going to receive as an inheritance; he went out, not knowing where he was going. By faith he stayed as a foreigner in the land of promise, living in tents with Isaac and Jacob, co-heirs of the same promise. For he was looking forward to the city that has foundations, whose architect and builder is God.

Have the children write the verses in their Bible Verse Memory Books and illustrate it.

WORKSHEETS FOR LESSON 15

ACTIVITY SHEET 1: MAP FOR IMAGINARY TRIP TO THE HOLY LAND

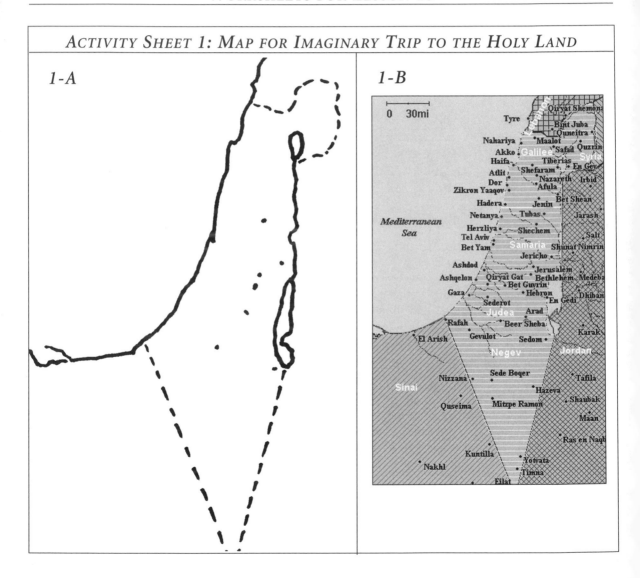

1-A

1-B

ACTIVITY SHEET 1-C: IMAGINARY TRIP TO THE HOLY LAND TRAVEL BROCHURE

Directions: Duplicate both pages of this brochure. Copy or paste the inside template onto the back of the outside template. Cut the pages and fold on the center line. On the cover, you might want to place an airplane and other pictures. List the things to see and do on page 2. On the next 2 pages, place or draw pictures of the things to see in Israel.

Outside template of brochure

Things to See	My Trip to Israel
	by: _____

Inside template of brochure

What to See and Do in Israel	Things to See
1.	
2.	
3.	
4.	
5.	
6.	
7.	
8.	
9.	
10.	
11.	

ACTIVITY SHEET 4-A: THE TRAVELS OF ABRAHAM

Directions: Write the names of the significant cities, rivers, and countries where Abraham visited. These would include Ur, Haran, the Tigris River, the Euphrates River, the Mediterranean Sea, the Dead Sea, the Jordan River, the Sea of Galilee, Mesopotamia, Palestine, and Egypt. Why is this area called the Fertile Crescent?

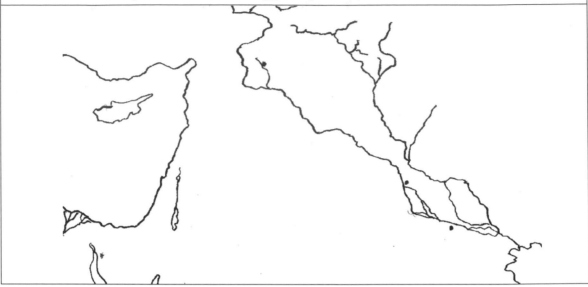

ACTIVITY SHEET 4-B: WHAT ABRAHAM'S LIFE WAS LIKE

Directions: Using the material in the handbook, "The Travels of Abraham," compare Abraham's experience with your experience today.

1. Home—What was Abraham's home in Ur like? How does it compare with my home today? How did a home then differ from one today?
Abraham's home:_____
My home:_____

2. Religion—What was the religion of Ur like? How does your Christian faith differ? Which faith would you rather have and why?
Religion in Ur:_____
My Christian faith: _____

3. Transportation—How did Abraham travel from Ur to Haran and on to the Promised Land? How do we travel today? How do the kinds of transportation differ? How would you rather travel—as they did then or now?
Transportation in Abraham's day: _____
Transportation today:_____

4. Safety—How safe was the land in Abraham's day? How safe is it where you live today? What are the differences? Is it safer today or then?
Safety in Abraham's day: _____
Safety today:_____

ACTIVITY SHEET 4-C: THE PATRIARCHS CROSSWORD PUZZLE

Directions: Find the appropriate words and complete the crossword puzzle.

Across

3. _____ Crescent
4. country southwest of Israel
8. wife of Jacob
9. next to what river do you find Haran?
11. Terah took Abram's family
12. a group of travelers and their pack animals
14. Abraham's nephew
15. wicked city destroyed by fire

Down

1. sea without any outlet
2. large building that appears to have large steps
5. wife of Isaac
6. father of Abram
7. son of Hagar and Abraham
10. city where Abram was born
13. a wanderer from place to place

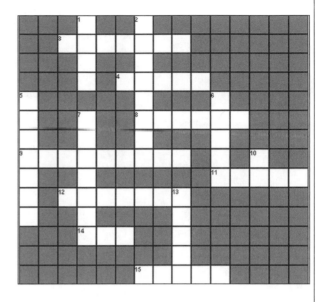

ACTIVITY SHEET 5: THE EXODUS WORDFIND

Directions: Find the words that are capitalized in the wordfind paragraph below. The words may be found side to side, up and down, diagonally, or backwards.

MOSES was born in EGYPT. God protected Moses. He was taken from the NILE River and raised by Pharaoh's daughter. When he was an adult, God called him to lead the Israelites from Egypt. They traveled in the WILDERNESS. They came to Mount SINAI, the mountain of God. There, God gave Moses and his people the Ten Commandments. Continuing in the wilderness, they came to KADESH BARNEA. The people sinned against God and were punished. They had to stay in the wilderness for many more years. After Moses died, God chose JOSHUA to lead the people into the Promised Land. They crossed over the JORDAN River and marched around the walls of JERICHO. The walls fell and God guided the people into the Promised Land of CANAAN.

B	X	D	W	N	R	P	E	E	V	M	H	I	R	J
F	U	R	N	G	J	E	R	I	C	H	O	D	M	G
U	C	G	A	U	S	N	E	L	I	N	C	J	D	F
Q	W	D	A	Z	E	E	A	J	C	A	U	X	G	G
P	C	P	N	C	K	G	S	D	T	W	N	I	Z	G
L	V	S	A	U	R	J	Y	O	R	B	S	I	B	D
Y	B	S	C	V	A	K	H	P	M	O	E	F	S	X
Q	H	E	H	S	E	D	A	K	T	S	J	Y	F	K
E	Z	N	Y	K	I	G	M	B	G	W	A	B	B	R
W	F	R	Y	E	C	X	W	Y	X	F	U	E	B	O
A	W	E	Y	A	Z	W	P	O	H	J	H	P	L	F
P	J	D	S	U	U	R	T	Z	D	E	S	L	O	H
R	Q	L	U	H	B	R	E	A	X	W	O	C	O	Q
D	E	I	K	L	E	J	F	I	H	X	J	P	R	G
X	X	W	G	T	T	B	I	G	H	H	P	W	U	W

LESSON 1

Activity Sheet 1
Books of the Law
1. Genesis
2. Exodus
3. Leviticus
4. Numbers
5. Deuteronomy

Books of Poetry and Wisdom
1. Job
2. Psalms
3. Proverbs
4. Ecclesiastes
5. Song of Solomon

Books of History
1. Joshua
2. Judges
3. Ruth
4. 1 Samuel
5. 2 Samuel
6. 1 Kings
7. 2 Kings
8. 1 Chronicles
9. 2 Chronicles
10. Ezra
11. Nehemiah
12. Esther

Books of Major Prophets
1. Isaiah
2. Jeremiah
3. Lamentations
4. Ezekiel
5. Daniel

Books of Minor Prophets
1. Hosea
2. Joel
3. Amos
4. Obadiah
5. Jonah
6. Micah
7. Nahum
8. Habakkuk
9. Zephaniah
10. Haggai
11. Zechariah
12. Malachi

Activity Sheet 3
GOD:
Keeps promises
Is love
Created everything
Is holy
Hates sin
Sovereign
All-powerful
Knows everything
Present everywhere
Protects believers
Perfect

SATAN:
Enemy of mankind
Morning star
Rebelled against God
Tries to hurt believers
Made some angels sin
Has some power
Intelligent

Activity Sheet 5
1. A   6. D
2. D   7. D
3. D   8. A
4. A   9. A
5. A   10. A

LESSON 2

Activity Sheet 4
Adam
Eve
Eden
walked
fruit
one

Serpent
God
die
Satan
doubt
good
Eve
Adam

God
clothes
fig
hid
sin
hard
Redeemer
peace

Activity Sheet 5
Cain
Son of Adam and Eve
Older son
He was a farmer
He brought sacrifices of fruits from his land to God
God was not pleased with his sacrifice
He killed his brother

Abel
Son of Adam and Eve
Younger son
He was a sheep herder
He brought a lamb sacrifice to God
God was pleased with his sacrifice

LESSON 3

Activity Sheet 1
e. 1
g. 2
h. 3
d. 4
c. 5
f. 6
b. 7
a. 8

Activity Sheet 2
Characteristics of Adam
10. Created directly by God
12. Father of all mankind
4. Disobeyed God
11. Failed to trust God
14. Named the animals
6. Blessed by God at the beginning

Characteristics of Abraham
5. Father of Israel
1. Obeyed God
3. Trusted God
9. Demonstrated faith in God
2. Blessed by God at the end
15. Given God's covenant

Characteristics of Both
8. Loved by God
7. Married to a wife
13. Father of a son

Activity Sheet 3
1. We must trust God completely.
2. Abraham
3. That God would bless Abraham and make of his family a great nation.
4. Believe in God and trust God that He will protect and love me. [There are other possible answers to this question.]
5. Yes!

Activity Sheet 4
Across
3. Haran
6. Sarah
8. Jacob
9. inheritance
12. Leah
14. angry
15. Laban

Down
1. blessing
3. Abraham
4. Rachel
5. goats
7. Rebekah
10. Isaac
11. dream
13. Esau

Activity Sheet 6
JUDAH
ISSACHAR
DAN
JOSEPH
BENJAMIN
REUBEN
ZEBULUN
LEVI
NAPHTALI
ASHER
DINAH
GAD
SIMEON
MANESSAH
EPHRAIM

Activity Sheet 7
1. Jacob
2. coat
3. dreams
4. hated
5. well
6. sell
7. blood
8. sad
9. Potiphar
10. prison
11. baker
12. cupbearer
13. second
14. famine
15. Egypt
16. frightened
17. protected
18. reunited

LESSON 4

Activity Sheet 7:
1. gods
2. statue
3. Lord
4. Sabbath
5. mother, father
6. kill
7. unfaithful
8. steal
9. falsely
10. envy

LESSON 5

Activity Sheet 2
1. Moses
2. Promised Land
3. foot
4. Great Sea (the Mediterranean Sea today)
5. strong
6. obey
7. Book
8. do
9. prosperous
10. fearful

Activity Sheet 3
1. spies
2. Jericho
3. captured
4. Rahab
5. Israelites
6. Egypt
7. stalks
8. protected
9. rope
10. three
11. cord

Activity Sheet 9

```
O  J  V  J  O  P  G  O  T  X  X  C  N  Z  P
H  W  Y  K  O  G  E  S  L  U  A  S  T  R  Z
P  E  A  O  P  X  E  R  P  T  J  H  B  N  J
W  Z  D  P  V  I  U  I  J  B  W  W  X  Y  U
A  Q  W  L  R  H  A  M  A  R  Y  S  Y  L  D
T  N  W  P  T  E  H  P  O  R  P  A  M  R  G
P  Z  H  F  Q  X  U  Z  S  A  F  D  O  N  E
B  Z  W  V  P  S  B  A  M  U  V  Y  W  X  J
P  Q  N  O  K  U  B  C  O  U  J  F  Z  B  G
L  F  Y  O  D  Y  X  U  F  M  N  I  F  L  J
Z  D  I  I  Q  M  T  K  X  X  H  G  X  U  K
K  C  V  C  E  I  H  L  M  N  M  P  R  J  D
C  A  O  E  H  A  N  N  A  H  I  A  A  T  M
D  H  E  C  U  O  E  M  C  J  D  B  V  W  I
W  O  M  W  X  A  O  P  I  W  F  Z  Q  T  S
```

LESSON 7

Activity Sheet 1
1. Prophets
2. Jeremiah
3. God
4. Repent
5. Dishonest
6. Incense
7. Punishment

Activity Sheet 2
Situation 1—They asked to be allowed to eat the kind of food they desired for ten days and to have the king compare them with the other princes. The food, allowed by the Hebrew Law produced healthier young men. They were allowed to continue.

Situation 2—Shadrach, Meshach, and Abednego were thrown into the fiery furnace by the king. Instead of dying in the flames, there were four in the furnace. God protected them, and they were not harmed or even singed by the fire. The king then threw his men in the furnace and they were killed.

Situation 3—The other princes were jealous of Daniel and persuaded the king to order no prayer to anyone but to the king. The punishment was to be thrown into the lion's den. Daniel was thrown into the lion's den, but God protected Daniel, and he came out the next morning unharmed. The king's evil princes were thrown to the lions and devoured.

Activity Sheet 10
Across
3. Belshazzar
4. Darius
5. Nehemiah
6. Daniel
7. Jeremiah
8. Ezra
9. Esther

Down
1. Haman
2. Nebuchadnezzar

LESSON 6

Activity Sheet 2

David	*Goliath*
Small	Big
Slingshot	Sword and shield
Faith in God	Faith in himself
No armor	Heavy armor
Won the fight	Lost his life

Activity Sheet 3
Repent means to tell God that you are sorry for sin and to turn away from that sin.

Activity Sheet 4
Early Days
Kindness
Love for the Lord
Wise, discerning heart
Administered justice
Had insight and understanding
Last Days
Loved many wives
Wives turn his heart away from God
Did evil in the sight of God

Activity Sheet 5
1. Jerusalem
2. altar of burnt offerings
3. laver
4. Holy Place
5. menorah
6. incense
7. shew bread
8. veil
9. Holy of Holies
10. sacrifice
11. Ark of the Covenant
12. throne

Activity Sheet 10
1. Saul
2. Goliath
3. Elijah
4. Josian
5. Sheba
6. King Ahab
7. Uriah
8. Naboth
9. Jonathan
10. Jereboam
11. Nathan
12. Jonah

LESSON 8

Activity Sheet 3
Gospels
1. Matthew
2. Mark
3. Luke
4. John
The Book of History
1. Acts

The Letters of Paul
1. Romans
2. 1 Corinthians
3. 2 Corinthians
4. Galatians
5. Ephesians
6. Philippians
7. Colossians
8. 1 Thessalonians
9. 2 Thessalonians
10. 1 Timothy
11. 2 Timothy
12. Titus
13. Philemon
The General Letters
1. Hebrews
2. James
3. 1 Peter
4. 2 Peter
5. 1 John
6. 2 John
7. 3 John
8. Jude
The Book of Prophecy
1. Revelation

Activity Sheet 5
1. Matthew, Mark, Luke, John
2. Gospels
3. Acts
4. Paul
5. General Letters
6. Revelation
7. 27

LESSON 9

Activity Sheet 2
1. Early Life
2. Galilean Ministry
3. Judean Ministry
4. Triumphal Entry
5. First Year
6. Resurrection
7. First Year
8. Second Year
9. Third Year

Activity Sheet 4
1. John
2. James
3. Judas
4. Andrew
5. Philip
6. Peter
7. Matthew
8. Thomas
9. Simon
10. James
11. Thaddaeus
12. Bartholomew

Activity Sheet 9

```
X L E L S I G L G C C A N Y E
X S B O R T H P W A N D R E W
Z U L N C C J J E P Q B S W S
U E J T V J R R G X U N A M
G A W A L F U M K R D T M G Z
T D P E Z E T D E Z Q O O Z N
M D K V M Q B T A F N S H C X
A A M O W O E P Z S S V T R H
P H Q L E P L X P G J O H N J
O T M B H P E O J Y S T A S A
J E U H T I P H H S V E Y U M
Q R M Y T L L B J T P I M M E
F Q P C A I Y A I D R U J A S
Q V Q W M H N T X N F A D M J
W X E Z Z P K K A Q Y D B M B
```

Activity Sheet 9
1. Mary, Martha, Lazarus
2. Martha
3. Lazarus
4. Mary
5. Mary, Martha
6. Lazarus
7. Martha

LESSON 10

Activity Sheet 9

```
W J W K R W O T D W M A R Y M
N F G A S C E N S I O N M A V
M N L A F N N X D C O C G S M
F V R Q L O O C C J K D J O X
K L E H N I N I Q T A Z V L K
O S S I Z S L O T L O W K D V
Q G U S M S F E E A L G C I N
Z C R X A I U N E R V F G E M
H K R T U M E A N G E L S R E
A M E K T M O Z M O J Z A S Z
R P C S R O K H J M P T N S Z
Z V T Q K C S Q T I E D R E U
C F I Y J Q P M N X O J J C F
I I O J J O B E X C R V E Z L
C T N I U D Q B T E D X F N G
```

LESSON 11

Activity Sheet 6
Gospel
Power
Salvation
Conditional
Response

Activity Sheet 8
Across
7. Ephesus
8. Pentecost
9. Lydia

Down
1. Caesar
2. Ephesus
3. Damascus
4. John
5. Lystra
6. Jerusalem

Activity Sheet 9
1. d
2. f
3. a
4. e
5. b
6. g
7. c

LESSON 12

Activity Sheet 1
1. Sunday
2. Jesus rose from the dead
3. God created light
4. first
5. Sunday
6. first
7. new
8. Sunday

Activity Sheet 3
1st Bound Jesus and sent him to Caiaphas
2nd Death sentence—charge of blasphemy
3rd Death sentence made legal by chief priests and elders
4th Not guilty
5th Not guilty
6th Not guilty, but turned Jesus over to Jews

LESSON 14

Activity Sheet 2

```
J C E U J J Z H B U N Y X I Y
F P Q B N B I D L S T W M I N
K S T J N P R E T E P X I B M
C W Z C E A K S X J J N W L B
G A S T V S E D W D G V D N L
V J U D A S J H K C W I V U Z
J H K R E O L V W C S Y S Y G
D H Y P H V O W F C V T V Q Y
Y A E N M E V P U J C G O C
O M C B V R E P Y F C Z D Q O
S K W R A H L A Y C H R S Q J
D U B E W E R M P V D Z O N L
O Z C A S T U P T N C F R S J
G J O D E Q F Y D T Z S J Z S
E K W B S F F B T P A G V R G
```

Activity Sheet 5
1. Magdalene
2. Peter
3. guards
4. women
5. Emmaus
6. Peter
7. ten
8. disciples
9. hundred
10. disciples

Activity Sheet 7
A. Great Fish of Jonah
B. Easter egg
C. Easter lily
D. Peacock
E. Butterfly
F. Lamb of God
G. Phoenix

LESSON 15

Activity Sheet 4A

Activity Sheet 4C
Across
3. Fertile
4. Egypt
8. Rachel
9. Euphrates
11. Haran
12. caravan
14. Lot
15. Sodom

Down
1. Dead
2. ziggurat
5. Rebekah
6. Terah
7. Ishmael
10. Ur
13. nomad

Activity Sheet 5

```
B X D W N R P E E V M H I R J
F U R N G J E R I C H O D M G
U C G A U S N E L I N C J D F
Q W D A Z E E A J C A U X G G
P C P N C K G S D T W N I Z G
L V S A U R J Y O R B S I B D
Y B S C V A K H P M O E F S X
Q H E H S E D A K T S J Y F K
E Z N Y K I G M B G W A B B R
W F R Y E C X W Y X F U E B O
A W E Y A Z W P O H J H P L F
P J D S U U R T Z D E S L O H
R Q L U H B R E A X W O C O Q
D E I K L E J F I H X J P R G
X X W G T T B I G H H P W U W
```

244